Multimedia Systems and Content-Based Image Retrieval

Sagarmay Deb
University of Southern Queensland, Australia

IDEA GROUP PUBLISHING
Hershey • London • Melbourne • Singapore

Acquisition Editor:	Mehdi Khosrow-Pour
Senior Managing Editor:	Jan Travers
Managing Editor:	Amanda Appicello
Development Editor:	Michele Rossi
Copy Editor:	Angela Britcher
Typesetter:	Jennifer Wetzel
Cover Design:	Lisa Tosheff
Printed at:	Integrated Book Technology

Published in the United States of America by
　　　　Idea Group Publishing (an imprint of Idea Group Inc.)
　　　　701 E. Chocolate Avenue, Suite 200
　　　　Hershey PA 17033
　　　　Tel: 717-533-8845
　　　　Fax: 717-533-8661
　　　　E-mail: cust@idea-group.com
　　　　Web site: http://www.idea-group.com

and in the United Kingdom by
　　　　Idea Group Publishing (an imprint of Idea Group Inc.)
　　　　3 Henrietta Street
　　　　Covent Garden
　　　　London WC2E 8LU
　　　　Tel: 44 20 7240 0856
　　　　Fax: 44 20 7379 3313
　　　　Web site: http://www.eurospan.co.uk

Library of Congress Cataloging-in-Publication Data

Multimedia systems and content-based image retrieval / Sagarmay Deb, editor.
　　　p. cm.
Includes bibliographical references and index.
　ISBN 1-59140-156-9 (hardcover) -- ISBN 1-59140-157-7 (ebook)
　1. Multimedia systems. 2. Image processing--Digital techniques. 3.
Database management. I. Deb, Sagarmay, 1953-
　QA76.575.M8519 2004
　006.7--dc22
　　　　　　　　　　　　2003014942

Paperback ISBN 1-59140-265-4

British Cataloguing in Publication Data
A Cataloguing in Publication record for this book is available from the British Library.

All work contributed to this book is new, previously-unpublished material. The views expressed in this book are those of the authors, but not necessarily of the publisher.

Multimedia Systems and Content-Based Image Retrieval

Table of Contents

SECTION VII: DYNAMIC USER INTERFACE

Preface

Multimedia systems and content-based image retrieval are very important areas of research in computer technology. Plenty of research works are being done in these fields at present.

These two areas are changing our life-styles because they together cover creation, maintenance, accessing and retrieval of video, audio, image, textual and graphic data. But still lots of important issues in these areas remain unresolved and further research works are needed to be done for better techniques and applications.

The primary objective of this book is to combine these two areas of research together as one is related to the other and provide an up-to-date account of the works being done. We addressed research issues in these fields where some progresses have been made already. Also we encouraged researchers, academics and industrial technologists to provide new and brilliant ideas on these fields which could be pursued for further research.

Content-based image retrieval (CBIR) is a bottleneck of the multimedia systems. Although attempts have been made to perform CBIR on an efficient basis based on shape, color, texture and spatial relations, it has yet to attain maturity. A major problem in this area is computer perception. It is very difficult to make a computer think like a human being to sense what the image or object within the image is. In other words, there remains a big gap between low-level features like shape, color, texture and spatial relations and high-level features like table, chair, car, etc. This means to find the semantic meanings out of an image are still very difficult. Only to some extent, success has been achieved and only in certain categories of images. No universally accepted software package is available to find semantic or high-level meanings out of an object. Another issue in this area of research is image segmentation. This is also a problem of computer perception. Plenty of research is being done to have meaningful and thorough image segmentation based on color, texture, and shape. Only limited success is achieved in certain specific types of image while no universally accepted software package is available for any kind of image. We addressed these two issues in Section III and IV. Issues related to video shot transitions and video content-based retrieval techniques are also covered in Section III and IV.

Section I of the book is the introduction. We have given a general introduction of the two areas, namely, multimedia systems and content-based image retrieval, from the very elementary level. We discussed the problems in these areas and some of the works done in the field of content-based image retrieval since the beginning of last decade of the last century.

Section II covers research works done in multimedia structures and security. Digital watermarking techniques are applied for content protection of multimedia data. It is a relatively new field of research. New solutions are provided for music sheets to overcome the drawbacks of raster-oriented watermarking algorithms for images, which is applied for music sheets. Also, this section covers face recognition technology with an emphasis on facial scan or face recognition and a Chinese duplicate image retrieval system.

In Section V, we present the research works to provide home users with effective and efficient tools to organize and access large digital images and video albums. We introduce new concepts of emergence index in image retrieval where we consider hidden or implicit meanings of an image in addition to explicit meaning for indexing purposes.

Section VI deals with various content-based image retrieval techniques and Section VII talks about user interfaces. The area of user interfaces is also a very important area of research in multimedia systems as it is the medium between the system and the end user. Successful content-based image retrieval is not possible without proper user interface through which the search process begins. We provided a state-of-the-art review of research on user interface including researches on face animation.

The audience for this book would be researchers who are working in these two fields. Also, researchers from other areas who could start-up in these fields could find the book useful. It could be a reference guide for researchers from other related areas. Reading this book can also benefit undergraduate and post-graduate students, who are interested in multimedia technology.

CHAPTER HIGHLIGHTS

Chapter 1: Multimedia Systems and Content-Based Image Retrieval

In this chapter, we present a basic introduction of the two very important areas of research in the domain of information technology, namely, multimedia systems and content-based image retrieval. The latter is still a widely unresolved problem. We discuss some of the works done so far in content-based image retrieval in the context of multimedia systems.

Chapter 2: A Duplicate Chinese Document Image Retrieval System Based on Line Segment Feature in Character Image Block

With the rapid progress of digital image technology, the management of duplicate document images is also emphasized widely. As a result, this chapter suggests a duplicate Chinese document image retrieval (DCDIR) system, which uses the ratio of the number of black pixels to that of white pixels on the scanned line segments in a character image block as the feature of the character image block. Experimental results indicate that the system can indeed effectively and quickly retrieve the desired duplicate Chinese document image from a database.

Chapter 3: Technology of Music Score Watermarking

Content protection for multimedia data is widely recognized especially for data types that are frequently distributed, sold or shared using the Internet. Particularly, the music industry, in dealing with audio files, realized the necessity for content protection. Distribution of music sheets will face the same problems. Digital watermarking techniques provide a certain level of protection for these music sheets. But classical raster-oriented watermarking algorithms for images suffer several drawbacks when directly applied to image representations of music sheets. Therefore, new solutions have been developed which are designed regarding the content of the music sheets. In comparison to other media types, the development for watermarking of music scores is a rather young art. The chapter reviews the evolution of the early approaches and describes the current state of the art in the field.

Chapter 4: Face Recognition Technology: A Biometric Solution to Security Problems

Face recognition technology is one of the most widely used applications in computer vision. It is widely used in the applications related to security and human-computer interfaces. The two reasons for this are the wide range of commercial and law enforcement applications and the availability of feasible technologies. In this chapter, the various biometric systems and the commonly used techniques of face recognition, Feature Based, Eigen Face Based, Line Based Approach and Local Feature Analysis are explained along with the results. A performance comparison of these algorithms is also given.

Chapter 5: Histogram Generation from the HSV Color Space Using Saturation Projection

In this chapter, we make an in-depth analysis of the visual properties of the HSV (Hue, Saturation, Intensity Value) color space and describe a novel histogram generation technique for color feature extraction. In this new approach, we extract a pixel feature by choosing relative weights of hue and intensity based on the saturation value of the pixel. The histogram retains a perceptually smooth color transition between its adjacent components that enables us to do a window-based smoothing of feature vectors for the purpose of effective retrieval of similar images from very large databases. The results have been compared with a standard histogram generated from the RGB color space and also with a histogram similar to that used in the QBIC system (Niblack et al., 1993).

Chapter 6: Video Content-Based Retrieval Techniques

The increasing use of multimedia streams nowadays necessitates the development of efficient and effective methodologies and systems for manipulating databases storing these streams. These systems have various areas of application such as video-on-demand and digital libraries. The importance of video content-based retrieval (CBR) systems motivates us to explain their basic components in this chapter and shed light on their underlying working principles. In general, a content-based retrieval system of video data consists of the following four stages:

- Video shot boundary detection
- Key Frames (KFs) selection
- Features extraction (from selected KFs)
- Retrieval stage (where similarity matching operations are performed)

Each one of these stages will be reviewed and expounded based on our experience on building a Video Content-based Retrieval (VCR) that has been fully implemented from scratch in JAVA Language (2002). Moreover, current research directions and outstanding problems will be discussed for each stage in the context of our VCR system.

Chapter 7: Object-Based Techniques for Image Retrieval

To overcome the drawback of using only low level features for the description of image content and to fill the gap between the perceptual property and semantic meaning, this chapter presents an object-based scheme and some object level techniques for image retrieval. According to a multi-layer description model, images are analyzed in different levels for progressive understanding, and this procedure helps to gain comprehensive representations of the objects in images. The main propulsion of the chapter includes a multi-layer description model that describes the image content with a hierarchical structure, an efficient region-based scheme for meaningful information extraction; a combined feature set to represent the image at a visual perception level; an iterative training-and-testing procedure for object region recognition, a decision function for reflecting common contents in object description and a combined feature and object matching process, as well as a self-adaptive relevance feedback that could work with or without memory. With the proposed techniques, a prototype retrieval system has been implemented. Real retrieval experiments have been conducted, results show that the object-based scheme is quite efficient and the performance of object level techniques have been confirmed.

Chapter 8: Object-Based Video Analysis and Interpretation

In this chapter, we present a novel scheme for object-based video analysis and interpretation based on automatic video object extraction, video object abstraction, and semantic event modeling. In this scheme, video objects (VOs) are first automatically extracted, followed by a video object abstraction algorithm for identifying key frames to reduce data redundancy and provide reliable feature data for the next stage of the algorithm. Semantic feature modeling is based on temporal variation of low-level features of a video object. Dynamic Bayesian networks (DBNs) are then used to characterize the spatial-temporal nature of the video objects. The system states in the proposed DBNs directly correspond to the physical concepts. Thus, the decoding of the DBN system states from observable variables is a natural interpretation of the behavior of the video objects. Since the video objects are generally considered as the dominant semantic features of video clips, the proposed scheme provides a powerful methodology for content description, which is critical for large scale MPEG-7 applications.

Chapter 9: Advances in Digital Home Photo Albums

With rapid advances in sensor, storage, processor, and communication technologies, home users can now afford to create, store, process, and share large digital images and subsequently, video albums. With more and more digital albums being accumulated, home users need effective and efficient tools to organize and access images and videos in a semantically meaningful way without too much of a manual annotation effort. To address this genuine need, an international collaboration project (2000-2003) among CNRS, France, School of Computing, National University of Singapore, and Laboratories for Information Technology, Singapore was formed to develop the next generation Digital Image/Video Album (DIVA) for home users. The goal of this chapter is to explain the work carried out in the DIVA international project. In particular, we will describe the needs of users in the domain of management and retrieval of still images, before explaining the research work done in semantic indexing and retrieval of still images

Chapter 10: Algorithm for the Retrieval of Image with Emergence Index in Multimedia

In this chapter, we discuss emergence phenomenon where we study the hidden meanings of an image. We present this concept in image database access and retrieval of images using this as an index for retrieval. This would give an entirely different search outcome than ordinary searches where emergence is not considered, as consideration of hidden meanings could change the index of a search. We talk about emergence, emergence index and accessing multimedia databases using emergence index to locate geographic areas in this chapter along with the algorithm.

Chapter 11: An Efficient Content-Based Retrieval System for Large Image Database

Content-based image retrieval has become more desirable for the development of large image database, due to the accessibility of user preferred images in many applications, such as a photo database. This chapter presents an efficient method of retrieving images from an image database. Our system combines color, shape and spatial features to index and measure similarity of images. Several color spaces that are widely used in computer graphics are discussed and compared for color clustering. In addition, this chapter proposes a new automatic indexing scheme of image databases according to our clustering method and color sensation, which could be used to retrieve images efficiently. As a technical contribution, a Seed-Filling-like algorithm that could extract the shape and spatial relationship feature of an image is proposed. Due to the difficulty of determining how far objects are separated, this system uses qualitative spatial relations to analyze object similarity. Also, the system is incorporated with a visual interface and a set of tools, which allows the users to specify or sketch the images conveniently for query purposes. Besides, the feedback learning mechanism enhances the precision of retrieval. The experience shows that the system is able to retrieve image information efficiently by the proposed approaches.

Chapter 12: A Spatial Relationship Method Supports Image Indexing and Similarity Retrieval

The increasing availability of image and multimedia-oriented applications markedly impacts image/multimedia file and database systems. Image data are not well-defined keywords such as traditional text data used in searching and retrieving functions. Consequently, various indexing and retrieving methodologies must be defined based on the characteristics of image data. Spatial relationships represent an important feature of objects (called icons) in an image (or picture). Spatial representation by 2-D String and its variants, in a pictorial spatial database, has been attracting growing interest. However, most 2-D Strings represent spatial information by cutting the icons out of an image and associating them with many spatial operators. The similarity retrievals by 2-D Strings require massive geometric computation and focus only on those database images that have all the icons and spatial relationships of the query image. This study proposes a new spatial-relationship representation model called "Two Dimension Begin-End boundary string" (2D Bε-string). The 2D Bε-string represents an icon by its MBR boundaries. By applying "dummy objects," the 2D Bε-string can intuitively and naturally represent the pictorial spatial information without any spatial operator. A method of evaluating image similarities, based on the modified "Longest Common Subsequence" (LCS) algorithm, is presented. The proposed evaluation method can not only sift out those images of which all icons and their spatial relationships fully accord with query images, but for those images some of whose icons and/or spatial relationships are similar to those of query images. Problems of uncertainty reflection of images, the query targets and/or spatial relationships thus solved. The representation model and similarity evaluation also simplify the retrieval progress of linear transformations, including rotation and reflection, of images.

Chapter 13: A Stochastic and Content-Based Image Retrieval Mechanism

Multimedia information, typically image information, is growing rapidly across the Internet and elsewhere. To keep pace with the increasing volumes of image information, new techniques need to be investigated to retrieve images intelligently and efficiently. Content-based image retrieval (CBIR) is always a challenging task. In this chapter, a stochastic mechanism, called Markov Model Mediator (MMM), is used to facilitate the searching and retrieval process for content-based image retrieval, which serves as the retrieval engine of the CBIR systems and uses stochastic-based similarity measures. Different from the common methods, our stochastic mechanism carries out the searching and similarity computing process dynamically, taking into consideration not only the image content features but also other characteristics of images such as their access frequencies and access patterns. Our experimental results demonstrate that the MMM mechanism together with the stochastic process can assist in retrieving more accurate results for user queries.

Chapter 14: Mind the Gap: Content-Based Image Retrieval and the User Interface

The user interface provides the medium between the end user and the system, and is instrumental in facilitating effective human-computer interaction. Despite being identified as one of the major research areas of the field, few studies have investigated the design of existing or new user interface metaphors or paradigms for specifying visual queries. Research has demonstrated that the design of the user interface must match the tasks, activities, and goals of the end user population for whom it is being developed. Currently, there is little empirical evidence to support the use of any interface metaphor or paradigm. What type of user interface is required to support human-computer interaction in a content-based image retrieval environment is an open research issue. This chapter presents an overview of user interface research activity and related areas in the field of content-based image retrieval.

Chapter 15: Face Animation: A Case Study for Multimedia Modeling and Specification Languages

This chapter will discuss the multimedia modeling and specification methods, especially in the context of face animation. Personalized Face Animation is and/or can be a major user interface component in modern multimedia systems. After reviewing the related works in this area, we present the ShowFace streaming structure. This structure is based on most widely accepted industry standards in multimedia presentations like MPEG-4 and SMIL, and extends them by providing a higher level Face Modeling Language (FML) for modeling and control purposes, and also by defining image transformations required for certain facial movements. ShowFace establishes a comprehensive framework for face animation consisting of components for parsing the input script, generating and splitting the audio and video "behaviours," creating the required images and sounds, and eventually displaying or writing the data to files. This component-based design and scripted behavior make the framework suitable for many purposes including web-based applications.

Acknowledgments

The editor would like to extend his thanks to all the authors who contributed to this project by submitting chapters. The credit for the success of this book goes to them.

Sincere thanks goes to all the staff at Idea Group Publishing for their valuable contributions — particularly to Mehdi Khosrow-Pour, Senior Academic Editor, Michele Rossi, Development Editor, and Carrie Skovrinskie, Office Manager, who provided valuable suggestions and guidance during the development process.

Finally, the editor would like to thank his wife, Ms. Clera Deb, for her support and cooperation during the venture.

Sagarmay Deb
Editor
University of Southern Queensland, Australia

Section I

An Introduction to Multimedia Systems and Content-Based Image Retrieval

Chapter I

Multimedia Systems and Content-Based Image Retrieval

Sagarmay Deb, University of Southern Queensland, Australia

ABSTRACT

In this chapter, we present a basic introduction of the two very important areas of research in the domain of information technology, namely, multimedia systems and content-based image retrieval. The latter is still a widely unresolved problem. We discuss some of the works done so far in content-based image retrieval in the context of multimedia systems.

INTRODUCTION

Research on multimedia systems and content-based image retrieval has gained tremendous momentum during the last decade. This is due to the fact that multimedia databases cover the text, audio, video and image data which help us to receive enormous amounts of information and which has brought fundamental changes in our life style. Content-based image retrieval (CBIR) is a bottleneck of the access of multimedia databases simply because there remains vast differences in the perception capacity between a human being and a computer. We give an introduction of these two areas in this chapter along with an idea of the research being conducted in CBIR over the last few years in the context of multimedia systems. The section on multimedia databases describes general background of multimedia databases. The section on Content-based image retrieval talks about general background, problems and some of the works done so far in content-based image retrieval. A summary is presented at the end.

MULTIMEDIA DATABASES

General Background

Multimedia environment, much talked-about topic in computers, is adding new dimensions in the area of information technology and all relevant fields. Multimedia and imaging applications are enriching existing applications by integrating images, voices, text and video. The ultimate goal is to have all information types digitized and computerized. As we proceed to convert enormous amounts of non-digitized information into multimedia objects, the outcomes are extremely significant with its effects in various activities of life.

The available literature talks about certain advanced technologies which are:

- Computer-aided design and manufacturing (CAD/CAM) using 2-D and 3-D graphics, animation and visualization
- Network standard, such as asynchronous transfer mode (ATM) and fibre distributed data interface (FDDI) which allow multimedia information to flow through wide area networks (WANS) as well as local area networks (LANS)
- Image processing systems which include more sophisticated techniques to segment and process images
- Character and object recognition systems using pattern recognition and neural networks
- Software systems such as object-oriented languages, databases and operating systems
- Hardware components such as video cameras, video boards, sound boards and high-resolution monitors
- Storage devices such as optical disks and magneto-optic technologies

All of the above developments in information technology are lending support to multimedia information technology.

Multimedia environments can be available in PC-based systems, then in more advanced Power PCs with built-in audiovisual capabilities and to more advanced and sophisticated UNIX workstations.

There are some similarities between object-oriented databases and multimedia databases. Just as an object-oriented database tries to depict the real world as much as possible so are multimedia databases because of their ability to capture and play back the sounds and images of the real world as realistically as possible.

Other features of multimedia databases are:

1. Automatic feature extraction and indexing where image processing and pattern recognition systems for images often extract the various features and content of multimedia objects. When large amounts of non-digitized information are converted into digital multimedia objects, quite a few automatic indexing features are

utilized. This is particularly true where paper documents are converted into scanned digitized images that are eventually recognized by optical character recognition (OCR) products.

2. Interactive querying, relevance feedback and refining where user queries involve a graphical user interface where the construction of the query can be performed interactively. In multimedia databases, it is common to have domains or lists of various existing multimedia objects so that the user can construct a query interactively. The result of the query can be shown with more relevant selections first followed by less relevant selections and the user can select relevant objects, refine the query and resubmit, etc.

3. Content-based indexing where a video could contain the frame number of the start of each clip or scene for each video. For images containing objects arranged spatially, iconic indexing through 2-D strings contains the location and relative position of each element or object in the whole image.

4. Single and multikey (dimensional) indexing where spatial and multidimensional indexes are used. A geometric region has X and Y coordinates. Spatial indexes, such as R trees or multidimensional structures such as grid files or k-d trees will produce better access times for queries covering all the dimensions of the multidimensional attribute being retrieved.

5. Storage organization for Binary Large Objects (BLOB) where multimedia databases allow the users to create and store BLOBs. Because the BLOB interfaces typically allow the user to access and update byte or bit streams, the multimedia storage manager makes use of the positional indexes to store the BLOBs. This permits very fast access to continuous streams of bytes or bits starting at a particular position. Positional indexes also accelerate the insertions and appends of byte streams in BLOBs.

6. Spatial data types and queries where the spatial relationships between various elements of the image are studied.

7. Query optimization where a multimedia database management system that integrates hierarchical storage optimization, information/content-retrieval modules and complex object managers must decide on the best way to perform execution.

8. Complex object clustering where to provide efficient access to a multimedia complex object, the storage management layer has to incorporate complex object clustering storage techniques. The goal would be to minimize I/O access time for the complex object and its sub-objects and also the processing time needed to reconstruct the complex object.

Multimedia Database Management Systems

Multimedia Database Management Systems (MDBMS) deal with audio, video, text and image data. We can create, update, delete and enquire these data in the multimedia databases. Ordinarily, data are BLOBS. Multimedia objects can take lot of storage space and that requires very efficient storage management systems for fast and efficient access of the data.

There are three layers in a multimedia database. The interface layer deals with browsing and query. Then, the object composition layer handles managing objects and the storage layer deals with clustering and indexing.

Research Issues

Some of the important research problems are: (1) watermarking technology, which is very useful in protecting digital data such as audio, video, image, formatted documents and three dimensional objects; (2) synchronization and timeliness, which are required to synchronize multiple resources like audio and video data; (3) quality of service (QoS), which is relevant to high-speed networks to achieve low end-to-end delay, loss rate and optimum data transmission with the available resources; and (4) reusability, where browsing of objects give the users the facility to reuse multimedia resources. (5) Since the multimedia data is voluminous and occupy a lot of storage space, developing efficient storage techniques is essential for fast accessing and retrieval of information. (6) For video content-based retrieval, efficient shot boundary detection, key frames selection, feature extraction and retrieval are important research issues at the moment.

CONTENT-BASED IMAGE RETRIEVAL

General Background

Images are being generated at an ever-increasing rate by various sources. They include military purposes, aviation satellites, biomedical purposes, scientific experiments and home entertainment.

Application areas in which CBIR is a principal activity are numerous and diverse. They are:

- Art galleries and museum management
- Architectural and engineering design
- Interior design
- Remote sensing and management of earth resources
- Geographic information systems
- Scientific database management
- Weather forecasting
- Retailing
- Fabric and fashion design
- Trademark and copyright database management
- Law enforcement and criminal investigation
- Picture archiving and communication systems (Gudivada & Raghavan, 1995)

Previously there were two approaches to CBIR.

The first one is the attribute-based representation advocated by database researchers where image contents are modeled as a set of attributes extracted manually and managed within the framework of conventional database management systems. Queries are specified using these attributes. This entails a high-level of image abstraction.

The second approach propagated by image interpretation researchers depends on an integrated feature-extraction/object-recognition subsystem to overcome the limitations of attribute-based retrieval. This subsystem automates the feature-extraction and object-recognition task that occurs when the image is inserted into the database. This automated approach to object recognition is computationally expensive, difficult and tends to be domain specific.

Recent CBIR research tries to combine both of the above mentioned approach and has given rise to efficient image representations and data models, query-processing algorithms, intelligent query interfaces and domain-independent system architecture.

There are two major categories of features. One is primitive, which is concerned with extracting boundaries of the image and the other one is logical, which defines the image at various levels of detail.

Regardless of which approach is used, the retrieval in CBIR is done by color, texture, sketch, shape, volume, spatial constraints, browsing, objective attributes, subjective attributes, motion, text and domain concepts (Gudivada & Raghavan, 1995).

Our study of the existing literature suggests, in recent times, there have been very many attempts to perform CBIR on an efficient basis based on feature, color, texture and spatial relations. Quite a few models have been developed which address the problem of image retrieval from various angles. Some of the models are QBIC (Query by Image Content), Virage, Pichunter, VisualSEEK, Chabot, Excalibur, Photobook, Jacob, and Digital Library Project (Seaborn, 1997).

One of the most well known packages is QBIC which was developed by IBM. It uses color, texture, shape, example images and sketches to retrieve images used in large image and video databases. Based on the same kind of approach developed by Virage which made use of color, composition (color layout), texture and structure (object boundary information) and is being applied in face recognition and in retrieval of ophthalmologic images. NEC Research Institute has developed Pichunter, which utilizes image properties like ratio of image dimensions, color percentages and global statistical and frequency properties. It is more applicable in database retrieval instead of feature detection and is also being applied in relevance feedback using Bayesian probability theory. VisualSEEK, developed at the Columbia University Centre for Telecommunication Research, uses color percentage method in content-based retrieval. Using regional colors and their relative locations, the image is segmented and this is quite a bit similar to the way we perceive an image. Chabot mainly uses texts to retrieve images. It uses to some extent color percentages to retrieve images automatically otherwise all features are input manually. Excalibur is of the same type as QBIC and Virage and uses standard metrics, color, shape and texture and like Pichunter uses image ratio. In addition, it extracts features like structure of brightness and color. It gives an option to the users to indicate which features are dominant. MIT's Vision and Modeling Group developed Photobook, which uses color percentages, textures and statistical analysis. The images are segmented here and then texts are made out of those segmentations using predefined templates and techniques. The images are retrieved based on these texts. Jacob uses a combination of color, texture and motion as features to retrieve video clips as this package is developed for video databases. The Digital Library Project of Berkeley University applies color percentage method and feature of dots. The user can define the quantity of various colors in the image and also can define colors and sizes of dots to be there in the image.

These models have brought this area of CBIR from its infancy to a matured stage. They study the various features of the images, make statistical analysis of color distribution as well as shape and texture and retrieve images from the contents of the image.

The developments in this field have been defined in three levels (Eakins & Graham, 1999).

Level one is the primitive level where low-level features like color, texture, shape and spatial locations are used to segment images in image databases and then find symmetry based on these segmentations with the input image. Plenty of research projects were being done during the past decade. As we mentioned earlier, many software packages have been developed for efficient image retrieval. Most of them have used a combination of text-based and content-based retrieval. Images are segmented manually, a priory and text are generated based on these manual segmentations and retrievals are conducted accordingly. But since the volume of images generated could be enormous in fields like satellite picturing, this method of manual part processing is time-consuming and expensive. Few automatic retrievals without human intervention have been developed like QBIC, Virage, and Excalibur which are now commercially being used in addition to packages developed which are not yet commercial. But they have limited applications in areas like trademark registration, identification of drawings in a design archive or color matching of fashion accessories based on input image. No universally accepted retrieval technique has yet been developed. Also, the retrieval techniques developed without human intervention are far from perfect. Segmentation has been done in some packages based on color where the segmented parts taken individually do not contribute to any meaningful identification (Ma et al., n.d.). They generate a vague symmetry between input objects and objects in image database. This level still needs to be developed further to have universal applications.

Level two deals with bringing out semantic meanings of an image of the database. One of the best known works in this field is of Forsyth et al. (1996) successfully identifying human beings within images. This technique had been applied for other objects like horses and trees.

Also, for example, a beach can be identified if a search is based on color and texture matching and the color selected is wide blue with yellow texture below.

Attrasoft Image Finder has developed an image retrieval technique where input images would be stored in various files. Also, images would be kept in directory files. There is an interface screen where users can provide the file name containing the input image and also can put various parameters like focus, background, symmetry, rotation type, reduction type and so on. The images from the directory would then be retrieved based on these inputs. The images in the directory are defined containing the sample segments or translated segments, rotated segments, scaled segments, rotated and scaled segments, and brighter or darker segments. This method goes to some extent in bringing out semantic meanings in an image in the sense that the user can specify an input image semantically, then corresponding input image is retrieved and based on that input image, image database is searched to find symmetry (Attrasoft, 2001). There are few other similar automatic image retrieval models available including Computer Vision Online Demos.

But this level also needs a lot more developments to achieve a universally accepted technique to bring out semantic meanings out of the image.

Level three attempts retrievals with abstract attributes. This level of retrieval can be divided into two groups. One is a particular event such as 'Find pictures of Australia playing cricket against another particular country.' A second one could be 'Find a picture which is a residential area.'

To interpret an image after segmentations and analyzing it efficiently requires very complex reasoning. This also requires a retrieval technique of level two to get semantic meanings of various objects. It is obvious this retrieval technique is far from being developed with modern technology available in the field.

Works Done So Far

In this section, we present some of the works done in the field of content-based image retrieval. Although plenty of research works have been done so far in the field, no universally accepted model has yet been developed. The research concentrated on image segmentation based on low-level features like color, shape, texture and spatial relations. But to find the semantic meanings or high-level meanings of an image like whether it is the image of human beings or a bus or a train and so on is still a problem. Attempts are being made to link low-level and high-level features. But it is proving difficult for the very simple reason there remains a vast gap between human perception and computer perception. We present a few references of the works done.

One approach is where document images are accessed directly, using image and object attributes and the relative positions of objects within images, as well as indirectly, through associated document components. This is based on retrieving multimedia documents by pictorial content. Queries may address, directly or indirectly, one or more components. Indirect addressing involves references from associated components, e.g., an image caption is a text component referring to an image component and so is an in-text reference to an image. A symbolic image consists, in general, of objects, relations among objects and descriptions of object and image properties. The properties of objects and whole images are described by object and image attributes, respectively (Constantopoulos et al., 1991).

Then there is another method of querying and content-based retrieval that considers audio or visual properties of multimedia data through the use of MORE. In MORE, every entity in an application domain is represented as an object. An object's behavior is presented with a method, which activates the object by receiving a certain message. Objects bearing the same characteristics are managed as a single class. Generally, a class contains structural definitions, methods, or values that the objects in the class commonly posses (Yoshitaka et al., 1994).

Range searches in multi-dimensional space have been studied extensively and several excellent search structures have been devised. However, all of these require that the ranges in the different dimensions be specified independently. In other words, only rectangular regions can be specified and searched so far. Similarly, non-point objects can be indexed only in terms of their bounding rectangles. A polyhedral search of regions and polyhedral bounding rectangles can often provide a much greater selectivity in the search. How to use multi-attribute search structures for polyhedral regions, by mapping polyhedral regions into rectangular regions of a higher dimensions has been shown (Jagadish, 1990).

In human design processes, many drawings of shapes remain incomplete or are executed inaccurately. Cognitively a designer is able to discern these anomalous shapes, whereas current CAAD systems fail to recognize them properly so that CAAD systems are unable to match left-hand-side conditions of shape rules. As a result, current CAAD systems fail to retrieve right-hand-side actions. Multi-layered neural networks are constructed to solve the recognition and transformation of ill-processed shapes in light of recent advances of connectionism in cognitive psychology and artificial intelligence (Liu, 1993).

Attempts have been made to retrieve a similar shape when shapes are measured by coordinate systems (Mehrotra & Gary, 1995).

Then, MIRO (Multimedia Information Retrieval) is researching new methods and techniques for information storage and retrieval so that all types of media can be handled in an integrated manner through adaptive interaction with a user. Topics include human-computer interaction, logical and probabilistic models of information retrieval, run-time support for multimedia information retrieval and evaluation of retrieval effectiveness (Thanos, 1995).

A parallel computing approach to creating engineering concept spaces for semantic retrieval has been developed through the Illinois Digital Library Initiative Project. This research presents preliminary results generated from the semantic retrieval research component of the Illinois Digital Library Initiative (DLI) project. Using a variation of the automatic thesaurus generation techniques, to which is referred to as the concept space approach, it is aimed to create graphs of domain-specific concepts (terms) and their weighted co-occurrence relationships for all major engineering domains. Merging these concept spaces and providing traversal paths across different concept spaces could potentially help alleviate the vocabulary (difference) problem evident in large-scale information retrieval. Experiments had been done previously with such a technique for a smaller molecular biology domain (Worm Community System, with 10+ MBs of document collection) with encouraging results (Chen et al., 1996).

A system named MARCO (denoting MAp Retrieval by COntent) that is used for the acquisition, storage, indexing and retrieval of map images is presented. The input to MARCO is raster images of separate map layers and raster images of map composites. A legend-driven map interpretation system converts map layer images from their physical representation to their logical representation. This logical representation is then used to automatically index both the composite and the layer images. Methods for incorporating logical and physical layer images as well as composite images into the framework of a relational database management system are described. Indices are constructed on both the contextual and the spatial data thereby enabling efficient retrieval of layer and composite images based on contextual as well as spatial specifications. Example queries and query processing strategies using these indices are described. The user interface is demonstrated via the execution of an example query. Results of an experimental study on a large amount of data are preserved. The system is evaluated in terms of accuracy and in terms of query execution time (Samet, 1996).

Fingerprint databases are characterized by their large size as well as noisy and distorted query images. Distortions are very common in fingerprint images due to elasticity of the skin. In this article, a method of indexing large fingerprint image databases is presented. The approach integrates a number of domain-specific high-level features such as pattern class and ridge-density at higher levels of the search. At the lowest level, it incorporates elastic structural feature-based matching for indexing the database. With a multilevel indexing approach, the search space is reduced. The search engine has also been implemented on Splash 2 — a field programmable gate array (FPGA)-based array processes to obtain near ASIC level speed of matching. This approach has been tested on a locally collected test data and on NIST-S, a large fingerprint database available in the public domain (Ratha et al., 1996).

Focussing has been done on the use of motion analysis to create visual representations of videos that may be useful for efficient browsing and indexing in contrast with traditional frame-oriented representations. Two major approaches for motion based representations have been presented. The first approach demonstrated that dominant 2-D and 3-D motion techniques are useful in their own right for computing video mosaics through the computation of dominant scene motion and/or structure. However, this may not be adequate if object level indexing and manipulation is to be accomplished efficiently. The second approach presented addresses this issue through simultaneous estimation of an adequate number of simple 2-D motion models. A unified view of the two approaches naturally follows from the multiple model approach: the dominant motion method becomes a particular case of the multiple motion method if the number of models is fixed to be one and only the robust EM algorithm without the MDL stage employed (Sawhney, 1996).

Image content-based retrieval is emerging as an important research area with application to digital libraries and multimedia databases. The focus is being put on the image processing aspects and, in particular, using texture information for browsing and retrieval of large image data. It proposed use of Gabber wavelet features for texture analysis and provided a comprehensive experimental evaluation. Comparisons with other multi-resolution texture features using the Brodatz texture database indicate that the Gabor features provide the best pattern retrieval accuracy. An application to browsing large air photos is illustrated (Manjunath & Ma, 1996).

A method is developed for the content-based retrieval of multi-spectral satellite images using invariant representations. Since these images contain a wide variety of structures with different physical characteristics it is useful to exploit several classes of representations and algorithms. Working from a physical model for multi-band satellite image formation, existing algorithms for this application have been modified and integrated. The performance of the strategy has been demonstrated for image retrieval invariant to atmospheric and illumination auditions from a database of 166 multi-band images acquired at different times over areas of the U.S. (Healey & Jain, 1996).

The problem of retrieving images from a large database is addressed using an image as a query. The method is specifically aimed at databases that store images in JPEG format and works in the compressed domain to create index keys. A key is generated for each image in the database and is matched with the key generated for the query image. The keys are independent of the size of the image. Images that have similar keys are assumed to be similar, but there is no semantic meaning to the similarity (Shneier & Abdel-Mottaleb, 1996).

The Multi-mission VICAR Planner (MVP) is described in an article. It is an AI planning system which uses knowledge about image processing steps and their requirements to construct executable image processing scripts to support high-level science requests made to the Jet Propulsion Laboratory (JPL) Multi-mission Image Processing Subsystem (MIPS). This article describes a general AI planning approach to automation and application of the approach to a specific area of image processing for planetary science applications involving radiometric correction, color triplet reconstruction and mosaicing in which the MVP system significantly reduces the amount of effort required by image processing experts to fill a typical request (Chien & Mortensen, 1996).

Another paper presents how morphological transformations can be related to representations of a set on different lattices. (A hierarchical definition of structuring element conveys to a class of multi-grid transformations Pk that handle changes on discrete representations of regions.) The transformations correspond to upward and downward processes in a hierarchical structure, based on multi-grid transformations, a method to delineate non-perfectly-isolated objects in an nxn image requiring O(log n) time is presented. The approach considers grey level regions as sets and processes through a pyramid to carry out geometric manipulations. Extending the concept of boundary to cope with hierarchical representations of a set, a second method, which identifies the boundaries in an image is discussed (Montiel et al., 1996).

IMEDIA project, which is related to image analysis, is the bottleneck of multimedia indexing concerns about image analysis for feature space and probabilistic modelisation, statistics and information theory for interactive browsing, similarity measure and matching. To achieve these goals, research involves the following topics: image indexing, partial queries, interactive search, multimedia indexing (Boujemma et al., 2000).

In a project named Efficient Content-Based Image Retrieval, the focus is the development of a general, scalable architecture to support fast querying of very large image databases with user-specified distance measures. They have developed algorithms and data structures for efficient image retrieval from large databases with multiple distance measures. They are investigating methods for merging their general distance-measure independent method with other useful techniques that may be distance measure specific, such as keyword retrieval and relational indexing. They are developing both new methods for combining distance measures and a framework in which users can specify their queries without detailed knowledge of the underlying metrics. They have built a prototype system to test their methods and evaluated it on both a large general image database and a smaller controlled database (Shapiro et al., 2000).

There is another work that addresses the issue of a gap existing between low-level visual features addressing the more detailed perceptual aspects and high-level semantic features underlying the more general aspects of visual data. Although plenty of research works have been devoted to this problem, so far, the gap still remains (Zhao et al., 2002).

Another chapter provides a state-of-the-art account of Visual Information Retrieval (VIR) systems and Content-Based Visual Information Retrieval (CBVIR) systems. It provides directions for future research by discussing major concepts, system design issues, research prototypes and currently available commercial solutions (Marques et al., 2002).

SUMMARY

A general introduction of the subject-area of the book has been given in this chapter. Both multimedia systems and content-based image retrieval have been discussed from the introductory level. Also, focus has been made to specify current problems in both of these fields and research efforts being made to solve them. Some of the research works done in the field of content-based image retrieval have been presented to give an idea of the research being conducted. All these should give a broad picture of the contents of issues, covered in these areas.

REFERENCES

Attrasoft (2001, May). *Attrasoft*, P.O. Box 13051, Savannah, GA. 31406, USA.

Boujemma, N. et al. (2000, February). *IMEDA Project*, INRIA.

Chen, H., Scatz, B., Ng, T., Kirchhoff, A., & Lin, C. (1996). A parallel computing approach to creating engineering concept spaces for semantic retrieval: The Illinois digital library initiative project. *IEEE Transactions on Pattern Analysis and Machine Intelligence,* (18).

Chien, S.A. & Mortensen, H.B. (1996). Automating image processing for scientific data analysis of a large image database. *IEEE Transactions on Pattern Analysis and Machine Intelligence,* 18(8).

Constantopoulos, P., Drakopoulos, J., & Yeorgaroudakis, Y. (1991). Retrieval of multimedia documents by pictorial content: A prototype system. *International Conference on Multimedia Information Systems '91.* The Institute of Systems Science, National University of Singapore, 35-48.

Eakins, J.P. & Graham, M.E. (1999). Content-based image retrieval: A report to the JISC technology application programme. Institute for Image Data Research, University of Northumbria at Newcastle, UK.

Forsyth, D.A et al. (1996). Finding pictures of objects in large collections of images. In Heidon, P.B & Sandore, B. (Eds.), *Digital Image Access and Retrieval: 1996 Clinic on Library Applications of Data Processing,* (pp. 118-139). Graduate School of Library and Information Science, University of Illinois at Urbana-Champaign.

Gudivada, V.N. & Raghavan, V.V. (1995). Content-based image retrieval systems. *IEEE,* September 1995.

Healey, G. & Jain, A. (1996). Retrieving multispectral satellite images using physics-based invariant representations. *IEEE Transactions on Pattern Analysis and Machine Intelligence,* 18(8).

Jagadish, H. V. (1990). Spatial search with polyhedra. *IEEE,* 311-319.

Liu, Y. (1993). A connectionist approach to shape recognition and transformation. *CAAD Futures '93,* 19-36.

Ma, W.Y., Manjunath, B.S., Luo, Y., Deng, Y., & Sun, X. (n.d.). *NETRA: A Content-Based Image Retrieval System.* Dept. of Electrical and Computer Engineering, University of California, Santa Barbara, California, USA.

Manjunath, B.S. & Ma, W.Y. (1996). Texture features for browsing and retrieval of image data. *IEEE Transactions on Pattern Analysis and Machine Intelligence,* 18(8), August 1996.

Marques, O. & Furht, B. (2001). Content-based visual information retrieval. *Distributed Multimedia Databases: Techniques and Applications,* 37-57.

Mehrotra & Gary. (1995). Similar-shape retrieval in shape data management. *IEEE,* September 1995.

Montiel, M.E., Aguado, A.S., Garza-Jinich, M.A., & Alarcdn, J. (1996). Image manipulation using m-filters in a pyramidal computer model. *IEEE Transactions on Pattern Analysis and Machine Intelligence, 18(8).*

Ratha, N.K., Karu, K., Chen, S., & Jain, A.K. (1996). A real-time matching system for large fingerprint databases. *IEEE Transactions on Pattern Analysis and Machine Intelligence, 18(8).*

Samet, H. (1996). MARCO: Map retrieval by content. *IEEE Transactions on Pattern Analysis and Machine Intelligence, 18(8)*.

Sawhney, H. & Ayer, S. (1996). Compact representations of videos through dominant and multiple motion estimation. *IEEE Transactions on Pattern Analysis and Machine Intelligence, 18(8)*.

Seaborn, M.A. (1997). Image Retrieval Systems.

Shapiro, L.G. et al. (2000). *Efficient Content-Based Image Retrieval.* Department of Computer Science and Engineering, University of Washington.

Shneier, M. & Abde-Mottaleb, M. (1996). Exploiting the jpeg compression scheme for image retrieval. *IEEE Transactions on pattern Analysis and machine Intelligence, 18(8)*.

Thanos, C. (1995). Multimedia information retrieval. *Sven MiiBig.*

Yoshitaka, A., Kishida, S., & Hirakawa, M. (1994). Knowledge-assisted content-based retrieval for multimedia databases. *IEEE Multimedia,* (Winter), 12-21.

Zhao, R. & Grosky, W.I. (2001). Bridging the semantic gap in image retrieval. *Distributed Multimedia Databases: Techniques and Applications*, 14-36.

SECTION II

MULTIMEDIA STRUCTURES AND SECURITY

Chapter II

A Duplicate Chinese Document Image Retrieval System Based on Line Segment Feature in Character Image Block

Yung-Kuan Chan, National Huwei Institute of Technology, Taiwan

Tung-Shou Chen, National Taichung Institute of Technology, Taiwan

Yu-An Ho, National Taichung Institute of Technology, Taiwan

ABSTRACT

With the rapid progress of digital image technology, the management of duplicate document images is also emphasized widely. As a result, this paper suggests a duplicate Chinese document image retrieval (DCDIR) system, which uses the ratio of the number of black pixels to that of white pixels on the scanned line segments in a character image block as the feature of the character image block. Experimental results indicate that the system can indeed effectively and quickly retrieve the desired duplicate Chinese document image from a database.

INTRODUCTION

With the widespread popularity of electronic documents as well as electronic books, more and more people have started reading these new sorts of publications. Most of the electronic books and electronic documents are stored in an image format. As for traditional newspapers or magazines, they can also be transformed into digital image formatted data by using the tool like a scanner, and then saved in a computer for the purpose of data backup. Meanwhile, by combining with the characteristic of rapid data processing of a computer, the data of the duplicate documents can be quickly acquired and retrieved.

Because the technology of Optical Character Recognition (OCR) has been improved to a degree, a document image can be transformed to become the data with Big5 code format, and only the Big5 codes are stored so as to reduce the required memory space. However, using the technique of OCR may cause some errors in document contents because of recognition failure. Moreover, in order to preserve the original contents and states of a document, transforming a document into an image and storing the image in a database is sometimes necessary.

The primary function of a duplicate document image retrieval (DDIR) system is to transform the data in document format into those represented in digital image format. This transformation would be completed by using the tool like a scanner. Then, the DDIR system will store these images and their corresponding features in a database for data backup purpose. Here the document image is called a duplicate document image. When intending to retrieve a duplicate document image, users can also use the tool like a scanner to input the first several text lines of the original document into the system, and to create a query document image and figure out the feature of the image. The DDIR system finally transmits the users the duplicate document image whose image feature is similar to that of the query document image.

In the aspect of extracting the feature from a document image, many techniques have been proposed (Caprari, 2000; Doermann, Li, & Kia, 1997; Peng et al., 2001). Caprari (2001) used the method of document template to measure the overlapping ratio of black pixels and white pixels between two document images when their two templates overlap. Generally, the higher the overlapping ratio is, the more similar these two documents are. Doermann, Li and Kia (1997) encoded the heights of English letter shapes and used these codes as the feature of the English document image. Meanwhile, by comparing and matching these feature codes, the duplicate document images that are stored in the database can be searched and retrieved. Besides, Peng et al. (2001) applied the block sizes and locations to be the feature of a document image, and suggested a component block list matching technique based on this feature for the duplicate document image retrieval.

The features mentioned above are only suitable for stating the characteristic of an English document image. The characteristics of Chinese characters are different from those of English ones, and the strokes and shapes of Chinese characters are much more complicated than those of English characters. Therefore, this paper suggests a line segment feature, which is appropriate for stating the characteristics of the Chinese character image blocks in a Chinese document image, and applies this feature to construct a duplicate Chinese document image retrieval (DCDIR) system.

The next section will give a brief review of some related works. The following section will describe the line segment feature in a character image block proposed in this chapter. Then, the chapter will delineate how to make use of this proposed feature to create a DCDIR system. This is followed with a statement on the experimental and analyzed results. This is followed by a discussion on the future trends of the duplicate document image retrieval system. At last, the conclusions will be given.

BACKGROUND

The feature of a text image plays an important role in a DDIR system. Many techniques of the text image feature extraction have been proposed, such as the features of line segmentation, page segmentation, text block, and shape code (Caprari, 2000; Doermann, Li, & Kia, 1997; Peng et al., 2001). This section will give them a briefly description.

Caprari (2000) proposed a method for document image retrieval. He uses the document template technique to calculate the proportion of overlap area that contains both black pixels and white pixels when two templates overlap, as the feature of a document image. In general, the higher the overlapping ratio is, the more similar both documents are.

Doermann, Li and Kia (1997) presented a document image retrieval system. This system classifies and encodes character types based on the condition that four base lines cross each text line, and uses the codes as the feature of the document image. Meanwhile, the duplicate document images in the database can be retrieved by comparing their feature codes.

Later, Peng et al. (2001) also proposed a component block list matching method to retrieve the duplicate document image from a database. In this method, the size of each component block containing a paragraph text image in a duplicate document image as well as its relative location are regarded as the features of the duplicate document image.

DATABASE CREATION

The proposed duplicate document image retrieval system includes two parts — database creation and data retrieval. This section introduces the part of database creation in detail, and the next section will explain the part of data retrieval. When creating a duplicate document image database, one can use the tool like a scanner to scan each original document to generate a duplicate document image, and store the duplicate document image in the database. Each duplicate document image is a binary image, which only consists of black and white pixels.

When scanning a document to generate a duplicate document image, the position of the document on the scanner may be misplaced so that the duplicate document image becomes inclined. Figure 1(a) shows an original image and Figure 1(b) is its duplicate document image that appears inclined. The inclined condition of a document image would bring about inconvenience to users and cause errors in extracting its image feature values. Peng et al. (2000) used a correlation-based method to detect the inclination of an image, and then they applied an interpolation method to turn the image back according to the detected inclination. This method can be effectively used to adjust the inclined condition of a duplicate document image. Therefore, this paper uses the method to turn the inclined document image back. Figure 1(c) is the duplicate document image after inclination adjusting.

However, as in Figure 1(c), after the duplicate document image is turned back, the frame of the duplicate document image would become inclined. The inclination condition affects the appearance of the document and makes it inconvenient to read the document. Therefore, it is necessary to cut off the border blank of the document image. While

Figure 1: The Normalization of an Inclined Document Image

(a) An original document

(b) The duplicate document image after scanning

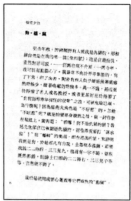

(c) The duplicate document image after inclination adjusting

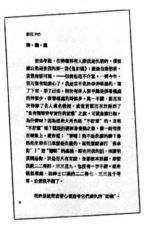

(d) The duplicate document image after cutting off the border blank

removing the border blank, the system starts scanning the duplicate document image, which is turned correctly, from the most left-top pixel. Then, from left to right and top to bottom, each pixel is scanned until one certain black pixel P is found. Finally, all pixels located on the lines, which are prior to the line containing P, are removed in order to cut off the top border blank of the document image. By using the same method, the bottom, left and right border blanks of the document image are removed as well. Figure 1(d) demonstrates the final duplicate document image after cutting off the border blank of the document image illustrated in Figure 1(c).

Afterwards, the duplicate document image that has been normalized (i.e., inclination adjusting and cutting off the border blank) is then stored in a database. At the same time, the character image features of the duplicate document image are extracted and then stored in a database as well. The features are used as the index of the duplicate document image. Before extracting out the character image features of the duplicate document image, the system has to first perform the text line segmentation toward the duplicate document image so as to make every line image block containing only the complete image of one certain line text in the original document. Then, the system segments out all character image blocks from each previously segmented line image block so that every character image block contains only one Chinese character. Finally, the feature of each character image block is then extracted out.

Concerning the steps of segmenting line image blocks from a duplicate document image, first, all the black pixels in the duplicate document image are projected in a horizontal direction onto a projection vertical axis. For example, Figure 2(b) is the result from the horizontal projection of Figure 2(a). On the projection vertical axis, the distribution borders of black pixels and white pixels are the locations of the top and bottom boundaries of line image blocks, as shown in Figure 2(c). The length of a black section on the projection vertical axis is the height of the corresponding text line containing the character images whose black pixels are projected onto the black section.

Next, all the black pixels in every line image block are projected in a vertical direction to a certain projection horizontal axis. For example, Figure 3(b) shows the result that the line image block in Figure 3(a) is projected onto a projection horizontal axis. In this case, the distribution borders of the black pixels and white pixels on the projection horizontal axis are the locations of the left and right boundaries of character image blocks. Figure 3(c) shows the result of segmenting the line image block in Figure 3(a) into character image blocks. On the projection horizontal axis, the length of a black section is the width of the corresponding character image block, whose black pixels are projected onto the black section.

According to the statistics from experiments, the heights of many Chinese punctuation symbols (such as '，', '。', '、') are generally smaller than three-fourths of the height of most Chinese characters, and the width is also smaller than three-fourths of the width of most Chinese characters, too. Therefore, when the height of a certain character image block **CB** is smaller than the third-fourth of the average height of all character image blocks in the document image, and the width of **CB** is also smaller than the third-fourth of the average width of all character image blocks, the system will then regard the character in **CB** as a noise or a punctuation and then remove it. In accordance with above

Figure 2: The Text Line Segmentation of a Document Image

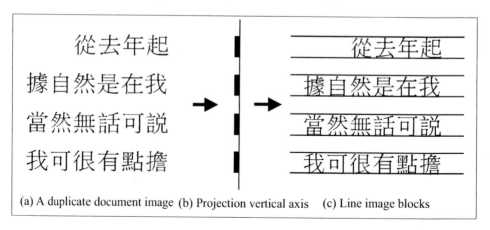

(a) A duplicate document image (b) Projection vertical axis   (c) Line image blocks

situation, however, some punctuation symbols (like '?', '|', '—') would not be removed. This system would regard them as the ordinary Chinese characters. In the DCDIR system, both the query document and the desired duplicate document image are from the same original document and they are processed by the same procedure. Thus, these unremovable punctuation symbols would not affect the final retrieval result.

After all the character image blocks are segmented out from a duplicate document image, three horizontal scanning lines are drawn on each character image block. These three horizontal scanning lines respectively located at $1/4{\times}H$, $2/4{\times}H$ and $3/4{\times}H$ character height in the block. Here H represents the height of the character image block. Then, according to the ratio of the total number of the black pixels to that of the white pixels that the scanning line goes through, an encoding process is executed to reduce the memory space required to store the feature of the character image block. The way of encoding is shown as follows:

$$X_i = \begin{cases} 0, \text{if } D_{i,b} \times m > D_{i,w} \\ 1, \text{if } D_{i,b} \times m \leq D_{i,w} \end{cases}, \text{for } i = 0, 1, \text{and } 2.$$

In this equation, $D_{i,w}$ and $D_{i,b}$ are respectively the total numbers of white pixels and black pixels that the i-th scanning line passes through, and m is the weight (a given constant value) for the ratio from the total numbers of black pixels and white pixels on the scanning line. Thus, each character image block can be represented by a three-bit $(X_0X_1X_2)$ code; we name the code the feature code of the character image block. As a result, there are 8 total kinds of different combinations for a feature code. These eight binary codes are respectively $000, 001, 010, 011, 100, 101, 110,$ and 111, and their corresponding decimal feature codes are respectively $0, 1, ...,$ and 7.

Figure 3: Segmentation of Character Image Blocks

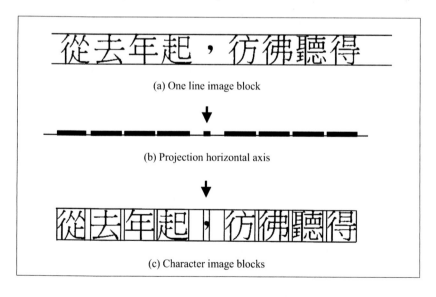

(a) One line image block

(b) Projection horizontal axis

(c) Character image blocks

Figure 4: The Three Scanning Lines of the Character '徙 '

First scanning line

Second scanning line

Third scanning line

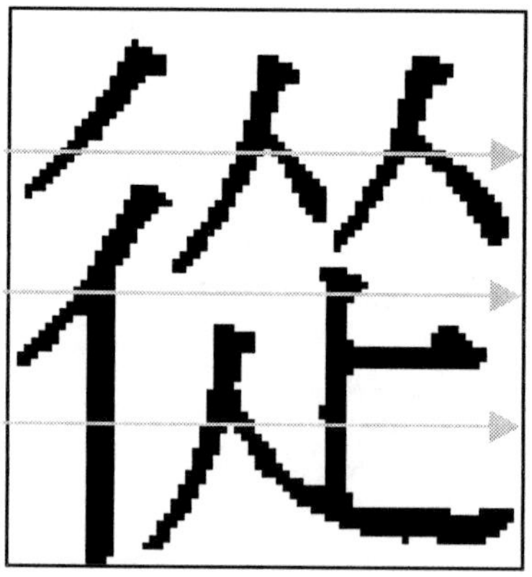

Suppose $m = 3$, Figure 4 shows the three scanning lines of the character '徙 '. The first scanning line has **21** black pixels and **52** white pixels, so $X_0 = 0$. The second scanning line has **11** black pixels and **62** white pixels, so $X_1 = 1$. In addition, the third scanning line has **14** black pixels and **59** white pixels, so $X_2 = 1$, too. Therefore, the binary feature code $X_0 X_1 X_2$ of the character image block is **011** (and its corresponding decimal feature code is **3**).

Because the resolution setup of a scanner may be different, the same original document may be scanned to become the duplicate document images of different sizes. This proposed feature adopts the ratio from the number of black pixels and white pixels, so the feature encoding would not be affected due to the scale variant of images. Moreover, the desired duplicate document image and the query document image are both from the same original document. Therefore, the problem that the font type and style of the characters in the query document are different from those in the desired duplicate document image would not occur in this system.

DATA RETRIEVAL

When intending to search a duplicate document image I_d, users can use the tool as a scanner to scan the first several lines of text in its original document in order to create a query document image I_q. By repeating the same method mentioned above, the feature codes of all character image blocks are extracted from the query document image. Let $Q = q_1 q_2 \ldots q_l$ be the feature code of the query document image, and the length of the feature code is l. Next, the system extracts the first feature codes with the length l from every duplicate document image in the database. Let the extracted feature codes be $D = d_1 d_2 \ldots d_l$. Then, the system estimates the similarity between D and Q.

In this estimation process, the system compares the corresponding bit pair q_i and d_i between Q and D from left to right, respectively. When $q_i = d_i$, the system adds **1** to the value of S. $S = 0$ initially. The final value of S is the similarity between I_q and I_d. Finally, the duplicate document image, which has the largest similarity value, is found out.

EXPERIMENTAL RESULTS AND ANALYSIS

The experimental platform used in the system includes AMD Duron 750 CPU, *448* MB RAM, and Microsoft Windows 2000 operating system. In addition, the programming tool is java version 1.2.1, and the database system is Microsoft SQL Server.

The goal of the first experiment is to explore the constant weight value *m*. This value denotes the weight with the number of black pixels to that of white pixels on the scanning lines in a character image. As for different values of *m*, in this experiment, according to the difference of feature codes, *5,401* commonly used Chinese characters among Big5 codes are categorized into eight groups each of which corresponds to one feature code. Table 1 shows the number of members in each group for *m* = 2, 3, and 4. The various variances σ^2_c for *m* = 2, 3, and 4 are also respectively calculated in the experiment, where:

$$\sigma^2_c = \frac{\sum_{i=0}^{7}(c_i - \mu_c)^2}{8}.$$

In the above equation, c_i is the number of members in group *i*, and μ_c is the mean value of c_i's for a certain value of *m*. From the experimental results, one can know that, when *m* = 3, the variance σ^2_c has the minimum value. This means, when *m* = 3, all Chinese character image blocks can be most uniformly mapped to various kinds of feature codes. As a result, the following experiments of this paper will adopt the condition *m* = 3 to perform the feature encoding.

The purpose of the following experiment is to explore the performance of the proposed DCDIR system. This experiment prints out the image file of the electronic book "朝花夕拾・呐喊" to create a document, and then scans each page in the document to become an image by using a scanner. Moreover, by using the feature extracting technique

Table 1: The Results of the First Experiment

m Feature code	2	3	4
000(0)	372	1253	2266
001(1)	596	773	763
010(2)	262	387	402
011(3)	813	525	312
100(4)	337	564	628
101(5)	817	591	324
110(6)	390	374	262
111(7)	1798	918	428
Variance (σ^2_c)	220549	74523	387785

Table 2: The Result of the Second Experiment

Chinese character lines Testing result	First 3	First 5	First 6	First 7	First 10
Database image	336	336	336	336	336
Testing image	101	101	101	101	101
Correctly retrieving the desired image	99	100	100	101	101
Accuracy rate (%)	98.0	99.0	99.0	100	100

proposed in this chapter, the feature values of the document images are extracted and stored in a database, where the resolution of the scanner is set to be *300* dpi. In this experiment, there are *336* sheets of duplicate document images in the database, each of which contains *2148×3251* pixels. The font type and size are "新細明體" and *12* points, respectively, and each image has at least *10* text lines.

This experiment rescans *101* sheets of the original document and uses these document images to generate the query document images. In this experiment, the first three, five, six, seven, and ten text lines of the *101* original document sheets are respectively used as the contents of the query document images. When performing the query, the system executes the anti-inclined processing on the query image, extracts the feature values of the query image, and then compares them with the feature values of each duplicate document image in the database.

From the experimental results, even if only the first three text lines of a document sheet are used as the content of a query document image, the accuracy rate of correctly retrieving the desired document image could still reach more than *98.0%*. In addition, when the first seven text lines are used as the content of the query document image, the accuracy rate of precisely seeking the desired image could reach *100%*; moreover, the average searching time is approximately *8* seconds. Table 2 shows the results of this experiment.

FUTURE TRENDS

Up to now, many techniques about the duplicate document image retrieval system have been proposed (Caprari, 2000; Doermann, Li, & Kia, 1997; Peng et al., 2000; Peng et al., 2001). However, these techniques are only suitable for the duplicate English document images. Because an English document is mostly made up of approximately *70* commonly-used characters, which contains *52* English letters (including uppercase and lowercase letters) and punctuation marks, the classification and encoding procedure based on the feature of these characters' font types are possible. However, these methods are not suitable for the duplicate Chinese document image retrieval because the number of all different Chinese characters is about *45,000*, in which about *5,401* are commonly used, and the strokes and shapes of most Chinese characters are more complicated than those of English characters.

To effectively manage the duplicate Chinese document images, it is necessary to develop a feature, which can offer an excellent identification capacity to classify Chinese characters by only using a little extra memory space. In order to reduce the extra memory space, it is feasible to segment a duplicate document image into blocks, each of which contains a set of adjacent characters, and to extract the features from the blocks. The image features are then regarded as the feature of the duplicate document image. However, the number of the blocks in a duplicate document image is much less than that of the characters in an identical duplicate document image. The feature dimensions are quite reduced; therefore, its identification capability is lessened, either.

After a paper document is used over a long period of time, the document may be stained or worn away, such that its content is indistinct. How to develop an effective image feature insensitive to these variations is an important task in the future.

CONCLUSION

This chapter introduces a line segment feature to represent a character image block and presents a DCDIR system based on this feature. The proposed image feature takes down the ratio of the number of black pixels to that of the white pixels contained in the scanning lines on a character image block. Thus, this feature would not work abnormally due to different sizes of document images, either would it cause the problem of different character font types and formats. Experimental results also indicate that the proposed DCDIR system can provide an excellent function of retrieval.

REFERENCES

Caprari, R. S. (2000). Duplicate document detection by template matching. *Image and Vision Computing, 18*(8), 633-643.

Doermann, D., Li, H., & Kia, O. (1997). The detection of duplicates in document image databases. *Proceedings of the Fourth International Conference on Document Analysis and Recognition, 1*, (pp. 314-318).

Peng, H., Chi, Z., Siu, W. C., & Long, F. (2000). PageX: An integrated document processing software for digital libraries. *Proceedings of the International Workshop on Multimedia Data Storage, Retrieval, Integration, and Applications, Hong Kong*, (pp. 203-207).

Peng, H., Long, F., Chi, Z., & Sui, W. C. (2001, July). Document Imaging Template Matching Based on Component Block List. *Pattern Recognition Letters, 22*(9), 1033-1042.

Chapter III

Technology of Music Score Watermarking

M. Monsignori, University of Florence, Italy and EXITECH, Italy

P. Nesi, University of Florence, Italy

M. Spinu, University of Florence, Italy and EXITECH, Italy

ABSTRACT

Content protection for multimedia data is widely recognized especially for data types that are frequently distributed, sold or shared in digital and via Internet. Particularly, the music industry dealing with audio files realized the necessity for content protection. Distribution of music sheets will face the same problems. Digital watermarking techniques provide a certain level of protection for music sheets. Classical image-oriented watermarking algorithms for images suffer from several drawbacks when directly applied to image representations of music sheets. Therefore, new solutions have been developed which are designed regarding the content of the music sheets. In comparison to other media types, the development of watermarking algorithms for music scores is a rather young technology. The chapter reviews the evolution of the early approaches and describes the current state of the art in the field.

INTRODUCTION

In the case of black and white (b/w) images, most of the approaches used for color images are unusable. For example, for b/w pictorial images, it is unsuitable to work in the frequency based transform domain since this implies generating an unacceptable noise for the musicians. Some other techniques proposed for watermarking can be also considered as possible approaches in music scores watermarking.

The copyright owners (the music publishers, authors and/or distributors) have in their archives high quantities of music scores. In classical music, the original music is normally stored on paper since it was produced several years ago. Presently, only new light and popular music pieces are in symbolic notation formats. Light and popular music have a limited life span in terms of time duration in comparison with classical music pieces. Publishers keep their distance from transforming their classical music pieces in digital format for e-commerce purposes since whenever distributing in this way their copyright ownership is not protected. Therefore, classical music risks remaining in the archives of publishers and libraries since its distribution is too dangerous for the future business of the copyright owners. The life of the copyrights for that kind of music is close to 60 to 80 years. Current copyright infringement is only via photocopy process. Internet distribution risks being an efficient vehicle for losing control on this material. The situation is different for light and popular music where the market life is shorter.

E-commerce for music distribution is not acceptable for publishers without the support of adequate protection mechanisms. Publishers prefer to protect their music and at the same time to allow the users exploiting content functionalities according to the permissions and prices established by the publishers. To cope with these problems, mechanisms for protecting musical objects include:

- Encryption techniques to support the transferring music objects;
- Watermarking audio files in different formats;
- Watermarking images of music score sheets;
- Watermarking music sheets while they are printed from symbolic notation files; and
- Definition of Digital Rights Management policies.

If a good and complete protection model will be developed and profitably validated, many publishers could decide to publish their classical music pieces on the Internet and this will have surely positive effects on the music sheet market. These include:

- The music should be bought in real-time.
- The distribution will not be limited to geographical areas.
- A further evolution of music software (editors, delivering systems, commercial tools, etc.) might be expected.
- Moreover, very ancient music sheets are interesting for artistic and historical aspects, especially if handwritten.

The field of music application quickly evolves, giving to the publishers, or in general to the music copyright owner, the possibility to use the new technologies in order to improve their activity.

The chapter continues with a brief description of several possible approaches for watermarking music sheets and with a complete description of a technique that was implemented as the best result of our research. Please note that the work available on watermarking music sheets is really limited to two research groups that produced the results for the research and development project called WEDELMUSIC.

BACKGROUND

The music scores availability changed during the years. At the beginning, the music was described with a low number of symbols by using the state-of-the-art technologies. The paper was used as a support for the music scores until few years ago. Today, the symbolic representation of music has conquered more application fields and numerous musicians started to use new technologies for writing and manipulating music.

Music on sheets not always satisfies the music consumers that frequently need to make changes (adding annotations) on the music that they buy. The music scores are really used day by day. This is quite different with respect to a book that is typically read once or twice.

If a user makes copies their quality quickly is not good. Digitized music sheets could give a lot of advantages in that sense. A musician could print several copies of the music that he bought, and changes could be saved into a safe digital format.

A first possible, low cost solution can be to acquire the music sheet with a scanner. An image music score is only a photographic copy; it has a number of considerable disadvantages. The most important is that the technology capabilities in manipulating digital contents are not used. The music scores in image format are not editable. This important issue is the reason that motivate young musicians to buy music editors. They manipulate what we call *Symbolic Music Notation.* The symbolic notation it is obviously stored in digital in files of the computer and can be used for producing the music sheet as well as for producing an annotated version of it, if the changes are made with the same music editor used for creating the music sheet.

A digital symbolic music score at any given moment can be edited and copied an infinite number of times, with a far superior quality of print. Also, the symbolic music editors allow the synchronization between various types of digital music (symbolic, images, MIDI audio, MP3 audio, etc.) (Bellini et al., 2001; Bellini et al., 2003).

In order to understand each musical symbol, an analysis can be performed on the musical content and not only on the music external characteristics it is needed to consider the capability of music editor. For instance, by using a music editor it is possible to search specific sequences of notes in numerous scores, to make transposition for different instruments, to make a piano reduction, to change the lyric, and to annotate and make deeper changes in the structure of the music.

Today the music scores are available on paper at 90 percent. The situation changes rapidly since a big number of publishers started to digitize in a massive manner their music scores archives.

Watermarking Music Sheets — Approaches Description

In this section, before presenting the possible algorithms and techniques for watermarking music sheets, some general requirements are exposed and discussed. Also, an analysis of the embedded data is shown. Most of the described approaches were analyzed and tested during the early phases of our research. Others were collected from the literature (Busch et al., 2000; Funk et al., 2001; Schmucker et al., 2001; Zhao et al., 1995). A possible application in music score watermarking of the approach shown in Maxemchuk and Low (1997) is also introduced.

Requirements

The requirements have been collected by means of a set of interviews with the experts of WEDELMUSIC project user group. The user group is mainly inclusive of musicians, copyists and music publishers. The identified requirements can be divided in three categories:

Content Requirements:

- The embedded data has to contain the publisher identification, the music piece identification and the music distributor identification. In alternative, the embedded data may contain a simple identification code, ID, that allows getting the former information by simply consulting a WEB service.

Visual Requirements:

- The watermark inserted in the printed music sheet has to be invisible for musicians or at least it must not disturb them during the music playing.
- The watermark has to be present inside the music printed by the final user in any format if the music is available in symbolic format. Thus, the watermark reading has not to depend on the availability of the music sheet's reference image.

Resistance Requirements:

- The cost to remove watermarks must be extremely expensive if compared to regular buying.
- The watermark must resist during sheet manipulation until the music printed becomes unreadable. Five levels of photocopy are sufficient to make music unreadable or of low quality.
- The watermark should also be readable by processing a smaller piece of music sheet (greater than three-fourths of the whole music sheet page) although a copy of a small part of the score does not represent a high commercial value.
- Processes of digital filtering, zooming, rotations, cropping, noise addition, flipping, etc., must be considered less probable manipulations since they are strongly time consuming (their cost can be comparably similar to the price of the music sheet, for a music score can include 30 pages) and too technical for the majority of end-users whose background is that of a musician.

Other typical watermark parameters have been taken into account in order to analyze the technique capability.

- The amount of embedded information has a direct influence on watermark robustness. The more information is embedded, the lower the robustness becomes. This is due to the following reason. The hidden code is repeated several times in the same page; therefore when the code is big, the number of times it can be repeated is lower, thus decreasing the general robustness.

- Embedding strength — There is a trade-off between watermark embedding robustness and quality. Increased robustness requires a massive embedding of hidden bits. This increases music score degradation and watermark visibility.

Data Capacity

A very important question is the information that should be stored during the watermarking process. This is limited by the number of music notation symbols that can be changed and how these symbols can be changed without degrading the readability. This is generally called the capacity of the information channel used for watermarking.

Watermarked Code

Another important question is what kind of information the watermark should contain.

It is necessary to embed the copyright information for the identification of the right owner and also to keep a trace about the origin of the scores in order to find the path of distribution.

According to the analysis performed in our research, the whole watermark code should be divided in two parts:

1. Copyright Watermark:
   <publisher ID code><component type><component number>
   In total there are 12 digits alphanumeric number = 72 bits
2. User Watermark:
   <LDID>
   The content of this part will be the distributor ID, which is a six digit alphanumeric number = 36 bits

The total number of bits to be embedded into the image can be 108. Some control sequences (hash, CRC or start/end sequences) should be needed. This information can be changed during the algorithm development and the number of bits should be variable because of synchronization problems.

Implementation Environment

The great majority of the music scores are still on paper in the publisher's archives. A first way to transform them into digital documents can be to transform them into images using a scanner. Another possible way can be to transform them in symbolic music by using a music editor. Obviously, the second way is very expensive since the music has to be totally retyped. The comparison of very efficient OMR (Optical Music Recognition) software similar to the OCR (Optical Character Recognition) seems to be quite improbable in the near future.

After the digitalization of the music images or symbolic music are obtained, these digital documents are different in quite all their characteristics. For example, in the case of text acquisition, the scanned image is just a photo of the original. The retyped text file instead, gives to the user the possibility to use all the text editor capabilities to manipulate

Figure 1: Music Score Digitalization

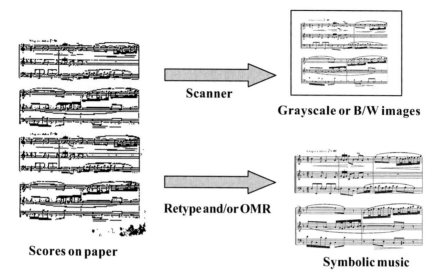

it. In the case of the images, no successive music manipulation is possible and only few changes can be performed to the image. An advantage is that the images can be easily viewed in any operating system and with an infinite number of applications.

The symbolic music allows the user to modify the music, justify it, change the page settings, etc. It can be considered as a kind of source code for the music. The disadvantage is that all these operations can be performed only if the music editor is available, and professional music sheets are typically produced by expensive and professional music editors. On the other hand, music editor builders provide simple viewers that in most cases do not guarantee the digital right management, DRM.

It is well known that the music sheets are distributed in paper format between the musicians. Therefore, it seems that the digitizing process is useless. In practice, music sheet distribution via Internet, from publishers to consumers, can be realized only by using digital formats. The distribution among consumers such as now with the photocopy could be even via digital music sheets, as occurred with audio files on Napster. Please note that on peer-to-peer (P2P) application there is also a quite significant distribution of music scores.

Also, by using the digital formats the music will be converted again on paper (today the musicians play the music only from paper sheet). This means that some printing capabilities have to be given to each software tool that manipulates music scores.

After printing, the music score comes back to the original format after changes are performed in digital format.

Watermarking images or watermarking symbolic music lead to obtain the same result. The watermarked music (symbolic or image) should remain in digital format in some not changeable file formats (like PDF) or in difficult changeable formats (PostScript).

In the next section, the described approaches are intended for the above mentioned two digital formats of the music scores. The implementation of the related algorithm for music watermarking is completely different in the two cases.

Figure 2: System Architecture for Music Sheet Watermarking while Printing

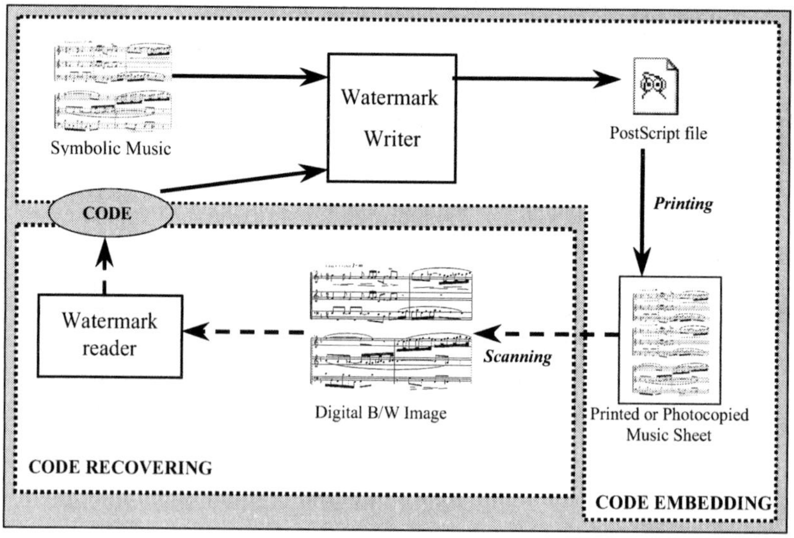

System Architecture for Watermarking while Printing Symbolic Music

The system architecture provides (as any other watermarking system architecture) a watermark writer process and a watermark reader process (see Figure 2).

The code is inserted in the music score when the print command is activated in a music editor (such as WEDELMUSIC). The process may generate a PostScript file or may send the information directly to the printer. In order to read the code hidden in the watermarked music sheet, it has to be scanned and the resulted image has to be elaborated with the watermark reader, which reconstructs the embedded code.

Approaches Overview

In this section, a short overview of several experiments on watermarking music sheets is reported. According to the requirements of publishers, the printed music sheets must be produced at high resolution and quality. In appreciated music sheets, there is no noise, meaning that the information is in black and white and therefore no space is left to hide information inside noise or in any kind of noise added-image. It means that the hidden code can be included only in the shape or in the position of music notation symbols. According to such a purpose, some common elements of music sheets can be considered: staff lines, stems, note head, bar lines, etc.

While stepping into such a direction, it is necessary to find a compromise between quality and watermark readability. It is hard work since quality is very important for musicians and some minor changes could produce readability problems for them. They pay attention to the design of musical symbols and any variation may be detectable and may disturb the musician during the music playing.

The techniques herewith considered can be split in two categories:
- Transformation of music elements
- Adoption of different fonts for the same symbol

In the approaches based on transformation, music symbols such as staff lines, bar lines, beams, stem or slurs (ties) are manipulated. The most significant examples are:
- Modifying the orientation of note stems,
- Modifying the position of the notes on the staff,
- Modifying the orientation of beam lines,
- Adding white dots in the middle of other bigger music notation symbols,
- Modulating staff lines by giving them different thickness, and considering thinner segments 0 and deeper as 1,
- Modulating staff lines to give them a sort of sinusoidal behavior, etc.

In general, the information to be hidden can be included in the changes considering both their presence and absence, as 1 and 0, respectively. In some cases, the magnitude of the change can be used for hiding more bits, for example in the orientation, the angle can be variable in order to add more bits.

Stem Rotation

The major problems of hiding information in the stem rotation (Busch et al., 2000) are the music score degradation and the low capacity in terms of hidden bits. As depicted in Figure 3, a non-expert musician is capable of identifying that kind of change into the music score. This method bothers the musicians when the music is read. In addition, it needs the original music page for watermark reading.

Beam Thickness Modification

By modifying the orientation or thickness of beam lines it is possible to hide only a few bits. Another important problem is that the presence of beams is not guaranteed

Figure 3: Stem Rotation Approach

into the music page. Musicians may easily detect the thickness variation when the beam is placed near to a staff line. In addition, this method requires the original music page in order to perform the watermark reading.

Noteheads Shifting

The approach chosen by Schmucker et al. (2001) consists of shifting note heads (see Figure 4). The distance between the notes has a musical significance. Therefore, in several cases the approach may disturb the music reading. In the figure, the second chords from the left were moved to the left and the musicians may detect the missed alignment of the chords. The displacement has been highlighted with the line below the staff and the gray lines. The movement of notes may generate problems when the notes are marked with ornaments, accents, expressions, etc., in those cases, the movement becomes more evident creating a misalignment with the markers. The idea is good but unfortunately is feasible only for specific music scores: with a large amount of notes and if the nearly staffs do not contain beams.

The idea is suitable to hide a significant code length if a sufficient number of noteheads are present into the score page. Typically, the number of notes in a score image is quite low, it ranges from 10 to 50 for each music staff. A score page may have from seven to 15 music staffs. This solution requires the original music page for watermark reading since the difference with the original position of the notes has to be taken.

If considering the main score, the shifted notes are quite easy to be detected by the musicians reading them (according to the needs of simultaneity among parts/layers/voices), while it turns out to be quite invisible in single parts. Such a watermark is easy to be detected by musicians in regular groups of notes provided that the distance among successive notes of the same beam is non-regular/periodic. If the shift is too evident, it may become a problem for the musicians, since it might give the impression that some changes in the note duration were imposed.

Adding White Dots

This approach consists of adding small white dots into larger music notation symbols (see Figure 5). The results can be quite easily detected by musicians and are not annoying while playing music. This is not a robust approach, since a mere photocopy

Figure 4: Shifting Beamed Notes Approach

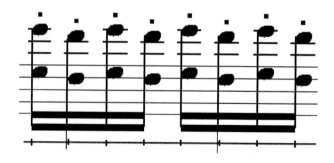

Figure 5: Inserting a White Dot into a Note Head

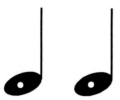

may destroy the dots when they are small enough to be acceptable by musicians. This solution encounters the same failure and problems as previously explained for the low number of noteheads, which are present in a core page. The number of bits, which can be hidden in the music page, depends on the number of notes, which are on the same page.

The approaches based on changing single music notation symbols are unsuitable since they neither allow hiding a high number of bits nor permit replicating the code several times in the same score page to increase code robustness.

Different Fonts for the Same Music Symbol

According to this technique, different fonts for the selected music symbols are used to hide either 1 or 0, depending on the font used. This implies that the font has to be easily recognized in the phase of watermark reading. The approach was proposed for text watermarking by Maxemchuk et al. (1997).

Figure 6 shows an example of possible font modification. The original character (on left) was changed by modifying flag thickness (on center) or length of the hook (on right). An undefined number of small changes can be performed on musical symbols in order to add the watermark. In some cases, the same character may present four different forms in order to hide two bits of the watermark code. The problem in using this technique is related to the channel capacity (since it is also a method based on symbol modification). The difference with respect to text watermark is that in music language the number of "characters" on a page is smaller. Therefore, it may become difficult to hide the whole code in a single music score page.

Image Watermarking Approach for Music Sheets

Binary images consists either of '1s' or '0s' (white or black pixels). The frequency domain cannot be used for embedding a watermark. The only possibility to store information is to exploit the relationship of black and white pixels in a certain environment

Figure 6: Different Font for the Same Note

(i.e., a block) as information carrier (Funk & Schmucker, 2001). Therefore, the method of Zhao and Koch (1995) is based on blocks of distinct size. The ratio of 1s and 0s in a certain block b is used to embed a watermark.

The rate (percentage) $P_1(b)$ of black pixels in a selected block b is defined as:

$$P_1(b) = N_1(b) / \#b$$

where $N_1(b)$ is the number of '1s' in the block b and $\#b$ its size.

The sum of percentages of black and white pixels in block is 100 percent. Therefore, the rate (percentage) $P_0(b)$ of white pixels is:

$$P_0(b) = N_0(b)/ \#b = 100-P_1(b).$$

On the one hand, a '0' is embedded in a block b if $P_1(b)$ is greater than a given threshold t_{upper}. On the other hand, a '1' is embedded if $P_1(b)$ is less than another given threshold t_{lower}. Embedding is done by flipping some of the pixels in a block until the rate $P_1(b)$ is in a certain embedding range which is given by λ which should be considered as a robustness degree. So the resulting rates of the watermarked blocks are:

- Embedding a '1': $P_1(b) <= t_{lower}$ and $P_1(b) >= t_{lower} - \lambda$
- Embedding a '0': $P_1(b) >= t_{upper}$ and $P_1(b) <= t_{upper} + \lambda$

Two different areas in binary images are distinguished by Zhao and Koch, according to the distribution of black or white pixels in it. These areas are treated different in the process of flipping pixels.

- In dithered blocks where black and white pixels are well interlaced the modifications are well distributed in the whole blocks.
- In sharply contrasted blocks with clear boundaries between black and white pixels the process of flipping pixels is applied at the boundary of black and white pixels.

In Funk and Schmucker (2001) a technique based on Koch and Zhao method has been presented. In order to improve robustness and invisibility some changes were performed on the number of blocks, thresholds and block size. A more important change has been to separate the image black pixels in two sets in order to differentiate between pixels belonging on musical symbols and pixels belonging to line segments (horizontal or vertical).

The final idea is to embed the watermark only on the black pixels belonging to the staff lines. The fact that the pixel is on a line does not guarantee that it is on the staff line. For this purpose only horizontal segments having a length greater than a fixed threshold were considered.

MAIN THRUST OF THE CHAPTER

The techniques previously introduced have several problems in satisfying the user requirements. Some of them are not capable of hiding the needed code length; others are based on the image manipulation (see also Deseilligny et al., 1998) so cannot be used for a real time print from the symbolic music editors. A good music score watermarking system should be useful also when the user can manipulate the music in a symbolic format (change number of staffs per page, eliminate some measures or add comments and then printing the modified score in the printer at home). The watermarker has to be quick enough in order to embed the code after the user pushes the print command and before the printer goes to perform the action. Also, the research on text watermarking produces some valuable results (Brassil et al., 1995; Brassil et al., 1999; Low et al., 1995; Maxemchuk et al., 1994). Unfortunately, most of these techniques are not useful for music sheet watermarking except for those based on using different fonts (Maxemchuk et al., 1997).

Solution and Recommendations

Different possible approaches already presented in Monsignori et al. (2001a), Monsignori et al. (2001b), and Monsignori et al. (2001c) are better analyzed in the next sections since they seem to offer more guarantees in satisfying the user requirements.

Line Thickness Modulation Approach

Figure 7 shows an example of the line modulation. It consists of modifying the lines' thickness in order to insert a binary code made up of several bits. Modulated lines can be easily noted if their presence is known, whereas they are not perceived if their presence is unknown. This was confirmed during our validation phase by a group of experts.

This approach enables one to hide a considerable number of bits in several instances per page. This makes the solution particularly suitable and robust to permit the watermark reading even out of small parts of the music sheet.

Watermark Embedding Process

As described before, the process to insert the code into a digital document is called watermark embedding. For this approach, if the symbolic music notation is available, the embedding process can be performed during the printing of a music score from a

Figure 7: Staff Lines Thickness Modification

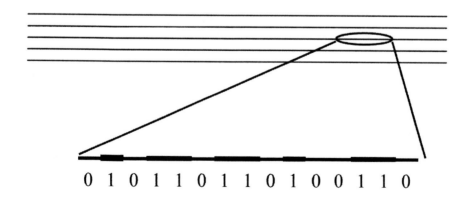

Figure 8: Embedding Process Phases

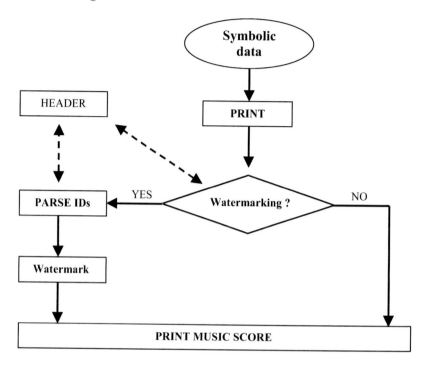

WEDELMUSIC editor. The data needed for the code creation are stored in an encrypted file stored on the reseller server. In Figure 8, this file is called "header." During the music editing/visualizing no changes are made on the display. When the "print" command is activated the editor printing process includes the watermark, the hidden code that allows one to identify the music piece univocally as produced by the right owner.

To ensure optimal results for the reading process without degrading the music sheet, several decisions have been taken for implementing the approach:

- The length of the single bit in terms of dot per inch (dpi) in the printed music sheet is calculated before the generation of the printed page. It mainly depends by the length of the staff.

- For the thickness of the line in case of zeros and ones, the 2/300 dpi and 3/300 dpi values were chosen after analysis of quality degradation and watermark reading results.

- Before a preliminary analysis, it was decided to place the starting point of the code after the (first) clef founded in the staff (see Figure 9). This decision was taken because the clefs cover a large part of the staff lines and thus that area is not usable to hide the data. The systematic misdetection of the beginning of the code covered by the clef could be recovered by the processing of the replicated code on all the staff lines at the expense of the robustness.

- During the image acquisition for watermark reading some deformations could be found. For a better estimation of the code length, between the two codes inserted

Figure 9: Code Positioning in a System

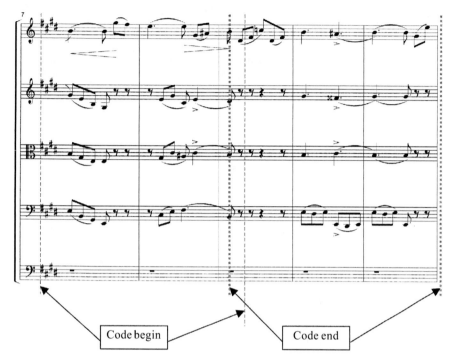

on the same line, a number of zero bits coded were added (see Figure 9) to get the perfect beginning of the code. In addition, in order to correct some wrongly detected bits a CRC, cross check control bits, were added.

As previously described the watermarked code can be built as follows:
- Copyright Watermark: comprised of 12 alphanumeric digits = 72 bits;
- User Watermark: comprised of six alphanumeric digit = 36 bits.

For a total of 108 bit + 1 start byte + 5 bytes of CRC = 160 bits. In order to improve the approach robustness, some CRC blocks were added. On every set of three bytes a CRC was added, finally a CRC to verify the correctness of the partial CRCs gas been also added. In this way errors in receiving wrong bits can be easily corrected.

Watermark Reader

In this section, the algorithm used for reading the watermark code from a scanned music sheet is described. According to the solution chosen, in order to read the watermark it is not needed to have the original music sheet with or without a watermark since the watermark is directly read from the line modulation. The bitmap image of the music sheet on which the user has to verify the presence of a watermark has to be acquired by using a scanner. The scanned music sheet is elaborated in order to enhance its contrast. After this first phase, a set of steps has to be performed in order to read the watermark code:

1. Delimitation of staffs. This task is performed using the classical segmentation algorithms based on histogram profiles of OMR such as in Marinai and Nesi (1999).
2. Delimitation of single staff lines. Also in this case, detection is performed using histograms as above.
3. Tuning phase to: (i) estimate the thickness values assigned to 1 and 0 values of the thickness line modulation; (ii) to verify the presence of the watermark (see in the following).
4. Recognition of the watermarked lines (see in the following).
5. Extraction/reading of the watermark code (see in the following).
6. Verification by means of control/correction bits of the correctness of the read code and eventual corrections. It consists of processing the binary sequence obtained in order to verify its correctness. To this end, together with the effective watermark code, some control/correction bits have been inserted in order to identify, and in some cases correct, the presence of wrong bits.

In the following, only the most important steps are described.

3. *Tuning Phase*

The phase of tuning is performed in order to estimate the thickness values of the line modulation representing the 1 or 0 of the watermark code. These values are influenced by the operations that have been performed on the music sheet. For instance, a music sheet printed 300 dpi and acquired at 600 dpi may have a line thickness between four and six pixels. When the image is photocopied the thickness typically changes to an unpredictable amount due to the scaling effect of photocopying. The precision of estimation of line thickness corresponding to 1 and 0 is fundamental for the correct reading of the watermark. Therefore, the first step is to verify if the score music under elaboration is watermarked or not, and at the same time to estimate the thickness values associated with 1 and 0 bit values. To this end, the following estimations are performed.

The following function h represents the thickness of the staff lines:

$$h_k[i][j]$$

where:

*   **k** is the staff number in the page (from one to number of staves in the page, MAXSTAVES)
*   **i** is the line number in the staff (from one to five)
*   **j** is the horizontal position in pixels (the maximum value, jMAX, depends on the acquired resolution. For a 600 dpi scanner resolution jMAX is close to 4500.

If we establish a running window around the staff line that runs from the left to right of the page, the value of the above function is comprised between 0 and the height of the running window, Hmax. For any value of $x \in (0, H \max)$ the following counting function is defined as:

$$V_i^k(x) = \sum_{j=0}^{jMAX} \gamma(h_k[i][j], x)$$

where

$$\gamma(h_k[i][j], x) = \begin{cases} 1 & if(x = h) \\ 0 & otherwise \end{cases}.$$

$V_i^k(x)$ is calculated for each staff line of the page (or part) under analysis. Then, a mean value $M(x)$ is calculated as:

$$M(x) = \frac{\sum_{k=0}^{MAXSTAVES} \sum_{i=1}^{5} V_i^k(x)}{5 * MAXSTAVES}$$

In addition, the mean value of the displacement with respect to the mean value of $M(x)$ is obtained as:

$$F(x) = \sum_{k=0}^{MAXSTAVES} \sum_{i=1}^{5} \hat{V}_i^k(x)$$

where

$$\hat{V}_i^k(x) = \left| V_i^k(x) - M(x) \right|.$$

Plotting $F(x)$ function a cumulative histogram of the line thickness is produced as reported in Figure 10. In this graph two peaks are present. The position of the peaks represent the thickness associated with 0 and 1, respectively. The example shows a case in which the line thickness associated with 0 has measured to be seven pixels while the line thickness associated to 1 was of nine pixels.

Please note that non-watermarked lines contribute to the lower peak, while in watermarked lines a comparable number of 1 and 0 can be foreseen. When only one peak is present the music score under analysis does not present the watermark or it is not anymore readable.

4.   *Identification of the Watermarked Lines*
A statistics analysis about the line thickness performed on each staff line allows distinguishing the lines that have been marked from those that are non-marked. For

Figure 10: Cumulative Histogram of the Line Thickness, F(x)

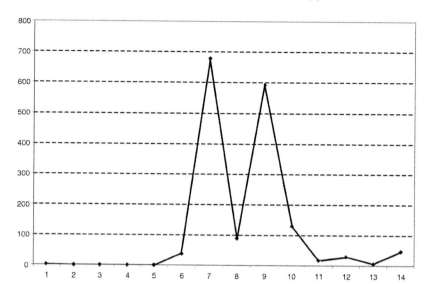

each staff line, the displacement, $\widetilde{V}(x)$, with respect to the mean value $m(x)$ is estimated:

$$\widetilde{V}_i^k(x) = V_i^k(x) - m_k(x)$$

where

$$m_k(x) = \frac{\sum_{i=1}^{5} V_i^k(x)}{5}$$

Plotting $\widetilde{V}(x)$ different results are obtained for marked and not marked lines (see Figure 11).

The graph on the left side represents the behavior in the case of absence of a watermark, while that on the right denotes the presence of the watermark. The first peak is positive in the first figure and negative in the second. This method is used for distinguishing watermarked lines.

Obviously, the identification of the marked lines is influenced by the presence of musical symbols on the lines (noteheads, beams, etc.). On the other hand, the estimations are performed on about 4500 points. This makes the estimation confident. For example, the graphs reported in Figure 12 show the same functions after the third photocopy.

Figure 11: The $\tilde{V}$ (x) Function for the Staff after Scanning the Music Sheet

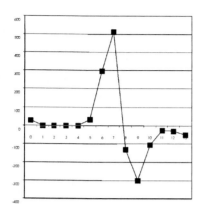
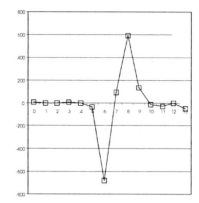

5.   *Extraction of the Watermark Code*

Once the watermarked lines are identified, it is possible to proceed at the watermark reading. The watermark code is included twice for each line. A code is comprised of 160 bits and thus 320 bits for each line. Since a staff is about 4500 points we used about 14 points for each bit.

In order to make it less visible only two staff lines on the five of the pentagram are marked. Thus, four watermark codes are included for each staff. Typically in an A4 page about 10 staffs are present, then each page presents 40 copies of the same watermarked code. This confers a high robustness at the approach.

On the acquired images on which the watermark has to be read a horizontal distortion of the image and rotations can be present. These can be due to the acquisition by means of scanners or due to the photocopy. The rotation can be easily removed by using histogram-based approaches. The horizontal distortion leads to transform in an unpredictable manner the length of the watermarked code.

Figure 12: Plotting Results for Watermarked (Right) and not Watermarked Lines (Left)

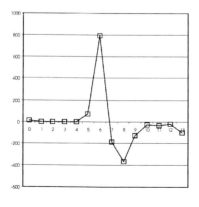
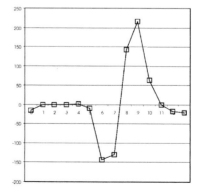

In order to solve this problem, the beginning and the end of the watermark code are marked with a sequence of bits (11001100), one byte. In this way, the position of the watermark code is identified. This allows to:

1. Align the watermark codes read from all the available staff lines, up to 40 in a page, to obtain a cumulative function $\widetilde{V}(x)$ for all the watermarked codes.

2. Superimpose a grid to read each single bit with the sequence of the values of cumulative function $\widetilde{V}(x)$.

In some cases, musical symbols cover a part of the staff line and thus, the watermark code becomes unreadable in that point. On the other hand, the possibility to align more watermarked codes (of the same staff or of other staffs) allows overcoming this problem.

The code recovering process uses the principle of the embedding process. For each staff, it is determined the modulation step p_j, that is the length of the line segment on which the single bit is encoded. The value of p_j is calculated by dividing the staff line length with 360 (number of bits encoded). This value is a good approximation of the real value of the segment (in practice each value has to be verified and reestimated because of the distortion inserted by the photocopying process). It is assumed that the staff was not cut (in that case the music is useless).

After to have identified the starting point s_j, the end point e_j and the modulation step p_j the single bit intervals $\left(b_k^j, b_{k+1}^j\right)$ are evaluated.

It is known that $b_0^j = s_j$ and $b_k^j = s_j + kp_j$ where $k = 1, 2, \ldots N_{bit} - 1$.

In some cases, as a music sheet manipulation effect, or because of symbols covering the staff lines, some thickness values can be useless for the bit value calculation. These values have to be eliminated. If H_0 and H_1 are the thicknesses associated to 0 and 1, respectively, a parameter ε is introduced as maximal variation. The thickness values out from the interval $(H_0 - \varepsilon, H_1 + \varepsilon)$ and the values equal to $(H_0 + H_1)/2$ are replaced with the thickness predominant value (H_0 or H_1). By making this, the final estimation will gain in precision.

The mean value for the thickness is calculated as:

$$\overline{\overline{H}}_k = \frac{\sum_{j=0}^{N_{seq}} \overline{H}_{b_k^j}}{N_{seq}}$$

The binary value of bit k is given by:

$$B_k = \begin{cases} 0 \text{ if } \overline{\overline{H}}_k \leq \dfrac{H_0 + H_1}{2} \\ 1 \qquad \text{otherwise} \end{cases}$$

In the previous formula, the value $(H_0 + H_1)/2$ was assigned to the low bit value. The decision was taken for several reasons:

Figure 13: First Phase — Staff Line Detection

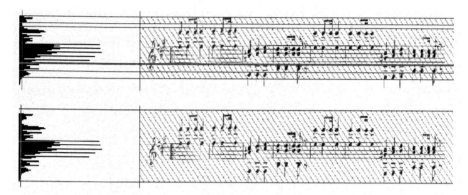

- For each thickness value a bit value has to be assigned;
- The probability to have the mean value is very low; and
- The zero bit is less subject to distortion (H_1 can be found also in case of symbol overlap or in case of distortion, H_0 can be considered as indicated the zero embedded value).

Figures 13 and 14 describe the watermark reading process.

Figure 14: The Screen Shot of the Watermark Reading tool (The considered image was obtained after the acquisition of the original. In the bottom-right corner the CRC verification results are listed.)

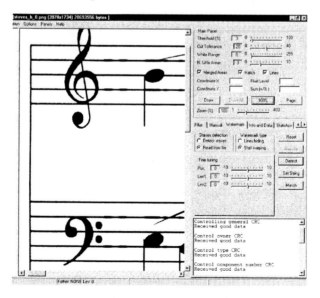

Approach Validation

Our primary goal has been to embed a high number of bits to satisfy the user requirements. Obviously this constraint penalized some other aspects of the watermark requirements as the robustness.

Since an objective assessment was needed, the validation of the method was performed in some meetings with several people working on music: the user group of expert of WEDELMUSIC project, plus other musicians of a local music school. The total validation has been based on the opinions of 28 people: musicians, copyists, publishers, computer music technicians and music teachers. Great part of the group were musicians, while only four were copy editors and three publishers.

The group was formed in this manner to cover the different needs. In fact, publishers have to accept to publish watermarked music. In turn, publishers use copy-editors, which are music engravers/copyists, for formatting music. Therefore, they are a very important category for the watermark validation. In general, it is possible to get a very good assessment from musicians. Obviously, a specific watermark approach can be unacceptable for the musicians if the music sheet is not readable or annoying for the presence of evident changes. Typically, copyists are the most exigent.

We asked to assess a sequence of 15 different music scores. Some of them were watermarked others were not watermarked music sheets. Different watermark approaches were used for different music sheets. Different levels of photocopy of the same watermarked or not watermarked music sheets were included. Different resolutions of the same music sheets were also used to assess the minimum acceptance level of people involved in the validation. All music sheets were printed at the same magnitude, thus the dimension of the staff line was constant. Its value has been chosen according to that most commonly used in printed sheets.

They were informed about the main concepts of watermark and not about the specific changes that we made on the music score. They performed the assessment singularly without the possibility to compare the different pages of music and the opinions of each other. After the assessment, we explained the techniques and we had a discussion. In the following, only a part of the results obtained are reported. In most cases, during the assessment, the watermark was not detected from the participants in all music sheets in which it was present. Only after having informed them and explained how to see it, they were capable of detecting it.

In Table 1, the results of the ITU results are reported. The mean vote is 3.45 that means a judgement between fair and good.

Line Mask Approach

The watermarking approach proposed in this section can be applied to images of a music sheet or during the printing of the music score from a symbolic music notation file. The approach consists of marking some points on the music score for virtually hiding a number of lines connecting them. A line based techniques for watermarking color images was presented in Maes et al. (1998). The position and the orientation of the hidden lines are used as the vehicle to hide the watermark code. The first step in implementing such a technique is to create a mask consisting in a number of lines (see Figure 15). Each line angle encodes a number of bits.

Table 1: Results of the Validation

Rating	Quality	Number of answers	Percentage
5	Excellent	11	19.64%
4	Good	25	44.64%
3	Fair	4	7.14%
2	Poor	9	16.07%
1	Bad	7	12.50%

In particular, the angle between the hidden line and the vertical axis has been used for hiding the information (see Figure 16). The idea is not based on writing black lines on the music score (this may lead only to destroy the music sheet). The effective implementation consists in marking some points aligned to some hidden lines. The points that identify the hidden line may be placed in the intersection among the hidden line and the staff lines such as the points that in Figure 16 are marked with circles. In the solution taken, groups of the lines contributing to encoding the same code start from a common points.

The problems related to this approach are:

- The definition and identification of the starting point of the lines that encode the same code. The starting points have to be clearly identifiable.
- The identification of the vertical axis to estimate the angle.
- The identification of the hidden lines in the music score even when they are intersected with each other.
- The estimation of the angle of the hidden line with respect to the reference vertical axis with a given precision.
- The insertion of a watermark comprised of at least 60 bits per page, considering that it has to be repeated several times on the page to make it robust enough for the reading.

Since the music scores may be deformed during successive photocopying, some of the above problems have to cope with distortions during the watermark reading. The resulted points circled in Figure 16, or only a part of them, have to be marked in some way.

Figure 15: Line Mask

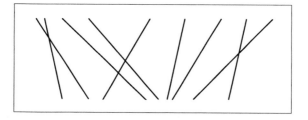

Figure 16: Possible Points to be Marked in the Music Score Resulted after Overlapping the Hidden Lines

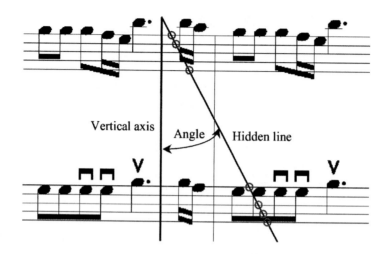

The intersection points located on the staff lines which are covered by other musical symbols have to be eliminated from the group of "markable" points. For marking points different techniques may be used (cutting the staff line with a white line, modifying staff line thickness, etc.) considering that the image score has to remain in two colors.

In Figure 17, an example of the solution taken is presented. The marked points have been obtained by deleting a little part of staff lines. The inserted watermark is visible and absolutely a not bother for the musicians. Please note that the real music score is normally smaller that the one depicted in Figure 17.

In order to better retrieve the lines and to avoid false watermark detection, the set of "markable" points has been divided in two subsets for any staff. The first contain the points on the first, third and fifth staff line, the second subset contains the points on the second and the fourth staff lines (see Figure 18). Between the possible 16 positions for the pairs, we have used the first set and for the odds the second one.

Embedding Process

Once the approach was introduced some implementation details have to be exposed.

Line Mask Definition

The line mask creation is the first step in the approach implementation. The code to be embedded has a total of 108 bits divided in three groups of 24 bits and a group of 36 bits (LDID). The angle of hidden lines has to be maintained in small range since the adoption of horizontal (or quite horizontal) lines leads to cut only few staffs and vertical lines may overlap bar lines. If a line angle ranges from three degrees to 48 degrees then the line may assume 16 different positions to embed four bits. For hiding 24 bits, six lines are needed and for hiding 36 bits nine lines are needed. Thus, means that for the 108 bits

Figure 17: Watermarked Music Score

27 lines are totally needed. The lines were divided in four groups. The first group will be placed on the top left half page, the second on the top right half page, the third on the bottom left half page and the last on the bottom right of the page. For the lines staying on the right side of the sheet, the rules are the same but the angle will change from -3 degrees to -48 degrees.

Figure 18: Points Chosen to be Marked in the Music Score

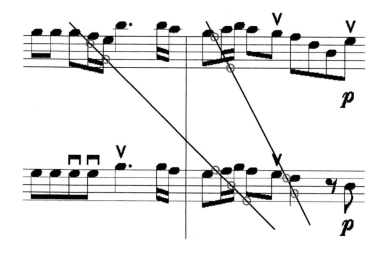

Figure 19: Line Angle Variation Depends on the Line Position

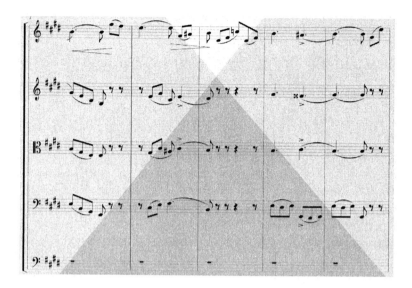

As shown in Figure 19, the areas covered by the two sets of lines overlap in the middle bottom zone. Here some marked points belonging to both areas can be found. However, their alignment determines the right line. The area covered by the both sets of lines increases from top to bottom. If a little number of staves is used to hide a set of lines it will be smaller. On the other hand, the code redundancy increases if more staves are used. At the final choice, a compromise has to be accepted between the two parameters.

Starting Points

During the marking phase, the lines are placed over a block of staves, starting from fixed points on the first/second line of the first staff. This ensures the possibility of reading the watermark also if we are not capable to find the first marked point. The first (last) starting point is after (before) 1/100 of the staff length. The starting points of the hidden lines are spaced by 5/100 of the staff length. In our experiments, we have placed one half of the hidden lines starting from the beginning of the staff to the middle. They have an angle oriented to the right-down side of the score page (as in the previous figures). The other half of the hidden lines, those that begin from the second half of the first staff line, are oriented on the opposite direction, left down. In this case, the hidden line direction is up towards the music staffs. A total of 20 hidden lines can be included.

Number and Position of the Marked Points

During the watermark reading process finding the marked points means finding the lines and thus the watermarked code.

In a given area, it is possible to find several marked points, whether those points belong to the same line or not.

Figure 20: The Areas where it is Possible to Find Marked Points are Overlapped from the Second Staff

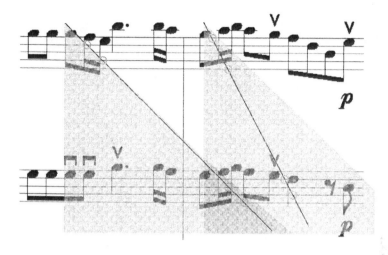

If it is supposed that the code is searched on three staves the next hypothesis can be considered:

- Each line marks three points on each staff;
- The areas covered by two successive lines are overlapped by 1/3 on the second staff and 1/2 on the third.
- The probability to find points belonging to other line (bad points) are $P(1) = 0$ on the first staff, $P(2) = 0.4$ on the second and $P(3) = 0.8$ on the third.

That means that the mean value for the number of good points founded on a given area will be:

$$P_{GP}=3-P(1)*3+3-P(2)*3+3-P(3)*3=5.4 \text{ points.}$$

Thus, for each nine searched points it is possible to find 3.6 wrong points. Considering three staves, the probability to find all nine good points is:

$$P_{GP} = \frac{\text{number of good points}}{\text{total number of points}} = \frac{9}{9+3.6} = 0.714$$

If only two staves are considered the same probability will be:

$$P_{GP} = \frac{6}{6+1.2} = 0.83$$

since the mean value for the number of good points founded on a given area is:

$$P_{GP}=3-P(1)*3+3-P(2)*3=4.8\,\text{points.}$$

The founded values are quite good and can be subsequently increased if the point's alignment is considered. In order to eliminate some practical problems and increase the probability of true angle recognition, other tricks can be used in the implementation phase.

If the problem of areas overlapping is considered then it is possible to change the marked points for two consecutive lines as shown in Figure 20. In this case, the problem is eliminated and for each set of points the line can be found without problems.

It is also possible to suppose to differently mark the points obtained from two successive angles. As it is easy to observe in Figure 21 two successive angles (the step between the angles is three degrees) of the same line.

Watermark Reading

The process of watermark reading is mainly divided into five steps as reported in the following:

1. *Image Segmentation*
    The image segmentation has basically the goal of detecting the staff lines. It was already illustrated in the previous chapter where it was performed for the same purpose. The process is mainly composed by two phases:

*   A first image scanning estimates the distance between the lines and between the staves.

*   A second scanning finds five sequences of black pixels and four sequences of white pixel patterns with the previous determinate dimensions.

2. *Finding all Reference Points of the Hidden Lines over the Staves*
    This is necessary to establish if a sufficient number of marked points exists in order to recognize the presence or not of the watermark. The number of points used is known

Figure 21: Two Angles that Differ by Three Degrees should be Easily Confused

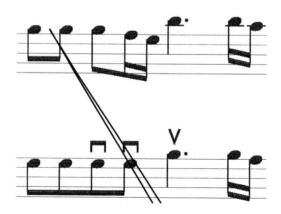

Figure 22: By Differently Marking the Points for Two Successive Angles the Possibility to Confuse is Practically Eliminated

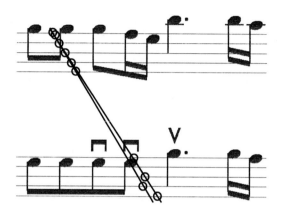

on the basis of the algorithm parameters. The acceptance threshold is to detect the 40 percent to 50 percent of points inserted during the marking phase. In order to find these points, each staff line is scanned and the vertical profile estimated. In order to search the reference points, a sub-image window of dimension W x H has been used. The dimension H is 20 percent bigger than the staff line thickness. This depends on the resolution of acquisition and is dynamically determined. The dimension W is estimated by using a histogram-based approach (it is equal to the staff wideness) (Marinai et al., 1999). If E(x, y) is the image brightness gray level of a pixel inside the scanning window, the V(x) profile is obtained as:

$$V(x) = \sum_{i=1}^{H} E(x,i), \quad x = 1, 2...W$$

The V(x) profile (see Figure 23) presents some minimums where the staff line is interrupted even after several levels of photocopy. These minimums are as the marked points of the hidden lines. The profile is processed with a low-pass filter to reduce the noise. Potential marked points of hidden lines are found when a given set of consecutive points of profile V(x) is under the threshold. The threshold is 35 percent to 40 percent of maximum V(x) value (the peak seen in Figure 23 and Figure 24 are not considered for the calculus of the maximum value). In Figure 24, the histogram resulted after the analysis of the second photocopy is shown. The marked points can be easily found. In Figure 24, the axis and the threshold level are shown. If $P_{cut(k)}$ are the points resulted at the intersection of t_s with V(x), (in Figure 24 there are six *k* points), then the couple of $P_{cut(k)}$ and $P_{cut(k+1)}$ defines the x value where the marked point is found on the staff line.

For each $x \in (P_{cut(k)}, P_{cut(k+1)})$ will be $V(x) < t_s$ where t_s at 40 percent from the maximum value of V(x) means that if the line thickness is 40 percent from the mean line thickness in that point a marked point will be considered.

The mean value is considered as the horizontal position of the correspondent marked point[1].

$$x_{mp(\frac{k+1}{2})} = \frac{P_{cut(k)} + P_{cut(k+1)}}{2}$$

3. *Finding the Starting Points of Each Line*
    On the basis of the above mechanism for positioning the starting points, they are searched at the calculated position for the specific staff line (first or second staff line) from which the hidden line is supposed to begin. The processes of photocopy and image acquisition by means of a scanner introduce horizontal distortions. To cope with this problem a quite large tolerance is used. If the starting points are missing, the lines could be recovered by using a combinatorial Hough transform working on points detected on the image (Nesi et al., 1995).

4. *Finding the Points Matching the Lines*
    For each starting point and for a fixed set of possible line slopes the detected potential marked points identified at the first step are verified. The potential marked points considered are those located inside an image transversal scanning segment (see Figure 26), placed over the staves, for each given slope of the hidden line[2]. This ensures to examine only a few points near to the line and at the same time, to compensate distortions.

The gray image segment highlighted in Figure 26 has an angle α corresponding to the searched bit sequence and the thickness w. The thickness is used as a parameter and may vary from three to 10 pixels. The angle may vary between three and 48 degrees.

If x_i and y_i are the coordinates of the $N_{\alpha k}$ points (named P_i) founded into the gray window then the line will be determined by $y = ax+b$. The points inside the scanning segment are

Figure 23: Horizontal Histogram of a Staff Line Segment (The white hole corresponds to the marked points.)

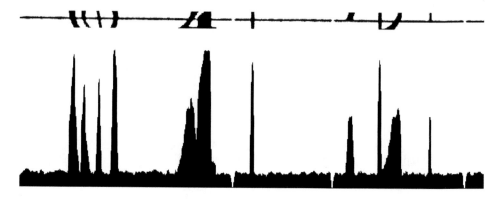

Figure 24: The Same Histogram Performed on an Image Obtained from the Second Photocopy (Due to the line thickness increases some points are difficult to see on the line but the histogram allows their exact determination. On the images, the horizontal and vertical axis and the threshold are shown.)

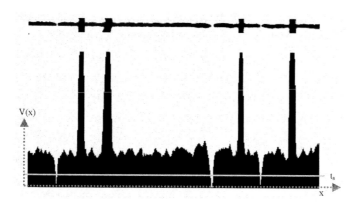

considered in order to estimate the slope, a, of the hidden line. To calculate a the next formula can be used:

$$a = \frac{N_{\alpha k}\sum_{i=0}^{N_{\alpha k}}x_i y_i - \sum_{i=0}^{N_{\alpha k}}x_i \sum_{i=0}^{N_{\alpha k}}y_i}{N_{\alpha k}\sum_{i=0}^{N_{\alpha k}}x_i^2 - \left(N_{\alpha k}\sum_{i=0}^{N_{\alpha k}}x_i\right)^2}$$

Unfortunately, the previous formula does not give the expected result in practice since the number of used points ($N_{\alpha k}$) is too low. The slope and its variance are estimated, in reading the watermark, by using each possible couple of points such as in Nesi et al. (1995).

With $N_{\alpha k}$ points:

$$N_{\alpha x} = \frac{N_{\alpha k} * (N_{\alpha k} - 1)}{2}$$

combinations of two points (P_i and P_j with $i \neq j$) are possible.

For each line (built with the two points) the slope is calculated. This slope is subject to distortion so a threshold of one degree is accepted. In Figure 25, the distribution of couples of points angles are shown. Reading the watermark from the original printed music score gave no problems in identification of the right slope.

The obtained most likelihood slope is accepted if:

Figure 25: The Number of Points Founded in a Couple of Windows Angled at 27 and 45 Degrees Respectively

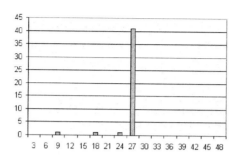

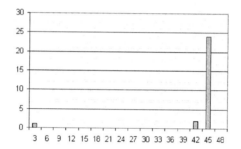

- The number of detected potential points is higher than a predefined threshold;
- The value is close to the reference value of the scanning segment;
- The variance is lower than a predefined threshold; and
- The distribution can be considered Gaussian (to this end a statistic test is performed).

Considering nine good points and 3.6 wrong points for three staves the good combination of couple of points is:

$$C_{GP} = \frac{N_{GP}(N_{GP} - 1)}{2} = \frac{9*8}{2} = 36$$

The combinations of wrong points will be:

$$C_{WP} = \frac{N_{WP}(N_{WP} - 1)}{2} = \frac{4*3}{2} = 6$$

$$P_{GP} = \frac{\text{number of good comb.}}{\text{number of total comb.}} = \frac{36}{36+6} = 0.837$$

The combinations of mixed points were not considered since they can be easily eliminated by considering their alignments. For only two staves, with six good points and 1.2 wrong points, the probability is 0.937. Both the probabilities are greater with respect the normal ones.

If a false point and missed detections are considered it is possible to suppose that:

$$N_{fc} = K_{fc} * N_w$$

and

$$N_{ff} = K_{ff} * N_g$$

Where:

- N_{fc}, number of false cuts;
- N_{ff}, number of missed point detection (fully false points);
- N_w, number of wrong points (real marked points from the other hidden line);
- N_g, number of good points (marked point of the searched hidden line);
- K_{fc}, the probability to have false cuts;
- K_{ff}, the probability to have false full.

It is reasonable to suppose that Nw = Ng*0.3 (since two successive zones may overlap by 1/3 on the second staff). If K_{fc} is really smaller than 10 percent, then K_{ff} should be supposed to be around 20 percent.

In this case the probability to have good line angle estimation can be calculated as:

$$P = \frac{N_g - N_g * K_{ff}}{N_w + N_w * K_{fc} + N_g - N_g * K_{ff}} = \frac{N_g\left(1 - K_{ff}\right)}{N_w\left(1 + K_{fc}\right) + N_g\left(1 - K_{ff}\right)}$$

replacing K_{ff}, K_{fc} and N_g in the previous formula the P value can be calculated to be:

$$P = \frac{N_g\left(1 - K_{ff}\right)}{N_w\left(1 + K_{fc}\right) + N_g\left(1 - K_{ff}\right)} = \frac{N_g\left(1 - K_{ff}\right)}{N_g * 0.3 *\left(1 + K_{fc}\right) + N_g\left(1 - K_{ff}\right)} =$$

$$\frac{1 - 0.2}{0.3 *\left(1 + 0.1\right) + 1 - 0.2} = \frac{0.8}{1.13} = 0.707$$

Figure 26: The Scanning Window for Watermark Reader in Case of Forensic Detection (The gray zone is scanned for marked points.)

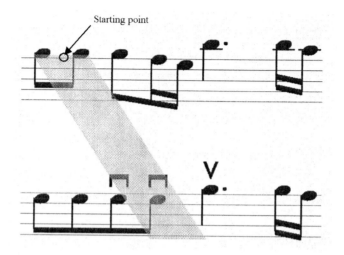

This means that also if a reasonable probability of false detection is considered the probability to perform good angle estimation remains at acceptable level.

5.   *Watermark Code Reconstruction*
This is the last step of the reading process. The code will have N blocks of four bits if N is the number of hidden lines. The angle of each line determines the value of respective blocks.

$$b_k = \frac{\alpha_k - 3}{3}$$

where α_k is the angle of the line k and b_k is a number between 0 and 15 thus a sequence of four bits.

Notes

The approach may be used also in case of blind detection. The blind detection means to start scanning the image without previously knowing the line angle. The watermark reader has to consider all the points found in the area and then try to determine the most probable angle. The difference is that the scanning window has to be greater than the precise one in order to cover all the possible positions where marked points should be found (see Figure 27). The previous calculated probability is referred to in this case since the probability of zone overlapping was considered as 1/3 for the second staff and 1/2 for the third staff (see also Figure 20).

Figure 27: The Scanning Window for Watermark Reader in Case of Blind Detection (The gray zone is scanned for marked points.)

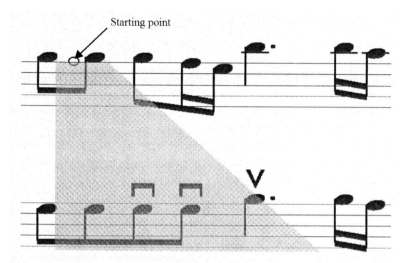

Mask Approach Validation

Our primary goal has been to embed a sufficient number of bits to satisfy the user requirements. This constraint penalized a bit of the robustness since the total number of embeddable bits are limited. The first step to be performed for the validation has been to evaluate the quality of the printed watermarked music sheets by using a scale as the one presented in (Kutter & Peticolas, 1999), based on the Human Visual System.

The presented technique was validated by the previously described user group of WEDELMUSIC project. For the validation, we asked that the user group members assess a sequence of 15 different music scores and only five of them were watermarked. In most cases, during the assessment, the watermark was not detected from the participants in all music sheets in which it was present. Only after having informed them and explained how to see it, they were capable of detecting it. In Table 2, the results of the analysis are reported. The mean vote is 3.71 that means a judgement between fair and good.

To obtain the end-users' acceptance of the watermark solution we have tested the watermark robustness against several levels of photocopying. The results were encouraging. The watermark can be easily read after five levels of photocopying. The robustness mostly depends on the technique used for marking points.

Non-Watermark-Based Approach for Music Sheet Protection

During the research performed for watermarking techniques a different approach for copy control was analyzed.

The problem is to find something that disables the music sheets photocopying. A solution can be to find something that when the music is photocopied act as a content destroyer.

Table 2: Results of the ITU Validation

Rating	Quality	Number of answers	Percentage
5	Excellent	6	10.71%
4	Good	29	51.78%
3	Fair	9	16.07%
2	Poor	6	10.71%
1	Bad	0	0.00%

No solution seems to offer this capability since the photocopying machine act as a passive instrument.

It is known that when adding yellow lines to a page, the black and white photocopy hardware will transform the yellow lines in dark gray. The idea to add yellow shapes on the music sheet is not suitable since the printing is normally performed on black and white printer and the yellow share will be lost.

The idea should be to add some light gray shapes. Some tries were performed by adding a light gray rectangle around the music as a kind of background (see Figure 28).

The quality of the photocopied music sheet decreases very rapidly and at the third level of photocopy the music sheet is almost no more readable.

It is interesting to observe how the areas more rich (dense) in symbols are the first to loose readability. The result seems to offer a future field of investigation in music sheet copy control.

Figure 28: Music Printed on a Light Grey Background

Figure 29: The Music Sheet after the First Photocopy

Figure 30: The Music Sheet after the Second Photocopy

Figure 31: The Music Sheet after the Third Photocopy (The originally light grey pixels change to a dark grey color and the music is no longer readable.)

CONCLUSIONS AND FUTURE TRENDS

The protection of music sheets is very important since they are entering into the digital market and distribution. The watermarking of music sheets is a new area of research and new solutions and algorithms are expected. The main problems are related to the fact that music is mainly black and white information while a great part of the techniques adopted for images are based on the presence of colors. The music sheet watermarking can be also considered a good way to understand when the music sheet has been illegally copied rather than to be capable of demonstrating the violation of copyright. In fact, the copyright for the music sheet is in several cases related to the visual shape of the music; that is the music formatting of music.

Recently, some optical music recognition, OMR, systems have been proposed. They can be considered killer applications for the music sheet watermarking as the OCR for textual watermarking. On the other hand, the quality of OMR systems is not presently satisfactory to be considered a real risk for music sheet watermarking technologies.

As shown in the chapter, some of the techniques proposed are strong enough to provide watermarks that persist after a significant number of photocopy levels. When the degradation of the photocopy process has reduced the quality and thus the value of the music sheet the watermarking can be lost but not before. This is extremely promising for the publishers.

REFERENCES

Bellini, P., Bethelemy, J., Bruno, I., Nesi, P., & Spinu, M. B. (2003). Multimedia music sharing among mediateques, archives and distribution to their attendees. *Journal on Applied Artificial Intelligence*, Taylor and Francis (in press). Found at: www.wedelmusic.org.

Bellini, P., Della Santa, R., & Nesi, P. (2001). Automatic formatting of music sheets. *Proceedings of the First International Conference on WEB Delivering of Music*, WEDELMUSIC-2001, (November 23-24, pp. 170-177). Florence, Italy.

Brassil, J. T., Low, S., & Maxemchuk, N. F. (1999). Copyright protection for the electronic distribution of text documents. *Proceedings of the IEEE, 87*(7), 1181-1196.

Brassil, J. T., Low, S., Maxemchuk, N. F., & O'Gorman, L. (1995). Electronic marking and identification techniques to discourage document copying. *IEEE Journal on Sel. Areas in Communication, 8*, 1495-1504.

Busch, C., Rademer, E., Schmucker, M., & Wothusen, S. (2000). Concepts for a watermarking technique for music scores. *Proceedings of the Third International Conference on Visual Computing*, Visual 2000. Mexico City.

Deseilligny, M. P. & Le Men, H. (1998). An algorithm for digital watermarking of binary images, application to map and text images. *Proceedings of the International Workshop on Computer Vision.* Hong Kong.

Funk, W. & Schmucker, M. (2001). High capacity information hiding in music scores. *Proceeding of the International Conference on WEB Delivering of Music, WEDELMUSIC2001,* (pp. 12-19). Florence, Italy: IEEE Press.

Kutter, M. & Petitcolas, F.A.P. (1999). A fair benchmark for image watermarking system. *Proceedings of SPIE Security and Watermarking of Multimedia Contents, 3657,* (pp. 226-239). San Jose, CA: SPIE.

Low, S. H., Maxemchuk, N. F., Brassil, J. T., & O'Gorman, L. (1995). Document marking and identification using both line and word shifting. *Proceedings of INFOCOM 95,* (pp. 853-860). Boston, MA.

Maes, M.J.J.B & Van Overveld, C.W.A.M. (1998). Digital watermarking by geometric warping. *Proceedings of IEEE International Conference on Image Processing, ICIP98,* (Vol. 2, pp. 424-426). Chicago, IL: IEEE Press.

Marinai, S. & Nesi, P. (1999). Projection based segmentation of musical sheets. *Proceedings of the Fifth International Conference on Document Analysis and Recognition, ICDAR'99,* (pp. 515-518). Bangalore: IEEE Press.

Maxemchuk, N. F. (1994). Electronic document distribution. *ATT Technical Journal,* 73(5), 73-80.

Maxemchuk, N. F. & Low, S. (1997). Marking text documents. *Proceedings of International Conference on Image Processing, ICIP97, 3.* Santa Barbara, CA: IEEE Press.

Monsignori, M., Nesi, P., & Spinu, M.B. (2001a). Watermarking music sheets. *Proceedings of IEEE Second Pacific RIM Conference on Multimedia, PCM2001, LNCS 2195,* (pp. 646-653). Beijing: Springer Press.

Monsignori, M., Nesi, P., & Spinu, M.B. (2001b). A high capacity technique for watermarking music sheets while printing. *Proceeding of IEEE Fourth Workshop on Multimedia Signal Processing, MMSP2001,* (pp. 493-498). Cannes: IEEE Press.

Monsignori, M., Nesi, P., & Spinu, M.B. (2001c). Watermarking music sheet while printing. *Proceeding of the International Conference on WEB Delivering of Music, WEDELMUSIC2001,* (pp. 28-35). Florence, Italy: IEEE Press.

Nesi, P., Del Bimbo, A., & Ben-Tzvi, A. (1995). A robust algorithm for optical flow estimation. *Computer Vision and Pattern Recognition,* 62(1), 59-68.

Schmucker, M., Busch, C., & Pant, A. (2001). Digital watermarking for the protection of music scores. *Proceedings of IS&T/SPIE 13ᵗʰ International Symposium on Electronic Imaging 2001, Conference 4314 Security and Watermarking of Multimedia Contents III,* 4314, (pp. 85-95). San Jose: SPIE Press.

Zhao, J. & Koch, E. (1995). Embedding robust labels into images for copyright protection. *Proceedings of the International Congress on Intellectual Property Rights for Specialized Information, Knowledge and New Technologies,* (pp. 242-251). Vienna.

ENDNOTES

[1]   The vertical position of the marked points results from image segmentation phase

[2]   During watermark reading, the estimation of the vertical axis orientation is performed on the basis of the location of the staff barlines (vertical lines separating measures).

Chapter IV

Face Recognition Technology: A Biometric Solution to Security Problems

Sanjay K. Singh, Purvanchal University, India

Mayank Vatsa, Purvanchal University, India

Richa Singh, Purvanchal University, India

K. K. Shukla, Institute of Technology (IT-BHU), India

Lokesh R. Boregowda, Honeywell SSL, India

ABSTRACT

Face recognition technology is one of the most widely used problems in computer vision. It is widely used in applications related to security and human-computer interfaces. The two reasons for this are the wide range of commercial and law enforcement applications and the availability of feasible technologies. In this chapter the various biometric systems and the commonly used techniques of face recognition, Feature Based, eigenface based, Line Based Approach and Local Feature Analysis are explained along with the results. A performance comparison of these algorithms is also given.

INTRODUCTION

Biometrics is defined as the automated use of physiological or behavioral characteristics to determine or verify an identity. A biometric device compares unique personal characteristics to identify the individuals. The two major categories of biometric devices are Physiological and Behavioral. Physiological biometric identification measures unique body characteristics such as fingerprint details, retina blood vessel patterns, features of the iris, the size and shape of a hand or facial scan. It compares these characteristics against a pattern recorded during an enrollment process. Behavioral measurements identify unique learned traits such as a person's signature, voice scan, and keystrokes scan. The major biometric technologies that are being used nowadays are:

- Finger scan
- Iris scan
- Hand scan
- Voice scan
- Retina scan
- Signature scan
- Facial scan

It is clear that the events of September 11 had a profound effect on security-based systems. Clearly, the recent events will have a significant impact on the future demand in the biometrics industry.

In this chapter, the main emphasis is on "facial scan or face recognition." Face recognition is distinguishing people's faces. Humans have the capability to recognize faces. A large database of human faces is stored in our brain and to identify any face the face of the person is matched with the face database of persons stored in our memory. If a successful result is obtained, a person recalls the identity of the face or else it is added into the database of faces in the brain. This performance is related to neurons and all but actually what happens in the brain during recognition is still not clear. Here, a brief description of the major biometric technologies is given.

Finger-Scan Technology

Finger-scan biometrics is based on the distinctive characteristics of the human fingerprint. A fingerprint image is read from a capture device, features are extracted from the image, and a template is created. If appropriate precautions are followed, what results is a very accurate means of authentication. Following are the terminology for the method:

Fingerprints vs. Finger-scans — Fingerprint Characteristics — Feature Extraction — Silicon, Optical, Ultrasound

Fingerprints vs. Finger-Scans

The aura of criminality that accompanies the term "fingerprint" has not significantly impeded the acceptance of finger-scan technology, because the two authentication methods are very different. Fingerprinting, as the name suggests, is the acquisition and

Figure 1: Sample of Fingerprint

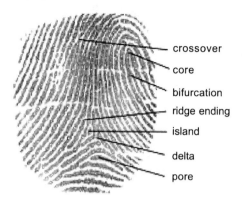

storage of the image of the fingerprint. They require 250kb per finger for a high-quality image. Finger-scan technology also acquires the fingerprint, but does not store the full image. It stores particular data about the fingerprint in a much smaller template, requiring 250 to 1,000 bytes. After the data is extracted, the fingerprint is not stored. Significantly, the full fingerprint cannot be reconstructed from the finger-scan template. The key is the template — what is stored is not a full fingerprint, but a small amount of data derived from the fingerprint's unique patterns.

Fingerprint Characteristics

The human fingerprint is comprised of various types of ridge patterns, traditionally classified according to the decades-old Henry system: left loop, right loop, arch, whorl, and tented arch. Loops make up nearly two-thirds of all fingerprints, whorls are nearly one-third, and perhaps five to 10 percent is arches. These classifications are relevant in many large-scale forensic applications, but are rarely used in biometric authentication. This fingerprint is a right loop.

Minutiae (Figure 1) are the discontinuities that interrupt the otherwise smooth flow of ridges. These are the basis for most finger-scan authentication. Codified in the late 19th century as Galton features, minutiae are at the most rudimentary ridge endings i.e., the point at which a ridge stops and bifurcations are the point at which one ridge divides into two. Many types of minutiae exist, including dots (very small ridges), islands (ridges slightly longer than dots, occupying a middle space between two temporarily divergent ridges), ponds or lakes (empty spaces between two temporarily divergent ridges), spurs (a notch protruding from a ridge), bridges (small ridges joining two longer adjacent ridges), and crossovers (two ridges which cross each other).

Feature Extraction

Once a quality image is captured, it must be converted to a usable format. If the image is grayscale, areas lighter than a particular threshold are discarded, and those darker are made black. The ridges are then thinned from five to eight pixels in width down to one pixel, for precise location of endings and bifurcations. Minutiae localization begins with this processed image. At this point, even a very precise image will have distortions and false minutiae that need to be filtered out.

Optical, Silicon, Ultrasound

Getting good images of the distinctive ridges and minutiae is a complicated task. The fingerprint is a small area from which to take measurements, and the wear of daily life affects which ridge patterns show most prominently. Increasingly sophisticated mechanisms have been developed to capture the fingerprint image with sufficient detail and resolution. The technologies in use today are optical, silicon, and ultrasound.

Hand Scan Technology

This approach uses the geometric shape of the hand for authenticating a user's identity. Authentication of identity using hand geometry is an interesting problem. Individual hand features are not descriptive enough for identification. However, it is possible to devise a method by combining various individual features to attain robust verification.

Unlike fingerprints, the human hand isn't unique. One can use finger length, thickness, and curvature for the purposes of verification but not for identification. For some kinds of access control like immigration and border control, invasive biometrics (e.g., fingerprints) may not be desirable as they infringe on privacy. In such situations, it is desirable to have a biometric system that is sufficient for verification. As hand geometry is not distinctive, it is the ideal choice. Furthermore, hand geometry data is easier to collect. With fingerprint collection, good frictional skin is required by imaging systems, and with retina-based recognition systems, special lighting is necessary. Additionally, hand geometry can be easily combined with other biometrics, namely fingerprint. One can envision a system where fingerprints are used for (infrequent) identification and hand geometry is used for (frequent) verification.

Hand-scan is a relatively accurate technology, but does not draw on as rich a data set as finger, face, or iris. A decent measure of the distinctiveness of a biometric technology is its ability to perform one-to-many searches, i.e., the ability to identify a user without the user first claiming an identity. Hand-scan does not perform 1-to-many identification, as similarities between hands are not common. Where hand-scan does have an advantage is in its FTE (failure to enroll) rates, which measure the likelihood that a user is incapable of enrolling in the system. Finger-scan by comparison is prone to FTEs due to poor quality fingerprints; facial-scan requires consistent lighting to enroll a user properly. Since nearly all users will have the dexterity to use hand-scan technology, fewer employees and visitors will need to be processed outside the biometric.

Retina Scan Technology

Retina scan is perhaps one of the most accurate and reliable biometric technologies and among the most difficult to use. Film portrayals of retina scan devices reading at an arm's length with a non-stationary subject are false. In its current incarnation, retina scan biometrics requires a cooperative, well-trained, patient audience, or else the performance will fail dramatically.

Figure 2: Eye Structure Iris Scan Technology

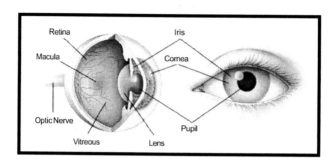

Even when those unfamiliar with the rudimentary anatomy of the eye are reminded that all vision is based upon light passing through the pupil to the retina, there is still measurable resistance to retinal technology. This is perhaps due to an unusually high degree of sensitivity with issues of the eye. Iris scan biometrics, which read the patterns of the iris and require less effort on the part of the user, are frequently met with similar expressions of hesitation. Despite its relative sophistication, retina scan is actually one of the oldest biometrics. As far back as the 1930s, research suggested that the pattern of blood vessels on the back of the human eye were unique from person to person. Further investigation showed that these patterns, even between identical twins, were indeed unique. With the exception of some types of degenerative eye diseases, or cases of severe head trauma, retinal patterns are stable enough to be used throughout one's life.

The retina as shown in Figure 2 is a thin nerve (1/50th of an inch) on the back of the eye, it is that part of the eye that senses light and transmits impulses through the optic nerve to the brain — the equivalent of film in a camera. Blood vessels used for biometric identification are located along the neural retina, the outermost of the retina's four cell layers. Retina scan devices read through the pupil, which requires the user to situate his or her eye within a one-half inch of the capture device, and to hold still while the reader ascertains the patterns. The user looks at a rotating green light as the patterns of the retina are measured at more than 400 points. By comparison, a fingerprint may only provide 30 to 40 distinctive points (minutia) to be used in the enrollment, template creation, and verification process. This leads to a very high level of accuracy in comparison to most other biometrics. No reliable statistics are available regarding the FTE rate, or the number of users who are simply unable to perform an acceptable enrollment. Based on experience, it is fair to conclude that a statistically significant number of people, perhaps five to 10 percent, may be unable to perform a satisfactory enrollment.

Iris recognition leverages the unique features of the human iris to provide an unmatched identification technology. So accurate are the algorithms used in iris recognition that the entire planet could be enrolled in an iris database with only a small chance of false acceptance or false rejection. The technology also addresses the FTE problems, which lessen the effectiveness of other biometrics. The tremendous accuracy of iris recognition allows it in many ways, to stand apart from other biometric technologies. All iris recognition technology is based on research and patents held by Dr. John Daugman.

Iris recognition is based on the visible (via regular and/or infrared light) qualities of the iris. A primary visible characteristic is the trabecular meshwork; (permanently formed by the eighth month of gestation) a tissue which gives the appearance of dividing the iris in a radial fashion. Other visible characteristics include rings, furrows, freckles and the corona to cite only the most familiar. Expressed simply, iris recognition technology converts these visible characteristics into a 512 byte IrisCode(tm), a template stored for future verification attempts. 512 bytes is a compact size for a biometric template, but the quantity of information derived from the iris is massive. From the iris of 11mm diameter, Dr. Daugman's algorithm provides 3.4 bits of data per square mm. This density of information is such that each iris can be said to have 266 unique "spots," as opposed to 13 to 60 for traditional biometric technologies. This 266 measurement is cited in all iris recognition literature. After allowing for the algorithm's correlative functions and for characteristics inherent to most human eyes, Dr. Daugman concludes that 173 "independent binary degrees-of-freedom" can be extracted from his algorithm — an exceptionally large number for a biometric.

Iris identification is a very accurate biometric technology. Only retinal scan can offer nearly the security that iris scan offers, and the interface for retina scan is thought by many to be more challenging and intrusive. More common biometrics provide reasonably accurate results in verification schematics, whereby the biometric verifies a claimed identity, but they cannot be used in large-scale identification implementations like iris recognition.

Facial Scan Technology

Just as with finger scan and voice scan biometrics, facial scan technology recognizes people by various methods. All share certain commonalities, such as emphasizing those sections of the face, which are less susceptible to alteration, including the upper outlines of the eye sockets, the areas surrounding one's cheekbones, and the sides of the mouth. Most technologies are resistant to moderate changes in hairstyle, as they do not utilize areas of the face located near the hairline. All of the primary technologies are designed to be robust enough to conduct a one-to-many search that is to locate a single face out of a database of thousands, even hundreds of thousands, of faces. The system designs for facial scan verification vs. identification differ in a number of ways. The primary difference is that identification does not require a claimed identity. Instead of employing a PIN or user name and then delivering confirmation or denial of the claim, identification systems attempt to answer the question, "Who am I?" If there are only a handful of enrollees in the database, this requirement is not terribly demanding; as databases grow very large, into the tens and hundreds of thousands, this task becomes much more difficult. The system may only be able to narrow the database to a number of likely candidates and then require human intervention at the final verification stages.

Facial scan systems, depending on the exact type of implementation, may also have to be optimized for non-cooperative and uncooperative subjects. Non-cooperative subjects are unaware that a biometric system is in place, or don't care, and make no effort either to be recognized or to avoid recognition. Uncooperative subjects actively avoid recognition, and may use disguises or take evasive measures. Facial scan technologies are much more capable of identifying cooperative subjects, and are almost entirely incapable of identifying uncooperative subjects.

Voice Recognition

Voice recognition employs the basic fact that no two individuals can produce exactly the same voice patterns. Thus, the fundamental procedure in such a system is to first obtain the input, converge it into a digital format and compare it with a previously stored database. It is possible to represent the vocal-tract in a parametric form as the transfer function H(z). In order to estimate the parameters of H(z) from the observed speech waveform, it is necessary to assume some form for H(z). Ideally, the transfer function should contain poles as well as zeros. However, if only the voiced regions of speech are used then an all-pole model for H(z) is sufficient. Furthermore, linear prediction analysis can be used to estimate the parameters of an all-pole model. Finally, it can also be noted that the all-pole model is the minimum-phase part of the true model and has identical magnitude spectra, which contains the bulk of the speaker-dependent information.

FACE RECOGNITION TECHNOLOGY

Automatic human face recognition, a technique which can locate and identify human faces automatically in an image and determine "who is who" from a database, are gaining more and more attention in the area of computer vision, image processing and pattern recognition over the last two decades. There are several important steps involved in this problem: detection, representation and identification. Based on the different representations, various approaches can be grouped into feature-based and image-based. Feature-based approaches, especially those relying on geometrical features, represent the face as a multi-dimensional feature vector and determine the identification by the Euclidean distance between different feature vectors. Image-based approaches rely on the entire image, instead of some features. In its simplest form, the face is represented as a 2-D array of intensity values. The feature-based approach has the advantage over the image-based approach that it requires less data input but suffers from the incompleteness of features and the difficulty of automatic feature detection. By carefully choosing the region of interest (ROI) and possibly appropriate transformations, the image-based approaches can give more reliable results than the feature-based approach. In the simplest version of image-based approaches, faces are represented as a 2-D array of intensity values and recognition is normally based on direct correlation comparisons between the input face and all other faces in the database. The image with the highest correlation is chosen as the best match (a perfect match gives a value of 1.0). This approach obtains satisfying results only when conditions are ideal (with equal illumination, scale and pose, etc.). However, ideal conditions are not present in most of the cases. In order to make this method more feasible, face images should be registered first. In addition, conducting correlation in the whole image scale is easily interfered by the background and is too time-consuming. Therefore, using smaller special ROIs, which are referred to as templates, is a better alternative option. Methods that are more complicated include the elastic template technique, principal component analysis method using eigenfaces and the neural network approach but most of these recognition systems have a similar disadvantage that they cannot work effectively under varying poses. The strategy adopted in our system is also based on gray level images. To overcome all the drawbacks mentioned above we incorporate a landmark-based affine registration algo-rithm to normalize image scales and orientations. To make the system work under varying head poses, we create a database with multi-view faces. Therefore, there are four major components in our face recognition system: modeling, feature detection, normalization and identification.

Fundamental Issues in Face Recognition

The requirement for reliable personal identification in computerized access control has resulted in an increased interest in biometrics. Biometrics being investigated includes fingerprints, speech, signature dynamics, and face recognition. Sales of identity verification products exceed $100 million. Face recognition has the benefit of being a passive, non-intrusive system for verifying personal identity. The techniques used in the best face recognition systems may depend on the application of the system. We can identify at least two broad categories of face recognition systems:

1.   We want to find a person within a large database of faces (e.g., in a police database). These systems typically return a list of the most likely people in the database. Often only one image is available per person. It is usually not necessary for recognition to be done in real-time.
2.   We want to identify particular people in real-time (e.g., in a security monitoring system, location tracking system, etc.), or we want to allow access to a group of people and deny others (e.g., access to a building, computer, etc.). Multiple images per person are often available for training and real-time recognition is required.

We are interested in recognition with varying facial detail, expression, pose, etc., and do not consider invariance to high degrees of rotation or scaling — a minimal preprocessing stage is available if required. We are interested in rapid classification and hence do not assume that time is available for extensive preprocessing and normalization. (Good algorithms for locating faces in images can be found in Vincent, J. M.)

Robust face recognition requires the ability to recognize an identity despite many variations in appearance that the face can have in a scene. The face is a 3-D object that is illuminated from a variety of light sources and surrounded by arbitrary background data (including other faces), therefore, the appearance a face has when projected onto a 2-D image can vary tremendously.

If we wish to develop a system capable of performing non-contrived recognition, we need to find and recognize faces despite these variations. In fact, 3-D pose, illumination and foreground-background segmentation have been pertinent issues in the field of computer vision as a whole. Additionally, our detection and recognition scheme must also be capable of tolerating variations in the face itself.

The human face is not a unique rigid object, there are billions of different faces and each of them can assume a variety of deformations. Inter-personal variations can be due to race, identity, or genetics while intra-personal variations can be due to deformations, expression, aging, facial hair, cosmetics and facial paraphernalia. Furthermore, the output of the detection and recognition system has to be accurate. A recognition system has to associate an identity or name for each face it comes across by matching it to a large database of individuals. Simultaneously, the system must be robust to typical image-acquisition problems such as noise, video-camera distortion and image resolution. Thus, we are dealing with a multi-dimensional detection and recognition problem.

One final constraint is the need to maintain the usability of the system on contemporary computational devices (100 MIPS). In other words, the processing involved should be efficient with respect to run-time and storage space.

Research in intensity image face recognition generally falls into two categories: holistic (global) methods and feature-based methods. Feature-based methods rely on the identification of certain fiducial points on the face such as the eyes, nose, mouth, etc. The location of those points can be determined and used to compute geometrical relationships between the points as well to analyze the surrounding region locally. Thus, independent processing of the eyes, the nose, and other fiducial points is performed and then combined to produce recognition of the face. Since detection of feature points precedes the analysis, such a system is robust to position variations in the image. Holistic methods treat the image data simultaneously without attempting to localize individual points. The face is recognized as one entity without explicitly isolating different regions in the face. Holistic techniques utilize statistical analysis, neural networks and transformations. They also usually require large samples of training data. The advantage of holistic methods is that they utilize the face as a whole and do not destroy any information by exclusively processing only certain fiducial points. Thus, they generally provide more accurate recognition results. However, such techniques are sensitive to variations in position, scale and so on that restricts their use to standard, frontal mug-shot images.

Just as with finger scan and voice scan biometrics, facial scan technology recognizes people by various methods. All share certain commonalities, such as emphasizing those sections of the face which are less susceptible to alteration, including the upper outlines of the eye sockets, the areas surrounding one's cheekbones, and the sides of the mouth. Most of the technologies are resistant to moderate changes in hairstyle, as they do not utilize areas of the face located near the hairline. All of the primary technologies are designed to be robust enough to conduct one-to-many searches, that is, to locate a single face out of a database of thousands, even hundreds of thousands, of faces.

LITERATURE SURVEY

As one of the most successful applications of image analysis and understanding, face recognition has recently received significant attention, especially during the past few years.

The strong need for user-friendly systems that can secure our assets and protect our privacy without losing our identity in a sea of numbers is obvious. Although extremely reliable methods of biometric personal identification exist, e.g., fingerprint analysis and retinal or iris scans, these methods rely on the cooperation of the participants, whereas a personal identification system based on analysis of frontal or profile images of the face is often effective without the participant's co-operation or knowledge.

A general statement of the problem can be formulated as follows: given still or video images of a scene, identify or verify one or more persons in the scene using a stored database of faces. Available collateral information such as race, age, gender, facial expressions and speech may be used in narrowing the search (enhancing recognition). The solution to the problem involves segmentation of faces (face detection) from cluttered scenes, feature extraction from the face region, recognition or verification. In identification problems, the input to the system is an unknown face, and the system reports the determined identity from a database of known individuals, whereas in verification problems, the system needs to confirm or reject the claimed identity of the input face.

Commercial and law enforcement applications of FRT range from static, controlled format photographs to uncontrolled video images, posing a wide range of different technical challenges and requiring an equally wide range of techniques from image processing, analysis, understanding and pattern recognition. In some applications, such as computerized aging, one is only concerned with defining a set of transformations so that the images created by the system are similar to what humans expect based on their recollections. In is not an overstatement to say that face recognition has become an application of computer vision, pattern recognition and image understanding.

Face Recognition from Single Intensity or Other Images Segmentation

In the Conference on Audio and Video Based Person Authentication (1997-1999), an example-based learning approach to locating vertical frontal views of human faces in complex scenes is presented. This technique models the distribution of human face patterns by means of a few view-based "face" and "non-face" prototype clusters. At each image location, a different feature vector is computed between the local image pattern and the distribution-based model. This difference vector is then fed into a trained classifier to determine whether a human face is present at the current image location or not. The system detects faces of different sizes by exhaustively scanning an image for face-like local image patterns at all possible scales. The system performs following four steps:

- The input sub-image is scaled and a mask is applied to eliminate near boundary pixels. Normalization in intensity is done by first subtracting a best-fit brightness plane from the unmasked window pixels and then applying histogram equalization.
- A distribution-based model of canonical face and non-face-patterns is constructed from samples. The clusters are constructed by an elliptical k-means clustering algorithm using an adaptively varying normalization Mahalanobis distance metric.
- A vector of matching measurement is computed for each pattern.
- A MLP classifier is trained for face/non-face discrimination.

To detect faces in an image, preprocessing is done as in step 1, followed by matching measurement computation and finally the MLP is used for detection.

Feature Extraction

Feature extraction is the key to both face segmentation and recognition, as it is to any pattern classification task. There has been renewed interest in the use of the

Karhunen-Loeve (KL) expansion for the representation and recognition of faces. Note that the number of images M usually available for computing the covariance matrix of the data is much less than the row or column dimensionality of the covariance matrix, leading to singularity of the matrix. A standard method from linear algebra is used that calculates only the M eigenvectors that do not belong to the null space of the degenerate matrix. Once the eigenvectors are obtained, then an image in the ensemble can be approximately reconstructed using a weighted combination of eigen pictures. By using an increasing number of eigen pictures, one gets an improved approximation to the given image. Using this method one can find the eyes and mouth in a face. Edge detection and Gabor functions are a few other methods for implementing the task.

Recognition from Intensity Image

Statistical Approaches

Eigen pictures are used by P.J. Philips, P. Rauss and S. Der for face detection and identification. Given the eigenfaces, every face in the database can be represented as a vector of weights; the weights are obtained by projecting the image into eigenface components by a simple inner product operation. When a new test image for identification is given, that is also represented by its vector of weights. The images in the database whose weights are closest to the weights of the test image are located and the best match is found. By using the observation that the projection of a face image and a non-face image are quite different, a method of detecting the presence of a face in a given image is obtained. It was also reported that the approach is robust to changes in lighting condition, but degrades quickly as the scale changes. The approach works well as long as the test image is similar to the ensemble of images used in the calculation of eigenfaces. The approach was also extended to real time recognition of a moving face image in a video sequence.

More recently, practical face recognition systems have been developed based on eigenface representation. In Masser, Matas, Kittler, Leuttin and Maitre (1999), the eigenface method based on simple subspace restricted norms is extended to use a probabilistic measure of similarity. The proposed similarity measure is based on a standard Bayesian analysis of image differences of two categories: (1) intra-personal variations in the appearance of the same individual due to different expressions or lightning, and (2) extra personal variations in appearance due to difference in identity. The high dimensional probability density functions for each class are then obtained from training data using an eigen space density estimation technique and are subsequently used to compute a similarity measure based on the posteriori probability of membership in the intrapersonal class.

Neural Network Approach

The neural network (NN) approach has been used in face recognition to address several problems: gender classification, face recognition and classification of facial expressions. One of the earliest demonstrations of NN for face recall applications used Kohonen's associative map. Using a small set of face images, accurate recall was reported even when the input image was very noisy or when portions of the image were missing. This capability has also been demonstrated using optical hardware. Philips, McCabe and

Chellapa (1998) describe an NN approach to gender classification using a vector of sixteen numerical attributes such as eyebrow thickness, widths of nose and mouth, six chin radii, etc. Two Hyper BF networks were trained, one for each gender. The input images were normalized with respect to scale and rotation by using the positions of eyes; which were detected automatically. The 16-dimensional feature vector was also automatically extracted. The outputs of the two Hyper BF networks were compared; the gender label for the test image being determined by the network with greater output. When the feature vector from the training set was used as the test vector, then 92.5 percent correct recognition accuracy was reported and for faces not in the training set, the accuracy dropped to 87.5 percent. Same validation of the automatic classification results has been reported using humans.

Other than the Hyper BF method, other methods are also used in artificial the neural network approach for FRT. DLA (Dynamic Link Architecture), Gabor Filters, Elastic Bunch Graph Matching are few of them.

Other Sensing Modalities

Range Images

The discussion so far has considered only the face recognition method for the systems that use data obtained from the 2-D intensity images. Another topic being studied by researchers is face recognition from range image data. A range image contains the depth structure of the object in question. Although such data is not available, in most applications it is important to determine the value of the added information present in range data in terms of its effect on the accuracy of face recognition.

Chellapa, Wilson and Sirohey (1995) described a template-based recognition involving descriptors based on curvature calculation made on range image data. The data are obtained from a rotating laser scanner system with resolution better then 0.4mm. Surfaces are classified into planar, spherical, and surfaces of revolution. The data are stored in a cylindrical coordinate system. At each point on the surface the magnitude and directions of the maximum and minimum normal curvatures are calculated. To remove the noise, Gaussian filters are used. Surface regions are classified as convex, concave and saddle. Ridges and valley lines are determined by obtaining the maxima and minima of the curvatures. The strategy used for face recognition is as follows:

- The nose is located.
- Locating the nose facilitates the search for the eyes and mouth.
- Other features such as forehead, neck, cheeks, etc., are determined by their smoothness.
- This information is then used for depth template comparison. Using the location of the eyes, nose and mouth, the face is normalized into a standard position. This position is re-interpolated to a regular cylindrical grid and the volume of space between the two normalized surfaces is used as the mismatch measure.

Sketches and Infrared Images

In Samal and Iyengar (1992) and Johnston, Hill and Corman (1992), face recognition based on sketches, which are quite common in law enforcement, is described. Humans have a remarkable ability to recognize faces from sketches. This ability provides a basis for forensic investigations: an artist draws a sketch based on the witness' verbal description; then a witness looks through a large database of real images to determine possible matches. Usually the database of real images is quite large, possibly containing thousands of real photos. Therefore, building a system capable of automatically recognizing faces from sketches has practical value.

Kirby and Sirovich (1990) describe an initial study comparing the effectiveness of visible and infrared imagery for detecting and recognizing faces. The illumination problem can be solved by this method but the inferior resolution of IR images is a drawback.

So far, we have not distinguished between two concepts: face identification and face verification. Strictly speaking, recognition includes both identification and verification. In identification tasks, the input to the system is an unknown face and the system reports its identity using a database of known individuals whereas in verification, the system needs to confirm or reject the claimed identity of the input face.

Face Recognition from Image Sequence

In surveillance applications, face recognition and identification from a video sequence is an important problem. The task of recognizing individuals from a surveillance video is still difficult for the following reasons:

*   The quality of the video is low.
*   The face images are small.
*   The characteristics of human face objects may not be clear.

Video based FRT offers several advantages over still image-based FRT:

*   Video provides abundant image data; good frames can be selected on which to perform classification.
*   Video provides temporal continuity; this allows reuse of classification information obtained from high quality frames in processing low quality frames.
*   Video allows tracking of face images; hence phenomena such as facial expressions and pose changes can be compensated for, resulting in improved recognition.

COMPARISON OF POPULAR APPROACHES

This section is a detailed study of the following algorithms:

*   Feature Based Approach for Face Recognition
    *   ➤ (Cox, Ghosn, & Yianilos)
*   Face Recognition using eigenfaces
    *   ➤ (Turk & Pentland)
*   Line Based Face Recognition
    *   ➤ (de Vel & Aeberhard)

- Local Feature Analysis
  - ➢ (Penev)

Feature Based Approach for Face Recognition Using Mixture Distances

Just as with finger scan and voice scan biometrics, facial scan technology recognizes people by various methods. All share certain commonalities, such as emphasizing those sections of the face, which are less susceptible to alteration, including the upper outlines of the eye sockets, the areas surrounding one's cheekbones and the sides of the mouth. Most of the technologies are resistant to moderate changes in hairstyle as they do not utilize areas of the face located near the hairline. All of the primary technologies are designed to be robust enough to conduct one-to-many searches that is, to locate a single face out of a database of thousands, even hundreds of thousands of faces. There are about 80 nodal points on a human face. Here are a few of the nodal points that are being measured. (See Table 1.)

These nodal points are measured to create a numerical code; a string of numbers that represents the face in a database. This code is called a face print. The various steps being followed are given below:

1. Detection — When the system is attached to a video surveillance system, the recognition software searches the field of view of a video camera for faces. If there is a face in the view, it is detected within a fraction of a second. A multi-scale algorithm is used to search for faces in low resolution. (An algorithm is a program that provides a set of instructions to accomplish a specific task.) The system switches to a high-resolution search only after a head-like shape is detected.
2. Alignment — Once a face is detected, the system determines the head position, size and pose. A face needs to be turned at least 35 degrees toward the camera for the system to register it.
3. Normalization — The image of the head is scaled and rotated so that it can be registered and mapped into an appropriate size and pose. Normalization is performed regardless of the head's location and distance from the camera. Light does not impact the normalization process.

Table 1: Examples of Nodal Points Measured on a Human Face

❖ Distance between eyes
❖ Width of nose
❖ Depth of eye sockets
❖ Cheekbones
❖ Jaw line
❖ Chin

4. Representation — The system then translates the facial data into a unique code. This coding process allows for easier comparison of the newly acquired facial data to store the facial data.
5. Matching — Finally, the newly acquired facial data is compared to the stored data and (ideally) linked to at least one stored facial representation.

Normalization

One of the most critical points when using a vector of geometrical features is that of proper scale normalization. The selected image must be somehow normalized (or aligned) in order to be independent of position, scale and rotation of the face in the image plane. Translational dependency can be eliminated once the origin of coordinates is set to a point, which can be detected with good accuracy in each image. The approach we have followed achieves scale and rotation invariance by setting the inter-ocular distance and the direction of the eye-to-eye axis. The inter-ocular distance chosen is about 28-pixels in the image of 100x125 pixels.

Constructing Image Vectors

Some of the feature points taken on the face are illustrated in Figure 3 and Table 2.

Given a database of facial feature vectors $Y = \{y_i\}$ each corresponding to a different person, and a query q consisting of a facial feature vector for some unidentified person is assumed to be represented in Y, our objective is to locate the y_i corresponding to q. In the absence of error and assuming that no two people are alike, we would have only to search Y for an exact match to q, but in practice q will not match to anything in Y perfectly because of many sources of error. These include the feature extraction errors associated with the human limitations, while constructing the feature vector from a photograph variation in the subject's pose, unknown camera optical characteristics and physical variations in the subject itself. Clearly, the nature of these error processes should influence the way in which we compare queries and database elements. The difficulty lies in the fact that we can't directly observe them given that only a single example of each person exists in Y.

Figure 3: Feature Points

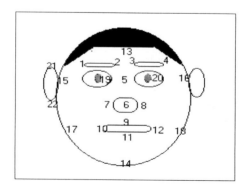

Table 2: Feature Points on the Human Face

Feature	Part of the face
1	Left corner of the left eyebrow
2	Right corner of the left eyebrow
3	Left corner of the right eyebrow
4	Right corner of the right eyebrow
5	Midpoint of the two eyes
6	Tip of the nose
7	Corner of left nostrils
8	Corner of right nostrils
9	Upper center of lip-line
10	Left corner of the lips
11	Midpoint of the lower lip line
12	Right corner of the lips
13	Uppermost central forehead
14	Lowermost point of the chin
15	Left hairline
16	Right hairline
17	Left cheek line
18	Right cheek line
19	Left eye-pupil
20	Right eye-pupil
21	Upper tip of the ear
22	Lower tip of the ear

The various steps in our recognition algorithm are the construction of the query vector q using the same method of construction of the feature vector in which the original database was constructed to minimize the local errors. We also choose an error vector ε in mean pixels depending upon the magnitude of the error, which might have crept up during the process of construction of the feature vector. The value of this error vector ε is ±3 pixels in construction of the feature vector phase, while in pixel matching the value is chosen as ±0.2 of the maximum absolute gray scale, i.e., 255.

Another step in our algorithm consisted of finding the cost function for the images during matching. In case the vector element matches with the test image, the cost function is assigned value 0 or else it is assigned 1. The total cost of the image match is then calculated and the various images are ranked according to the increasing cost. Out of these sorted images, those for which the cost function was at most evaluated to be 4 were chosen and were then assigned to as the input for the other modules of the algorithm.

The three different modules of the algorithm consisted of simple feature vector matching, pixel matching by tolerant subtraction employed for the input images with that of the test image and the third one consisted of edge detection and later subtraction of thus, found edge binary images.

Face Recognition Using Eigenfaces

Until Kirby and Sirovich in the *International Journal of Computer Vision* (1998) applied the Karhunen-Loeve Transform to faces, face recognition systems utilized feature-based techniques, template matching or neural networks to perform the recognition. The groundbreaking work of Kirby and Sirovich not only resulted in a technique that efficiently represents pictures of faces using Principal Component Analysis (PCA), but also laid the foundation for the development of the "eigenface" technique of Turk and Pentland at the Conferences on Automatic Face and Gesture (1995-1998), which has now become a de facto standard and a common performance benchmark in face recognition (Brunelli & Poggio, 1993).

Starting with a collection of original face images, PCA aims to determine a set of orthogonal vectors that optimally represent the distribution of the data. Any face images can then be theoretically reconstructed by projections onto the new coordinate system. In search of a technique that extracts the most relevant information in a face image to form the basis vectors, Turk and Pentland proposed the eigenface approach, which effectively captures the variations within an ensemble of face images.

The notion of direction of variance in a high dimensional space can be extracted from the covariance matrix of the data points. The eigenvectors of the covariance matrix define a space in which the covariance among dimensions is zero, so the matrix takes on a diagonal form. The problem is essentially solved by computing the eigenvectors of the covariance matrix and projecting the data points into this new space. Consider an image φ_i among a collection of M images, define ψ as the average image:

$$\Psi = 1/M * \sum_{i=1}^{M} \phi_1 \tag{1}$$

Every image differs from the mean by a vector $\Gamma_i = \varphi_i - \psi_i$. The covariance matrix of the data is thus defined as:

$$C(\{\phi_i\}) = \sum_{i=1}^{M} \Gamma_i^T \Gamma_I = AA^T \tag{2}$$

where, A is a column-wise concatenation of all the φ_is.

$$A = [\Gamma_1, \Gamma_2, \dots \Gamma_M] \tag{3}$$

Note that C has dimension $wh \times wh$ where w is the width of the image and h is the height. The size of this matrix is enormous, but since we only sum up a finite number of image vectors M the rank of this matrix cannot exceed $M-1$. We note that if v_i are the eigenvectors of A^TA (note the order of multiplication):

$$A^TAv_i = \mu_i v_i \tag{4}$$

where, μ are the eigenvalues, then $A\,v_i$ are the eigenvectors of $A\,A^T = C$ as we see by multiplying on the left by A the previous equation:

$$AA^TAv_i = A\mu_i v_i = \mu_i Av_i \tag{5}$$

but $A\,A^T$ is only of size $M\,X\,M$. So defining u_i the eigenvectors of C we have:

$$u_i = Av_i \sum_{k=1}^{M} v_{ik} G_k \tag{6}$$

From here we assume that the order of i is such that m_i the eigenvalues are decreasing (these values are the variances along the new coordinate space). They decrease in exponential fashion, meaning that roughly 90 percent of the total variance is contained in the first five to 10 percent of the dimensions.

We decide to project a face image Γ onto only $M' << M$ dimensions by computing:

$$\Omega(\Gamma) = \{\omega_\kappa\} \text{ where } \omega_\kappa = u_\kappa.\Gamma \text{ and } 1 \le k \le M' \tag{7}$$

ω_k is the k-th coordinate of Γ in the new system. The vectors u_k are actually images, and are called eigen images/eigenfaces. Figure 9 displays some eigen images and we see that they do resemble the original faces with the variations from all other faces also included making them look more like multiple border images. We have an interesting by-product, which is the reconstruction of a projected image that could be used for compression or validation purposes:

$$\Gamma' = \sum_{i=1}^{M'} \omega_i u_i \text{ so we have } \phi' = \Gamma' + \Psi \tag{8}$$

So now each image is a vector $\Omega_i = \Omega(\Gamma_i)$ of size M'. The similarity is simply defined as the distance between projections:

$$\delta(\Gamma_i, \Gamma_j) = \| \Omega_i - \Omega_j \| \tag{9}$$

If this distance is small, we say the images are similar and we can decide which the most similar image in the database is. In order to increase the robustness to minor changes in expression, slight variations of view angles and illumination, we consider that each of the L persons is represented in the database by N images. We can then form a class C_i = $\{\Gamma\}$ of images for that person and consider as a representative image the artificial average of the projections of each image in the class:

$$\Omega(X_i) = 1/N * \sum_{i=1}^{N'} \Omega\Gamma_i \tag{10}$$

We can then use $\Omega(C_i)$ in Equation 9 as one of the two vectors to compare.

Since the process involves projections, we might end up having two different images with the same coordinates, specifically if one of them is not a face at all, leading to unwanted results. The solution is to estimate the difference between an image and its reconstruction. Faces should fall close to their reconstructions, whereas non-faces should fall far away. We define:

$$\epsilon(\Gamma) = \|\Gamma - \Gamma'\| \tag{11}$$

where, the Γ comes from Equation 8.

The recognition of an image knowing these two measure δ and ϵ happens as follows:
- ϵ small and δ_i is small for some class of faces $l \Rightarrow$ recognize the person l.
- ϵ small and δ_i is big for all $l \Rightarrow$ it is an unknown face.
- ϵ big, regardless of the value $\delta \Rightarrow$ the image is probably not a face.

So the preprocessing for recognition is the following:
- Compute the matrix A on a reasonable subset of all face images using Equation 3.
- Then compute the eigenvectors and eigenvalues of $A^T A$.
- Sort them by decreasing eigenvalue, and compute the eigen-images u_i with the help of Equation 6.
- Project all faces into the space defined by the u_i's yielding at Ω_i by Equation 7.
- For each class l of faces compute the average $\Omega(C_i)$ Equation 10.
- Store the u_i, and Ω_i and Ω_c for future use.

When we want to recognize an incoming test image Γ, we do the following:
- Compute its projection Ω from Equation 7.
- Compute the closeness of reproduction $\epsilon(\Gamma)$. If it is larger than a threshold $\hat{\epsilon}$, we decide the image is not a face at all.
- Else we compute distances to all of the L known classes: $\delta(\Omega, \Omega(C_i))$. Then find the smallest one that yields a class $*l$. If it is smaller than a threshold $\hat{\delta}$, we decide the recognized person is $*l$, else we conclude the image is not a known person.

Line Based Face Recognition

The basis for the line based face recognition algorithm is that even though each line segment only predicts a correct face marginally better than random, the combination of line segments from a unique face image leads to a high probability of correct face classification. We extend the idea that 3-D object recognition can effectively be undertaken using multiple redundant 2-D views of an object to the idea that a combination of a set of randomly placed 1-D line segments in a 2-D object view exploits the coherence in that view. Therefore, the basis for image representation is the simple rectilinear line segment primitive form.

We are interested in classifying K faces, $F_k(k = 1, 2, 3, ...)$, given $V_k \oplus D$ image views of each unique face F_k, obtained by regular sampling in the viewing sphere. The aim is to recognize one of the K faces from test image views.

A face image is modeled as a regular lattice of $w \times h$ pixels, with each pixel P having a depth equal to the $\Im_p$ image planes. We first classify the pixels in $\Im$ into two classes — $C_{p,1}$ and $C_{p,2}$. Class $C_{p,1}$ consists of all those pixels that represent a face such that $C_{p,1} \cap C_{p,2} = \varnothing$. We are interested in those pixels in $C_{p,2}$ having neighbors in $C_{p,1}$ and call the set of those face boundary pixels β.

Consider l pixel values extracted along a straight line or "chord" between two points in an image comprising of $l \times \Im_p$ bits of data. The number of line pixels is small enough for efficient classification but of course may not capture the information necessary for correct classification. However, with some reduced probability (larger than random), the line predicts the correct face class. The algorithm we propose is based on the observation that the classification of many such lines from a face image $\Im$ leads to an overall probability of correct classification (PCC) which approaches 1. This observation serves as the main motivation for the algorithm.

For any two points $B_1 \in \beta$ and $B_2 \in \beta$ in an image view V_k such that the Euclidean distance B_1 and B_2 is greater than a minimum D_{min}, let $L(B_1, B_2) \equiv (L^{(1)}, L^{(2)}, ...L^{(l)})$ be a vector of length l, where l is the number of equi-spaced connected intensity values $L^{(q)} = P(L)_q$ (where $q = 1, 2, ..., l$) along the image rectilinear segment from B_1 to B_2. We note that in the algorithm, the points B_1 and B_2 need not necessarily belong to the set of face boundary pixels b. Indeed, rectilinear line segments may span any two pixels that are outside the face boundary, i.e., $B_1, B_2 \subseteq C_{p,2}$. The relative performance of the algorithm will depend on the coverage of the face by the set of the line segments and maximum performance will generally be achieved when $B_1, B_2 \in \beta$.

The line segment length l is a constant parameter determined a priori; larger values of l result in better classification rates at the expense of increased processing times. All lines are scaled to the value l by pixel interpolation. We call $L(B_1, B_2)$ a lattice line, denoted by L. The exact interpolation of L need not lie on the corner of the boundary pixels B_1 and B_2.

For each face class in the training set of V_k image views, we randomly generate $N_k = V_k \times N_v$ lattice lines (N_v lines per image view per face class), $L_{i,k} \equiv (L_{i,k}^{(1)}, L_{i,k}^{(2)}, ...L_{i,k}^{(l)})$ for $i = 1, 2, ..., N_k$ such that N_k lattice lines for K face classes. The set of lattice lines for all K face classes is given by:

$$\Psi = \bigcup_{k=1}^{K} \bigcup_{i=1}^{N_k} L_{i,k}$$

We define the distance $D(L_{r,s}, L_{m,n})$ between two lattice lines $L_{r,s}$ and $L_{m,n}$ as:

$$D(\boldsymbol{L}_{r,s}, \boldsymbol{L}_{m,n}) = \Sigma\left((L_{r,s}^{(q)} - (L_{m,n}^{(q)} + \Delta))^2\right),$$

for $r, m = 1, 2, \dots N_k$ and $s, n = 1, 2, \dots K$, where $\Delta = \mu(L_{r,s}) - \mu(L_{m,n})$ and $\mu(L_{r,s}) = \Sigma_i L_{r,s}/l$. The value of Δ has the effect of shifting the two lines towards the same average value, making the distance measure invariant to illumination intensity.

Consider now a set of test lines sampled from one or more face views in the viewing sphere (for the same face subject). Given an unseen test lattice line L_j, where generally $L_j \notin \psi$, we define $L_{j,*}$ such that $D(L_j, L_{j,*})$ is a minimum, where $L_{j,*} \in \psi$. The nearest neighbor classifier (NNC) maps L_j to the class F_k to which L_j belongs. We choose the nearest neighbor classifier since it has a good performance over a range of problem domains.

We assume that there are N test lines L_j for a given test face, where $j = 1, 2, \dots, N$. and, for each line, we have obtained an $L_{j,*}$ and a D_j. Let $D_{max} = k_1 * max_{1 \le j \le N}\{D_j\}$ for some value of k_1 between $0 < k_1 \le 1$ and $D_{min} = min_{1 \le j \le N}\{D_j\}$. We define the cumulative l_1-norm error statistic for line L_j, $err_j = (\Sigma_{q=1}^{l}(|L^{(q+1)}_{j,*} - L^{(q)}_{j,*}|))/(l-1)$ for $q = 1, 2, \dots, l-1$ and the maximum cumulative error statistic, $err_{max} = max_{1 \le i \le N}\{err_i\}$.

We define $conf_j$ as the measure of confidence that NNC (L_j) is correct:

$$\begin{aligned} conf_j \ &= 0 \qquad\qquad\qquad\qquad\qquad\qquad \text{if } D_j > D_{max} \\ &= \{W_1 (D_{max} - D_j)/(D_{max} - D_{min})\}^{p1} * \{(err_j/err_{max})W_2\}^{p2} \qquad \text{otherwise} \end{aligned}$$

where p_1, p_2, w_1, and $w_2 \in IR_\oplus$. The variables p_1 and p_2 control the shape of the confidence function, whereas w_1 and w_2 are the weight magnitudes of the distance and cumulative error statistic components, respectively.

To classify a face F_t for which we know its boundary pixel set β, we randomly select N lattice lines $L_j, j = 1, 2, \dots, N$. For each face class $F_k = 1, 2, \dots, K$, define $TC_k = \Sigma_{j=1}^{N} conf_j$, such that $NNC(L_j) = F_k$. We assign F_t to class F_g such that TC_g is the maximum. That is:

If $TC_g = max\{TC_k\}$
Then $F_g \leftarrow F_t$ for $F_g = 1, 2, \dots K$.

Because F_t is assigned to class F_g based on the combination of many assignments of individual lines, we may assess the likelihood that our decision is correct by the agreement within the line assignments. Specifically, we define the *confidence measure factor* as the ratio:

$$CMF = [TC_g - TC_j^{(2)}]/TC_j^{(2)},$$

where $TC_j^{(2)}$ is the second largest compounded confidence measure that a class obtained. As our decision is based on the maximum score, the associated confidence CMF is proportional to the difference with the second largest score. The denominator normalizes CMF for different numbers of testing lines.

It is a considerable advantage that if a classifier were to supply a confidence measure factor with its decision, as the user is then given information about which assignments are more likely to be wrong so that extra caution can be exercised in those cases. Our implementation makes use of the confidence measure factor by means of several decision stages. First, the number of testing is to be kept small, an initial decision is arrived at quickly and the confidence measure factor is evaluated. Second, if the confidence measure factor is smaller than twice the minimum confidence measure factor threshold CMF_{min}, then the number of testing lines is doubled and a second decision is made at the cost of extra time. Finally, if the second confidence measure factor is smaller than CMF_{min}, the number of testing lines is doubled again one last time. Thus by specifying a larger value for CMF_{min}, the number of test lines will be increased and hopefully improve the rate of correct classification. However, by increasing the number of test lines there will be a commensurate increase in the time required for classification. Therefore, depending on the application task, the user can choose whether to seek a high classification rate at the expense of larger classification times or to achieve a lower classification rate with an accompanying reduction in classification times.

Local Feature Analysis

Local Feature Analysis (LFA) is derived from the eigenface method. To reduce the dimensionality, many algorithms are being worked out like Principal Component Analysis, Gaussian Component Analysis, Independent Component Analysis, Factorial Learning, Infomax, Matching Pursuit and symplectic maps. So far, however, the most practical and systematic method which has been developed is *Principal Component Analysis (PCA)*, also known as *Karhunen-Loeve Procedure.* PCA assumes that the probability density of the input ensemble in the space of receptor activation patterns is significantly nonzero only in a low dimensional linear subspace, which is subsequently parameterized with a linear expansion in the eigenvectors of the correlation matrix of the ensemble. This method of PCA is incapable of capturing, in a natural way, some of the symmetries present in the original ensemble. For example, PCA is not capable of extracting local features like structure in objects, which have been hypothesized to be important for recognition. Also, in general PCA produces global linear filters whose output is not very naturally amenable to subsequent processing. Local representations are desirable since they offer robustness against variability due to changes in localized regions of the objects.

This is obtained by the two-step procedure known as LFA. It initially derives a dense set of linear filters with local support that are defined at each point of the receptor grid and are different from each other; the filters are optimally matched to the input ensemble and their outputs are de-correlated. At the first step of LFA, the receptor activation pattern due to any incoming object is filtered with this dense sense of receptor fields. (Because the object ensemble is, in general, with reduced dimensionality, the dense set of LFA outputs, entirely contained in the PCA subspace is linearly independent.) Therefore, full de-correlations cannot be achieved, and outputs necessarily contain residual correlations. At the second step of LFA, the residual correlations are used to sparsify the output; it is represented as a small subset of all output units.

LFA can be described as the irreducible set of building elements. It contains individual features instead of relying on only a global representation of the face. The system selects a series of blocks that best define an individual face. The features are the building blocks from which all facial images can be constructed. It anticipates that the slight movement of a feature located near one's mouth will be accompanied by relatively similar movements of adjacent features. Since feature analysis is not a global representation of the face, it can accommodate angles up to about 25^0 in the horizontal plane and 15^0 in the vertical plane. Problems arise when the input picture taken at different angles and lightning conditions might have a different selection of blocks than the one from the same person in the face-bank. In that case, two possibilities may occur:

- Match is not found; then another selection of block is generated until match is successful.
- Match is found; in this case, there is the probability that face matched is not the one being searched.

Therefore, we must generate another block and try to find the match again. This method depends greatly on tuning the choice of block generation. Increasing the number of "local features" can improve the performance of the method.

Experimental Database

The input into the system and, consequently, into the first face location module will be either a still image or a frame from a video sequence. Analysis of the complex scene will then be performed to output an estimated location of the face.

The face normalization module will then aim to transform the image into a standardized format, where varying scaling factors, rotational angles of faces, lighting conditions, background environment, and facial expressions of faces will be considered. The normalized faces can be then entered into the face recognition module, either to add a new face into the database or to recognize a face from the existing database.

As discussed above much research and focus has been placed upon the face recognition stage, and most developmental work has been performed using image databases and still images that were created under a constant predefined environment. Since a controlled environment removes the need for extensive normalization adjustments, reliable techniques have been developed to recognize faces with reasonable accuracy provided the database contain perfectly aligned and normalized face images. Thus, the challenge for face recognition systems does not lie in the recognition of the faces, but in normalizing all input face images to a standardized format that is compliant with the strict requirements of the face recognition module. Although there are models developed to describe faces, such as texture mapping with the Candide model (Manjunath & Chellapa, 1991), currently, there are no developed definitions or mathematical models that define what the important and necessary components are for describing a face.

Using still images taken under restraint conditions as input, it is reasonable to omit the face normalization stage. However, when locating and segmenting a face in complex scenes under unconstraint environments such as in a video scene, it is necessary to define and design a standardized face database. As a result, numerous configurations and schemes have been proposed and reviewed throughout the design of this face recognition system in order to create such a database. Techniques such as alignment of faces relative to the face centroid, center of mass of skinned surfaces, and distances between the eyes and the nose, have all been considered.

Preparation of Image Database

To prepare the image database we have adopted the following methodology:

- The face/faces in the scene should be facing the camera with a maximum of 30 degrees freedom for the face in all directions — up/down/sideways/forward, etc.;
- Avoiding occlusion of one face by another (no overlap in case of multiple faces);
- Control the illumination so that there is no glaze/too much shine on any part of the scene — in particular on the face region;
- Let the person walk normally towards the camera from a distance of about two to three meters at maximum and one meter minimum;
- Let the background be static (without much motion) and non-complex (less variation in terms of relative brightness and color). Take the video shot for about five seconds at least and not more than 10 seconds and maintain frame rate of either 15 or 30 fps, which are the normal standards;
- Let the dimension of the grabbed video be any of the following standards used in other parts of the world:
  - ➢ 320 X 200 (width by height)
  - ➢ 352 X 288
  - ➢ 176 X 144.

In the experiment, the resolution for still capture is of 1024 X 768 and for video capture is 320 X 240. Per person, we have taken the snapshots as follows:

- Face moving upward and downward (with a rotation at random angles);
- Face moving sideward left and right (with a rotation at random angles);
- Face tilting left and right.

All these cases are considered for three different zooms (1x, 1.5x, 2x). The same database is being extended with all the above cases for different illumination conditions (faded light, sufficient light and bright light). This database contains images of 100 different persons.

These data are the results of a project that compares several techniques for face recognition on a common database, thereby providing quantitative information on the performance of different recognition strategies. The results are obtained by implementing the algorithms of Feature based, eigen based and Line based technology on MATLAB 6.0 with the system configuration as P-III, 128MB RAM. The toolboxes used in MATLAB were Image Processing Toolbox, Neural Network Toolbox and various other general functions used in the software.

Samples of photographs taken for the image database are shown in Figure 4.

Figure 4: Database Images

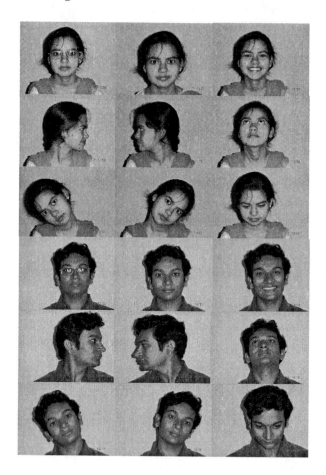

RESULT
Result of Feature Based Approach

The results are shown in the following pages, and are arranged in the manner of successful search, the partial successful match (if any) and the unsuccessful match, with a note on the specific result for all of the three algorithms we employed during the course of our experiment.

Test 1: Feature Matching

In this test, the feature vectors of database images are compared with those of test images, and images having a maximum number of similar (exact) features are selected. The three best selections are displayed (see Figure 5).

The first three images are the example of a successful result when the search in the database is successful, while in the last case, the algorithm shows that the test image is

Figure 5: Results of Feature Matching

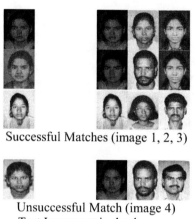

Successful Matches (image 1, 2, 3)

Unsuccessful Match (image 4)
Test Image not in database

not available in the database. Image 4 shows that in case the test image is not present in the database, the algorithm gives the three nearest matches found.

Test 2: Feature Matching and Pixel Matching

In this test, the feature vectors of database images are compared with those of test images and a few images with the nearest match are selected. Then, on these selected images pixel matching is done. (See Figure 6.)

The first two images are the example of a successful result when the search in the database is successful, while in the other two, the algorithm shows that the test image is not

Figure 6: Results of Feature Matching and Pixel Matching

Test Image   Best Matched Images

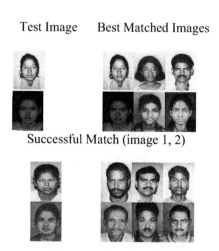

Successful Match (image 1, 2)

Figure 7: Results of Feature Matching and Edge Detection

Test Image   Best Matched Images

Successful Match (image 1, 2)

Partially Successful Match (image 3)
(Note that the 2nd best match is the original image)

Unsuccessful Match (image 4)
Test Image not in database

available in the database. This result shows that if the image is not available in the database then it will display the three nearest matches and, if available, then the first best-matched image is the same as the test image.

Test 3: Feature Matching and Edge Detection

In this test, the feature vectors of the database images are compared with those of test images and a few images with the nearest match are selected. Then, on these selected images edge detection and tolerant subtraction is done. (See Figure 7.)

The first three images are the example of a successful result when the search in the database is successful, while in the last case the algorithm shows that the test image is not available in the database. This result also shows that the images may not be exactly the same in the case of a successful search as in image two as well as that the search may not give the same image as the first best match as in case of image three. Image four shows that in case the test image is not present in the database, the algorithm gives the three nearest matches found. The results of feature based algorithm can be shown as in Table 3.

Result of Eigen Face Approach

To demonstrate the capability and the accuracy of the recognition stage, a selected database of ten faces and several recognition results are presented. The database presented in Figure 8 is a small database that was used during the development of the

Table 3: Results of Feature-Based Algorithms

Criterion	Experimental Results
Procedure	Semi automatic
Same image with different name	100% accuracy
Same image with different brightness	Independent of brightness – 100%
Same image with different contrast	Independent of contrast – 100%
Different image of same person	• With same posture & head orientation – 85% • It can't work if features are not available
Zoom and Blur-ness	• Handles the zoom factor – 90% • Blur-ness – 95%
Angle Orientation	Can manage the rotation up to 10%
+ ve points	• High accuracy rate on slightly different images • Very fast after user inputs • Gives the best three matched images
- ve points	Semi automatic, i.e., it needs lots of user interaction which causes the effect on results. The result is heavily dependent upon the users' accuracy.

design to test the recognition ability of the system. The faces presented are the inputs into the training stage where a representative set of eigenfaces were determined. After training, the face from the test image is detected and normalized and then the normalized face is given for recognition. Comparing the weights of the test face with the known weights of the database performs identification. Mathematically, a score is found by calculating the norm of the differences between the test and known set of weights, such that a minimum difference between any pair would symbolize the closest match.

Figure 8: Input Training Images

Figure 9: Eigenfaces Corresponding to the Training Images

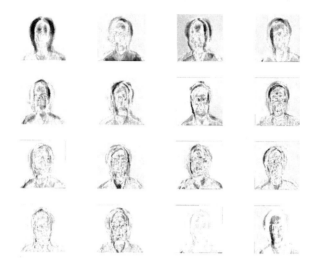

The eigenfaces were calculated from the previous training images. When the eigenfaces are displayed, they look like a ghostly face. The eigenfaces are displayed in Figure 9. In this case, 10 eigenfaces were chosen. This was based on the eigen-vectors with the highest eigenvalues.

Recognition is done by finding the training face that minimized the "face" distance with respect to the input face, i.e., which of the training faces was more similar to the input face. This was based on determining the Euclidian distance.

$$\varepsilon_k = || \Omega - \Omega_k ||$$

Recognition was performed on 16 faces of the training subjects. A 100 percent recognition rate was achieved over the training set. Several pictures not related to the training images were input into the program to determine if the algorithm would recognize them. If an unknown image is input, the algorithm will return a message that it does not recognize the image.

The program will prompt the user for an image to be detected among the database. When an image is entered into the database, the program is able to process and detect what face image closely resembles the input image. The algorithm will return the image that closely matches the index of the input image (Figure 10).

If we give some other images, which are not trained than the accuracy decreases, and it depends upon the quality and specification of the input image. To make the results more clear, Table 4 will be helpful.

Results of Line Based Face Recognition Method

To investigate the effect of various parameter settings on classification and correctness, we ran four experiments varying each parameter at a time. In each experiment,

Figure 10: Results of Eigenface Algorithm

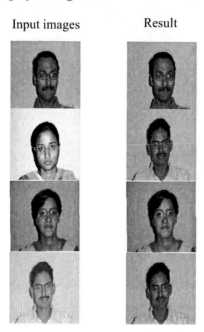

the parameters were resampled over the combined face database. For example, for evaluating the probability of correct classification (PCC) for different numbers of test lines, each set of test lines was obtained by resampling the combined face database.

In the first experiment, the number of test lines N was varied from 20 to 400. The number of training lines, N_k, was set to $l = 32$, and the minimum confidence factor to 200, the line dimensionality t to $l = 32$, and the minimum confidence factor to zero. This

Table 4: Results of Eigenface Algorithm

Criterion	Experimental Results
Procedure	Automatic
Same image with different name	100% accuracy
Same image with different brightness	• If slight change – 95% • If large difference then – 8%
Same image with different contrast	• If slight change – 80% • If large difference then – 60%
Different image of same person	• With same posture and head orientation • With large differences – fails
Zoom and Blur-ness	• Fails on zoom • With little blur-ness (70%)
Angle Orientation	Can manage rotation up to 2%
+ ve points	• Very fast (take around one to three seconds to recognize) • Speed depends upon the size of image • Can handle little bit of blur-ness
- ve points	• Ca not work on different rotations, angles and orientations

corresponds to a ratio in the number of training pixels to image size equal to 0.078, equivalent to an effective dimensionality reduction for model storage by a factor equal to 12.8. As expected, both the computation time and the classification accuracy increase almost monotonically with the number of test lines. The increase in time is approximately linear while the accuracy first increases rapidly and then levels out.

In the second experiment, the number of training lines was varied from 50 to 400. The number of testing lines was fixed at 150, the line dimensionality was set to 32, and the minimum confidence parameter was set to 0.

Both the time and the classification accuracy increase with increasing number of training lines. Increasing the number of test lines only decreases the variance in the procedure that forms a decision from the classification of all test lines.

In the third experiment, the minimum confidence measure factor value was varied from 0.0 to 0.4. The number of training lines was set to 300, initial number of testing lines to 50, and the line dimensionality as 32. The experiment was repeated with the number of initial testing lines set to 100. An improved accuracy for the case when the initial number of test lines is doubled is observed. For example, for a time equal to 0.7 seconds, both cases achieve near 100 percent accuracy for the people and greater than 90 percent accuracy for the views. Thus, we can conclude that we can decrease the number of initial testing lines without ill-effect so long as we increase the minimum confidence measure accordingly and vice versa.

In the last experiment, the line dimensionality l varied from eight to 64. The number of training lines was set to 300, the initial number of testing lines to 100, and the minimum confidence value to 0.1. The classification accuracy first increases rapidly, then stabilizes with the change occurring between $l = 16$ to 24. The timing first decreases and then it increases. This is because the confidence value is not set to zero and small dimensionalities triggered frequent increases in the number of test lines. However, it is perhaps surprising that, for $l = 16$, the classification rate for persons is already 100 percent.

The results indicate that despite very low PCC of individual lines combining a large number of such classifications, results in an overall PCC, which is much higher. A number of training and test lines per face view were chosen to be equal to 280, respectively. A dimensionality of 32 and minimum confidence measure factor to 0.4 were selected. (See Figure 11.)

Results of Local Feature Analysis

In this method of Local Feature Analysis, the images used must be in the canonical form, i.e., they should contain the face part only. In the experiment, local features of the database image are calculated. For recognition, the local features of even the query face are calculated and the query face is then reconstructed using the local features and the database images. This reconstructed image is then used to calculate the minimum distance from the database images and the image with minimum distance is the closest matched image.

Figure 11: Results of Line Based Algorithm

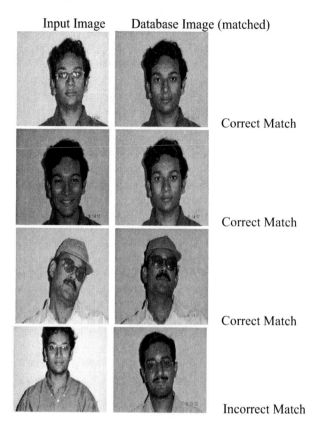

Input Image	Database Image (matched)	
		Correct Match
		Correct Match
		Correct Match
		Incorrect Match

In Figure 12, the test image is the one given for recognition; this image is not there in the database. The second image is showing all the features obtained in the query face by the local feature analysis, and last one is the image best matched with the query image in the database.

Table 7 shows that maximum recognition rate is obtained at an eigenvector of about 30 to 40. The maximum recognition obtained with it is around 95 percent. The minimum distance classifier is applied with the closest distance of 3.0.

Table 5: Different Results of the Line-Based Algorithm

Training Procedure	Classification Accuracy in Recognition (%)		Training Time per view (sec)	Test Time per view (sec)
	Face	View		
Random	90	60	1.20	1.15
Selected	90	65	1.22	1.10
Selected	85	50	1.94	7.20

Table 6: Results of Line-Based Algorithm

Criterion	Experimental Results
Procedure	Semi automatic, user dependent
Same image with different name	90% accuracy
Same image with different brightness	Independent of brightness changes
Same image with different contrast	Independent of illumination changes
Different image of same person	• With same posture & head orientation – 80% • With different image Up to 5^0 - 65% Up to 10^0 – 50% Up to 20^0 or more - Fails
Zoom and Blur-ness	• Fails on zoom (15%) • With little blur-ness (70%)
Angle Orientation	Can manage the rotation up to 10%
+ ve points	• Independent of brightness, contrast and blur-ness • Little differences on images of same person can be managed
- ve points	• Semi automatic, results dependent upon user's accuracy • Fails on zoom and rotation

Figure 12: Steps in Local Feature Analysis

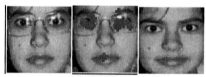

Test **Features** **Recognized**
Image **in Image** **Image**

Table 7: Accuracy Chart of LFA

No. of Eigenvector	10	20	30	40	50	60	70
Recognition (%)	76.2	84.6	94.8	95.3	93.1	88.4	81.9

CONCLUSION

While the problem of recognizing faces under gross variations remains largely unsolved, a thorough analysis of the strength and the weakness of the face recognition algorithms (feature based, eigenface, line based and local feature) has been presented and discussed.

The results are shown in the above pages, and are arranged in the manner of successful search, the partial successful match (if any) and the unsuccessful match, with a note on the specific result for all of the four algorithms we employed during the course of our experiment. Some salient features of the results are:

- The feature matching method gave a 100 percent result.
- The pixel matching method too yielded an impressive figure, but for some cases in which the query image was among the best three rather than the best match. Also, certain query images, with different orientation than the database image of the same person, did not match.
- The edge detection method on the contrary was able to identify query images in different orientations and poses than the image in the database, but this too yielded, in certain cases, the correct image as one among the best three, rather than the best-matched image.
- The algorithm has an added advantage of a very compact representation and thus high matching speed.

The attained performance suggests that recognition by means of a vector of geometrical features can be useful for small databases or as a screening step for more complex recognition strategies.

Figure 13: Sample Results of LFA

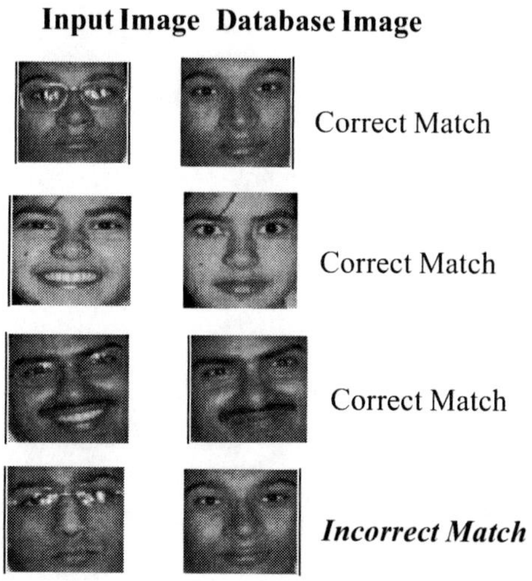

Input Image Database Image

Correct Match

Correct Match

Correct Match

Incorrect Match

Table 8: Results of Local Feature Analysis

Criterion	Experimental Results
Procedure	Automatic
Same image with different name	100% accuracy
Same image with different brightness	Independent of brightness changes
Same image with different contrast	Independent of illumination changes
Different image of same person	• With same posture & head orientation –95% • With different image Up to 5^0 - 94% Up to 10^0 – 91% Up to 20^0 – 82%
Zoom and Blur-ness	• On zoom – 86.4% • Blur-ness – 89.7%
Angle Orientation	Can manage the rotation up to 25^0
+ ve points	• Independent of brightness, contrast and blur-ness • Little differences (up to 25^0) on images of same person can be easily recognized • Automatic
- ve points	• Fails on zoom and rotation

Face recognition using eigenfaces requires one major criterion — an ideal database. This single criterion has lead to the design of numerous other similar eigen-decomposition algorithms and the research into the improvement of face detection and normalization methods. While under a perfectly aligned and standardized database, unfailingly accurate face identification can be assured; such a database is generally not available and obtainable in practice. As mentioned continuously, much of the limitations in eigenface recognition lie in the inability of the system to normalize a database of faces reliably. The bridge between transforming an image of a face into a standardized extraction of a face is one of the biggest challenges confronted by engineers. Since the eigenface requires such strict alignment of faces, any inaccuracies in aligning the face will degrade the recognition and generalization ability of the database. While many research groups have published successful results on face recognition using eigenfaces, very few in fact achieved their results based on a generalized ideal set of the eigenfaces. Without such ensemble of eigenfaces, it is highly probable that the recognition is performed based on erroneous information, such as the orientation, scaling or illumination of the faces. Since there are so many complicated disadvantages related to the eigenface, it is logical to consider other alternatives that can be used to perform face recognition. Eigenfaces is the most popular method and is in essence, a statistical analysis of a two-dimensional image.

Careful observation would reveal that the researches conducted on eigenfaces are in fact based on gray scale images. The color contents of the face images are generally omitted. This poses the question of why color eigenfaces have not been investigated. Furthermore, since human faces are three-dimensional objects, it is worth considering why a two-dimensional method has been utilized. A simple answer is that this area of research is still extremely new and the development of new algorithms generally takes time and investments by many research groups. However, future research into the area of 3-D modeling and recognition including color will become revolutionary in the image-processing field and will pave the pathway towards a new paradigm of image analysis. Amazing explorations are yet to be completed in this dynamic area of research.

In the line base method, a computationally efficient view based face recognition algorithm using random rectilinear line segments of face images has been described. The algorithm is robust to slightly rotated views, variations in scale and change in illumination intensity and shows some robustness to change in facial expressions, but the algorithm has the drawback of some user interaction in detecting the human face boundary. If the boundaries are largely indistinguishable from the background then the performance of the current algorithm will be reduced.

In the local feature analysis, matching is performed based on the various prominent features and the reconstructed image. The algorithm can work with the head orientation up to a certain extent and is even robust to the brightness and contrast changes in the image. The drawback with the algorithm is that it fails on rotated views and zooms.

All the above algorithms have their own advantages and drawbacks, which can be removed by combining their advantages and removing the drawbacks.

ACKNOWLEDGEMENT

Authors wish to acknowledge Prof. A.K. Jain, Prof. Y.V. Venkatesh, Prof. A. Rosenfeld, and other people for their kind support and guidance.

REFERENCES

Achermann, B. & Bunke, H. (n.d.). *Combination of Face Classifiers for Person Identification.*

Aizawa, K. et al. (1993). Human facial motion analysis and synthesis with application to model based coding. In *Motion Analysis and Image Sequence Processing,* (pp. 317-348). Boston, MA: Kluwer Academic.

Akamatsu, S., Sasaki, T., Fukamachi, H., & Suenaga, Y. (1991). A robust face identification scheme — kl expansion of an invariant feature space. In *SPIE Proceedings Vol. 1607: Intelligent Robots and Computer Vision X: Algorithms and Techniques,* (pp. 71-84).

Brunelli, R. & Poggio, T. (1992). Hyperbf networks for gender classification. In *Proceedings of the DARPA Image Understanding Workshop,* (pp. 311-314).

Brunelli, R. & Poggio, T. (1993). Face recognition: Features versus templates. *IEEE Trans. on PAMI,* 15(10), 1042-1052.

Buck, M. & Diehl, N. (1993). Model based image sequence coding. In *Motion Analysis and Image Sequence Processing,* (pp. 285-315). Boston, MA: Kluwer Academic.

Chellappa, R., Wilson, C.L., & Sirohey, S. (1995). Human and machine recognition of faces: A survey. *IEEE.*

Cox, I. J., Ghosn, J., & Yianilos, P. N. (1996). *Feature Based Approach for Face Recognition Using Mixture Distance.*

Cox, L. J., Jacobe, D. W., Krishnamachari, S. & Yianillos, P. N. (1994). Experiments on feature-based face recognition. *NEC Research Institute.*

de Vel, O. & Aeberhard, S. (1997). Line based face recognition. *PAMI IEEE*.

Edelman, S., Roisfield, D., & Yeshurun, Y. (n.d.). *Learning to Recognize Faces from Examples*.

Golomb, B. & Sejnowski, T. (1998). Sex Recognition from faces using Neural Network. *International Journal of Computer Vision*.

Johnston, A., Hill, H., & Carman, N. (1992). Recognizing faces: Effects of lightning direction, inversion and brightness reversal. *Cognition*.

Kanade, T. (1977). *Computer Recognition of Human Faces*. Stuttgart, Germany: Birkhauser Verlag.

Kanade, T. (n.d.). *Picture Processing by Computer Complex and Recognition of Human Faces*.

Kirby, M. & Sirovich, L. (1990). *Application of the Karhunen –Loeve Procedure for the Characterisation of Human Faces*.

Lavine, D., Lambird, B. & Kamal, L. (n.d.). Recognition of Spatial Point Patterns.

Lawrence, S., Giles, C., Tsoi, A. & Back, A. (1997). *Face Recognition: A Convolutional Neural Network Approach*.

Li, H., Roivainen, P., & Forchheimer, R. (1993). 3-D motion estimation in model based facial image coding. *IEEE Trans. Pattern Analysis and Machine Intelligence*, 15, 545-555.

Lin, S., Kung, S., & Lin, L. (1997). *Face Recognition/Detection by probabilistic decision based Neural Network*.

Manjunath, B.S. & Chellappa, R. (1991). A computational model for boundary detection. *Proceedings of IEEE Computer Society Conference on Computer Vision and Pattern Recognition*, (June), 358-363.

Messer, K., Matas, J., Kittler, J., Leuttin, J., & Maitre, G. (1999). XM2VTSDB: The extended m2vts database. *International Conference on Audio- and Video-Based Person Authentication*.

Moses, Y., Adini, Y., & Ullman, S. (1994). Face recognition: The problem of compensating for changes in illumination direction. In J. O. Eldundh (Ed.), *Third European Conference On Computer Vision* (pp. 286-296).

Philips, P.J., McCabe, R.M., & Chellappa, R. (1998). *Biometric Image Processing and Recognition*.

Philips, P.J., Rauss, P., & Der, S. (n.d.). FERET (face recognition technology) recognition algorithm development and test report.

Proceedings of the International Conferences on Automatic Face and Gesture Recognition, 1995-2002.

Proceedings of the International Conferences on Audio-and Video-Based Person Authentication, 1997-1999.

Reisfeld, D. & Yeshurun, Y. (1992). Robust detection of facial features by generalized symmetry. *Proceedings of International Conference on Pattern Recognition*.

Sakamoto, S. & Tajima, J. (1994). Face feature analysis for human identification. *NEC Central Research Laboratory*.

Samal, A. & Iyengar, P. (1992). Automatic recognition and analysis of human faces and facial expressions: A survey. *Pattern Recognition*.

Turk, M. & Pentland, A. (1991). Eigenfaces for recognition. *Journal of Cognitive Neuroscience*.

Vincent, J.M. (n.d.). Face Finding in Images. *Applications of Neural Networks*.

White, S. (1992). Features in face recognition algorithms. *Part of the Area Exam for Area II Course VI*. MIT, (February).

SECTION III

MULTIMEDIA ACCESS AND FEATURE EXTRACTION TECHNIQUES

Chapter V

Histogram Generation from the HSV Color Space Using Saturation Projection

Shamik Sural, Indian Institute of Technology, India

ABSTRACT

In this chapter, we make an in-depth analysis of the visual properties of the HSV (Hue, Saturation, Intensity Value) color space and describe a novel histogram generation technique for color feature extraction. In this new approach, we extract a pixel feature by choosing relative weights of hue and intensity based on the saturation value of the pixel. The histogram retains a perceptually smooth color transition between its adjacent components that enables us to do a window-based smoothing of feature vectors for the purpose of effective retrieval of similar images from very large databases. The results have been compared with a standard histogram generated from the RGB color space and also with a histogram similar to that used in the QBIC system (Niblack et al., 1993).

INTRODUCTION

Content-based image retrieval (CBIR) is an important research topic covering a large number of domains like image processing, computer vision, very large databases and human computer interaction (Smeulders et al., 2000; Carson et al., 1999; Gevers & Smeulders, 2000; Ma & Manjunath, 1997). In the field of multimedia systems, images play an important role due to their extensive use in various forms including those in web pages, scanned documents, medical databases and others. In spite of the abundance of their presence, research in the field of content-based image retrieval is yet to attain sufficient maturity especially for the viable commercialization of developed products. Most of the available image search engines either belong to the academic domain or are constrained by several limitations. The search results are not yet up to the satisfaction level of common users in contrast to the text search engines with fairly high usage like Google (Brin & Page, 1998). It is imperative that a lot of effort is still required to improve both the efficiency and the accuracy of content-based image retrieval systems. The development of modern day CBIR systems needs to lay stress on the users' perception about their requirements and building of intuitive interfaces that do not translate technological constraints into usability restrictions.

The focus of this chapter is image retrieval in the context of very large databases including the web, where users can use image feature-based searches through friendly interfaces. After working on different approaches to image retrieval including color, texture and shape, we have felt that the color histogram based approach is the most suitable for such an application since color matching generates the strongest perception of similarity to a common user. Also, it is more important to efficiently retrieve images with visually similar colors than to, comparatively, slowly match images having exact color distribution as in a query image. In many situations, presence of some of the dominant colors in the retrieved images is considered a better match than an exact matching with a number of non-dominant colors in the query image. It should be noted that for many domain specific applications, it may be required to capture information from various other features like texture, shape, etc., to create an even more controlled result set. However, even in such applications, color still plays an important role in retrieval. Use of associated text and other application specific features for semantic classification of images can be incorporated in our system in the future.

BACKGROUND

Color Based Image Retrieval

In color-based image retrieval, there are primarily two methods: one based on color layout (Wang et al., 2001) and the other based on color histogram (Swain & Ballard, 1991; Deng et al., 2001). In the color layout approach, two images are matched by their exact color distribution. This means that two images are considered close if they not only have similar color content but also if they have similar color in approximately the same positions. While this approach tends to reduce false positives, it is inherently slow due to higher computational complexity, especially when retrieval is done on a very large database.

In the second approach, a histogram corresponding to a query image is compared to the histograms of all the images stored in the database. A histogram is a vector whose components represent a count of the number of pixels having similar colors in the image. Thus, a histogram may be considered as a signature extracted from a complete image. Since the process of histogram generation having n components, converts an image into a point in the n-dimensional vector space, a standard distance measure like the Euclidean distance can be used for the comparison of these vectors. Research has also been done to improve the retrieval performance by using a few other distance measures like the Manhattan distance and the Earth Mover's distance (Rubner et al., 1997). We have also explored the possibility of using Vector Cosine angle as a distance measure in image database searches, a common form of distance metric used in text searches (Sural et al., 2002).

Existing Approaches to Color Histogram Generation

A standard way of generating a color histogram is to concatenate the higher order two bits for each of the Red (R), Green (G) and Blue (B) values in the RGB space. The histogram then has 2^{3N} bins that accumulate the count of pixels with similar color. It is also possible to generate three separate histograms, one for each channel, and concatenate them into one (Jain & Vailaya, 1996). Smith and Chang (1996) have used a color set approach to extract spatially localized color information and provided for efficient indexing of the color regions. In their method, the large single color regions are extracted first, followed by multiple color regions. They utilize binary color sets to represent the color content. Ortega et al. (1998) have used the HS coordinates to form a two-dimensional histogram. The H and S dimensions are divided into N and M bins, respectively, for a total of NxM bins. Each bin contains the percentage of pixels in the image that have corresponding H and S colors for that bin. They use "intersection similarity," which captures the amount of overlap between two histograms.

A New Approach to Color Histogram Generation

We use a one-dimensional histogram that exploits the inherent properties of the HSV color space. Instead of partitioning the color space or a suitable subspace as suggested by the other researchers, we analyze the properties of the HSV space with emphasis on the visual properties of the three dimensions, namely, hue, saturation and intensity value. Our approach to histogram generation from the HSV space is different from the existing methods since we have a one-dimensional histogram and it uses the hue and intensity values only based on the saturation of each pixel. A perceptually smooth transition of colors is retained in the generated histogram that can be used for a window-based comparison of feature vectors for similar image searches.

MAIN THRUST OF THE CHAPTER
Analysis of the HSV Color Space

We describe a new method of histogram generation from the HSV color space where each pixel contributes weighted values of its hue 'H' and intensity 'V' based on its

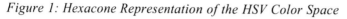

Figure 1: Hexacone Representation of the HSV Color Space

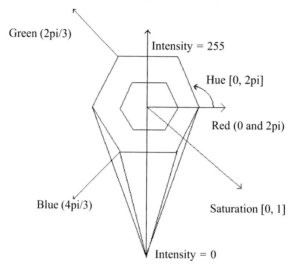

saturation 'S.' The generated vector consists of a number of "color" components and a number of "gray" components. The color components store contribution from the hue of each pixel and the gray components store contribution from the intensity value of each pixel. Each of the two contributions is determined by the pixel saturation. In this section, we analyze the properties of the HSV color space and establish a framework for color feature extraction suitable for histogram generation.

A three dimensional representation of the HSV color space is a hexacone (Shapiro & Stockman, 2001), where the central vertical axis represents the intensity as shown in Figure 1. Hue is defined as an angle in the range $[0,2\pi]$ relative to the red axis with red at angle 0, green at $2\pi/3$, blue at $4\pi/3$ and red again at 2π. Saturation is the depth or purity of color and is measured as a radial distance from the central axis with a value between 0 at the center to 1 at the outer surface. For $S = 0$, as one moves higher along the intensity axis, one goes from black to white through various shades of gray. On the other hand, for a given intensity and hue, if the saturation is changed from 0 to 1, the perceived color changes from a shade of gray to the most pure form of the color represented by its hue. Looked at from a different angle, any color in the HSV space can be transformed to a shade of gray by sufficiently lowering the saturation. The value of intensity determines the particular gray shade to which this transformation converges. When saturation is near 0, all pixels, even with different hues, look alike and as we increase the saturation towards 1, they tend to get separated out and are visually perceived as the true colors represented by their hues.

Thus, for low values of saturation, a color can be approximated by a gray value specified by the intensity level while for higher saturation values, the color can be approximated by its hue. The saturation threshold that determines this transition is once again dependent on the intensity. For low intensities, even for a high saturation, a color is close to the gray value and vice versa. Saturation gives an idea about the depth of color and the human eye is less sensitive to its variation compared to variation in hue or intensity. We, therefore, use the saturation value of a pixel to determine whether the hue or the intensity is more pertinent to human visual perception of the color of that pixel and ignore the actual value of the saturation. This nature of the HSV space is central to our method of histogram generation.

Conversion Between Color Spaces

An image in one of the standard file formats like JPEG is first read and the RGB values of each pixel are determined. The next step is to convert the RGB values into corresponding HSV values. Using the suggestions given in (Shapiro & Stockman, 2001), a pseudocode for converting RGB values to HSV values may be written as follows:

```
FUNCTION rgb2hsv
    // Initialize
    maxrgb = max(r,g,b); minrgb = min(r,g,b);
    // Determine Intensity
    v = maxrgb;
    // Determine Saturation
    if (v > 0.0)
        s = (v-minrgb)/v;
    else
        s = 0.0;
    // Determine Hue
    if (s = 0.0)
        h = (-1.0);
    else
        {
            diff = v - minrgb;
            if (r == v) h = (pi/3)*(g-b)/diff;
            else if (g==v) h = (2*(pi/3)) + ((pi/3)*(b-r)/diff);
            else if (b==v) h = (4*(pi/3)) + ((pi/3)*(r-g)/diff);
            // Remove Extraneous Values if Any
            if (h < 0.0) h= h + (2*pi); if (h > 2*pi) h = 2*pi;
        }
    return [hsv];
```

Color Histogram Generation

We extract a color histogram as the feature vector from each image having two parts: (i) A representation of the hue value between 0 and 2π quantized after a transformation and (ii) A quantized set of gray values.

We use a new idea termed as "saturation projection" to determine the weights by which each pixel should contribute its hue to a color component of the histogram and its intensity to a gray component of the histogram. The term saturation projection denotes relative distribution of saturation to the hue and the intensity axes. Thus, every pixel in an image contributes to two distinct components in the histogram, a color component and a gray component. The weight is dependent on saturation and the sum of the relative weights of the two contributions equals unity. The weight of the hue component, $w_h(s)$ should satisfy the following properties.

- $w_h(s) \in [0,1]$
- For $s_1 >= s_2$, $w_h(s_1) >= w_h(s_2)$, i.e., $w_h(s)$ is a monotonically increasing function in $[0,1]$
- For $s = 0$, $w_h(s) = 0$; for $s = 1$, $w_h(s) = 1$
- $w_h(s)$ changes slowly with s for high values of s ($s \approx 1$)
- $w_h(s)$ changes sharply with s for low values of s ($s \approx 0$)

Considering, the above requirements, we choose the weight function as follows:

$$w_h(s) = s^r \text{ where } r \in [0,1] \tag{1}$$

A plot of $w_h(s)$ with s for different values of r is shown in Figure 2.

A typical value of r that we choose in our system is 0.2. This value of r distributes the saturation into hue and intensity axes in a manner that matches well with human visual perception of the same.

The weight of the intensity component w_I is then derived as:

$$w_I(s) = 1 - w_h(s) \tag{2}$$

A plot of $w_h(s)$ and $w_I(s)$ for different values of s is shown in Figure 3 for $r = 0.2$.

We now determine the size of the feature vector, which is the number of components in the color histogram. Since the color histogram is comprised of hue components as well as gray components, we calculate them separately.

As discussed before, hue varies continuously between 0 and 2π. So we need to multiply it by a constant factor to spread out the values that can be effectively quantized to represent distinct colors in the histogram.

The number of components in the feature vector based on hue is, thus, given by:

$$N_h = \text{Round}(2\pi \text{MULT\_FCTR}) + 1 \tag{3}$$

Figure 2: Variation in $w_h(s)$ with s for Different Values of r

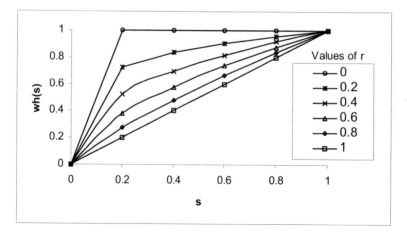

Figure 3: Variation in $w_h(s)$ and $w_l(s)$ with s for r = 0.2

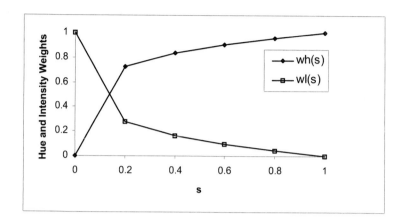

Here MULT_FCTR is the multiplying factor that determines the quantization level for the hues. We typically choose a value of 9. With this value of MULT_FCTR, the total number of hue components N_h becomes 58.

The value of intensity varies between 0 and 255. So we use an appropriate quantization level to group together similar gray values in the histogram. We divide the pixel gray values by a constant factor. Then, the number of components representing gray values becomes:

$$N_g = Round(I_{max}/DIV\_FCTR) + 1 \tag{4}$$

Here, I_{max} is the maximum value of the intensity, usually 255, and DIV_FCTR is the dividing factor that determines the number of quantized gray levels. We, typically, choose DIV_FCTR = 50. With this value of DIV_FCTR, the total number of gray components N_g becomes 6 (subscripted 0 to 5).

Thus, the total number of components in the complete histogram is:

$$N = N_h + N_g \tag{5}$$

For the above-mentioned values of MULT_FCTR and DIV_FCTR, we get an N = 64-component color histogram for each image. Choosing suitable values of the normalization factors will generate a histogram of a different size.

The quantized values of hue in the histogram may be considered circular since hue ranges from 0 to 2π, both the end points being red. This circular nature of the hue values as well as the uniform transition of color in the histogram forms the basis of a window-based smoothing of feature vectors during image retrieval. The feature vector may be represented as a logical combination of two independent vectors.

The algorithm for generating the color histogram (Hist) can now be written as follows:

For each pixel in the image:

Read the RGB value
Convert RGB to HSV
Update histogram as follows:
Hist[Round(H.MULT_FCTR)]
   = Hist[Round(H.MULT_FCTR)]+w_h(s)
Hist[Round(2πMULT_FCTR)+Round(V/DIV_FCTR)]
   = Hist[Round(2πMULT_FCTR)+
            Round(V/DIV_FCTR)]+W_i(s)

It is seen that one color and one gray component of the histogram are updated by the value of the corresponding weights. In Table 1, we show the color histogram components that will be updated and the corresponding weights for a number of pixel HSV values to explain the process of histogram generation. The value of r used is 0.2. For brevity, in the last column we show the index of the gray component updated and

Table 1: Histogram Components Updated for Different HSV Combinations

Hue	Saturation	Intensity	Color Component Update (component, value)	Gray Component Update (component, value)
0	0	255	0,0	5,1
0	1	255	0,1	5,0
0	0	0	0,0	0,1
0	1	0	0,1	0,0
2π/3	0	200	19,0	4,1
2π/3	1	200	19,1	4,0
2π/3	0.5	200	19,0.87	4,0.13
2π/3	0.5	100	19,0.87	2,0.13
4π/3	0	200	38,0	4,1
4π/3	1	200	38,1	4,0
4π/3	0.5	200	38,0.87	4,0.13
4 π3	0.5	100	38,0.87	2,0.13
2π	0	200	57,0	4,1
2π	1	200	57,1	4,0
2π	0.5	200	57,0.87	4,0.13
2π	0.5	100	57,0.87	2,0.13

not its exact position in the complete histogram. We extract feature vectors from all the available images and store them in the database after image size normalization.

Window-Based Smoothing of Image Features

It has been observed that when color histograms are extracted from two similar images, often two neighboring components in the histograms contain high values. This is due to the fact that two colors that appear close to the human eye may have a small difference in shade and map to two neighboring components in the histogram. When a standard measure like the Euclidean distance is used to compare such feature vectors, the result shows a high distance value. The specialization property inherent in the process of histogram comparison suppresses the generalization capability required by an application like image retrieval. Reducing the quantization level does not solve the problem since: (i) it tends to add neighboring pixel counts from one end of the feature vector and (ii) a lower quantization level, and hence, a less number of components, reduces the precision of color representation. In the QBIC system, a matrix is used to put weights that combine different histogram component values at the time of comparison. However, that is a very static representation that is also computationally expensive.

To overcome this drawback, we compare two histograms through smoothing windows instead of comparing the vector components directly. All the conventional color histograms fail to provide the requisite perceptual gradation of colors in the feature vectors required by such a smoothing operation. The histogram presented in this chapter, retains this property in the feature vector. For the jth component ($j \in [0, N_h + N_v - 1]$), with a smoothing window size of $2N+1$, we calculate the average value as follows:

$$\text{Hist}_w[j] = \sum_{i=j-N}^{j+N} w(i - j)\text{Hist}[i] \text{ where } w(i\text{-}j) = 2^{-|i-j|} \tag{6}$$

Since we derive both the hue and the gray level features using the HSV space, there are two independent color continuums in the histogram, one from Red→Green→Blue→Red and the other from Black→Gray→White. The circular nature of the hue components and the discontinuity at the hue-intensity component boundary are taken care of programmatically. The use of the new histogram shows an improved performance over conventional histograms generated from the RGB color space. The smoothing window further tunes the result of retrieval.

Results

Comparison of retrieval results for image databases is a non-trivial task. One of the main difficulties is the amount of subjectivity involved in deciding the correct result set. The input is typically a set of keywords or an example image. The idea of similarity between the query and the result set images depends on the individual performing the query. As a result, accurate ground-truthing of the image databases has not yet been done. A standard way of judging the result is through the calculation of recall and precision. Recall and precision are defined as follows:

$$\text{Recall} = \frac{Re\,levantObjects\,Re\,trieved}{TotalNumberof\,Re\,levantObjects}$$

$$\text{Precision} = \frac{Re\,levantObjects\,Re\,trieved}{TotalNumberofObjects\,Re\,trieved}$$

Since these measures are influenced by the relevant set, which in turn is often undefined, one needs to justify the results very carefully. We have done our experiments using relevant sets suggested by a number of different individuals for each set of query images. We then take an average of the recall and precision values for these different observers, each with 100 queries. This brings in a strong degree of objectivity in our results. We compare our results with those obtained from a standard RGB histogram and also with the histogram used in the QBIC system. The reason for choosing the standard histogram is the ease of implementation and one can easily replicate our experimental procedure. The QBIC histogram was chosen since it is one of the most influential research projects that shaped the initial days of work in the area of content-based image retrieval.

We have developed an interface using Java applet that displays images similar to a query image from a database, which currently has 20,000 images. Figures 4(a) and 4(b) show the recall and precision of image retrieval using a standard RGB histogram (obtained by concatenating two high order bits from each of the three channels, R, G and B), the histogram used in the QBIC system and the histogram developed by us.

For the new histogram, we show results for different widths of the smoothing window. In these figures, HSVnn represents use of the HSV histogram with a smoothing window of width nn. It is seen that the new HSV-based histogram has a much better retrieval performance than the standard RGB as well as the QBIC histogram. In most cases, recall and precision values are higher for the same number of nearest neighbors. It is also observed that application of a window of small width improves the result set. Again, for a very large window, different distinct colors tend to get added up and hence we do not see better results anymore. Such a comparison cannot be done with RGB features due to the lack of color continuity in the generated histogram. Some of the preliminary results of our work are available in Sural et al. (2002b).

We see that based on the color histogram itself, we are able to retrieve a number of relevant images from a large database.

DIRECTIONS FOR FUTURE RESEARCH

Multimedia databases and content-based image retrieval is a very important and exciting research area. Researchers from many related fields are contributing to improve the current state-of-the-art. A lot of new areas of research in this field are also coming up. In this section, we suggest some of the research directions that can be considered as direct extensions of the work described in this chapter.

Use of saturation projection for histogram generation from the HSV color space is a novel concept introduced by us. This is a method orthogonal to the existing mathematical approaches to histogram generation. The interpretation of the properties of the HSV

Figure 4: (a) Recall and (b) Precision Variation of the New Histogram, a Standard RGB Histogram and the QBIC Histogram

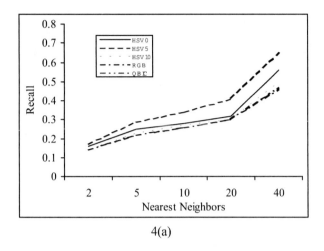

4(a)

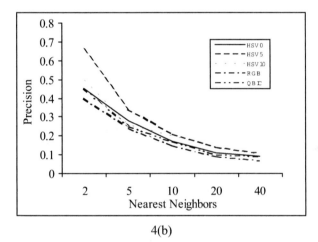

4(b)

color space and its application in feature generation can be extended to feature extraction for image segmentation problems as well.

It is clear from our discussions that comparison of images has been reduced to a problem of finding nearest neighbors between high dimensional vectors. There are a number of issues associated with the interpretation of nearest neighbors in such high dimensions as found in image database searches (Beckman et al., 1990; Berchtold et al., 1996). The very notion of nearest neighbor may not truly exist in high dimensions. Also, it is very difficult to build index structures that can efficiently retrieve data from very large databases. Often it is convenient to introduce the concept of approximate nearest neighbors to determine a result set efficiently without losing a lot of accuracy (Kushilevitz et al., 1998).

Interpretation of result sets is also an important research topic in the field of content-based image retrieval. For very large databases like the web where it may not even be possible to know the relevant set and hence the parameters recall and precision may have to be redefined. Recall may not be of much use while precision can be defined in terms of the number of images retrieved that are considered valid by a particular user. Thus, precision will have a dynamic nature since for the same result set, its value will depend on the user performing the experiment. Other areas of research in the area of content-based image retrieval may be found in Smeulders et al. (2000).

CONCLUSION

We have studied some of the important properties of the HSV color space and have developed a framework for extracting features that can be used for color histogram generation. Our approach makes use of the saturation value of a pixel to determine if the hue or the intensity of the pixel is more close to human perception of color than the pixel represents. In this process, we are able to generate a histogram that enables us to perform a window-based smoothing of the vectors during retrieval of similar images. While it is well established that color itself cannot retain semantic information beyond a certain degree, we have shown that retrieval results can be considerably improved by choosing a better histogram.

REFERENCES

Beckmann, N., Kriegel, H.-P., Schneider, R., & Seegel, B. (1990). The R*-tree: An efficient and robust access method for points and rectangles. *ACM SIGMOD*, 322-331.

Berchtold, S., Keim, D.A., & Kriegel, H.-P. (1996). The X-tree: An index structure for high-dimensional data. *VLDB*, 28-39.

Brin, S. & Page, L. (1998). The anatomy of a large-scale hypertextual web search engine. *Seventh International World Wide Web Conference*, (pp. 217-225). Brisbane, Australia.

Carson, C., Thomas, M., Belongie, S., Hellerstein, J.M., & Malik, J. (1999). Blobworld: A system for region-based image indexing and retrieval. *Third International Conference on Visual Information Systems*, 421-430.

Deng, Y., Manjunath, B.S., Kenney, C., Moore, M.S., & Shin, H. (2001). An efficient color representation for image retrieval. *IEEE Transactions on Image Processing*, 10, 140-147.

Gevers, T. & Smeulders, A. W. M. (2000). PicToSeek: Combining color and shape invariant features for image retrieval. *IEEE Transactions on Image Processing,* 9, 102-119.

Jain, A. & Vailaya, A. (1996). Image retrieval using color and shape. *Pattern Recognition*, 29, 1233-1244.

Kushilevitz, E., Ostrovsky R., & Rabani, Y. (1998). Efficient search for approximate nearest neighbor in high dimensional spaces. SIAM *Journal on Computing*, 30, 457-474.

Ma, W.Y. & Manjunath, B.S. (1997). NeTra: A toolbox for navigating large image databases. *IEEE International Conference on Image Processing*, (pp. 568-571).

Niblack, W., Barber, R., Equitz, W., Flickner, M., Glasman, E., Petkovic, D., Yanker, P., Faloutsos, C., & Taubin, G. (1993). The QBIC project: Querying images by content using color, texture and shape. *SPIE International Society Optical Engineers, in Storage and Retrieval for Image and Video Databases, 1908*, (pp. 173-187).

Ortega, M., Rui, Y., Chakrabarti, K., Warshavsky, A., Mehrotra, S., & Huang, T.S. (1998). Supporting ranked boolean similarity queries in MARS. *IEEE Transactions on Knowledge and Data Engineering, 10*, 905-925.

Rubner, Y., Guibas, L.J., & Tomasi, C. (1997). The Earth Mover's Distance, multi-dimensional scaling, and color-based image retrieval. In *ARPA IUW,* (pp. 661-668).

Shapiro, L. & Stockman, G. (2001). *Computer Vision.* Prentice Hall.

Smeulders, A.W.M., Worring, M., Santini, S., Gupta, A., & Jain, R. (2000). Content based image retrieval at the end of the early years. *IEEE Transactions on Pattern Analysis and Machine Intelligence, 22*, 1-32.

Smith, J.R. & Chang, S.F. (1996). VisualSeek: A fully automated content based image query system. *ACM Multimedia Conf.,* (pp. 317-327). Boston, MA.

Sural, S., Qian, G., & Pramanik, S. (2002). A histogram with perceptually smooth color transition for image retrieval. *Fourth Int. Conf. on CVPRIP*, (pp. 664-667). Durham.

Sural, S., Qian, G., & Pramanik, S. (2002b). Segmentation and histogram generation using the HSV color space for content- based image retrieval. *IEEE International Conference on Image Processing*, (pp. 589-592). Rochester, NY.

Swain, M. & Ballard, D. (1991). Color indexing. *International Journal of Computer Vision, 7*, 11-32.

Vailaya, A. (1996). Image retrieval using color and shape. *Pattern Recognition, 29*, 1233-1244.

Wang, J.Z., Li, J., & Wiederhold, G. (2001). SIMPLIcity: Semantics-sensitive Integrated Matching for Picture Libraries. *IEEE Transactions on Pattern Analysis and Machine Intelligence, 23*, 947-963.

Chapter VI

Video Content-Based Retrieval Techniques

Waleed E. Farag, Indiana University of Pennsylvania, USA

Hussein Abdel-Wahab, Old Dominion University, USA

ABSTRACT

The increasing use of multimedia streams nowadays necessitates the development of efficient and effective methodologies and systems for manipulating databases storing these streams. These systems have various areas of application such as video-on-demand and digital libraries. The importance of video content-based retrieval (CBR) systems motivates us to explain their basic components in this chapter and shed light on their underlying working principles. In general, a content-based retrieval system of video data consists of the following four stages: (1) Video Shot Boundary Detection, (2) Key Frames (KFs) selection, (3) features extraction (from selected KFs), and (4) retrieval stage (where similarity matching operations are performed). Each one of the above stages will be reviewed and expounded based on our experience in building a Video Content-based Retrieval (VCR) system that has been fully implemented from scratch in JAVA Language (2002). Moreover, current research directions and outstanding problems will be discussed for each stage in the context of our VCR system.

INTRODUCTION

Recently, multimedia applications are undergoing explosive growth due to the monotonic increase in the available processing power and bandwidth. This incurs the generation of large amounts of media data that need to be effectively and efficiently organized and stored. While these applications generate and use vast amounts of multimedia data, the technologies for organizing and searching them are still in their infancy. These data are usually stored in multimedia archives utilizing search engines to enable users to retrieve the required information.

Searching a repository of data is a well-known important task whose effectiveness determines, in general, the success or failure in obtaining the required information. A valuable experience that has been gained by the explosion of the web is that the usefulness of vast repositories of digital information is limited by the effectiveness of the access methods (Brunelli, Mich, & Modena, 1999). In a nutshell, the above statement emphasizes the great importance of providing effective search techniques. For alphanumeric databases many portals (Baldwin, 2000) such as *google, yahoo, msn,* and *excite* have become widely accessible via the web. These search engines provide their users a keyword-based search model in order to access the stored information but the inaccurate search results of these search engines is a known drawback.

For multimedia data, describing unstructured information (such as video) using textual terms is not an effective solution because they cannot be uniquely described by a number of statements. That is mainly due to the fact that human opinions vary from one person to another (Ahanger & Little, 1996), so that two persons may describe a single image by totally different statements. Therefore, the highly unstructured nature of multimedia data renders keyword-based search techniques inadequate. Video streams are considered the most complex form of multimedia data because they contain almost all other forms such as images and audio in addition to their inherent temporal dimension. The central role of video data among all other multimedia forms motivated us to focus in this chapter on proposing an effective search paradigm for that particular media.

One promising solution that enables searching multimedia data, in general, and video data in particular is the concept of content-based search and retrieval. The basic idea is to access video data by their contents; for example, using one of the visual content features. Realizing the importance of content-based searching, researchers have started investigating the issue and proposing creative solutions (Chang, 1998). Most of the proposed video indexing and retrieval prototypes have the following two major phases (Flinkner et al., 1995):

- Database population phase, consisting of the following steps:

  ➤ Shot boundary detection. The purpose of this step is to partition a video stream into a set of meaningful and manageable segments (Idris & Panchanathan, 1997), which then serve as the basic units for indexing.

  ➤ Key frames selection. This step attempts to summarize the information in each shot by selecting representative frames that capture the salient characteristics of that shot.

  ➤ Extracting low-level features from key frames. During this step, a number of low-level spatial features (color, texture, etc.) are extracted in order to use them as indices to key frames and hence to shots. Temporal features (e.g., object motion) can be used too.

- The retrieval phase: In this stage, a query is presented to the system that in turn performs similarity matching operations and returns similar data (if found) back to the user. One technique that is commonly used to present queries to video databases is QBE (Query By Example) (Yoshitaka & Ichikawa, 1999). In this technique, an image or a video clip is presented to the system and the user requests the system to retrieve similar items.

In this chapter, we present a new paradigm for solving the problem of content-based indexing and retrieval of video data. The proposed system tries to achieve its objectives by developing novel and effective approaches to tackle the problem at hand.

In spite of the fact that a number of video indexing and retrieval prototype systems have been introduced by other researchers, we believe there are still essential problems that require better solutions. These solutions should aim at improving the reliability, efficiency, and effectiveness of video retrieval systems. The first shortcoming of most of the current video retrieval systems is the lack of reliability of the shot boundary detection stage (Hanjalic & Zhang, 1999). The multiplicity of video streams, their varying contents, and the huge amounts of data involved are some obstacles against the design of robust and efficient techniques for detecting shot boundaries. Moreover, the lack of reliability of this particular stage not only affects its performance but also impacts the performance of the whole retrieval system. That is because the output of this stage plays a significant role in determining the results of all subsequent stages. The developed system introduces a novel paradigm to detect scene changes that is both reliable and efficient; thus, solving the problems exhibited in other shot boundary detection methodologies.

The second problem that will be addressed is how to devise an efficient algorithm to abstract the large amount of information found in each segmented shot. Most of the current approaches are either oversimplified so that they cannot perform the right choice or too complex that it renders them unsuitable for online processing. Two efficient algorithms to select key frames are introduced with the goal of avoiding the aforementioned shortcomings.

Deriving content indexes from the selected key frames is the next stage in which we use two low-level features (color and texture) as the basic components of the generated metadata. These metadata will be used in any further processing or similarity matching operations. The effectiveness of the retrieval stage is the last issue we are concerned with. This problem is so critical in determining the success of a content-based retrieval system for video data. Currently, retrieval systems overlook a very essential fact while measuring the similarity of video data. That fact can be stated as similarity matching has significance only if it can model what humans do. On the contrary of other techniques, the proposed retrieval system introduces a new similarity matching approach that attempts to model the way humans perceive multimedia data and judge their similarity. The developed retrieval module handles a number of shortcomings in current prototypes; thus, improving the overall performance of the retrieval system.

In a nutshell, the main objective of this chapter is to explain the working principles of a novel video content-based indexing and retrieval system whose main task is to endow its users with an easy-to-use, effective, and efficient scheme for retrieving the required information.

BACKGROUND

In this section, we review some related work that aims at solving the problem of CBR (Content-Based Retrieval) of video data, highlighting the challenges and the inadequacies of current approaches. This review will cover all the stages of the developed CBR system. To start with, we first give a quick overview of the concept of indexing and retrieving digital images based on their contents (Rui, Huang, & Chang, 1999) due to its relevance to the problem at hand.

The ideal way to describe the content of an image is in terms of its objects. However, object recognition in a general image database is a very hard problem. Instead, researchers extract low-level features (color, texture, shape, structure, spatial relationships among objects, etc.) to describe the content of an image. These features are then employed as indices to the image. Extracting these features and storing them into the database constitute the first stage of indexing images by content. The main functionality of the second stage, the retrieval system, is to analyze the presented query image in order to extract the same features from it. After that, the retrieval system performs similarity matching operations among extracted features of the query and those stored into the database. A number of systems have been proposed in the literature that, in general, apply the above-mentioned approach to access and browse images based on their contents (Abbadi, 2000; Abdel-Mottaleb, Dimitrova, Desai, & Martino, 1996; Delp, 1999; Flinkner et al., 1995; Gupta & Jain, 1997; Hsu, Chua, & Pung, 1995; Krishnamachari & Adbel-Mottaleb, 1999; Ma & Manjunath, 1997; Petland, Picard, & Sclaroff, 1994; QBIC System, 2000; Sheneier & Abdel-Mottaleb, 1996; Smith & Chang, 1996; Stanford Digital Library Group, 1995; Virage Video Indexing System, 2000).

On the other hand, by looking at indexing and retrieving of video data, the problem becomes much more complicated simply because video data have both temporal and spatial dimensions (Idris & Panchanathan, 1997). In the following, we will survey some related work proposed by various researchers for each stage of a video retrieval system.

Related Work on Video Segmentation

Video data are rich sources of information and in order to model these data, the information content of the data has to be analyzed. Video analysis is divided into two stages (Rui, Huang, & Mchrotra, 1998a). The first stage is to divide the video sequence into a group of shots (shot boundary detection) while the second stage is the process of selecting key frame(s) to represent each shot. Generally, there are two trends to segment video data. The first one works in the uncompressed domain while the other one works in the compressed domain (Chang, 1995). The first trend is discussed first.

Methods in the uncompressed domain can be broadly classified into five categories, template-matching, histogram-based, twin comparison, block-based, and model-based techniques. In template matching techniques (Hampapur, Jain, & Weymouth, 1994; Zhang, Kankanhalli, Smoliar, & Tan, 1993), each pixel at the spatial location (i,j) in frame f_m is compared with the pixel at the same location in frame f_n and a scene change is declared whenever the difference function exceeds a pre-specified threshold. Using this metric it becomes difficult to distinguish between a small change in a large area and a large change in a small area. Therefore, template-matching techniques are sensitive to noise, object motion and camera operations.

One example of the use of histogram-based techniques is presented in Tonomura (1991) where the histogram of a video frame and a difference function (S) between f_n and f_m are calculated. If S is greater than a threshold, a cut is declared. That technique uses Equation (1) to calculate the difference function and declare a cut if the function is greater than a threshold.

$$S(f_m, f_n) = \sum_{i=1}^{N} |H(f_m, i) - H(f_n, i)| \tag{1}$$

The rationale behind histogram-based approaches is that two frames that exhibit minor changes in the background and object content will also show insignificant variations in their intensity/color distributions. In addition, histograms are invariant to image rotation and change slowly under the variations of viewing angle, scale, and occlusion (Swain & Ballard, 1991). Hence, this technique is less sensitive to camera operations and object motion compared to template matching-based techniques.

Another technique that is called twin-comparison has been proposed in Zhang, Kankanhalli, Smoliar and Tan (1993). This technique uses two thresholds, one to detect cuts and the other to detect potential starting frames for gradual transitions. Unfortunately, this technique works upon uncompressed data and its inefficiency is the major disadvantage. A different trend to detect shot boundary is called block-based technique (Idris & Panchanathan, 1997) that uses local attributes to reduce the effect of noise and camera flashes. In this trend each frame f_m is partitioned into a set of r blocks and rather than comparing a pair of frames, every sub-frame in f_m is compared with the corresponding sub-frame in f_n. The similarity between f_n and f_m are then measured. The last shot boundary detection technique working upon uncompressed data is termed model-based segmentation where different edit types, such as cuts, translates, wipes, fades, and dissolves are modeled by mathematical functions (Idris & Panchanathan, 1997). The essence here is not only identifying the transition but also the type of the transition.

On the other hand, methods for detecting shot boundaries that work in the compressed domain have been investigated. The main purpose of works in this trend is to increase efficiency. Again, we can roughly divide these methodologies into three categories. The first category (Chen, Taskiran, Albiol, Delp, & Bouman, 1999; Lee, Kim, & Choi, 2000; Yeo & Liu, 1995b) uses DCT coefficients of video compression techniques (Motion JPEG, MPEG, and H.261) in the frequency domain. These coefficients relate to the spatial domain, hence they can be used for scene change detection. In Chen et al. (1999), shot boundary detection is performed by first extracting a set of features from the DC frame. These features are placed in a high dimensional feature vector that is called the GT (Generalized Trace). The GT is then used in a binary regression tree to determine the probability that each frame is a shot boundary. Yeo and Liu (1995b) use the pixel differences of the luminance component of DC frames in MPEG sequences to detect shot boundaries. Lee et al. (2000) derive binary edge maps from AC coefficients and measure edge orientation and strength using AC coefficients correlations and then match frames based on these features.

The second category makes use of motion vectors. The idea is that motion vectors exhibit relatively continuous changes within a single camera shot while this continuity is disrupted between frames across different shots. Zhang et al. (1993) have proposed a technique for cut detection using motion vectors in MPEG videos. This approach is based on counting the number of motion vectors M in predicted frames. In P-frames, M is the number of motion vectors whereas, in B-frames, M is the smaller of the counts of the forward and backward nonzero motion. Then, M < T will be an effective indicator of a camera boundary before or after the B-and P-frames, where T is a threshold value close to zero.

The last category working into the compressed domain merges the above two trends and can be termed hybrid Motion/DCT. In these methods motion information and the DCT coefficients of the luminance component are used to segment the video (Meng, Juan, & Chang, 1995).

Other approaches that cannot be categorized under any of the above two classes are reviewed below. Vasconcelos and Lippman (1997) have modeled the time duration between two shot boundaries using a Bayesian model and the Weibull distribution then, they derived a variable threshold to detect shot boundaries. A knowledge-based approach is proposed in Low, Tian, and Zhang (1996), and Zhang, Tan, Smoliar, and Gong (1995), where anchorperson shots are found by examining intrashot temporal variations of frames. In order to increase the robustness of the shot boundary detection, Hanjalic and Zhang (1999) proposed the use of a statistical model to detect scene changes. In summary, techniques that work upon uncompressed video data lack the necessary efficiency required for interactive processing. On the other hand, although the other techniques that deal directly with compressed data are more efficient, their lack of reliability is a common problem. To address these shortcomings, we proposed a reliable and very efficient technique to solve the problem of shot boundary detection of video data.

Related Work on Key Frames Selection

A shot boundary based approach was proposed in Nagasaka and Tanaka (1991) that uses the *n-th* frame in each shot as the key frame. The main disadvantages are, this method uses only one key frame that may not be stable and may not capture the major visual content of the shot. Zhang et al. (1993) proposed a visual content based approach where the first frame is used as a key frame but in addition to it other frames could be selected as additional key frames if they have significant content change compared to the first one. Motion based criteria are also considered in this method. Another approach that is based on motion analysis was proposed in Wolf (1996). That technique calculates the optical flow (Singh, 1991) for each frame, then computes a motion metric. It finally analyzes that metric and selects KFs at the local minima of motion.

A clustering algorithm has been proposed in Zhuang, Rui, Huang and Mehrotra (1998). The algorithm assumes that there are N frames within a shot divided into M clusters. The similarity between frames is performed using color histograms. Then, the algorithm chooses KFs from representative clusters (those having the number of frames greater than N/M). The frame that is closest to the cluster centriod is chosen as a key frame.

In Yeung and Liu (1995), temporal sampling, selection of representative frames is achieved by using a nonlinear sampling process in which every frame is compared with the last chosen representative frame. If the difference is above a certain threshold, that frame is added to the set of representative frames for that particular shot. An alternative method is given in Yeo and Liu (1995b), where a set of KFs is used to represent a shot and the first frame in that shot is always selected as a KF. A different approach to represent the shot is proposed in Chen et al. (1999), where frames in the shot are organized in a tree structure in such a way that the root node is the most representative frame in the shot. As one progresses down the tree, frames are organized into representative groups. This tree representation is obtained through agglomerative (bottom-up) clustering, where color, texture, and edge histograms are the components of the feature vector and L1 norm is used to measure the feature distance.

Tonomura, Akutsu, Otsuji and Sadakata (1993) proposed a system that represents video sequences by using evenly spaced key frames while ignoring shot boundaries. The major problem with this system is that it selects more than the necessary number of key frames especially in long inactive shots. In Girgensohn and Boreczky (1999), a technique is introduced to detect key frames to represent the whole video without doing any shot boundary detection. The general idea is to use a clustering algorithm to divide the frames into a number of clusters, each one having similar frames, and then choosing a frame from each cluster. A different illumination invariant approach is proposed by Drew and Au (2000), to select key frames. Another hierarchical color and motion segmentation scheme that is based on a multi-resolution implementation of the recursive shortest spanning tree is proposed in Avrithis, Doulamis, Doulamis and Kollias (1999).

A number of the above-mentioned techniques are so primitive and, in most cases, cannot faithfully represent the shot or capture its salient characteristics. The other approaches may produce more accurate results but they are computationally expensive which precludes their use in real-time retrieval systems.

Related Work on Video Indexing

Ideally, CBR of video data should be accomplished based on automatic extraction of content semantics but most of the current techniques only check the presence of semantic primitives such as objects or represent the content using low-level features. There are mainly two major trends in the research community to extract indices for proper video indexing and annotation. The first one tries to propose methods to automatically extract these indices, while the second trend performs iconic annotation of video by manually (with human help) associating icons to parts of the video stream. One example of the latter trend can be found in Davis (1993). This research uses a multi-layered representation to perform the annotation task where each layer represents a different view of video content. In this way, the indices support access at different levels of detail based on the requirements of various applications. The system proposed in that work has a directory workshop where iconic descriptors are created. The user can accumulate one or more icons in a different palette. Icons can be dragged and dropped on a media time line to annotate the temporal media properties. Other techniques for CBR of video data have been reviewed (Bimbo, 1999; Lew, 2001) and some of them use SQL-like query languages to formulate queries.

On the other hand, works on the first trend, automatic extraction of content indices, can be divided into three categories.

- The first one derives indices for visual elements (color, texture, shape, etc.) of a video frame by using image-indexing techniques.

- The second category extracts indices for camera motion (panning, zooming, etc.).
- The third category attempts to derive indices for region/object motion.

In the following, we will try to give an overview of various systems that support automatic extraction of content indexes, where some of them may be categorized under only one of the above categories or may belong to more than one.

One technique to deduce indices for camera motion that works in the uncompressed domain is introduced in Zhang et al. (1993). At first, optical flow (motion vectors field) is calculated using the block-matching technique and is used to detect camera movements. Panning and tilting are detected by thresholding differences in absolute values of each motion vectors (Θ_k) and the modal vector (Θ) as described in Equation (2). Zooming is detected by observing that vertical components of motion vectors in the first and last row of the frame have opposite signs so their difference exceeds the magnitude of both components. In the same paper, the authors suggest the possible use of motion vectors derived directly from compressed MPEG video data to detect camera operations.

$$\sum_{k=1}^{N} |\Theta_k - \Theta| \leq \Theta_p \tag{2}$$

Another research effort that can be categorized under the third category is introduced in Zhang, Wang and Altunbasak (1997). This system analyzes key frames in order to detect major objects/regions within the frames and calls these objects key-objects (regions with coherent motion).

A new video model based on the stratification concept has been proposed in Kankanhalli and Chua (2000), while another video browser, an extension to the Four Eyes system (Minka, 1996; Minka & Picard, 1997; Picard, Minka, & Szummer, 1996), has been introduced by Wachman (1997). A prototype system is presented in Smoliar and Zhang (1994), where indexing is performed through a knowledge-based structure (frame-based database) and the retrieval stage uses low-level features as indices. Another prototype that uses color, texture, and motion as an indices system has been introduced in Deng and Manjunath (1997).

One more system for video CBR that belongs to the third category is introduced in Zhong and Chang (1997) where an object segmentation algorithm is first applied to segment objects that are found in video frames. Color, edge, and optical flow are the three features used. Adjacent regions of salient objects are then grouped based on similarity in motion while the sizes and durations are used to eliminate noisy and unimportant regions. The authors proposed a framework for spatio-temporal video searches by extending the concept of 2-D strings to be used for video data. A motion-based indexing technique is proposed by Sahouria and Zakhor (1997), where object trajectories are used to aid indexing. The system is queried by sketching the required trajectory that is in turn analyzed and compared to the indices stored into the database using the R^{16} Euclidean norm.

The QBIC system developed at the IBM Almaden research center (Flinkner et al., 1995; Niblack et al., 1993) performs both image and video indexing and retrieval and it belongs to the first category. Another system called ViBE (Chen et al., 1999) is a browseable and searchable paradigm for organizing video data containing large numbers of sequences. The Berkeley Digital Library Project (2000) has a large part of it focused on image and video analysis for retrieval and browsing. The aim is to improve the performance of the query stage by deriving feature vectors that have the following properties: rich descriptors, invariant under irrelevant variation, and associated with intuitive metrics. A digital video library called Informedia (Christel, Kanade, Mauldin, Reddy, Sirbu, Stevens, et al., 1995; Christel, Olligschlaeger, & Huang, 2000; Wactlar, Christel, Gong, & Hauptmann, 1999) was developed at CMU. This system investigates the utility of speech recognition, image processing, and natural language processing techniques to improve indexing and searching of video libraries. The system uses image processing techniques working in a compressed domain for generating indexing features to support video similarity matching.

The last stage in a video indexing and retrieval system is the retrieval phase. In this phase, the major commonly used technique to present the query is QBE (Yoshitaka & Ichikawa, 1999), which has the obvious advantage of expressing the query intuitively. Other models are also proposed to submit queries to video retrieval systems. One of them is introduced by Kuo and Chen (2000) that uses query languages based on the semantic levels. Another research effort (Assflag & Pala, 2000) proposes the use of 3-D interfaces and virtual reality instead of using the QBE model. The major disadvantage of the last two techniques is that they are difficult to use and require experienced users to apply them effectively.

The central task in the retrieval subsystem is the similarity measure operation. There are many techniques to measure similarity but almost all of them are criticized in Santini and Jain (1999). We address this problem by proposing a novel approach for measuring video data similarity. This approach is a central theme in this chapter and its details are given later in this chapter.

Related Work on Video Retrieval

One important aspect of multimedia retrieval systems is the browsing capability and in this context some researchers proposed the integration between the human and the computer to improve the performance of the retrieval stage. The main justification to this approach is the inaccuracies of automatic tracking algorithms. In Luo and Eleftheriadis (1999), a system is proposed that allows the user to define video objects on multiple frames. Then, the system can interpolate the video object contours in every frame. Another video browsing system is presented in Uchihashi, Foote, Girgensohn and Boreczky (1999) and Wilcox et al. (1999) where comic book style summaries are used to provide fast overviews of the video content while a different one uses the mosiacing technique (Irani, Anandan, & Hsu, 1995). One other retrieval system that supports 3-D images, videos, and music retrieval is presented in Kosugi et al. (2001). In that system each type of query has its own processing module, e.g., image retrieval is processed using a component called ImageCompass.

A very central and significant issue in multimedia (especially video) retrieval systems is how to determine the similarity between the submitted query and the media stored into the database. For that reason, the effectiveness of the similarity matching model is a crucial factor in determining the success of a video retrieval system. A number of researchers have proposed various approaches to measure video similarity and a quick review follows.

One technique was proposed in Cheung and Zakhor (2000) to use the metadata derived from clip links and the visual content of the clip to measure video similarity. Color histograms are used to represent the visual content in conjunction with a pruning algorithm to reduce the dimensionality of the feature vector. An extension to the video signature technique just described that uses clustering of stored data is introduced by Cheung and Zakhor (2001). In that article, the authors stated the need for a robust clustering algorithm to offset the errors produced by random sampling of the signature set. The clustering algorithm they proposed is based upon the graph theory. Another clustering algorithm was proposed in Liu, Zhuang and Pan (1999) to dynamically distinguish whether two shots are similar or not based on the current situation of shot similarity.

A different retrieval approach uses time-alignment constraints to measure the similarity and dissimilarity of temporal documents. In Yamuna and Candan (2000), multimedia documents are viewed as a collection of objects linked to each other through various structures including temporal, spatial, and interaction structures. The similarity model in that work uses a highly structured class of linear constraints that is based on instant-based point formalism.

In Tan, Kulkarni and Ramadge (1999), a framework is proposed to measure the video similarity. It employs different comparison resolutions for different phases of video search and uses color histograms to calculate frame similarity. Frames are aligned before applying the similarity formula based on a number of alignment constraints that are calculated using forward dynamic programming techniques. By using this method, the evaluation of video similarity becomes equivalent to finding the path with minimum cost in a lattice.

A powerful concept to improve searching multimedia databases is called relevance feedback (Rui, Huang, & Mehrotra, 1998b; Wu, Zhuang, & Pan, 2000; Zhou & Huang, 2002). In this technique, the user can associate a score to each of the returned hits and these scores are used to direct the following search phase and improve its results. One example to the relevance feedback was introduced in Zhou and Huang (2002) where the authors define the relevance feedback as a biased classification problem in which there are unknown number of classes but the user is only interested in one class. They used linear/non-linear bias discriminant analysis, that is, a supervised learning scheme to solve the classification problem at hand.

From this quick survey of the current approaches, we can observe that an important issue has been overlooked by almost all the above techniques. This issue can be stated as "similarity matching has significance only if it can emulate what humans do" (Santini & Jain, 1999). Our belief in the utmost importance of the above phrase motivates us to propose a novel technique to measure the similarity of video data. This approach attempts to come up with a model to emulate the way humans perceive the similarity of video data.

VIDEO SHOT BOUNDARY DETECTION ON THE VCR SYSTEM

In general, successive frames in motion pictures bear great similarity among themselves but this generalization is not true at boundaries of shots. A frame at a boundary point of a shot differs in background and content from its successive frame that belongs to the next shot (see Figure 1). In a nutshell, two frames at a boundary point will differ significantly as a result of switching from one camera to another, and this is the basic principle that most automatic algorithms for detecting scene changes depend upon.

Moreover, video data are rich media of information because they have both spatial and temporal dimensions. For that reason, it is desirable to reduce the amount of data processed when dealing with a complex medium such as video. Almost all video data are compressed using any one of the popular compression algorithms where the most famous one among them and the current international standard is the MPEG standard (ISO/IEC, 1999; LeGall, 1991).

To achieve efficient segmentation of video data, the VCR system (Farag & Abdel-Wahab, 2001a, 2001b) starts by extracting an abstract representation of the video data then performs almost all further processing upon this form. The DC sequence is then used as input to a neural network module to perform the shot boundary detection task.

Extracting the DC Sequence

This section formulizes the problem of extracting the DC sequence from MPEG files and introduces our proposed solution to solve it. To encode MPEG files each frame in the original video file is divided into 8X8 blocks then the DCT transform is applied to individual blocks. The encoded transform coefficients in addition to the motion information are the main constituents of the compressed file. The first coefficient of the DCT of a block is termed the DC coefficient and it is directly proportional to the average intensity of that block. The main concept is to use these DC coefficients to derive an abstract description of a frame directly from the compressed data without the need for decoding. Each block will be represented by only one term (its average intensity derived from the DC term) and the composition of these terms will form what is called a DC frame. A sequence of such frames is termed the DC sequence. This sequence still bears high similarity to the original frame sequence (Yeo & Liu, 1995a) with the added advantage that it can be directly and very efficiently derived from compressed data.

Figure 1: The Differences in Content and Background between Two Successive Frames at a Shot Boundary

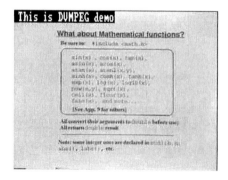

The general idea of using the DC sequence has been proposed in Shen and Delp (1995) and Yeo and Liu (1995b). The extraction of the DC frame from an I frame is trivial and can be calculated for each block as follows:

$$DC_I = \frac{1}{8} DC_{encoded}$$

(3)

where
DC_I: The derived DC for a specific block.
$DC_{encoded}$: The encoded value in that block (the first coefficient of the DCT).

As shown above deriving the DC terms from I pictures is a trivial task but for B and P pictures, it is not the same. One proposed solution (Shen & Delp, 1995) is to calculate the DC of a block in B or P frames using Equation (4).

$$DC_{P/B} = DC_{ref} + DC_{diff}$$

(4)

where
DC_{diff}: The encoded DC coefficient of a block in a P or B frame.
DC_{ref}: The average of the DC coefficients of the reference frame blocks (at max. four) overlapping with the predicted block.
Equation (5), given below, is the mathematical definition of the term DC_{ref}.

$$DC_{ref} = \frac{1}{64} \sum_{i=0}^{3} N_i DC_i$$

(5)

Figure 2: The Four Intersecting Blocks in the Reference Frame are to the Left while the Right Shape Shows the Predicted Block and the Motion Vector

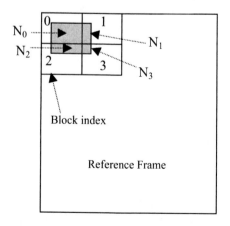
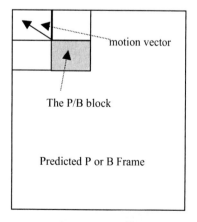

where

N_i: The intersecting area between the block in the P or B frame and the i-th block in the reference frame (see Figure 2).

DC_i: The DC coefficient of the i-th block in the reference frame.

Note that, right horizontal displacement and downward vertical displacement are considered positive displacements in MPEG terminology (Mitchell, Pennebaker, Fogg, & LeGall, 1997). Given the information in MPEG data and the proposed formulas described above, what is required is to determine two pieces of information in order to derive the DC sequence properly, these are:

- The intersecting areas of the blocks in the reference frame with the predicted block in the P or B frame. These areas are denoted N_0-N_3.
- The row and column indexes of each of the four intersecting blocks to be used in determining DC_i values, given the row and column indexes of the predicted block.

Three types of DC sequences, one for each color component used in MPEG (Y, Cr, Cb), are extracted but we use only the Y component because human eyes are more sensitive to the luminance component than the chrominance ones (Mitchell, Pennebaker, Fogg, & LeGall, 1997). If the block is bi-directionally predicted (has both forward and backward motion vectors), we propose to apply Equation (5) to both the forward and backward cases and take the average value. This is a similar technique to how the MPEG algorithm handles the reconstruction of pixel values during the decoding phase. Thus, in case of bi-directionally predicted blocks, Equation (6) below will be used to evaluate DC_{ref}.

$$DC_{ref} = \frac{1}{2}(\frac{1}{64}\sum_{i=0}^{3} N_i DC_i(forward) + \frac{1}{64}\sum_{i=0}^{3} N_i DC_i(backward)) \qquad (6)$$

To specify which blocks in the reference frame will contribute to the DC_{ref} formulas, Equations (5) and (6), we need to determine the rows and columns indexes of intersecting blocks in the reference picture and relate this information to the row and column index of the block under investigation. The influencing factors are the signs of the motion vectors. To derive the required relations, an investigation of the position of the considered block in relation to the other four intersecting blocks is performed. This investigation yields four sets of relations, one for each possible combination of motion vector signs. These relations for row and column indexes of the four overlapping blocks (B_0-B_3) are listed in Table 1, assuming the row and column of the predicted block are R and C, respectively. Similarly, all the intersecting areas (N_0-N_3) can be calculated using the geometry of Figure 2. By knowing the intersecting areas and the positions of the overlapping blocks in the reference frame, both Equations (5) and (6) can be evaluated.

All special cases have been handled by the algorithm, those include the case of large motion vectors magnitudes, boundary conditions check, the case of skipped Macroblocks (MB), and the case of non-coded blocks.

Table 1: Row and Column Indexes for Overlapping Blocks as Functions of the Signs of Motion Vectors and the Position of the Predicted Block

	+ΔX and +ΔY		+ΔX and -ΔY		-ΔX and +ΔY		-ΔX and -ΔY	
	Row	Col	Row	Col	Row	Col	Row	Col
B_0	R	C	R-1	C	R	C-1	R-1	C-1
B_1	R	C+1	R-1	C+1	R	C	R-1	C
B_2	R+1	C	R	C	R+1	C-1	R	C-1
B_3	R+1	C+1	R	C+1	R+1	C	R	C

Detecting Shot Boundaries

The DC sequence extracted in the previous section is used as input to a Neural Network (NN). The use of the NN (Beale & Jackson, 1991; Zurada, 1992) as a shot-boundary detection methodology is based on its desirable generalization and fault tolerance properties. Detecting shot boundaries in a video stream is a hard task, especially when we consider the multiplicities of video types (action movie, romantic movies, sports, news cast, etc.) and the different characteristics that each of these types has. Many of the current shot boundary detection algorithms fail to detect shot boundaries in cases of a fast camera or object motion or when a large object occupies the whole scene for a while. This lack of robustness in currently available techniques motivates us to propose a robust and efficient methodology to detect scene changes in various genres of video streams.

The first step in the design of the NNM is to determine a proper architecture of the network capable of solving the problem at hand (Farag, Ziedan, Syiam, & Mahmoud, 1997). Three architectures are investigated, in the first one, shown in Figure 3, the differences between corresponding DC terms in two adjacent DC frames are calculated and each difference value is used as input to a node at the input layer. Thus, for the jth element in the training/test set, the input to the input node i is given by Equation (7).

$$Input_i(j) = DC_i(j) - DC_i(j+1) \tag{7}$$

The second architecture diagrammed in Figure 4 uses only one node (in addition to the bias node) at the input layer. The input to that node is the sum of absolute differences between corresponding DC values in two successive DC frames. Equation (8) defines the value of the neural network input for the jth element of the training/test set, where n is the number of DC terms in a DC frame.

$$Input(j) = \sum_{i=0}^{n-1} |DC_i(j) - DC_i(j+1)| \tag{8}$$

The last considered network structure, illustrated in Figure 5, employs three input nodes, each one of them accepts input as the previous architecture but for DC frame

Figure 3: The Structure of the First Proposed Neural Network for Shot Boundary Detection, Assuming an Input MPEG Video Dimension of 320x240

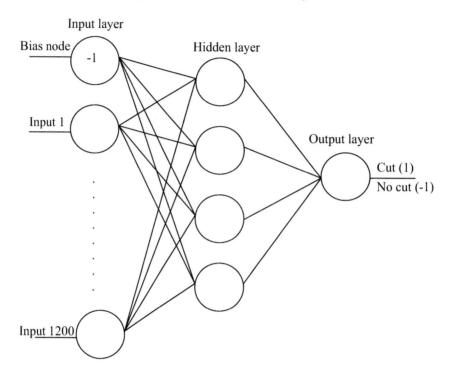

difference I (difference between j and j+1), I+1, and I+2, respectively. The inputs to this structure are formulated in Equations (9), (10), and (11), respectively.

$$Input_1(j) = \sum_{i=0}^{n-1} |DC_i(j) - DC_i(j+1)| \qquad (9)$$

$$Input_2(j) = \sum_{i=0}^{n-1} |DC_i(j+1) - DC_i(j+2)| \qquad (10)$$

$$Input_3(j) = \sum_{i=0}^{n-1} |DC_i(j+2) - DC_i(j+3)| \qquad (11)$$

The actual difference among the three architectures is the dimension of the pattern space presented to the network in order for it to learn the required classification task. In the first case the dimension of the pattern space is very large (it depends upon the input MPEG dimension), this implies a complex network and longer training and recall time. In the other two architectures, the input dimension is small (one and three, respectively). Our evaluation of these three architectures yields the following remarks.

Figure 4: The Structure of the Second Proposed Neural Network for Shot Boundary Detection

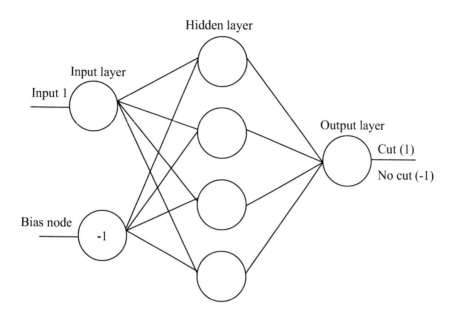

- The dependence of the first architecture upon the dimension of the input MPEG clip results in presenting a difficult problem that has a very large input space dimension to the network.
- The large input space dimension entails the use of complex networks that require a considerable amount of processing power to be trained or used in retrieving the embedded mapping information.
- Large and complex neural networks usually face difficulties to converge to acceptable training error levels.
- Even in cases where a complex network manages to converge, the performance of their recall phases is almost the same as the performance of other architectures.
- Both the second and the third structures are simple networks and there is no noticeable difference in the performance of their test phases.

Due to all of the above remarks, we opt to employ the second structure that is by far the simplest and most efficient one as will be illustrated in the next section. To train the neural network, we use a modified version of the back-propagation algorithm proposed by Rumelhart, Hinton and Williams (1986). To determine proper values for the parameters of the back-propagation algorithm and the neural network, many combinations of different values have been tested in order to select those that give better results. These parameters include the number of hidden layers, number of neurons in each hidden layer, the learning rate, the momentum coefficient, the slope of the sigmoid function, and

Figure 5: The Structure of the Third Proposed Neural Network for Shot Boundary Detection

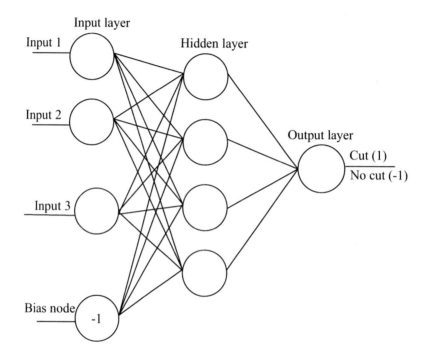

the number of nodes at the input and the output layers. Table 2 shows the best values obtained for these parameters out of our experimentations.

Segmentation Results

At first, the network is trained using a combination of two video clips. The first clip is a soccer match video that has one cut while the second one is a wrestling clip that has two cuts. The network learned the classification task quickly and stored the mapping between the inputs and outputs into its connection weights. In spite of the small training set used, the convergence behavior of the network was very good as shown in Figure 6 that depicts the learning error throughout the course of the training phase. The Y-axis of Figure 6 has a logarithmic scale to illustrate the rapid decay in learning error as training

Table 2: Neural Network and Back-Propagation Algorithm Parameters Used in Training and Testing

# of input nodes	# of hidden layers	# of nodes in each hidden layer	K	η	α	λ
structure dependent	1	4	1	0.4-0.8	0.2-0.4	1.0

Figure 6: The Error Value throughout the Neural Network Training Phase

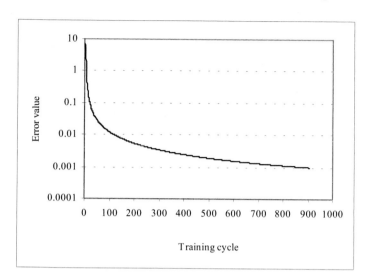

cycle increases. The next step is to test the generalization of the network during the recall phase. Many video clips (about 60) from various situations have been used in the testing phase. The results were very good in which the network was able to detect almost all cuts in these clips although they have never been presented to the network before. Table 3 shows shot boundary detection results for 12 clips from our database.

The detection performance observed from investigating Table 3 is very good. All cuts have been detected except in the documentary clip that has a lot of lighting variations that causes some misses. FAs are minimum, they happen in the racing-boats clip where a large object occupies the whole scene and in the newscast and documentary videos where dissolve-like transitions are incorrectly detected as cuts. Four flashlights out of five are detected in the celebration clip because of the weakness of the missed one. Based on the results in Table 3 the overall detection percent is almost 97% with 2.6% false

Table 3: Shot Boundary Detection Results for Various Video Genres

Video name	# of frames	# of cuts	# of detected cuts	False alarms
soccer	171	2	2	0
racing-boats	263	4	4	1
action-movie	178	2	2	0
carton	331	8	8	0
celebration	457	1-(5)	1-(4)	0
comedy	655	4	4	0
ads	759	10	10	0
class	2793	6	6	0
news-cast	2321	20	20	2
conf-discussion	4783	19	19	0
documentary	5094	41	35	2
tv-show	6139	72	72	0

alarms. These detection rates outperform the reported results of other proposed methods for detecting shot boundaries (Hanjalic & Zhang, 1999; Lee, Kim, & Choi, 2000). Moreover, we use various types of videos and most of the used clips contain very fast camera work or object motion. Other algorithms fail under these fast motions; on the contrary, ours performs very well in all these situations.

KEY FRAMES SELECTION

In this section, we present two algorithms to select KFs (Farag & Abdel-Wahab, 2002b). The first one uses the AFS (Accumulated Frames Summation) of DC terms to achieve its task while the second one employs the ALD (Absolute Luminance Differences) of Successive DC Frames. The first developed algorithm to select KFs could be described as follows:

- Initialize the representative set to be empty and select the first frame as the first element in that set.
- Initialize sum = 0 and flashIndex to the last detected flash position plus one.
- *For j = 0   To   N-2   do   {*
   if (j = flashArray[flashIndex])   /* only if ((j-1) >= 0) */
        sum = sum + diffArray[j-1]
   else if (j = (flashArray[flashIndex]+1))
        sum = sum + diffArray[j-2]
            flashIndex = flashIndex+1
   else
        sum = sum + diffArray[j]
   if (sum > δ_i)
        sum = 0
        Add j to the set of selected KFs
        Increment the number of selected KFs
   }

   where

$$diffArray[j] = \sum_{i=0}^{M-1} |DC_i(j) - DC_i(j+1)| \qquad (12)$$

N: The number of frames in a shot.
flashArray[]: An array containing indexes to flashlight positions.
δ_i: An initial threshold that determines the frequency of sampling.
DC_i: The DC of the luminance channel at location i.
M: The number of DC terms in a DC frame.

It is important to note that the occurrences of flashlights within shots are detected by the shot segmentation algorithm and those points are passed to the key frames selection module into *flashArray[]*. The KFs selection module employs this information

Table 4: Number of Selected KFs as a Function of Threshold Values with Second-Level Adaptation

Video name	$\delta_i = 150000$		$\delta_i = 250000$	
	# of KFs	Ave / shot	# of KFs	Ave / shot
soccer	16	5.3	10	3.3
racing-boats	15	2.5	10	1.7
action-movie	6	2.0	4	1.3
carton	22	2.4	16	1.8
celebration	11	5.5	7	3.5
comedy	7	1.4	6	1.2
ads	19	1.7	14	1.3
class	14	2.0	10	1.4
news-cast	51	2.2	37	1.6
conf-discussion	49	2.5	33	1.7
tv-show	121	1.7	93	1.3
Total Average		**2.66**		**1.82**

to avoid the inclusion of these pseudo peaks into the calculation of the accumulated summation used by the above algorithm. Instead, the algorithm substitutes each of these high-valued peaks by the last considered frame difference value (if any) as an approximation. In that way, the algorithm robustly excludes the effect of lighting changes occurred as the result of flashlights.

The algorithm uses two levels of threshold adaptations. The first-level adaptation mechanism solves the problem of various input size while the second level handles the tendency to select redundant key frames for long inactive shots and the possible failure to select a sufficient number of key frames in case of very active shots.

Threshold selection is the first step and some of the results are listed in Table 4. We select the initial threshold (δ_i) to be equal to 150,000 and the algorithm is allowed to adapt it to a value called δ_{a2}, the adapted threshold.

To study the behavior of the algorithm for each clip, a set of tables listing the selection results were created. For all the considered clips, the first-level threshold (δ_{a1}) will be a function of the input video dimension and the second-level threshold (δ_{a2}) will be computed for each shot based on its level of activity. Moreover, in these tables we include a parameter called AI (Activity Index) of each shot. This parameter is equal to the summation of frame differences all over a specific shot divided by the number of frame differences in that shot. Flashlights are discarded as explained before. The heuristic used in the second level adaptation process is to categorize a shot into one of three categories according to its activity index. These categories are low activity, medium activity, and high activity. Through a large number of experiments and observations of the video clips and their frame difference graphs, we define the value of two thresholds. Any shot with a normalized activity index (normalized with respect to its size) less than the first threshold is categorized as a low activity one. A shot with a normalized activity index between the two thresholds is considered a medium activity shot. Otherwise, the shot is considered a high activity one. The difference between the activity levels of two shots of the carton clip is shown in Figure 7.

Figure 7: The Activity Diagram for Shots 0 and 4 of the Carton Clip

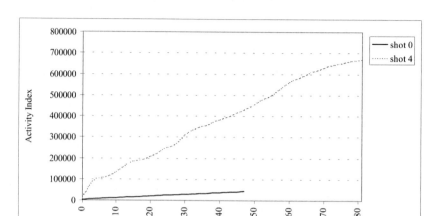

The selection results for the movie clip are listed in Table 5 while the three selected KFs for the third shot of the same clip are shown in Figure 8.

The ALD algorithm, the second one, could be described using the following steps:

- *Initialize the representative set to be empty and select the first frame as the first element in that set.*
- *Initialize i = 0 and flashIndex to the last detected flash position plus one.*
- *For   j = 1   To   N-1   do   {*

$$if (j = (flashArray[flashIndex]+1))$$
$$flashIndex = flashIndex+1$$
$$continue$$
$$if (Diff(i , j) > \delta_i)$$
$$i = j$$
Add j to the set of selected KFs
Increment the number of selected KFs

}

Table 5: KFs Selection for the Action-Movie Clip using $\delta_{a1} = 125,000$ with Second-Level Adaptation

Shot index	Range	# of frames	# of KFs	Index of selected KFs	AI	δ_{a2}
0	0-51	52	3	0, 31, 45	4621	93750
1	52-104	53	2	52, 86	3204	125000
2	105-177	73	1	105	1261	250000

Figure 8: Three Key Frames Better Abstract the First Shot of the Movie Clip because of the Various Positions the Character Takes

where

$$Diff(i, j) = \left| \sum_{k=0}^{M-1} DC_k(i) - \sum_{k=0}^{M-1} DC_k(j) \right|$$ (13)

N: The number of frames in a shot.
flashArray[]: An array containing indexes to flashlight positions.
δ_i: An initial threshold that determines the frequency of sampling.
DC_i: The DC of the luminance channel at location i.
M: The number of DC terms in a DC frame.

This algorithm bears some similarity to the AFS algorithm but it uses direct frame differences instead of the accumulated frame differences. ALD has been implemented and based on the previous experience from implementing the AFS algorithm where the same first level of adaptation was included. The second level of adaptation in ALD uses a different criterion to adapt the threshold on a shot-by-shot basis. In the AFS algorithm, we used the shot activity in the second level of adaptation but here we use a frame VI (Variance Index), the shot standard deviation, instead. The decision of using a frame variance comes from the nature of the selection method used. We use the direct difference between two consecutive frames and select another frame as a key frame if that difference is larger than a certain threshold. The problem here is that, we cannot use the same value of that threshold all over the whole video stream because different shots exhibit different lighting conditions and amounts of activity. In an attempt to avoid the effect of these different conditions on the accuracy of the selection algorithm, we calculate the standard deviation of the shot (we call it the variance index) while discarding flashlight values as done before. The variance index is then used to categorize the shot into a number of categories; e.g., very high variance and very low variance shots. Then, the shot threshold is adapted according to the category each shot belongs. For instance, the shot threshold is reduced in case of low variance in order to select more KFs to properly represent the shot and to account for the fact that there are small differences between DC frames of that shot. By implementing the above key frames selection module, we managed to design

Figure 9: The Number of Selected KFs for Each Shot of the Carton Clip using AFS and ALD

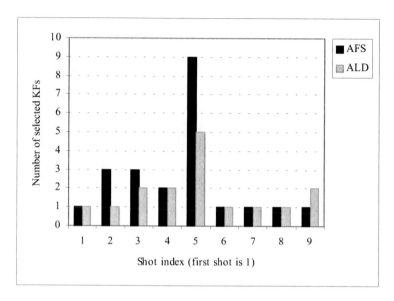

and implement an effective and efficient system for analyzing MPEG compressed video (Farag & Abdel-Wahab, 2002c).

Performance Comparison

We have proposed two algorithms in this section, the AFS and the ALD algorithms, and will attempt to give the pros and cons of each one of them:

- The AFS is generally biased towards selecting more KFs as the length of the shot increases. We introduce the second level of adaptation to effectively alleviate this natural bias. On the other hand this bias is not exhibited by the ALD.
- In general, ALD has a tendency to select less key frames per shot compared to those selected by the AFS. Figure 9 shows the number of selected KFs for each shot of the carton clip using both AFS and ALD.
- The ALD is more sensitive to lighting changes than the AFS.
- The distribution of KFs selected by the ALD may not be uniform over the length of the shot.
- We can conclude that the performance of the AFS, measured in terms of the number of selected KFs, is slightly better than that of the ALD as it captures the notion of activity in each shot in a better way. Therefore, the AFS takes more appropriate decisions in selecting each shot threshold and, hence, in determining the frequency of sampling for each individual shot. Those decisions have a direct impact on its effectiveness and applicability.

FEATURE EXTRACTION

The two stages first divide the video stream into its constituent shots then abstract each shot by using one or more representative frame(s). The next stage in most video content-based retrieval systems is to derive indexes from the selected KFs in order for these indexes to be used as metadata describing those shots.

Color and texture are commonly used indexing features in most video retrieval systems. To accomplish better understanding of how these features can be derived effectively, the techniques adapted by the VCR system are expounded below. Color feature extraction can work directly on the original decoded video frame or on its DC form. The adapted technique (Farag & Abdel-Wahab, 2002a) converts the color space of DC video frames (YCbCr in case of MPEG) to the traditional RGB color space and then derives color histograms from the RGB space. Deriving the histogram can be done in many ways. An efficient technique uses some of the most significant bits of each color component to form a codeword. Thus, we select the most significant two bits of each color component and concatenate the selected bits to end up with a six-bit codeword. This codeword forms a 64-bin color histogram that is used as the color feature vector. This histogram is a good compromise between computational efficiency and representation accuracy.

Many techniques were proposed in the literature to perform texture feature extraction. Some of them use auto-regression and stochastic models while others use power spectrum and wavelet transform (Drozdek, 2002). VCR employs a method that uses the Gabor wavelet transform to generate texture indexes. The Gabor wavelet transform of the KF image is first calculated then the mean and the standard deviation of each component of the Gabor filter (scale and orientation) are used as elements of the texture feature vector representing this particular KF.

THE RETRIEVAL SYSTEM

The final stage in most content-based video retrieval systems is the retrieval stage. In this stage, the user submits a query usually in the form of QBE (Query By Example) asking for similar material. The system starts by analyzing the input query and performing the similarity matching operations among the extracted features of the query and those features stored into the metadata of the system. It then returns any matches sorted according to the degree of similarity to the input query. The user can select any of the returned clips for replay or can submit any of the returned clips as a new query to the system to refine the search results. This refinement can continue until the user gets satisfactory results.

The Retrieval Subsystem

The first component of the retrieval subsystem, as mentioned before, is the user interface that represents the only interacting tool between users and the retrieval subsystem. The main functions of that interface are:
- To allow users to issue queries in an easy and intuitive way.
- To provide users with an effective visualization tool to enable them to browse through the results of their queries and to select any of the output clips to be played or to be used as a new search example.

The technique used to formulate a query is the QBE as mentioned before in which the user requires the system to retrieve similar items to the query example. The only assumption needed in order to use QBE is that the user has an image (or a video clip) to be used as a query. One issue here is the case where the user does not have a query example so the assumption required by QBE is not satisfied. To overcome this issue, the user can start by browsing the database and then selecting an item to be used as a query example.

A typical scenario for a search session is as follows. The user starts by supplying the system with a query (an image or a video clip) and requests the system to look for similar items. The system then searches all the available files and displays the results as key frames associated with file names of the clips containing these frames. The order of the displayed results will depend on the degree of similarity of each item with the query example. The user can then browse through the displayed results and choose any of them to start playing back at that point or as a new query.

Here, a very important issue arises that is the efficiency of the searching process. If the above algorithm is implemented as described, the time to retrieve the required video clip will be directly proportional to the number of clips stored into the database. In our research, we are addressing medium to large video archives and a direct linear search will result in very slow response time that prevents any type of interactivity. This will preclude the use of the proposed system as an online video search engine. To tackle this issue, we proposed a new scheme for improving the efficiency and scalability properties of the search process. The idea is to use a two-stage search procedure, these stages are:

- The filtering stage: Where the accuracy of the matching operation is not high. At the end of this stage most of the irrelevant items are excluded and the search space will be much more confined.

- The actual comparison stage: Where detailed matching operations are performed to find out relevant video data. These matching operations are performed over the results of the previous filtering stage.

The Filtering Algorithm

The algorithm we proposed to implement the filtering stage is a simple but effective way to reduce the size of the search space. It works only if the input query is a video clip and it does not apply to image queries. The basic concept is to derive a signature for each shot and compare these signatures (with some tolerance) at the beginning of the search process. If the signature of a query shot is approximately similar to a metadata shot signature, the database video clip containing this shot is considered relevant to that query shot. That database clip is now a candidate for the second search stage. One assumption we postulate here is that if one shot of a database clip is relevant to one of the query shots, the whole database clip will be elected as one input to the accurate comparison stage, the second one. The signature we used to represent each shot is the relative distance between selected key frames. For instance, shot 0 of the action-movie clip has three key frames with indexes 0, 31, 45 (see Table 5) so that its signature is a vector with two values (31, 14).

The filtering algorithm works as follows:

- Calculate the signature of the query shot and the database shot.
- If the length of the query signature is greater than the length of the current database shot signature, then the two shots are not relevant.
- If the two shots have the same signature length, check to see if the two signatures are approximately similar and, if so, the two shots are relevant, otherwise they are not relevant.
- If the length of the database shot signature is larger than that of the query, check if the signature of the query shot is a subset of this database shot signature and, if so, the two shots are relevant, otherwise they are not.

The above-proposed filtering algorithm is an effective tool to reduce the size of the search space and facilitate interactive query processing. The only problem we encountered while evaluating its performance occurs with queries that are edited versions of some database videos. In such cases, the signature of the edited clip is different from the signature of the original clip stored into the database. This may cause our filtering stage to exclude some database video clips albeit they might be relevant to the input query. To avoid such a situation, the system gives the user the ability to disable the filtering stage and this way the user can compromise the increase in the response time with the accuracy of the returned results. By giving the user such a control, the system becomes flexible enough to accommodate users with various requirements. The effectiveness of the filtering stage in speeding up the search process will be evaluated at the end of this section.

The User Interface and the Browsing Environment

We designed an easy-to-use user interface with two major goals in mind. The first one is to allow the user to navigate the video archive (or any other place in the storage devices) to select a query. Figure 10 shows the part of the interface that is created when the user presses the browse button. The stand-alone frame shown in Figure 10 enables the user to select a query and automatically disappear when the selection is done. Our second goal in designing the interface is to provide the user with an effective visualization tool to browse through the returned search results. A snapshot of part of the user interface displaying some of the retrieved clips is depicted in Figure 12.

The proposed browsing environment is worth some explanation at this point. We propose a visual browsing approach where each shot is represented (in the display interface) by its first key frame. The initial display of a set of shots will be their representative key frames (one for each shot). The results of a query will be displayed using the key frames organization just described and the same structure will allow the user to navigate the returned hits. One important point that is related to the browsing system is the ability given to the user to further refine the results of his search. So after he/she browses through the results produced by the system as a response to the first submitted query, one of the displayed items can be selected as a new query. This process can be repeated many times with the ultimate goal of improving the accuracy of the search results. In this scenario, both human experiences and the powerful features of computers are integrated in order to improve the performance of the retrieval system.

Figure 10: A Separate Frame of the Interface to Enable the Selection of the Query Example

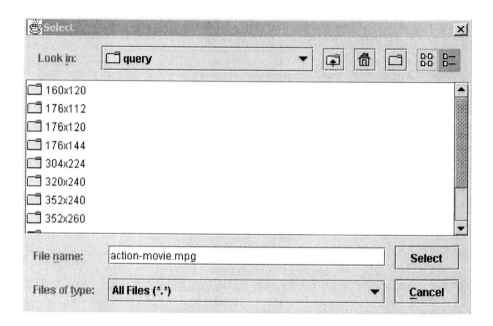

The Similarity Matching Model

The outputs of the filtering stage will be used as inputs to the second search stage that performs accurate similarity matching based on the contents of the query and those stored into the database. Here comes up one of our main contributions in the retrieval system in which a viable and distinguishable approach for performing the similarity matching phase, that constitutes the bulk of the search procedure, is proposed. This technique attempts to model the human perceptual way of judging video similarities. Although a faithful implementation of the human ability is beyond any proposed artificially automated system, a system that can partly model this ability can be proposed. The details of this similarity model are the topics of this section.

Before discussing the details of the proposed similarity model, let us define the three types of input queries that the retrieval system can receive, these are:

- A query image: In this case, neither the filtering stage nor the human-based similarity factors we propose are applicable because the image has no temporal dimension. The system extracts the color and texture features from an input image, in JPEG format (Pennebaker & Mitchell, 1993; Wallace, 1991) and compares these features with all the features vectors of candidate clips produced by the filtering stage. The hits are sorted and returned to the user based on how similar they are to the input query. Again, for the lack of time dimension, there is no meaning for similar shots in this context. Figure 11 illustrates an example of an unseen image query while Figure 12 shows the search results returned as a response of submitting the image in Figure 11 as a query to the system.

Figure 11: An Example JPEG Image Query

- A one-shot video clip: This is a special case of the next type and in these two types both the filtering stage and the similarity matching model are applicable. The returned search results will be the overall similarity hits, the most similar video clips to the input query as a whole. In addition, clips that are similar to the first shot will be retrieved too but in this particular case the two sets will be identical.
- Multi-shot video clip: This is the general case where the input is a normal video clip that has more that one shot. The retrieval system starts by analyzing the input clip, the same way performed during the data population phase, and producing an index

Figure 12: Results Obtained by Submitting the Image in Figure 11

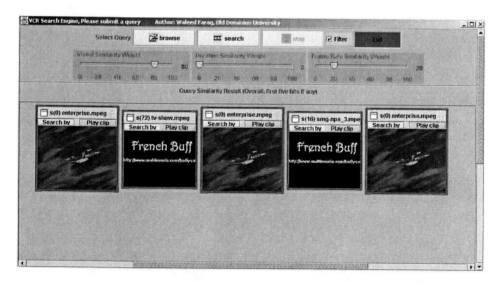

Figure 13: Part of the Search Results Obtained by Submitting the Action-Movie Clip as Query

file (in addition to other metadata information) for this particular query. Then the filtering stage will be applied producing a group of candidate clips for the accurate comparison stage. The latter stage measures the similarity between shots based on the shot content (using the color and the texture features as described in the indexing chapter). In addition to the visual content, a number of other factors aiming at modeling the human perception are also involved in determining the final similarity values. Figure 13 illustrates part of the interface obtained as a result of submitting the clip "action-movie" as a query example.

Starting from this point, our attention will be focused on input video queries, the last two types, because the assumptions and techniques that will be discussed cannot be applied to image queries. In order to lay the foundation of our similarity matching model, a number of assumptions will be listed first, these are:

- The similarity of video data is based on the similarity of their constituent shots. That is to say, we measure the similarity between shots and use these similarity values (along with other measures) to determine the overall clip-to-clip similarity.
- If the signature of the query shot is longer (in length) than the signature of a database shot, then the two shots are not relevant.

- If only one shot of the input query is relevant to a shot in one of the database clips, the whole database clip is considered relevant to the input query.
- The query clip is usually much smaller than the average length of the database clips otherwise the processing time at query invocation will be relatively large limiting the interactivity of the system.

The results of submitting a video clip as a search example is divided into two levels. The first one is the query overall similarity level which lists similar database clips sorted according to their degree of similarity to the input query. The second level gives a finer level of granularity in measuring the similarity of video data. In this level, the system displays a list of similar shots to each shot of the input query and this gives the user much more detailed results based on the similarity of individual shots. It has been reported that humans are fickle in their decisions from time to time (Picard & Minka, 1995). Thus, this finer level of measuring the similarity plays a vital role in improving the retrieval performance and helps the user to determine what they really are interested in. To illustrate the benefits of such an approach, we use the following example. Suppose a user submits a two-shot clip as a query and he is more interested in the content of the second shot of this query than that of the first shot. The system in response will retrieve a number of database clips that are similar to the input query as a whole. In addition, the system will return a list of similar database shots to each shot of the query. There is a high probability that overall similar clips will not be as important to the user as those shots returned by the system as similar to the second shot alone.

Shot Similarity Definition

In the above stated assumptions, we define video data similarity based on the similarity of individual shots, so let us go further and explain our definition of shot similarity. A shot is a sequence of frames so we need to formulate first frame similarity. In our model, the similarity between two video frames is defined based on their visual content where color and texture are used as visual content representative features. Color similarity is measured using the normalized histogram intersection while texture similarity is calculated using a Gabor wavelet transform technique discussed in the indexing section. We use Equation (14) to measure the overall similarity between two frames $f1$ and $f2$, where S_c (color similarity) is defined in Equation (15) and S_t (texture similarity) is defined as in Manjunath and Ma (1996).

$$Sim(f1, f2) = 0.5 * S_c + 0.5 * S_t \qquad (14)$$

$$S_c = \frac{\sum_{i=1}^{64} Min(H_{f1}(i), H_{f2}(i))}{\sum_{i=1}^{64} H_{f1}(i)} \qquad (15)$$

Equal weights have been used in Equation (14) to give equal emphasis to both the color and the texture features in determining frame similarity. One issue we need to highlight here regarding measuring the color similarity is the case of different dimension frames. We use various video clips in our database that vary in frame rate, length (number of frames), dimension (width and height in pixels), and other characteristics. When calculating the color histogram intersection, the variation of frame dimension should be considered. To solve this issue, the query frame histogram is scaled before calculating its normalized histogram intersection using Equation (16), where *size(fi)* is the product of the width and the height of frame i.

$$H_{f1}(i) = \frac{size(f2)}{size(f1)} * H_{f1}(i)$$
(16)

Suppose we have two shots *S1* and *S2*, each has *n1* and *n2* frames, respectively. An intuitive way to measure the similarity between these shots is to measure the similarity between every frame in *S1* with every frame in *S2* and form what we called the similarity matrix that has a dimension of *n1Xn2*. For the ith row of the similarity matrix, the largest element value represents the closest frame in shot *S2* that is most similar to the i-th frame in shot *S1*. Similarly, the largest element value in the j-th column represents the closest frame in shot *S1* that is most similar to the j-th frame in shot *S2*. By calculating the summation of these closest frames over all the rows and columns of the similarity matrix and dividing that summation by the total number of rows and columns in that matrix, we come up with a definition of the similarity between two video shots. Equation (17) is the mathematical definition of our shot similarity criterion.

$$Sim(S1,S2) = \frac{\sum_{i=1}^{n1} Max_{row(i)}(S_{i,j}) + \sum_{j=1}^{n2} Max_{col(j)}(S_{i,j})}{n1 + n2}$$
(17)

where
$Max_{row(i)}(S_{i,j})$: is the element with the maximum value in the ith row.
$Max_{col(j)}(S_{i,j})$: is the element with the maximum value in the jth column.
n1: is the number of rows in the similarity matrix.
n2: is the number of columns in the similarity matrix.

One can remark that direct application of Equation (17) is practically infeasible due to the large number of frames in video shots. For instance, a 10-second shot has 300 frames (assuming 30 frame/seconds rate). To avoid this computational complexity, we need to use an abstract form of the video shot to measure the similarity upon and a perfect candidate, we already used before, is the set of key frames. Thus, the set of key frames for each shot will be employed in calculating the shot similarity using Equation (17) and this results in a dramatic speed up in measuring shot similarity. For example, we got around 400 times improvement in computation time when applying Equation (17) upon key frames to calculate the similarity between two 60-frame shots with three key frames each.

Human-Based Similarity Factors

After we introduce our assumptions and expound the definition of shot similarity, the background has been established to explain our similarity matching model. It has been mentioned before that our similarity model attempts to emulate the way humans perceive the similarity of video material. This was achieved by integrating into the similarity measuring formula a number of factors that most probably humans use to perceive video similarity. These factors are:

- **The visual similarity:** Usually humans determine the similarity of video data based on their visual characteristics such as color, texture, shape, etc. For instance, two images with the same colors are usually judged as being similar. Our similarity model reflects this factor by using the color and texture of key frames as low-level features describing the visual content of the video/image data.

- **The rate of playing the video:** Humans tend also to be affected by the rate at which frames are displayed and they use this factor in determining the degree of video similarity. For example, two videos that have the same frame rate have a high probability of being judged as similar clips by a human observer. To take this factor into consideration, we included it in the final similarity calculation as will be explained later.

- **The time period of the shot:** The more the periods of video shots coincide, the more they are similar to human perception. We consider the duration factor in our similarity measuring formula to reflect the effect of this parameter.

- **The order of the shots in a video clip:** Humans always give higher similarity scores to video clips that have the same ordering of corresponding shots. Thus, our model includes the ordering factor in determining the similarity of video data.

As a result of the above discussion, we need to integrate these human-based similarity factors into the similarity calculation. Consequently, we include all these factors in one similarity matching formula given in Equation (18).

$$Sim(S1, S2) = W_1 * S_V + W_2 * D_R + W_3 * F_R \qquad (18)$$

where
S_V: The visual similarity calculated using Equation (17).
D_R: Shot duration ratio.
F_R: Video frame rate ratio.
W_1, W_2, and W_3: Relative weights used as parameters to the algorithm.

There are three parameter weights in Equation (18), namely, W_1, W_2, and W_3 that give the system indication on how important a factor is over the others. For example, stressing the importance of the visual similarity factor is achieved by increasing the value of its associated weight (W_1). The question now is "how to select the values of these weights to best reflect what humans do in measuring video similarity." Our first trial was to test various randomly selected combinations of these weight values to choose the best set of weights. A second idea is to use an optimization algorithm such as the Genetic Algorithm (Davis, 1991; Goldberg, 1989) to optimize the values of these weights and produce the best combination set. In the first case, we need a measure of similarity that should always work with various users, while in the second one, an evaluation function is required to give merits to individuals who perform better than other members of the population. Selecting fixed similarity criteria or evaluation function(s) by one or even a few individuals does not necessary reflect the opinion of other users of the system. The last statement is supported by the fact that a single individual is even fickle with respect to his/her opinions from time to time (Picard & Minka, 1995).

For the reasons mentioned in the previous paragraph, we found it too restrictive to select these parameters for the user in advance (either by using a pre-selected set of values or by using the genetic algorithm to select the best combination set). Consequently, we decided to give the user the ability to express his/her real need by allowing these parameters to be adjusted by the user before submitting the query. Three easy-to-use sliders, one for each weight parameter, are supplied into the interface (see Figure 12) to enable the user to select the values of these weights according to his preferences. For instance, if a user is interested in retrieving video clips that are mainly similar in visual content to the given query, he should select a large value for W_1 and small values (or even zeros) for the other two weights. Another example is a user that wants to retrieve videos that are similar in content and at the same time have similar frame rates to the query. In that case, the user should stress both W_1 and W_3. If the user is not decided or does not know what values of weights are better, then the system will select default values for these weights that stress visual similarity in calculating the similarity formula. This way, the system exhibits a great degree of flexibility to various situations and users opinions and flavors. A few clicks before issuing a new query is all that it takes to direct the system to what the user actually wants. The performance of the proposed similarity model will be evaluated at the end of this chapter.

To reflect the effect of the order factor, the overall similarity level should check if the shots in the currently investigated database clip have the same temporal order as the shots in the query clip. To achieve this goal, we propose an algorithm that restricts the candidate of the overall similarity set to clips that have the same temporal order of shots as the query clip. We still have a finer level of similarity that is based on individual query shots. This level can capture other aspects of similarity as discussed before.

Results

The performance of the system has been measured in terms of the recall and precision of the returned results based on a set of ground truth. Some of the results are listed below.

Figure 14 shows part of the retrieval interface displaying the first three hits obtained as a response to submitting the first shot (shot 0) of the racing-boats as a query. The obvious relevance of the returned shots to the query is quite evident in this figure. An example is shown in Figure 15 that displays the first twenty hits resulting from submitting shot nine of smg-npa-3 clip to the system. One can observe that all the retuned shots are shots that contain the same character pictured in the query shot and that the first hit, the most similar to the query, is the query shot itself. Moreover, some of the returned shots belong to the same clip in which the query shot is part of while the others are shots from a different clip. The performance of the system is very good in this query where all relevant shots were retrieved without any misses or false alarms.

Figure 14: The First Three Hits for Shot 0 of the Racing-Boats Clip

Figure 15: The First 20 Hits for Shot 9 of the smg-npa-3 Clip

FUTURE TRENDS

Before concluding this chapter, we need to shed the light on one of the most promising emerging multimedia standards, the MPEG-7 (Chang, Sikora, & Puri, 2001; Johnson, 2001; Vinod & Lindsay, 1999) and its relation to the developed system. This standard focuses on multimedia content description while complementing the other MPEG standard suite. Its basic goal is interoperability so it is designed to be an interoperable interface, which defines the syntax and semantics of various description tools. At the same time, MPEG-7 aims to provide a scalable framework for designing services that can be accessed from a variety of devices. To achieve its goals MPEG-7 provides three basic normative elements listed below.

1. Descriptors (Ds): define syntax and semantics of content features.
2. Description Schemes (DSs): specify the structure of relationships among Ds & DSs.
3. Description Definition Language (DDL): allows flexible definition of MPPEG-7 Ds and DSs based on XML schema.

Our system has a unified objective with the MPEG-7 standard in which both aim to provide effective search and retrieval techniques of stored multimedia data. Obviously, the new tools provided by MPEG-7 will make the video analysis task easier than in the case of MPEG-1 and MPEG-2 (used by our system). An important issue is that MPEG-7 does not specify or standardize how the features are extracted or applied. This property allows our proposed techniques to be applicable to MPEG-7 streams provided that the DC sequence extraction module is modified to parse MPEG-7 data.

CONCLUSION

In this chapter, we briefly review the need and significance of video content-based retrieval systems and explain their four basic building stages. Current research topics and work directions are covered along with the techniques proposed and implemented by our VCR system. The first stage, the shot boundary detection, divides video streams into their constituent shots. Each shot is then represented by one or more key frame(s) in a process known as key frames selection. The feature extraction stage, the third one, derives descriptive indexes such as color, texture, shapes, etc. from selected key frames and stores these feature vectors as metadata. Finally, the retrieval system accepts a user query, compares indexes derived from the submitted query with those stored into the metadata then returns search results sorted according to the degree of similarity to the query. At the end, we need to emphasize the importance of content-based video retrieval systems and assert that there are still a considerably large number of open issues that require further research to achieve more efficient and robust retrieval systems.

REFERENCES

Abbadi, M. (2000). *Content-based indexing and searching in image databases.* Doctorial dissertation. Department of Computer Science, George Washington University.

Abdel-Mottaleb, M., Dimitrova, N., Desai, R., & Martino, J. (1996). CONIVAS: Content-based image and video access system. *Proceedings of ACM International Conference on Multimedia*, (pp. 427-428).

Ahanger, G. & Little, T. (1996). A survey of technologies for parsing and indexing digital video. *Journal of Visual Communication and Image Representation*, 7(1), 28-43.

Assflag, J. & Pala, P. (2000). Querying by photographs: A VR metaphor for image retrieval. *IEEE Multimedia*, 7(1), 52-59.

Avrithis, Y., Doulamis, A., Doulamis, N., & Kollias, S. (1999). A stochastic framework for optimal key frame extraction from MPEG video databases. *Journal of Computer Vision and Image Understanding*, 75(1), 3-24.

Baldwin, R. (2000). Portals on edge. *IEEE Multimedia*, 7(1), 10-11.

Beale, R. & Jackson, T. (1991). *Neural Computing: An Introduction*. New York: IOP Publishing.

Berkeley Digital Library Project. (2000). University of California at Berkeley. Computer Science Department website: http://elib.cs.berkeley.edu/admin/proposal/proj-des/proj-des.html.

Bimbo, A. (1999). *Visual Information Retrieval*. San Francisco, CA: Morgan Kaufmann.

Brunelli, R., Mich, O., & Modena, C. (1999). A survey on the automatic indexing of video data. *Journal of Visual Communication and Image Representation*, 10(2), 78-112.

Chang, S.-F. (1995). Compressed domain techniques for image/video indexing and manipulation. *Proceedings of IEEE International Conference on Image Processing*, (Vol. 1, pp. 314-317).

Chang, S.-F., Chen, W., Meng, H., Sundaram, H., & Zhong, D. (1998, September). A fully automated content based video search engine supporting spatio-temporal queries. *IEEE Trans. Circuits and Systems for Video Technology*, 8(5), 602-615.

Chang, S.-F., Sikora, T., & Puri, A. (2001). Overview of the MPEG-7 standard. *IEEE Trans. Circuits and Systems for Video Technology*, 11(6), 688-695.

Chen, J., Taskiran, C., Albiol, A., Delp, E., & Bouman, C. (1999). ViBE: A video indexing and browsing environment. *Proceedings of SPIE/IS&T Conference Multimedia Storage and Archiving Systems IV, 3846*, (pp. 148-164).

Cheung, S. & Zakhor, A. (2000). Efficient video similarity measurement and search. *Proceedings of IEEE International Conference Image Processing*, (pp. 85-89).

Cheung, S. & Zakhor, A. (2001). Video similarity detection with video signature clustering. *Proceedings of IEEE International Conference Image Processing*, (pp. 649-652).

Christel, M., Kanade, T., Mauldin, M., Reddy, R., Sirbu, M., Stevens, S., et al. (1995). Informedia digital video library. *Communications of the ACM*, 38(4), 57-58.

Christel, M., Olligschlaeger, A., & Huang, C. (2000). Interactive maps for digital video library. *IEEE Multimedia*, 7(1), 60-67.

Davis, L. (1991). *Handbook of Genetic Algorithms*. New York: Van Nostrand Reinhold.

Davis, M. (1993). Media streams: An iconic visual language for video annotation. *Proceedings of IEEE Workshop on Visual Languages*, (pp. 196-201).

Delp, E. (1999). Video and image databases: Who cares? *Proceedings of SPIE/IS&T Conf. Storage and Retrieval for Image and Video Databases V, 3656*, (pp. 274-277).

Deng, Y. & Manjunath, B. (1997). Content-based search of video using color, texture, and motion. *Proceedings of IEEE International Conference Image Processing*, (Vol. 2, pp. 534-537).

Drew, M. & Au, J. (2000). Video key frame production by efficient clustering of compressed chromaticity signatures. *Proceedings of ACM International Conference Multimedia*, (pp. 365-367).

Drozdek, A. (2002). *Elements of Data Compression*. Brooks/Cole Publishing.

Farag, W. & Abdel-Wahab, H. (2001). *A new paradigm for detecting scene changes on MPEG compressed videos*. (Tech. Rep. No. TR_2001_02). USA: Department of Computer Science, Old Dominion University.

Farag, W. & Abdel-Wahab, H. (2001). A new paradigm for detecting scene changes on MPEG compressed videos. *Proceedings of IEEE International Symposium Signal Processing and Information Technology*, (pp. 153-158).

Farag, W. & Abdel-Wahab, H. (2002). A new paradigm for analysis of MPEG compressed videos. *Journal of Network and Computer Applications*, 25(2), 109-127.

Farag, W. & Abdel-Wahab, H. (2002). Adaptive key frames selection algorithms for summarizing video data. *Proceedings of 6th Joint Conference on Information Sciences*, (pp. 1017-1020).

Farag, W. & Abdel-Wahab, H. (2002). *Techniques for indexing MPEG compressed videos*. (Tech. Rep. No. TR_2002_01). USA: Department of Computer Science, Old Dominion University.

Farag, W., Ziedan, I., Syiam, M., & Mahmoud, M. (1997). Architecture of neural networks using genetic algorithms. *Proceedings of 5th International Conference Artificial Intelligence Applications (5th ICAIA)*.

Flinkner, M. et al. (1995). Query by image and video content: The QBIC system. *IEEE Computer*, 28(9), 23-32.

Girgensohn, A. & Boreczky, J. (1999). Time-constrained key frame selection technique. *Proceedings of IEEE International Conference Multimedia Computing and Systems*, (pp. 756-761).

Goldberg, D. (1989). *Genetic Algorithms in Search, Optimization, and Machine Learning*. Addison Wesley.

Gupta, A. & Jain, R. (1997). Visual information retrieval. *Communications of ACM*, 40(5), 70-79.

Hampapur, A., Jain, R., & Weymouth, T. (1994). Digital video segmentation. *Proceedings of ACM International Conference Multimedia*, (pp. 357-364).

Hanjalic, A. & Zhang, H-J. (1999). Optimal shot boundary detection based on robust statistical models. *Proceedings of IEEE International Conference on Multimedia Computing and Systems*, (pp. 710-714).

Hsu, W., Chua, S., & Pung, H. (1995). An integrated color-spatial approach to content-based image retrieval. *Proceedings of ACM International Conference on Multimedia*, 305-313.

Idris, F. & Panchanathan, S. (1997). Review of image and video indexing techniques. *Journal of Visual Communication and Image Representation*, 8(2), 146-166.

Irani, M., Anandan, D., & Hsu, S. (1995). Mosiac based representation of video sequences and their applications. *Proceedings of IEEE 5th International Conference on Computer Vision*, (pp. 605-611).

ISO/IEC 11172-2:1993/Cor 2. (1999): Information Technology — Coding of Moving Pictures and Associated Audio for Digital Storage Media at up to about 1.5 Mbit/s, Part 2: Video.

Java Language by Sun Microsystems. (2002). Located at: http://java.sun.com/products.

Johnson, R. (2001). Multimedia databases and MPEG-7. *Journal of Electronics and Communication Engineering*, 13(3), 98-99.

Kankanhalli, M. & Chua, T-S. (2000). Video modeling using strata-based annotation. *IEEE Multimedia*, 7(1), 68-74.

Kosugi, N. et al. (2001). Content-based retrieval applications on a common database management system. *Proceedings of ACM International Conference on Multimedia*, (pp. 599-600).

Krishnamachari, S. & Adbel-Mottaleb, M. (1999). Image browsing using hierarchical clustering. *Proceedings of 4th IEEE Symposium Computers and Communications*, 4, 301-309.

Kuo, T. & Chen, A. (2000). Content-based query processing for video databases. *IEEE Trans. Multimedia*, 2(1), 1-13.

Lee, S.-W., Kim, Y-M., & Choi, S. (2000). Fast scene change detection using direct feature extraction from MPEG compressed videos. *IEEE Trans. Multimedia*, 2(4), 240-254.

LeGall, D. (1991). MPEG: A video compression standard for multimedia applications. *Comm. of ACM*, 34(4), 46-58.

Lew, M. (ed.) (2001). *Principles of visual information retrieval*. Springer-Verlag.

Liu, X., Zhuang, Y., & Pan, Y. (1999). A new approach to retrieve video by example video clip. *Proceedings of ACM International Conference Multimedia*, (pp. 41-44).

Low, C., Tian, Q., & Zhang, H-J. (1996). An automatic news video parsing, indexing, and browsing system. *Proceedings of ACM International Conference Multimedia*, 425-426.

Luo, H. & Eleftheriadis, A. (1999). Designing an interactive tool for video object segmentation and annotation: Demo abstract. *Proceedings of ACM International Conference Multimedia*, 196.

Ma, W. & Manjunath, B. (1997). NeTra: A tool for navigating large image databases. *Proceedings of IEEE International Conference on Image Processing*, 1, 568-572.

Manjunath, B. & Ma, W. (1996). Texture features for browsing and retrieval of image data. *IEEE Trans. Pattern Analysis and Machine Intelligence*, 18(8), 837-842.

Meng, J., Juan, Y., & Chang, S-F. (1995). Scene change detection in an MPEG compressed video sequence. *Proceedings of IS&T/SPIE Symposium on Digital Video Compression: Algorithms and Technologies*, *2419*, (pp. 14-25).

Minka, T. (1996). *An image database browser that learns from user interaction.* Master's thesis, MIT Media Laboratory.

Minka, T. & Picard, R. (1997). Interactive learning using a society of models. *Pattern Recognition*, 30(4), 565-582.

Mitchell, J., Pennebaker, W., Fogg, C., & LeGall, D. (1997). *MPEG Video: Compression Standard.* Chapman and Hall.

Nagasaka, A. & Tanaka, Y. (1991). Automatic video indexing and full-video search for object appearance. *Proceedings of Visual Database Systems 2*, (pp. 113-127).

Niblack, W., Barber, R., Equitz, W., Flickner, M., Glasman, E., Petkovic, D., et al. (1993). The QBIC project: Querying images by content using color, texture, and shape. *Proceedings of SPIE Storage and Retrieval for Image and Video Databases*, *1908*, (pp. 173-187).

Pennebaker, W. & Mitchell, J. (1993). *JPEG Still Image Data Compression Standard.* Van Nostrand Reinhold.

Petland, A., Picard, R., & Sclaroff, S. (1994). Photobook: Tools for content-based manipulation of image databases. *Proceedings of SPIE: Storage and Retrieval for Image and Video Databases™, 2185*, (pp. 34-47).

Picard, R. & Minka, T. (1995). Vision texture for annotation. *Multimedia Systems*, 3, 3-14.

Picard, R., Minka, T., & Szummer, M. (1996). Modeling user subjectivity in image libraries. *Proceedings of IEEE International Conference on Image Processing*, (Vol. 2, pp. 777-780).

Query By Image Content System (2000) website: http://wwwqbic.almaden.ibm.com.

Rui, Y., Huang, T., & Chang, S-F. (1999). Image retrieval: Current techniques, promising directions, and open issues. *Journal of Visual Communication and Image Representation*, 10(1), 39-62.

Rui, Y., Huang, T., & Mchrotra, S. (1998). Browsing and retrieving video content in a unified framework. *Proceedings of IEEE Workshop on Multimedia Signal Processing*, (pp. 9-14).

Rui, Y., Huang, T., & Mehrotra, S. (1998). Relevance feedback techniques in interactive content-based image retrieval. *Proceedings of SPIE Conference Image Science and Technology (IS&T)*, (pp. 25-36).

Rumelhart, E., Hinton, G., & Williams, R. (1986). *Learning Internal Representation by Error Propagation*. In D. E. Rumelhart et al. (Eds.), *Parallel Distributed Processing*, (pp. 318-362). Cambridge, MA: MIT Press.

Sahouria, E. & Zakhor, A. (1997). Motion indexing of video. *Proceedings of IEEE International Conference on Image Processing*, 2, (pp. 526-529).

Santini, S. & Jain, R. (1999). Similarity measures. *IEEE Trans. Pattern Analysis and Machine Intelligence*, 21(9), 871-883.

Shen, K. & Delp, E. (1995). A fast algorithm for video parsing using MPEG compressed sequences. *Proceedings of IEEE International Conference on Image Processing*, 2, (pp. 252-255).

Sheneier, M. & Abdel-Mottaleb, M. (1996). Exploiting the JPEG compression scheme for image retrieval. *IEEE Trans. Pattern Analysis and Machine Intelligence*, 18(8), 849-853.

Singh, A. (1991). *Optical Flow Computation: A Unified Perspective*. IEEE Computer Society Press.

Smith, J. & Chang, S.-F. (1996). VisualSEEK: A fully automated content-based image query system. *Proceedings of ACM International Conference Multimedia*, (pp. 87-98).

Smoliar, S. & Zhang, H-J. (1994). Content-based video indexing and retrieval. *IEEE Multimedia*, 1(2), 62-72.

Stanford Digital Library Group. (1995). The stanford digital library project. *Communications of ACM*, 38(4), 59-60.

Swain, M. & Ballard, D. (1991). Color indexing. *Computer Vision*, 7(1), 11-32.

Tan, Y., Kulkarni, S., & Ramadge, P. (1999). A framework for measuring video similarity and its application to video query by example. *Proceedings of IEEE International Conference Image Processing*, (pp. 106-110).

Tonomura, Y. (1991). Video handling based on structured information for hypermedia systems. *Proceedings of ACM International Conference Multimedia Information Systems*, (pp. 333-344).

Tonomura, Y., Akutsu, A., Otsuji, K., & Sadakata, T. (1993). VideoMap and VideoSpaceIcon: Tools for anatomizing video content. *Proceedings of ACM INTERCHI*, (pp. 131-141).

Uchihashi, S., Foote, J., Girgensohn, A., & Boreczky, J. (1999). Video Manga: Generating semantically meaningful video summaries. *Proceedings of ACM International Conference Multimedia*, (pp. 383-392).

Vasconcelos, N. & Lippman, A. (1997). Towards semantically meaningful spaces for the characterization of video content. *Proceedings of IEEE International Conference Image Processing*, 2, (pp. 542-545).

Vinod, V. & Lindsay, A. (1999). MPEG-7: Its impact on research, industry, and the consumer. *Proceedings of IEEE International Conference Multimedia Computing and Systems*, 2, (pp. 406-407).

Virage Video Indexing System (2000). Located at: http://www.virage.com.

Wachman, J. (1997). A video browser that learns by example. Master's thesis. MIT Media Laboratory.

Wactlar, H., Christel, M., Gong, Y., & Hauptmann, A. (1999). Lessons learned from building a terabyte digital video library. *IEEE Computer*, 32(2), 66-73.

Wallace, G. (1991). The JPEG still picture compression standard. *Communications of ACM*, 34(4), 30-44.

Wilcox, L., et al. (1999). MBase: Indexing, browsing, and playback of media at FXPAL. *Proceedings of ACM International Conference Multimedia*, 204.

Wolf, W. (1996). Key frame selection by motion analysis. *Proceedings of IEEE International Conference Acoustic, Speech, and Signal Processing*, 2, (pp. 1228-1231).

Wu, Y., Zhuang, Y., & Pan, Y. (2000). Content-based video similarity model. *Proceedings of ACM International Conference Multimedia*, (pp. 465-467).

Yamuna, P. & Candan, K. (2000). Similarity-based retrieval of temporal documents. *Proceedings of ACM International Conference Multimedia*, (pp. 243-246).

Yeo, B-L. & Liu, B. (1995). On the extraction of DC sequence from MPEG compressed video. *Proceedings of IEEE International Conference Image Processing*, 2, (pp. 260-263).

Yeo, B-L. & Liu, B. (1995). Rapid scene analysis on compressed video. *IEEE Trans. Circuits and Systems for Video Technology*, 5(6), 533-544.

Yeung, M. & Liu, B. (1995). Efficient matching and clustering of video shots. *Proceedings of IEEE International Conference Image Processing*, 1, (pp. 338-341).

Yoshitaka, A., & Ichikawa, T. (1999). A survey on content-based retrieval for multimedia databases. *IEEE Trans. Knowledge and Data Engineering*, 11(1), 81-93.

Zhang, H.-J., Kankanhalli, A., Smoliar, S., & Tan, S. (1993). Automatically partitioning of full-motion video. *Multimedia Systems*, 1(1), 10-28.

Zhang, H.-J., Low, C., Gong, Y., Smoliar, S., & Tan, S. (1994). Video parsing using compressed data. *Proceedings of SPIE Image and Video Processing ™*, 2182, (pp. 142-149).

Zhang, H.-J., Tan, S., Smoliar, S., & Gong, Y. (1995). Automatic parsing and indexing of news video. *Multimedia Systems*, (Vol. 2, pp. 256-266).

Zhang, H.-J., Wang, J., & Altunbasak, Y. (1997). Content-based video retrieval and compression: A unified solution. *Proceedings of IEEE International Conference Image Processing*, (Vol. 1, pp. 13-16).

Zhang, H.-J., Wu, J., Zhong, D., & Smoliar, S. (1997). An integrated system for content-based video retrieval and browsing. *Pattern Recognition*, 30(4), 643-658.

Zhong, D. & Chang, S-F. (1997). Spatio-temporal video search using the object based video representation. *Proceedings of IEEE International Conference Image Processing*, (Vol. 1, pp. 21-24).

Zhou, X. & Huang, T. (2002). Relevance feedback in content-based image retrieval: Some recent advances. *Proceedings of 6th Joint Conf. On Information Sciences*, (pp. 15-18).

Zhuang, Y., Rui, Y., Huang, T., & Mehrotra, S. (1998). Adaptive key frame extraction using unsupervised clustering. *Proceedings of IEEE International Conference Image Processing*, (pp. 866-870).

Zurada, J. (1992). *Introduction to Artificial Neural Systems*. West Publishing Company.

SECTION IV

MULTIMEDIA CONTENT
ANALYSES

Chapter VII

Object-Based Techniques for Image Retrieval

Y. J. Zhang, Tsinghua University, China

Y. Y. Gao, Tsinghua University, China

Y. Luo, Tsinghua University, China

ABSTRACT

To overcome the drawback of using only low-level features for the description of image content and to fill the gap between the perceptual property and semantic meaning, this chapter presents an object-based scheme and some object level techniques for image retrieval. According to a multi-layer description model, images are analyzed in different levels for progressive understanding, and this procedure helps to gain comprehensive representations of the objects in images. The main propulsion of the chapter includes a multi-layer description model that describes the image content with a hierarchical structure; an efficient region-based scheme for meaningful information extraction; a combined feature set to represent the image at a visual perception level; an iterative training-and-testing procedure for object region recognition; a decision function for reflecting common contents in object description and a combined feature and object matching process, as well as a self-adaptive relevance feedback that could work with or without memory. With the proposed techniques, a prototype retrieval system has been implemented. Real retrieval experiments have been conducted; results show that the object-based scheme is quite efficient and the performance of object level techniques have been confirmed.

INTRODUCTION

Fast technique advancement and the rapid information increments mark the new century. Along with the progress of imaging modality and the wide utility of digital image in various fields, many potential content producers have emerged, and many image databases have been built. How to quickly access and manage these large, both in the sense of information contents and data volume, databases has become an urgent problem to solve. In the past 10 years, image retrieval techniques have drawn much interest, and content-based image retrieval (CBIR) techniques are proposed in this context to search information from image databases quickly and efficiently (Kato, 1992). With the advantage of comprehensive descriptions of image contents and consistence to human visual perception, research in this direction is considered as one of the hottest research points in the new century (Zhang, 2003).

Though many efforts have been put on CBIR, many techniques have been proposed and many prototype systems have been developed, the problems in retrieving images according to image content are far from being solved. Most of current techniques and systems for image retrieval just take into consideration low-level visual features, such as color and texture of image, or shape of objects and spatial relationships among different regions in images, to describe image contents. However, there is a considerable difference between the users' interest in reality, and the image contents described by only using the above low-level image features. In other words, there is a large gap between such image content description based on low-level features and that of human beings' understanding. As a result, these low-level feature-based approaches often lead to unsatisfying querying results in many cases.

In this chapter, a general scheme and some object-based techniques are proposed to efficiently fill the gap between the low-level feature and high-level semantic description of images. This is in the hope of making content-based image retrieval more like its real meaning, instead of just considering the visual perception. Throughout this chapter, several techniques are proposed, and all these techniques are gathered together into an object-based framework for image retrieval.

The proposed structure of this chapter is as follows: *Background*, (1) Extraction of Interesting Regions, (2) Object-level Processing, (3) Self-Adaptive Relevance Feedback; *Main Thrust of Chapter*, (1) Multi-Layer Description Model, (2) Meaningful Region Extraction, (3) Perceptual Feature Extraction, (4) Object Recognition, (5) Object Description and Matching, (6) Experiments and Discussions; *Direction of Future Research*; and *Conclusion*.

BACKGROUND

In content-based image retrieval, how to represent and describe the content of an image is a central issue. Many methods have been used, three broad categories are: synthetic, semantic and semiotic (Bimbo, 1999; Vailaya, 2000; Djeraba, 2002). The progress is enormous, however, due to the nature of this problem, many challenging tasks arose. Some of them are briefly discussed in the following.

Extraction of Interesting Regions

With the advantage of comprehensive descriptions of image contents, content-based image retrieval has become one of the hottest research aspects and many practical retrieval systems have been developed, such as QBIC (Lee, 1994), Photobook (Pentland, 1996), VisualSEEK (Smith, 1996), CAFIIR (Wu, 1997), and FourEyes (Minka, 1997), et al. However, most of the above image retrieval systems use low-level image features, such as color, texture, and shape, etc., to represent image contents directly. In fact, there is a considerable gap between semantics of images that the user is really interested in and the image content representation by the above low-level image features. Therefore, it is not surprising that the query results are often not much satisfying.

To closely capture the content of images and to efficiently represent the information of images, an object-based framework would be required. However, precise object segmentation in many cases is still beyond the capability of current computer techniques. Much work has been done in decomposing an image into regions with uniform low-level features such as color or texture. However, such a region may have few semantic meanings.

In this chapter, "meaningful region" extraction is proposed. The "meaningful region" is at the intermediate level between the original image and the interesting object of the image. This level is an effective visual level for the representation of images, according to humans' visual acuity. In addition, a meaningful region should be grouped in a higher feature space to have some suitable semantic meaning. Semantic meanings can be extracted from the meaningful region automatically and further object descriptions could be obtained with the help of a knowledge database.

Object-Level Processing

In the field of content-based image retrieval, a new research trend is to use high-level descriptions, instead of low-level features, in the match process. How to extract high-level descriptions from images and to fill the gap between the low-level features and human beings' understanding of image contents directly are critical. One promising technique to solve this problem is to describe the whole image with a hierarchical structure to reach progressive image analysis (Castelli, 1998; Jaimes, 1999; Hong, 1999). The contents of images can be represented in different levels (Amir, 1998), such as the three-level content representation, including feature level content, object level content and scene level content (Hong, 1999), and the five-level representation, including region level, perceptual region level, object part level, object level and scene level (Jaimes, 1999).

Among different structural levels, object level is considered the key linking the lower feature level and the higher semantic level. However, many existing methods treat the object level with traditional image segmentation and pattern recognition procedure, which would not be very feasible and could not greatly simulate human beings' understanding of image contents.

To extract semantics from an image, a number of current methods try to map low-level visual features to high-level semantics. In other words, to fill the semantic gap, one makes the system work with low-level features while the user puts more high-level knowledge in Zhou (2002). Two typical methods are the optimizing query request by relevance feedback and semantic visual template (Chang, 1998) and the using of interactive interface to progressively understand the contents of image (Castelli, 1998).

In this chapter, an object-level approach for content description and matching is proposed based on a multi-layer description model. A prototype system for retrieving images in object-level is also implemented. Differing from many other retrieval systems, there is no need for the user to provide sample images or sketch images. The user could submit his querying demand by just 'telling' the system what kind of objects should be included in the retrieved images, which is called object querying. Further, the user could require expected spatial relationships among selected objects, which is called relationship querying. Experiments with real images have been conducted using this system, and the effectiveness of object-based retrieval has been justified.

Self-Adaptive Relevance Feedback

It is generally accepted that high-level image features are crucial to improve the performance of content-based image retrieval up to so-called semantic-based querying. Among the related techniques, relevance feedback has been paid a lot of attention because it could combine the information from the user. In practice, many methods have been proposed to reach the goal of relevance feedback (Rui, 1998; Ciocca, 1999; Lee, 1999). In this way, through the selection of relevant and non-relevant images from the system interface, the semantic relationships between images are captured and embedded into the system by splitting/merging image clusters and updating the correlation matrix. There is a common point of these methods where the relevance feedback is based directly on the low-level image features and the operation of feedback is considered the approach to high-level semantics. However, relevance feedback is not exactly the representation of image semantics but the way to refine the querying results. Without a proper way to describe the image semantics, the function of relevance feedback could not be exerted well.

In this chapter, a new scheme for relevance feedback is proposed, which is integrated to a semantic-based image retrieval system. Unlike previous methods for relevance feedback, this scheme provides a self-adaptive operation. Based on multi-level image content analysis, the relevant images fed-back from the user could be automatically analyzed in different levels and thus, the gained result would be used to determine the querying scheme. In practice, to make the querying more convenient to the user, the procedure of relevance feedback could be led with memory or without memory. Experimental results show that the performance of the image retrieval could be greatly improved through the self-adaptive relevance feedback, both in accuracy and efficiency.

MAIN THRUST OF THE CHAPTER
Multi-Layer Description Model

How to describe image contents is a key issue in content-based image retrieval. In other words, among the techniques for image retrieval, the image content description model would be a crucial one. Humans' understanding of image contents possesses some fuzzy characteristics, which indicates that the traditional image description model based on low-level image features (such as color, texture, shape, etc.) is not always consistent to human visual perception. The gap between low-level image features and high-level image semantics makes the querying results sometimes disappointing. To improve the performance of image retrieval, there is a strong tendency in the field of image retrieval to analyze images in a hierarchical way and to describe image contents on a semantic level. A widely accepted method for obtaining semantics is to process the whole image on different levels, which reflects the fuzzy characteristics of image contents (Hong, 1999; Jaimes, 1999).

In the following, a multi-layer description model for image description is depicted (see Figure 1), which can describe the image content with a hierarchical structure to reach progressive image analysis and understanding (Gao, 2000b). The whole procedure has been represented in four layers: original image layer, meaningful region layer, visual perception layer and object layer. The description for a higher layer could be generated from the description from the adjacent lower layer, and establishing the image model is synchronously the procedure for progressive understanding of image contents. These different layers could provide distinct information of the image content, so this model is suitable to access from different levels.

In Figure 1, the left part shows that the proposed image model includes four layers, the middle part shows the corresponding formulae for the four layers' representation, while the right part gives some presentation examples of the four layers.

In this model, image content is analyzed and represented in four layers. There is a context between adjacent layers that the representation for the upper layer is directly extracted from that for the lower layer. The first step is to split the original image into several meaningful regions; each of them provides certain semantics in terms of human beings' understanding of image contents. Then, proper features should be extracted from these meaningful regions to represent the image content at a visual perception layer. In the interest of following up processing, such as object recognition, the image features should be selected carefully. The automatic object recognition overcomes the disadvantage of large overhead in manual labeling while it throws off the drawback of insufficient

Figure 1: Multi-Layer Description Model

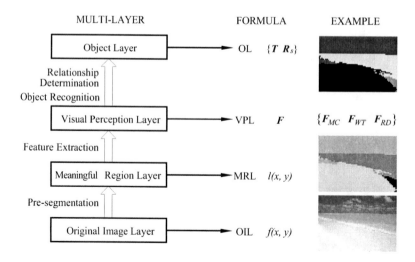

content information representation by using only lower level image features. Another important part of the object layer process is relationship determination, which provides more semantic information among the different objects of an image.

Based on the above statements, the multi-layer description model (*MDM*) could be expressed by the following formula:

$$MDM = \{OIL,\ MRL,\ VPL,\ OL\} \tag{1}$$

In Equation (1), *OIL* represents the lowest layer — original image layer — with the original image data represented by $f(x, y)$. *MRL* represents the labeled image $l(x, y)$ which is the result of meaningful region extraction (Luo, 2001). *VPL* is the description for the visual perception layer, and it contains three elements: $\vec{F}_{MC}, \vec{F}_{WT}$ and $\vec{F}_{RD}$, representing Mixed Color Feature, Wavelet Package Texture Feature and Region Descriptor, respectively (Gao, 2000a). One point that should be noticed is that the selection of *VPL* is flexible and should be based on the implementation. *OL* is the representation of object layer and it includes two components: T and R_s. The former T is the result of object recognition to indicate the attribute of each extracted meaningful region, for which detailed discussions would be given in the following. The latter R_s is a $K \times K$ matrix to indicate the spatial relationship between every two meaningful regions, with K representing the number of the meaningful regions in the whole image.

In brief, all the four layers together form a "bottom-up" procedure (implying a hierarchical image process) of multi-layer image content analysis. This procedure aims at analyzing the image in different levels so that the image content representation could be obtained step by step from low-level to high-level. In addition, this procedure is also the basis of the proposed self-adaptive relevance feedback.

Meaningful Region Extraction

Traditionally, image features are computed with the whole image, which makes further meaningful content representation and semantic extraction very difficult. Here, a process of pre-segmentation is suggested before further processes to extract different interest regions from the whole image (Pauwels, 1998). Differing from general image segmentation that leads to pixel-level precision, the goal of pre-segmentation is only to roughly extract semantically significant regions in image.

According to human visual perception theory, during visual perception and recognition process, human eyes move and successively fixate on the most informative parts of the image. These informative parts are named "meaningful regions" as they possess certain semantic meanings. The delineation of these meaningful regions will help the following perception feature extraction.

Flowchart

The flowchart for roughly extracting meaningful regions in an image is shown in Figure 2. Different modules will be detailed in the following subsections, here an overview is provided. First, the original images are classified into different image groups, according to their complexity index. For simple images with a lower complexity index, the meaningful regions could be extracted by using only hue information. The images with very high

Figure 2: The Flowchart for Roughly Extracting Meaningful Regions

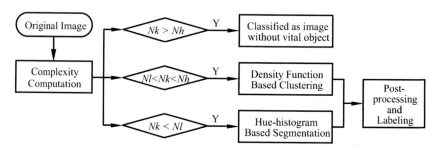

complexity indexes are exempted from further process, as the regions extracted from these images are hard to be recognized as significant objects. For other images, the extraction of meaningful regions will be based on some high-level features deduced from low-level features, and a non-parametric clustering algorithm based on weighted density function will be applied. Some image post-processing techniques are also employed such as noise removal and merging very small regions that do not contain significant semantic meaning.

Complexity Index

The complexity index N_k is determined by the following:

$$N_k = N \Big/ \sum_i R_k(i) \qquad\qquad (2)$$

where N is the image size (pixel number), k is the size of the neighborhood area considered, $R_k(i)$ is the ratio of the number of pixels labeled as the i-th pixel's label in its k-sized neighborhood. The complexity index N_k is a function of k, and for a given k, N_k is just a function of the complexity of images. The value of N_k is bigger if the complexity of the image is high.

According to the value of the complexity index, the images can be classified into different groups. Two limiting thresholds, N_l and N_h, can be used. If $N_k < N_l$, the image would be simple, and good segmentation results could be obtained by only using hue-histogram based segmentation. For a large number of images, the value of the complexity index would be moderate, $N_l < N_k < N_h$, so a clustering by using multidimensional feature analysis and in weighted-density space would be necessary. If $N_k > N_h$, the image would be too complex (composed of a large number of small regions) for further object recognition.

Hue-Histogram Based Segmentation

There are several color representation schemes, among them the Hue-Saturation-Intensity (HSI) color representation. It is used because the HSI color space represents the human concept of color well and it is more suitable for the segmentation of natural color images (Zhang, 1999).

Usually, in the HSI color space, intensity is used for texture analysis. The other two components have been used to extract the color information. The saturation is taken to produce the importance index, which indicates the weight of color information. The higher the saturation, the more reliable the color information and the process based on color information. The perception of color by human eyes is mainly obtained from the hue component, so a hue-histogram (weighted by saturation) based multi-threshold selection technique is employed for treating simple images.

Texture Feature

There is always very rich texture information in natural images and texture information should be considered in treating the most of images (Wouwer, 1999). People can easily differentiate different objects according to their texture. It has been shown that humans in the process use some perceptual texture features such as coarseness, contrast and direction to distinguish between textured images or regions. Among these, coarseness is the most fundamental property and, in a certain sense, it is the coarseness that determines the texture.

According to the coarseness index, whether an image is rich in texture information can be judged (Karu, 1996). Let C be the index of coarseness, the image contains more texture information if C is larger, and vice versa. In the image intensity space, let $E(i,j)$ = 1 if pixel (i,j) is a local extreme (either row maximum/minimum or column maximum/minimum) and $E(i,j) = 0$ if the pixel is not, then:

$$C = \frac{1}{N} \sum_{(i,j) \in image} E(i,j)$$

(3)

Coarseness estimation can help the determination of the weight for texture information.

Density Function

Perceptual salient regions in images are presumed to have relatively high data density than the boundary area (Coleman, 1979; Everitt, 1993). Suppose an image is represented by the data set $\{x_i \in R^n, i = 1, 2, ..., N\}$, convoluting it with a uni-model kernel function K can produce the density function (Pauwels, 1999):

$$f(x) = \frac{1}{N} \sum_{i=1}^{N} K_\sigma (x - x_i)$$

(4)

where the kernel can be a Gaussian kernel

$$K_\sigma (x) = (\frac{1}{2\pi\sigma^2})^{n/2} \exp\left(\frac{-\|x\|^2}{2\sigma^2} \right)$$

(5)

x_i is an n-D vector, and n is the number of the features used.

The density space can be obtained once having the density function. The cluster in the density space must be homogeneous in all the low-level feature space used (Hichem, 1999). In the density space, the local maximum that represents one object in the image can be computed by:

$$\frac{\partial^n f}{\partial F_1 \partial F_2 \cdots \partial F_n} = 0 \tag{6}$$

At the beginning, the cluster number could be overestimated by giving a low σ. Then, an optimal clustering can be obtained by grouping the image segments into more meaningful regions.

The distance between the i-th and j-th clusters can be defined by:

$$Dis(i, j) = \frac{d\xi^2}{W(i)W(j)} \tag{7}$$

where d is the Mahalanobis distance, ξ^2 is the variance of the scores on the line from cluster i and j, W is the size of the cluster. According to $Dis(i,j)$, two clusters with minimum distance will be merged.

To control the clustering procedure, an index S_k, is to be determined:

$$S_k = \frac{1}{K} \sum_{i=1}^{K} f(t_i) \tag{8}$$

Some K sub-regions in a cluster should be determined to find the local minimum density score $f(t_i)$. S_k is small if there are several low-density areas in a cluster. This means less similar regions are grouped together. With a small cluster number, S_k will be decreasing. The summation of S_k and N_k (as defined before) will indicate the optimal clustering result (Luo, 2001).

Weighted Non-Parametric Clustering

Early work in decomposing images into regions with uniform characteristics often used features such as color, texture or edge etc. Though a region can be defined as a set of homogeneous elements in the feature space, it may not have any semantic meaning. A meaningful region is grouped by a set of elements homogeneous in a higher level space, called Density Space, that contains more complicated information and more semantic meaning.

Different features have different contributions to image clustering. For example, the hue information is more reliable if the image is highly color saturated. The large variance of one feature always indicates that this feature would distinguish different objects clearly and it will play an important role in image segmentation and object recognition. So the following dynamic weighting mechanism could be employed:

$$W = \frac{\sigma}{d} \qquad (9)$$

where σ and μ are the standard deviation and the mean of feature sets. This weighting mechanism permits us to utilize all the features efficiently.

By using multi-dimensional low-level feature analysis (color, texture, etc.), the reliability of different features can be determined in order to adaptively weight the contribution of each feature to the segmentation process (Castagno, 1998). After determining the weight of different features, a new-weighted non-parametric clustering algorithm in the density space can be implemented. Weighting mechanisms are used to control the influence of each data source in the combined classification and to improve the combined classification accuracy.

One example is shown in Figure 3. Figure (a) is an original image, Figure (b) and (c) are the results obtained by using color feature and texture feature, respectively, Figure (d) shows the clustering result.

Perceptual Feature Extraction

After the processing of pre-segmentation, proper features should be extracted to represent the image at a visual perception level. Here, lower image features serve as the description of the visual perception level. In the interest of following processing, such as object recognition, the image features should be selected carefully. In the case of landscape images, we select color and texture features to represent the extracted meaningful regions.

In the visual perception layer, perceptual features are to be extracted. Both color feature and texture feature are used here, as people are more sensitive to color and texture information in a natural image. To represent the color information of images, a color feature set, which is a sub-space of the color space, is introduced to describe the image content in terms of human visual perception. Because such visual information representation deals with both hue and intensity, it is named Mixed Color Feature (MCF). In practice, based on MCF, a histogram of images is used to represent color visual information (Gao, 2000a). A proper distance measurement named Weighted Nearest Matching is also introduced in related processing, such as feature comparison.

Texture features based on wavelet are used since multi-resolution representations are widely employed in texture analysis for the sake of strong arguments found in psycho-

Figure 3: Example of Non-Parametric Clustering

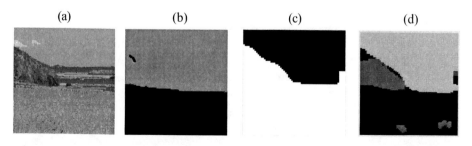

| (a) | (b) | (c) | (d) |

visual research. A typical hierarchical wavelet transform decomposes signals into a set of sub-images in the lower frequency band, which is enough in generic signal analysis. However, in the case of texture images, which possess a considerable proportion of energy in the intermediate frequency band, the higher frequency band should be further decomposed to capture more information. The wavelet package transform decomposes signals not only in the lower frequency band but also in the higher frequency band. In this section, a new texture descriptor is proposed. First, a Daubechies wavelet package transform is applied to the original image and as a result 18 sub-bands are generated. Then, for each sub-band, the average and standard variance of wavelet-coefficients are extracted as texture feature vectors.

Color Information Representation

In the *HSI* color model, color information is represented by three values: hue (*H*), saturation (*S*) and intensity (*I*). Among the three values, *H* is the closest to human vision and plays the key role in determining the color vision. Therefore, the value of *H* is often extracted as the color feature to reduce the dimension of feature space while reserving the color information of the original image as accurately as possible. Nevertheless, the color information uniquely represented by *H* sometimes performs badly, for example, in the case of $S = 0$, the value of *H* has no definition. In other words, such a definition of *H* could not include all the factors contributing to human visual perception. Here, another method to construct the color feature is presented. For the convenience of interpretation, a variable is introduced as follows:

$$Balance = \frac{\max(R, G, B)}{L_{Max}} \times 100\% \tag{10}$$

where L_{max} represents the maximal value of each color channel. The visual information can be divided into two parts, hue information and intensity information, in terms of the following criterions:

1. If the value of *S* is considerably small, the value of *H* could be neglected and only the intensity information should be considered.
2. If the value of *Balance* is considerably small, the visual information could also be described only by intensity information.

In this way, the visual information could be described by a combined vector *V*:

$$V = \{H_1, H_2, \cdots, H_{N_H}, I_1, I_2, \cdots, I_{N_I}\} \tag{11}$$

where N_H represents the dimension of hue part while N_I represents that of intensity part so that the total dimension of *V* is $N_H + N_I$.

It is evident that if *H* and *I* are orthogonal, the redundancy will be reduced to the minimal level (Zhang, 1998). So, a transformation in HSI space is carried out to make *H* and *I* to be easily separable and make the *H* distribution more uniform (Liu, 1998).

Distance Measurement

Since in MCF the H and I indicate different color information, the distance between two points in this sub-space could not be simply measured by the geometric distance. A segmental distance measurement is required. For the convenience of interpretation, the value of $H_i, i = 1, 2, \cdots N_H$ is scaled from $[0°, 360°]$ to $[0, N_H-1]$. Similarly, the value of $I_i, i = 1, 2, \cdots N_I$ is scaled from the region $[0, L_{Max}-1]$ to $[N_H, N_H + N_I -1]$. Suppose there are two points V_i and V_j among the vector V, the normalized distance between V_i and V_j could be defined as $Dis_{MCF}(V_i, V_j)$:

1.   If $V_i, V_j \in [H_1, H_2, \cdots, H_{N_H}]$,

$$Dis_{MCF}(V_i, V_j) = \begin{cases} \dfrac{|V_i - V_j|}{N_H/2} & |V_i - V_j| \le N_H/2 \\ \dfrac{N_H - |V_i - V_j|}{N_H/2} & |V_i - V_j| > N_H/2 \end{cases} \tag{12}$$

2.   If $V_i, V_j \in [I_1, I_2, \cdots, I_{N_I}]$,

$$Dis_{MCF}(V_i, V_j) = \frac{|V_i - V_j|}{N_I} \tag{13}$$

3.   If $V_i \in [H_1, H_2, \cdots H_{N_H}], V_j \in [I_1, I_2, \cdots, I_{N_I}]$

or $V_i \in [I_1, I_2, \cdots, I_{N_I}], V_j \in [H_1, H_2, \cdots, H_{N_H}]$,

$$Dis_{MCF}(V_i, V_j) = 1 \tag{14}$$

The above three equations define the normalized distance among the sub-space MCF.

Wavelet Package Texture Feature

Multi-resolution representations are widely used in texture analysis for the sake of strong arguments found in psycho-visual research. A typical hierarchical wavelet transform decomposes signals into a set of sub-images in the lower frequency band, which is enough in generic signal analysis. However, in the case of texture images, which possess a considerable proportion of energy in the intermediate frequency band, the higher frequency band should be further decomposed to capture more information. In the case of texture images, which possess a considerable proportion of energy in the intermediate frequency band, the wavelet package transform that decomposes signals not only in the lower frequency band but also in the higher frequency band could be used to decompose the higher frequency band to capture more information (Coifman, 1992).

Based on the above discussion, the following texture descriptor is proposed. First, a Daubechies wavelet package transform is applied to the original image and as a result

18 sub-bands are generated. Then, for each sub-band, the average and standard variance of wavelet coefficients are extracted as texture feature vectors.

Given the output of k-th sub-band, $x_k(i,j)$, $1 \le i,j \le M_k$ and the size of the sub-band, $M_k \times M_k$, $k = 1,2, \cdots, 18$, the average and standard variance could be computed by (using L_1-norm):

$$\bar{x}_k = \frac{1}{M_k^2} \|x_k\|_1 = \frac{1}{M_k^2} \sum_{i,j=1}^{M_k} |x_k(i,j)| \tag{15}$$

$$\sigma_k = \frac{1}{M_k^2} \sum_{i,j=1}^{M_k} |x_k(i,j) - \bar{x}_k| \tag{16}$$

Region Descriptor

To describe each meaningful region completely, some region descriptors, including regional area, centroid, and form factor, are also employed. Their definitions are given below. Let I represents the whole image, R represents meaningful regions of I, the normalized area of region R is:

$$A_R = \sum_{(x,y)\in R} 1 \bigg/ \sum_{(x,y)\in I} 1 \tag{17}$$

The centroid coordinates of region R are:

$$\begin{cases} \bar{x} = \dfrac{1}{X \cdot A_R} \sum_{(x,y)\in R} x \\ \bar{y} = \dfrac{1}{Y \cdot A_R} \sum_{(x,y)\in R} y \end{cases} \tag{18}$$

where X and Y represent the extents along direction x and y of the whole image, respectively. The form factor of region R is:

$$F = \frac{\|P\|^2}{4\pi S} \tag{19}$$

where P represents the perimeter of the region R while S represents the area of the region R.

Although color, texture and region features used here are low-level image features, these features are applied here on extracted meaningful regions and aimed at representing the outstanding character of the meaningful region but abandoning others' trivial visual perception. This is in contrast to traditional processes that apply feature computation on the whole image.

Object Recognition

Of the whole object layer, the key is to 'recognize' what a meaningful region represents in terms of human beings' knowledge. Automatic object recognition overcomes the disadvantage of large overhead in manual labeling while it throws off the insufficient image content description by lower image features.

In the following, an iterative procedure is used to approach the correct recognition result. The object recognition is basically a training-and-testing procedure. That is, the system would give its recognition result in terms of the knowledge having been stored in it. To make the problem simpler, it is assumed that there are finite types of interesting objects in a given image database. In fact, this requirement could often be satisfied in practice as only limited image contents are considered in one application. The object recognition is performed in an iterative way. Context-based knowledge would be obtained during this process, helping to reach the correct recognition result. There are three major steps included in this procedure: dynamic weight determination, multiple processes to recognition and multi-conditional judging. Experimental results in the context of content-based image retrieval have shown the advantage of this method, compared with traditional methods for object recognition.

Flowchart for Object Recognition

The flowchart for iterative recognition of objects based on extracted meaningful regions is shown in Figure 4. In Figure 4, the object recognition is considered as a training-and-testing procedure. That is, the system would give its recognition result in terms of the knowledge having been stored in it. To make the problem simpler, it is assumed that there are finite types of interesting objects in a given image database. In fact, this requirement could often be satisfied in practice as only limited image contents are considered. During the iterative procedure, context-based knowledge would be obtained and helped to reach the correct recognition result. The two major steps included in this procedure: dynamic weight determination and multiple processes to recognition, will be discussed briefly in the following.

Dynamic Weight Determination

To capture different aspects of images, multiple features are often used. How to determine the proportion of each feature in a description would heavily affect the performance of retrieval. The method proposed here is to count the distance between the feature obtained from an extracted meaningful region in the current image (F_m) and the i-th sample in the training feature set $\{F_t(i), i = 1, 2, ..., N\}$. In practice, the mean μ and standard variance σ of these distances are first computed as:

$$\mu = \frac{1}{N} \sum_{i=1}^{N} Dis[F_m, F_t(i)] \tag{20}$$

$$\sigma = \frac{1}{N} \sum_{i=1}^{N} \left| Dis[F_m, F_t(i)] - \mu \right| \tag{21}$$

Figure 4: Procedure for Object Recognition

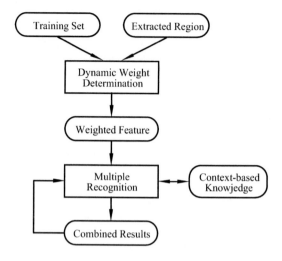

Then, the weight for feature *j* is determined by:

$$Weight = \frac{\sigma}{\mu} \tag{22}$$

In Equation (22), the weight is inversely proportional to the mean of the distance in order to normalize distance values from various image features. The weight is proportional to the variance, which indicates the dispersion of distance in the feature space between the meaningful region and each sample in the training set. In fact, the small variance indicates that this kind of feature plays a trivial role in object recognition. The large variance would heavily influence the result of recognition because the meaningful region is closer to the training set in the feature space. It could be seen from Equation (22) that the weight for each feature is not pre-determined in advance, but is determined dynamically.

Multiple Recognition

Due to the lighting conditions and/or variety of object appearance, the objects belonging to the same category can have different visual aspects. To recognize a particular object and the object set in an image correctly, two recognition processes are performed here.

The first one is, with respect to each meaningful region extracted from the image, to calculate the distances between the considered region and all object set *J* in the training set as described above. These distances are then ranked in an ascending order: $\text{Dis}[F_m, F_t(1)] < \text{Dis}[F_m, F_t(2)] < \cdots < \text{Dis}[F_m, F_t(N)]$. To capture the most significant objects in the training set while discarding trivial ones, only the first N_s distances are considered in recognition:

$$R_1 = Arg \max_{j \in J} \left\{ \sum_{k=1}^{N_s} \frac{E_j(k)}{Dis(F_m, F_t(k))} \right\} \tag{23}$$

where E_j is defined as:

$$E_j(k) = \begin{cases} 1, & \text{if} \quad F_t(k) \in j \\ 0, & \text{otherwise} \end{cases} \tag{24}$$

The second one is to consider all the objects in the training set together to calculate the feature distance to find the one that corresponds to minimal distance. In fact, the process is an instance of classification using minimal distance criterion.

$$R_2 = Arg \min_{1 < k < N} \left\{ Dis[F_{tm}, F_t(k)] \right\} \tag{25}$$

Based on the above two recognition criteria, a unique recognition result is generated by combination. This process can be iterated until the final recognition result is acceptable (in terms of the image composition, according to some *a priori* knowledge). In this process, some new knowledge, probably to be used in the next iteration, can be acquired and integrated to generate a current recognition result. With this iterative procedure, the context-based knowledge is gradually improved and the correct recognition result is gradually approached.

Object Description and Matching

Object Description

To describe objects in an image, a matrix T is defined. It is a diagonal matrix with each entry indicating the attribute of every meaningful region in the image. Let S be the set of all types of objects (totally M) in the image database, and s_i be the i-th object in S, then T could be expressed as:

$$T = Diag[t^1, t^2, \cdots, t^M] \tag{26}$$

where:

$$t^i = \begin{cases} 1 & \text{if} \quad s_i \in S \\ 0 & \text{otherwise} \end{cases} \quad i = 1, 2, \cdots, M \tag{27}$$

In addition, a relation matrix R_s is defined. It is a $K \times K$ matrix to indicate the spatial relationship between every two meaningful regions, with K representing the number of meaningful regions in the whole image. For instance, the spatial relationship between the i-th region and the j-th region could be represented by setting the value of r_{ij} in R_s, which is located in the i-th line and the j-th column.

Let $T_{r1}, T_{r2}, \cdots, T_{rN}$ be the content representation matrix of each relevant image, where subscript r indicates the set of relevant images and N is the number of relevant images. Then a correlation matrix C could be defined as follows:

$$C = Diag[c^1, c^2, \cdots, c^M] = \prod_{i=1}^{N} T_{ri}$$

$$= \begin{bmatrix} t_1^1 & & & \\ & t_1^2 & & \\ & & \ddots & \\ & & & t_1^M \end{bmatrix} \begin{bmatrix} t_2^1 & & & \\ & t_2^2 & & \\ & & \ddots & \\ & & & t_2^M \end{bmatrix} \cdots \begin{bmatrix} t_N^1 & & & \\ & t_N^2 & & \\ & & \ddots & \\ & & & t_N^M \end{bmatrix} \quad (28)$$

Finally, the decision function $B(N)$ could be defined as the sum of the diagonal elements in the matrix:

$$B(N) = tr[C] \quad (29)$$

It could be seen from Equations (26)~(29) that the decision function reflects whether all the relevant images have common contents, that is, the same objects. The system would present different querying criteria in terms of $B(N)$.

Object Matching

The object matching procedure is shown in Figure 5 (Zhang, 2002). The case of $B(N) = 0$ indicates that the relevant images do not have common objects. The case of $B(N) > 0$ indicates that the relevant images do have common objects. In the former case, feature based matching will be performed, while in the latter case, the matching will be based on objects as described in the following.

For object matching, the system would extract similarity information from the common objects in all relevant images to perform the match processing between the relevant images and candidate images. Let $F = \{f^i \mid i = 1, 2, \cdots, L\}$ be a set of representation for both the visual perception level and the object level, such as color, texture and spatial relationship. The weights in terms of the similarity information of all the relevant images should be updated as follows:

$$\tilde{d}^i = \frac{2}{N(N-1)} \sum_{j=1}^{N-1} \sum_{k=j+1}^{N} d^i(f_{rj}^i, f_{rk}^i) \quad i = 1,2,\cdots L \quad (30)$$

$$\sigma^i = \frac{2}{N(N-1)} \sum_{j=1}^{N-1} \sum_{k=j+1}^{N} \left| d^i(f_{rj}^i, f_{rk}^i) - \tilde{d}^i \right| \quad i = 1,2,\cdots,L \quad (31)$$

$$W^i = \frac{\tilde{d}^i}{\sigma^i} \quad i = 1,2,\cdots,L \quad (32)$$

Figure 5: Procedure of Self-Adaptive Relevance Feedback

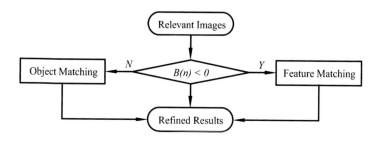

In Equation (30), the symbol r in the subscript of f_{rj}^i and f_{rk}^i means that this item is from the set of relevant images. Similarly, in the following, q would be used to indicate an image from the database. Unlike the general standard variation based on L_2 norm, σ^i in Equation (31) is based on L_1 norm, which has the advantage of simple calculation and shows good performance in practice. Equation (32) shows that the value of W^i is proportional to $\tilde{d}^i$ but inversely proportional to σ^i. Using σ^i as the denominator of W^i is based on such a hypothesis that the larger σ^i is, the less f^i could represent the similarity information of the relevant images. The goal of selecting $\tilde{d}^i$ as the numerator of W^i is to normalize the value of the distance so that different representations could be put together. Further interpretation about it would be given in the following. What should be stressed is that the above processing should be carried out with each common object of the relevant images. That is, there are different weights for all common objects of the relevant images.

Based on the above statements, the querying criterion for common information matching could be proposed with the similarity function. Let C be the correlation matrix for the relevant images and T_{qi} be the content representation matrix of the i-th image in the database. Then, a new decision function $B_{CIM}(qi)$ could be introduced as:

$$B_{CIM}(qi) = tr(C_{qi}) = tr\begin{bmatrix} c_{qi}^1 & & & \\ & c_{qi}^2 & & \\ & & \ddots & \\ & & & c_{qi}^M \end{bmatrix} = tr(CT_{qi}) \tag{33}$$

where C_{qi} represents the correlation matrix of the i-th image in the database. The proper candidate from the database should satisfy $B_{CIM}(qi) \geq B(N)$. Then, to each proper candidate, its similarity function could be calculated by:

$$S(qi) = \sum_{j=1}^{N} \sum_{1 \le k \le M, c_{qi}^k = 1} \vec{W}_k^{\tau} \vec{D}_k = \sum_{j=1}^{N} \sum_{1 \le k \le M, c_{qi}^k = 1} \sum_{l=1}^{L} w_k^l d^l (f_{qi,k}^l, f_{rj,k}^l) \qquad (34)$$

Going through the whole database by the proposed method for common information matching, each proper candidate would get its value of similarity, which could be used to order the returned querying results.

Experiments and Discussions

To test the performance of the proposed methods, a prototype retrieval system has been implemented based on the above-described techniques. The whole system could be divided into five modules, such as user input, system output, image database, querying mechanism and feedback mechanism (Gao, 2001). Each of them has its own function while connecting with each other to form an integrated system. Using this prototype system, the following three experiments have been conducted to verify the performance and effectiveness of the above presented techniques.

Object Recognition

Here we select landscape images as the data source. Seven object categories often found in landscape images are selected: mountain, tree, ground, water, sky, building and flower. There are two reasons for this selection. First, landscape images generally include complex color and texture information, and they are not easy to be treated by simple recognition procedures. Second, in landscape images, there are many objects having variable appearances under the same definition of objects. For instance, under the category 'sky,' there exist different appearances such as 'clear sky,' 'sunny sky,' 'cloudy sky' and so on. Instead of visual features, object recognition is mandatory in this case.

In Figure 6, four examples of test results about the object recognition are presented. The first row is for original images. The second row gives the extracted meaningful regions. As is mentioned above, the procedure of meaningful region extraction aims not at precise segmenting but rather at extracting major regions, which are striking to human vision. The third row represents the result of object recognition, with each meaningful region labeled by different colors (see the fourth row) to indicate the object category it belongs to.

Image Retrieval Based on Object Matching

Based on object recognition, the retrieval can be conducted in the object level. One example is shown in Figure 7. The user has submitted a query in which three objects "mountain," "tree" and "sky" are selected and thus, required. Based on this information, the system searches in the database and looks for images with these three objects, the returned images from the image database are displayed in Figure 7. Though the images in Figure 7 are different in the visual perception sense as they may have different colors or shapes or structure appearances, however, all these images have the required three objects.

In Figure 7, the ordering of these returned images is based on object similarity, which is provided by visual perception descriptors. One descriptor that can be used is the area of required object, as in general the larger the object in the image, the more interest to

Figure 6: Experimental Results for Pre-Segmentation and Object Recognition

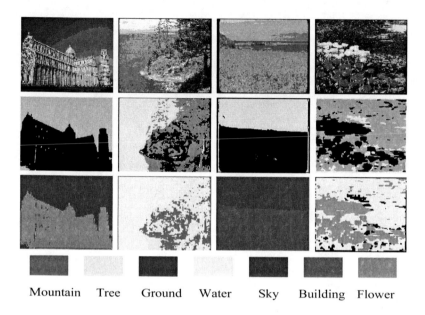

Mountain   Tree   Ground   Water   Sky   Building   Flower

the user. If the user selected the k-th object, then the ordering of returned images (have the required object) is made according to the normalized area of the k-th object (denoted by A_k) in these images. When the user selected totally K objects, then the ordering of returned images (have all required objects) will be made according to:

$$S = \sum_{k=1}^{K} A_k \qquad (35)$$

Figure 7: Experimental Results Obtained by Object Matching

Figure 8: Further Results Obtained by Object Relationship Matching

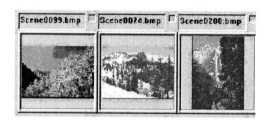

Based on object recognition, the retrieval can be further conducted using object relationship. One example is given in Figure 8, which is a result of an advanced search. Suppose the user made a further requirement based on the querying results of Figure 7, in which the spatial relationship between objects "mountain" and "tree" should also fulfill a "left-to-right" relationship. In other words, not only the objects "mountain" and "tree" should be presented in the returned images (the presentation of "sky" objects is implicit), but also the "mountain" should be presented in the images as the left side of the "tree" (in this example, the position of "sky" is not limited). The results shown in Figure 8 are just a sub-set of Figure 7.

Self-Adaptive Relevance Feedback

In the current content-based image retrieval system, relevance feedback has been often integrated into the system to grasp the description of images and refine the query results. However, the relevance feedback relying on the low-level features itself could not completely catch image semantics and thus, the performance of the system is heavily affected by the difficulty to meet users' requirements.

Based on the multi-level description model, the scheme of self-adaptive relevance feedback could be established. The main idea of the proposed scheme is to analyze the fed-back relevant images marked by the user in different levels to reach comprehensive similarity analysis. Then, a self-adaptive procedure is carried out to refine the query, by which different querying schemes could be used in terms of different results of similarity analysis. The final goal of the scheme is to make the querying results meet the user's demand as closely as possible.

The whole procedure will be carried out in two steps. First, similarity analysis is carried out on different levels of description along the relevant images to extract the relevant information. Then, different querying schemes would be used to search optimally matched images in terms of different results of similarity analysis. To this purpose, a decision function is calculated, which is based on the fed-back information obtained from the object layer. Then, one of the two matching processes, common information matching or respective information matching (see below), would be carried out according to the value of the decision function. In addition, the procedure of relevance feedback can be carried out with memory or without memory, which makes the feedback mechanism more flexible and convenient. In case of the feedback without memory, each feedback is an independent procedure, in which all of the relevant images selected in previous iterations would be ignored. In case of the feedback with memory,

Figure 9: Retrieval with Respective Information Matching

(a)

(b)

(c)

the relevant images selected in previous iterations would be taken into account in the current iteration. A time delay curve has been proposed to simulate human beings' memory mechanism in feedback with memory (Gao, 2001). In the following, two experimental examples are provided to show the results of relevant feedback based on object levels.

Figure 9 presents a typical instance that there is no common object of the relevant images. Figure 9(a) shows the sample images provided by the system. Here the No. 4 in the first row and No. 4 in the second row are relevant images selected. It could be easily seen that these two images have no common objects, leading to the respective information matching. The query result is shown in Figure 9(b). It should be noticed that since it is the first time of feedback, there is no difference using feedback with memory or without memory. From Figure 9(b), it could be seen that returned images include various

Figure 10: Retrieval with Common Information Matching

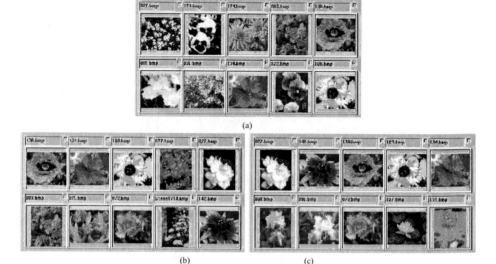

(a)

(b)   (c)

objects but they show some common characters. For example, they all somewhat show the color of 'yellow.' However, the user changes his interest to the two images No.1 and No.5 in the second row that show the common object of "building." Then, the feedback is carried out without memory and the result is given in Figure 9(c).

Figure 10 shows another instance of feedback but with common information matching. Figure 10(a) is the result of a first round retrieval, in which the object 'flower' is required. The three selected images (No. 5 in the first row as well as No. 3 and No. 5 in the second row) show the same character of 'large format' and the common information is utilized to find the optimally matching images. The returned result is shown in Figure 10(b). To obtain a more satisfying query result, two more images are selected (No. 5 in the first row and No. 5 in the second row) in Figure 10(b). The feedback with memory is carried out in this stage, reaching at the query result shown in Figure 10(c). It could be seen that the query result is gradually refined with the iterative feedback.

DIRECTION OF FUTURE RESEARCH

The procedure and techniques presented in the above could be further improved and pursued in a number of promising directions:

1.   The extraction of a meaningful region that is at the intermediate level between the original image and the interesting object of an image has played an important role for effective visual level process. Experiments have shown that successful extraction of meaningful regions from still images and video shots helps to integrate the unsupervised and adaptive clustering techniques in CBIR (content-based image retrieval) and CBVR (content-based video retrieval) systems (Luo, 2001). However, the robustness of extraction, especially with complicated images, needs to be

ameliorated. For this purpose, more characteristics of images should be further considered.

2.   The proposed object-based framework for efficient image representation has enabled flexible access and manipulation of image content. However, in the object layer, the semantic object delineation for general sources remains a challenging task. As image segmentation is not just a task that could be worked out at a low level, some high level knowledge should be incorporated (Zhang, 2001). In addition, as human beings are still far from knowing all the cognitive details from the real world, how to automatically form semantic objects is perplexing. How to efficiently describe semantic objects as congruous to humans' senses as possible should be studied.

3.   The multi-layer description model presented in Figure 1 only shows four layers. In fact, on the top of object layer, a scene layer that should be the highest layer in the proposed model should be considered. The description for a scene layer should be provided by the scene understanding, which is related to human knowledge for image contents, like the object recognition in the object layer. The process of scene understanding could be a training procedure, and the knowledge database for scene understanding could be updated during querying, in terms of the users' comprehension.

4.   Relevance feedback is useful to incorporate human intention and to approach the optimal retrieval results. However, feedback is just a method for refining the results so that it could not totally determine the performance of image retrieval systems, and how to make this process fast following the users' aspiration in the course of retrieval is interesting. When the system is based on lower level features, relevance feedback could only improve the retrieval results to some degree. The use of relevance feedback based on high-level content description in the object level could further improve the performance. On the other side, a potential direction would be to use association feedback based on feature elements (Xu, 2001).

CONCLUSION

In summary, this chapter proposed an object-based scheme for image retrieval and described the techniques to fulfill this task in detail (with principle description, algorithm implementation, and retrieval experimentation and result discussions).

On the basis of a multi-layer description model, a progressive procedure for image content understanding is presented. Starting from meaningful region extraction, some perceptual features are selected from extracted regions for the further recognition of corresponding objects. In the object level, the content description and object matching are carried out to efficiently retrieve expected images, and with self-adaptive relevance feedback, the results are refined according to users' wishes in an explicit manner. A prototype system based on these techniques has been implemented and real retrieval experiments have been conducted, the functionality and performance of the system has been verified.

Further research directions on improving the robustness of meaningful region extraction, on describing objects with more semantic meaning, on performing scene level process to fully understand the contents of images and on using feedback more efficiently are indicated.

ACKNOWLEDGMENTS

This work has been supported by the Grants NNSF-69672029, NNSF-60172025, HTP-863-317-9604-05 and TH-EE9906.

REFERENCES

Amir, A. & Lindenbaum, M. (1998). A generic grouping algorithm and its quantitative analysis. *IEEE PAMI, 20*(2), 168-185.

Bimbo, A. (1999). *Visual Information Retrieval*. Morgan Kaufmann, Inc.

Castagno, R., Ebrahimi, T., & Kunt, M. (1998). Video segmentation based on multiple features for interactive multimedia applications. *IEEE Trans. CSVT, 8*(5), 56-571.

Castelli, V., Bergman, L.D., & Kontoyiannis, I., et al. (1998). Progressive search and retrieval in large image archives. *IBM J. Res. Develop., 42*(2), 253-268.

Chang, S.F., Chen, W., & Sundaram, H. (1998). Semantic visual templates: Linking visual features to semantics. *Proceedings ICIP '98*, (pp. 531-535).

Ciocca, G. & Schettini, R. (1999). Using a relevance feedback mechanism to improve content-based image retrieval. *Proceedings Third International Conference, VISUAL '99*, (pp. 107-114).

Coifman, R.R. & Wickerhauser, M. V. (1992). Entropy-based algorithms for best basis selection. *IEEE Trans. Information Theory, 38*(3), 713-718.

Coleman, G. & Andrews, H.C. (1979). Image segmentation by clustering. *Proc. IEEE, 67,* (pp. 773-785).

Djeraba, C. (2002). Content-based multimedia indexing and retrieval. *IEEE, Multimedia,* (2), 18-22.

Everitt, B.S. (1993). *Cluster Analysis*. Edward Arnold.

Gao, Y.Y. & Zhang, Y.J. (2000a). Object classification using mixed color feature. *Proceedings of International Conference on Acoustics, Speech, and Signal Processing,* (Vol. 4, pp. 2003-2006).

Gao, Y.Y., Zhang, Y.J., & Merzlyakov, N.S. (2000b). Semantic-based image description model and its implementation for image retrieval. *Proceedings of the First International Conference on Image and Graphics*, (pp. 657-660).

Gao, Y.Y., Zhang, Y.J., & Yu, F. (2001). Self-adaptive relevance feedback based on multi-level image content analysis. *SPIE, 4315,* 449-459.

Hichem, F. & Krishnapuram, R. (1999). A robust competitive clustering algorithm with applications in computer vision. *IEEE Trans. PAMI, 21,* 450-465.

Hong, D.Z., Wu, J.K., & Singh, S.S. (1999). Refining image retrieval based on context-driven method. *SPIE Proceedings Storage and Retrieval for Image and Video Database VII,* (Vol. 3656, pp. 581-593).

Jaimes, A. & Chang, S.F. (1999). Model-based classification of visual information for content-based retrieval. *SPIE Proceedings on Storage and Retrieval for Image and Video Database VII,* (Vol. 3656, pp. 402-414).

Karu, K., Jain, A.K., & Bolle, R.M. (1996). Is there any texture in the image. *Pattern Recognition, 29,* 1437-1446.

Kato, T. (1992). Database architecture for content-based image retrieval. *SPIE, 1662,* 112-123.

Lee, C.S., Ma, W.Y., & Zhang, H.J. (1999). Information embedding based on user's relevance feedback for image retrieval. *SPIE, Proceedings Storage and Retrieval for Image and Video Database VI, 3846,* (pp. 294-304).

Lee, D., Barber, R., & NiBlack, W., et al. (1994). Indexing for complex queries on a query-by-content image database. *Proceedings 12th ICPR,* (pp. 142-146).

Liu, Z.W. & Zhang, Y.J. (1998). Color image retrieval using local accumulative histogram. *Journal of Image and Graphics, 3*(7), 533-537.

Luo, Y., Zhang, Y.J., & Gao, Y.Y., et al. (2001). Extracting meaningful regions for content-based retrieval of image and video. *SPIE, 4310,* 455-464.

Minka, T.P. & Picard, R.W. (1997). Interactive learning with a 'society of models.' *Pattern Recognition, 30,* 565-81.

Pauwels, E.J. & Frederix, G. (1998). Finding regions of interest for content-extraction. *SPIE, 3656,* 501-509.

Pauwels, E.J. & Frederix, G. (1999). Finding salient regions in images — non-parametric clustering for image segmentation and grouping. *Computer Vision and Image Understanding, 75,* 73-85.

Pentland, A., Picard, R.W. & Sclaroff, S. (1996). Photobook: Content-based manipulation of image database. *International Journal of Computer Vision, 18,* 233-254.

Rui, Y., Huang, T.S., & Mehrotra, S. (1998). Relevance feedback techniques in interactive content-based image retrieval. *SPIE Proceedings Storage and Retrieval for Image and Video Database V, 3312,* (pp. 25-34).

Smith, J.R. & Chang, S.F. (1996). Tools and techniques for color image retrieval. *SPIE Proceedings Storage and Retrieval for Image and Video Database IV, 2670,* (pp. 426-437).

Vailaya, A. & Jain, A. (2000). Detecting sky and vegetation in outdoor images. *SPIE, 3972,* (pp. 411-420).

Wouwer, G., Scheunders, P. & Livens, S., et al. (1999). Wavelet correlation signatures for color texture characterization. *Pattern Recognition, 32*(3), 443-451.

Wu, J.K. (1997). Content-based indexing of multimedia database. *IEEE Trans. Knowledge and Data Engineering, 9,* 978-989.

Xu, Y. & Zhang, Y.J. (2001). Association feedback: A novel tool for feature elements based image retrieval. *Lecture Notes in Computer Science 2195,* 506-513.

Zhang, Y.J. (1999). *Image Engineering (1): Image Processing and Analysis,* Tsinghua University Press.

Zhang, Y.J. (2001). *Image Segmentation.* Science Publisher.

Zhang, Y.J. (2003). *Content-based Visual Information Retrieval,* Science Publisher.

Zhang, Y.J., Gao, Y.Y., & Merzlyakov, N.S. (2002). Object recognition and matching for image retrieval. *Proceedings of the Second International Conference on Image and Graphics,* (pp. 1083-1089).

Zhang, Y.J., Liu, Z.W., & He, Y. (1998). Color-based image retrieval using sub-range cumulative histogram. *High Technology Letters, 4*(2), 71-75.

Zhou, X.S. & Huang, T.S. (2002). Unifying keywords and visual contents in image retrieval. *IEEE, Multimedia,* (2), 23-33.

Chapter VIII

Object-Based Video Analysis and Interpretation

Ying Luo, University of Washington, USA

Jeng-Neng Hwang, University of Washington, USA

Tzong-Der Wu, Chinese Culture University, Taiwan

ABSTRACT

In this chapter, we present a novel scheme for object-based video analysis and interpretation based on automatic video object extraction, video object abstraction, and semantic event modeling. In this scheme, video objects (VOs) are first automatically extracted, followed by a video object abstraction algorithm for identifying key frames to reduce data redundancy and provide reliable feature data for the next stage of the algorithm. Semantic feature modeling is based on a temporal variation of low-level features of video objects. Dynamic Bayesian networks (DBNs) are then used to characterize the spatio-temporal nature of the video objects. The system states in the proposed DBNs directly correspond to the physical concepts. Thus, the decoding of the DBN system states from observable variables is a natural interpretation of the behavior of the video objects. Since the video objects are generally considered as the dominant semantic features of video clips, the proposed scheme provides a powerful methodology for content description, which is critical for large scale MPEG-7 applications.

INTRODUCTION

The explosive growth of the amount of multimedia information, such as images, audio and video, calls for highly efficient methods for representing, indexing, retrieving and filtering of multimedia contents. Flexible and extensible representation schemes have been proposed with the advent of the MPEG-7 standard. To integrate MPEG-7 description schemes into multimedia applications, fully automatic algorithms for multimedia analysis and interpretation, i.e., content description, are the essential tools needed for large-scale multimedia applications. The discussion in this chapter will focus on the analysis and interpretation of video sequences. Nevertheless, the framework is readily extended to other multimedia applications.

The best method to demonstrate how a human understands video clips is by an example. When we watch the "Miss America" video sequence, our interpretation is that "a woman is talking." Two specific aspects of the video sequences are emphasized in the human interpretation: (1) It is the object (i.e., a woman) that is used by humans as the basic unit of understanding. (2) The interpretation is in terms of the semantics (i.e., talking) of the objects. It can be summarized that humans interpret the contents of video clips by the semantics of the objects in the video.

In contrast to the easy grasp of the contents of video clips by a human, fully-fledged interpretation of video sequences by computer is an extremely difficult task. The basic signal processing issue, i.e., the extraction of low-level features including both video and audio features such as motion, color and spectral features, is more or less a solved problem. In order for the computers to interpret the video sequences as a human does, there are two big gaps that need to be filled: one is the comprehensive algorithm that extracts the objects from low-level features. The other is the modeling of object behavior to a semantic level. The approach described in this chapter is trying to make a step toward the solving of these two problems.

The objective of this chapter is to describe an automatic video analysis and interpretation framework based on video object (VO) extraction, object-based abstraction and semantic feature mapping. Background about the definitions of the necessary concepts and a review of the literature are presented. The video object extraction and object-based abstraction are then described. Next, the mapping from object features to high-level semantic concepts by dynamic Bayesian networks is discussed. Finally, features of the proposed system are summarized and possible future work is discussed.

BACKGROUND

To design a complete video analysis and interpretation system we must solve two fundamental problems, i.e., what object-based features shall we count on and what mapping shall we use. For the first problem, we have both video and audio information at hand. In this chapter, we will only use video (visual) features extracted from segmented objects to demonstrate our idea. But the framework is readily extensible to include audio features. For the second problem, a dynamic Bayesian network approach is adopted to serve the purpose.

Video Feature Extraction

Current research in video feature extraction involves frame-based and object-based approaches. In frame-based approaches, low-level features such as color, histogram, texture and motion of frames (in uncompressed or compressed domains) are extracted. Using these low-level features for shot/scene detection (Boreczkey & Rowe, 2000) or for query-by-example (Rui & Huang, 1999) has become quite standard procedures. The advantage of frame-based features is that they are generally easy to compute. Their drawback is that it is very difficult to use them to address the fine-grained semantics of the video contents. In the frame-based approaches, all the features are in frame level, while one frame may include a hierarchy of interacting objects and background. For example, the very simple "hall monitor" sequence contains the hall and the people walking in the hall, while each person contains head, arms and legs. The frame-based feature vector does contain all of this information. More specifically, by extracting features in the frame level, the semantic information is implicit, and requires great effort to recover later. Pioneering work, such as Vasconcelos and Lippman (2000), exploits the frame-based features in the temporal direction and successfully establishes the mapping from the low-level features to high-level concepts. However, the frame-based features are generally very difficult to be used to get detailed semantic interpretation of video sequences and the results are basically macro-grained, e.g., the semantics information that can be eventually acquired is only the "class" (e.g., sports, news, etc.) of the video sequence.

In contrast to the frame-based approaches, the object-based approaches have been gaining popularity in recent years (Haering, Qian, & Sezan, 2000; Naphade & Huang, 2001; Zhong & Chang, 1999). In an object-based approach, low-level features from individual regions, instead of from frames, are the basic units for analysis. These regions are first extracted from video sequences by spatio-temporal segmentation procedures. Then, they are associated with semantic meaning by various mapping models. The advantage of the object-based approach is quite obvious; the semantic information can be explicitly expressed via the object features. Finer-grained semantic interpretation of video sequences can be obtained more easily by the features directly derived from objects. Moreover, it will be shown that the object-based approach gives us more flexibility in choosing complicated mapping models that are closer to human understanding of video sequences. The main drawback of this approach is that specific mapping models must be designed for different applications and will introduce larger computation complexity.

In our study, we also adopt an object-based approach. The critical difference of our work with other object-based approaches is that we go one step further by employing video objects (VOs) as the basic units for analysis. VOs are the concepts mainly introduced in MPEG-4. They are defined as spatio-temporal visual objects with semantic meaning, such as the human body in the continuous frames of a video sequences. In contrast, the objects mentioned in the above paragraph do not necessarily have semantic meaning. Instead, they might be regions generated by the spatio-temporal segmentation without specific semantics. One of the advantages of VOs is that they conform to the human understanding of the video sequences. Furthermore, after the VOs are success-fully extracted, they serve as the best vehicles for deriving the most part of the semantics from video sequences (see the "Miss America" example). Although a small part of the semantic information is lost during the VO extraction procedure, most of the irrelevant information is also removed. Thus, by only exploiting the features of VOs, we can obtain the critical semantics of the video sequence.

Dynamic Bayesian Networks (DBNs)

Many methodologies have been proposed to solve the second problem, i.e., the mapping problem. These methodologies include neural networks (Mittal & Cheong, 2001), hidden Markov models (HMMs) (Oliver, Rosario, & Pentland, 2000; Starner & Pentland, 1995), Bayesian networks (Naphade & Huang, 2001), factor graphs (Naphade, Kozintsev, & Huang, 2002), and support vector machines (Mittal & Cheong, 2001).

We specifically employ dynamic Bayesian networks (DBNs) for the mapping from low-level features to high-level semantics. DBNs are superset of HMMs, which can construct a direct mapping that will finally output a detailed interpretation of the VOs characteristics.

Bayesian Networks

It is assumed that the readers are familiar with HMMs since they are quite common in the modeling of temporal and spatial sequences nowadays. For a refresher, please refer to Rabiner (1989). In order to have a better understanding of DBNs, we need to present an introduction to basic concepts of Bayesian networks (BNs).

A basic concept in probability theory is that, as long as we know the joint probability distribution function (PDF) of all the random variables that model a physical domain, this

Figure 1: A BN Represents the Joint Distribution of W, X, Y, Z as P(W,X,Y,Z) = P(W)P(X)P(Y|W)P(Z|X,Y)

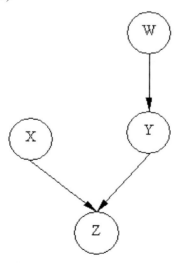

domain is considered as fully known. A Bayesian network of a physical domain represents the causal relationship between random variables, i.e., it explicitly "factorize" the random variables set to simplify the computation of joint PDFs. To illustrate this point, it's best to see an example as shown in Figure 1 where a BN representing a physical domain with four variables: W, X, Y and Z. We can see that W and X are independent variables, Y only depends on W, and Z depends on both X and Y. So, the joint PDF $P(W,X,Y,Z) = P(W)P(X)P(Y|W)P(Z|X,Y)$, is now factorized into several conditional PDFs that are much easier to compute or estimate.

Some of the basic points of BN are listed as follows:

1.   The BNs are directed acyclic graphs (DAGs). Each node of a BN represents a random variable and each edge indicates that the connected pair of nodes are causally related, i.e., dependent.

2.   Each node has a conditional probability distribution (CPD, continuous variable) or a conditional probability table (CPT, discrete variable). The CPD (CPT) basically defines the behavior of a node when its parent node states are changed.

3.   Inference: the procedure to derive the states of one part of the nodes when the states of the other part of the nodes are known.

4.   Learning: the procedure to learn the CPDs (CPTs) of the nodes when the behavior of part (or all) of the nodes is observed.

For a detailed discussion, please refer to Coweel, David, Lauritzen and Spiegelhalter (1999) and Murphy (2002).

Dynamic Bayesian Networks (DBNs)

A DBN is a Bayesian network with the same structure unrolled in the time axis as shown in Figure 2. The DBNs themselves are still Bayesian networks in nature, but they are generally considered as state-space models which model the system state dynamics

Figure 2: A Dynamic Bayesian Network which is Formed by a BN Unrolled in the Time Axis [It is a state-space model with state (hidden) nodes and observation nodes.]

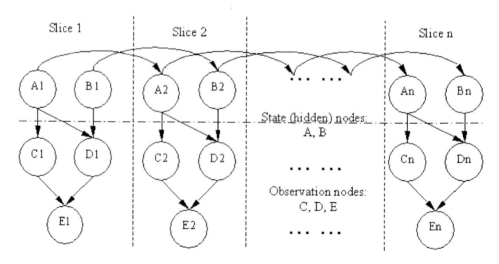

by observed variables, though it is not necessarily required that the system states be modeled explicitly as "hidden nodes" (in Figure 2, the system state is explicitly modeled as hidden nodes A and B). Their periodic structure can be taken advantage of to simplify the computation. Hidden Markov models (HMMs) and Kalman filters can be considered as special types of DBNs. They both have system states represented explicitly as hidden nodes. HMMs are DBNs with discrete state nodes, while Kalman filters are DBNs with continuous state and observation nodes. Although we will focus on temporal domain DBNs in this chapter, the BNs can in fact also be unrolled in the spatial domain (Muller, Eickeler, & Rigoll, 2001) and other domains. It is also possible to change the structure of the BNs at each time slice, which is called dynamic Bayesian multinets (DBM) as discussed in Bilmes (2000).

The DBNs for our application are similar to traditional HMMs, which are widely used in the modeling of temporal behavior of dynamic systems. The DBNs contain distinct observation nodes and discrete state (hidden) nodes. In comparison to HMMs, which allow one hidden node and one observation node at each time slice, general DBNs allow Bayesian networks with arbitrary structure at each time slice. Although this will introduce larger computational complexity, it gives the designers of DBNs great flexibility. Instead of packing all the features together into a feature vector represented by one observation node, it's possible to have one observation node for each physical feature at each time slice. Similarly, unlike the one-hidden-node requirement as in HMMs, there can be more than one hidden node representing the corresponding state of the physical world in DBN.

Since all the nodes of a DBN can be directly mapped from the corresponding physical world concepts, the causal relations between hidden nodes and observation nodes can be modeled according to data or human knowledge. In this case, the nodes are not necessarily fully connected. Actually, in most cases, they are not because there are always some nodes (variables) independent to each other (i.e., not all pairs of physical world concepts have a casual relationship). One of the advantages of general DBNs comes from the fact that the recognition of independent variables (nodes) will simplify the computation of joint probability distribution when a complex system with many variables is involved. Compared to DBNs, the HMMs compress all the hidden nodes and observation nodes into one hidden state and one observation node. Therefore, the search space in the training stage for HMM is much bigger, thus, more training overhead will be involved.

An example to show the differences between DBN and HMM by converting a DBN to an equivalent HMM is illustrated in Figure 3. A DBN with discrete hidden nodes can always be converted to an equivalent HMM (Zweig, 1998). In the DBN, the nodes A and B, which directly map the physical concepts, have four and three states, respectively. C, D, E, F are observation nodes. The arrows (edges) connecting different nodes indicate the dependency between two nodes. When we convert this DBN to the equivalent HMM, the HMM will have $3\times4 = 12$ states. The problem with the HMM is that by compressing all distinct hidden (observation) nodes of a DBN into one lumped hidden (observation) node, the dependency and independency relationships are all lost. During the training, a lot more data will be required for the HMM to converge to true distribution.

Except for the training efficiency for complex systems as discussed above, the other advantage of DBN is that each hidden node can represent a physical concept. For HMM, it is possible for the hidden nodes to represent some physical concepts in speech

Figure 3: A DBN Converted to an HMM

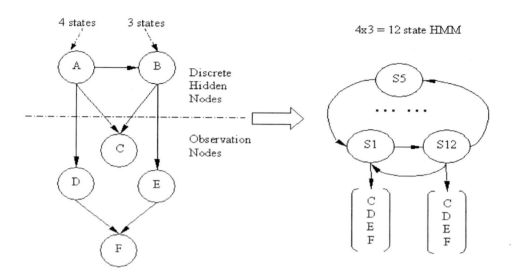

recognition (such as phonemes) (Rabiner, 1989) while in the video application of HMM, the hidden nodes generally represent some unknown middle states. When used in the interpretation of video events, only the final classification result is meaningful in HMMs. While by DBN, it's possible that when we finish interpretation, a detailed description of video events naturally comes out via the status of the hidden nodes. This makes DBNs, which are a direct modeling of human knowledge (i.e., physical concepts and their relationship), very attractive in terms of the ability to "describe" video events, which is critical in MPEG-7 applications. The other advantage is that it will make the design of the model much easier to follow and modify since it is a one-to-one mapping from human brain concepts to mathematical models.

Like Bayesian networks, the computation for DBNs also involves inference and learning. It is interesting to compare the computation of DBNs with HMMs. The three critical problems for HMM (Rabiner, 1989) also exist in the computation of DBNs. The first problem, "given the model, how to compute the probability of the observed sequences," can be solved by inference algorithms like junction trees and variational methods (Cowell, Dawid, Lauritzen, & Spiegelhalter, 1999; Murphy, 2002). The second problem, "the so-called most probable explanation (MPE) problem," can also be solved by inference algorithms which calculate marginal distributions for the nodes. The third problem, "the parameter learning problem," can be solved by the EM algorithm. The detailed discussion of the computation is beyond the scope of this chapter. Interested readers are referred to Murphy (2002) for more details.

VIDEO OBJECT EXTRACTION AND ABSTRACTION

The schematic diagram of our proposed framework is illustrated in Figure 4. The framework contains four modules: shot detection module, VO extraction module, video abstraction module and video modeling (mapping) module. After a video sequence is input into the system, it is first segmented into shots using frame-based features. The video objects are then extracted for each shot. Due to redundancy of video information, a video abstract procedure is employed to find key frames. Finally, the features derived from these key frames are used to model the video sequences, i.e., they act as the input for the mapping module.

Video Object Segmentation

After segmenting a video clip to shots (Taniquchi, Akutsu, & Tonomura, 1997), the first step is the extraction of VOs. There are two major categories of VO extraction, one is based on change detection, which is more suitable for video sequences with stationary backgrounds. The other is based on object tracking, which is mainly for video sequences with moving backgrounds. The change detection approach can be performed fully automatically, while the object tracking approach generally requires manual segmentation of a video object for the first frame.

We have two algorithms developed according to these two methodologies. The diagram of change detection algorithm (Kim & Hwang, 2002) is shown in Figure 5. The

Figure 4: Block Diagram of an Object-Based Video Analysis and Interpretation System

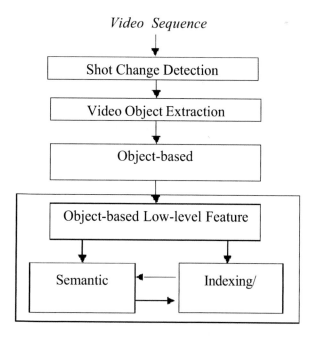

difference of two consecutive gray level images is calculated and the edge map DE_n is found by a Canny edge detector. Then, the moving edge ME_n of the current frame I_n is extracted based on the edge map DE_n of difference $|I_{n-1} - I_n|$, the current frame's edge map $E_n = \Phi(I_n)$, and the background edge map E_b, where E_b is calculated for the background when no object is present. Now we are ready to extract VO from ME_n. The horizontal candidates and vertical candidates are calculated according to ME_n. The horizontal candidates are declared to be the region inside the first and last edge points in each row of ME_n and the vertical candidates for each column. After finding both horizontal and vertical VOP candidates, intersection regions through logical AND operation are further processed by morphological operations. Finally, the extracted region is mapped back to the original image and the VO is obtained.

The diagram of object tracking based algorithm (Kim & Hwang, 2001) is shown in Figure 6. The manual video object extraction of the first frame is required for this

Figure 5: Block Diagram of Change Detection Video Object Extraction

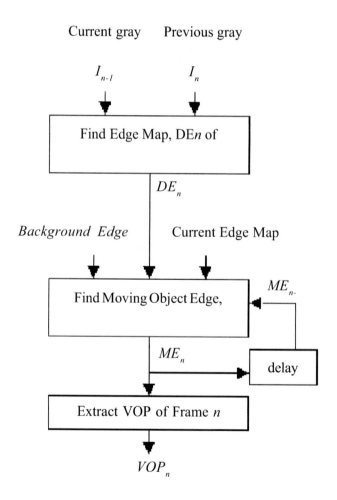

algorithm. For other frames, three steps, which are motion projection, model update and object post-processing, are required to extract the VOs. The first step is motion projection, which locates a video object with rough object boundary information, according to the previously extracted VO and estimated motion vectors. After this step, the projected points may not be exactly corresponding to the true positions of the video object in the current frame. So in the model update step, a procedure called modified histogram backprojection (Kim & Hwang, 2001) is used to correct the motion projected positions. Finally, object post-processing removes the errors (e.g., gulfs, small false regions) that still exist and at the same time smooths the object boundaries. For more details of these two algorithms, please refer to Kim and Hwang (2001, 2002).

In our proposed scheme, we interchangeably used the change detection and object tracking methods, depending on what kind of background a video sequence has. For still background video sequences, the change detection algorithm is used. For moving background video sequences, the object tracking algorithm is used.

Object-Based Video Abstraction

The purpose of the object-based video abstraction module is to identify key frames, which represent the most informative contents in a video shot, to reduce the redundancy of original video data, and to provide a good mechanism for semantic feature extraction and modeling. A video abstraction represents the content of a video sequence with concise information while the essence of the original message is preserved.

We have two algorithms for video abstraction proposed (Kim & Hwang, 2001; Kim & Hwang, 2002). The first algorithm is based on cluster analysis while the second one is based on sequential selection. Both of the two algorithms use Hu's moments as the features of VOs. The clustering approach divides one video shot into several segments (clusters), each segment contains frames similar enough, according to some criteria. Different segments should have sufficiently different characteristics. Then, key frames of each segment can be selected. The mean shift algorithm (Kim & Hwang, 2001) is adopted for the clustering.

Figure 6: Block Diagram of the Object Tracking Based VO Extraction

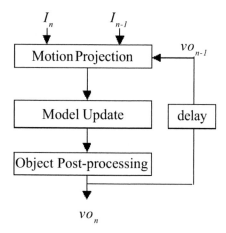

Figure 7: The Selected Key Frames from Clustering-Based Video Abstraction Scheme

The clustering approach works for video sequences with one VO and is an off-line algorithm. The sequential selection approach is an on-line algorithm and works for multiple VOs. The first frame is always chosen as a key frame. Then, the distance between the VO feature vectors is computed between the current frame VO, and the last extracted key frame VO. If this difference exceeds a given threshold, the current frame is selected as a new key frame. For more details of these two algorithms, please refer to Kim and Hwang (2001, 2002). Figure 7 shows the selected frames from clustering-based abstraction schemes on a hall monitor sequence, where the change detection algorithm is used to extract VOs.

VIDEO MODELING AND INTERPRETATION

Video object extraction and video abstraction provide a sound foundation for semantic modeling of the video clips. To obtain the semantics of the video clips, a mapping from low-level features to high-level semantic concepts is critically required. A dynamic Bayesian network (DBN) model is used in our proposed framework as the mapping tool.

Data Sets

To demonstrate our idea, we describe the feature extraction and DBN modeling for one-person sports video clips in this section. The collected video clips include five different types of sports events: downhill skiing, golf swing, baseball pitching, bowling, and ski jumping. Figure 8 shows typical image frames and the extracted objects of these five events.

The purpose of selecting one-person sports video modeling is to exploit the characterization of the human body motion. As seen in Figure 8, there are various lighting conditions for the video clips. So, ordinary color and texture features are unlikely to be reliable. A well-known fact is that the human body is an articulated structure whose motion can be decomposed into the various motion patterns of different body parts, i.e., head, trunk (its motion is likely to be closely associated with head in our data set), arms and legs. While the self-occlusion is very frequent during the body motion, it's not always possible to know the exact motion of different body parts. According to the observation, several assumptions about our data are made:

1. Since all the video sequences are captured from real scenarios, cluttered backgrounds and moving cameras are allowed.
2. Self-occlusion is allowed.
3. Various appearances are allowed for the athletes, i.e., various clothing and lighting condition, distinguishable or indistinguishable faces, and different body sizes can be present.
4. Whole body of the athlete is visible, i.e., no other occlusion.
5. The video event is complete. By "complete," we mean that during one sequence, an event happens from beginning to the end. A sports video is considered complete

Figure 8: Five Events — Bowling, Downhill Skiing, Golf Swing, Pitching and Ski Jump

if: the downhill athlete finishes a round of direction change and returns to the beginning direction in the downhill skiing procedure; the bowling athlete begins with raising the ball and finishes the throwing action; the ski jump athlete starts jumping and hits the ground; the golf athlete finishes a hit; and the pitcher finishes a baseball pitching.

From assumption 1 and the video object extraction approach described in the "Background" section, we can see that we must use the object tracking algorithm for moving background video sequences to obtain the VOs. Assumptions 2 and 3 present more difficulty in video object feature extraction. These two assumptions drove us to count on geometrical information of video objects as low-level features, which are considered to be the most reliable information presented in the sequences. Actually, our video abstraction algorithms also use geometrical features (i.e., Hu's moments) as the basis for computation. The last two assumptions, 4 and 5, are essential for the video modeling. Only when these two assumptions are confirmed, are the low-level feature to high-level semantics mapping meaningful.

Low-Level Video Object Feature Extraction

Our geometrical features are extracted from the shape of VOs. The observation of the data sets indicates that the motion of head, hands and legs has different characteristics for different sports events. With the key frame VOs as input, to extract the temporal position change of the head, hands and legs, we employ the following algorithm based on skeletonization of the human body shape:
1.   The VOs are binarized first.
2.   The Zhang-Suen/Stentiford/Holt combined algorithm, presented in Parker (1997), is employed to extract the skeleton of the binarized shape of VOs as shown in Figure 9b. The advantage of this algorithm is that it generates much less "spurs," which are frequently seen in some thinning algorithms (Parker, 1997), on the skeleton.

Figure 9: (a) Original VO, (b) Shape and Skeleton, (c) End Points and COG

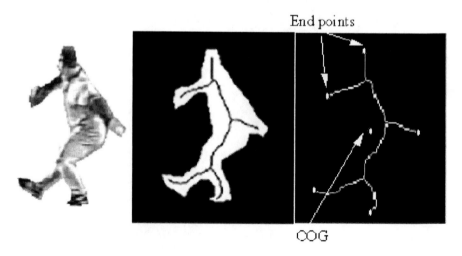

3.   The center of gravity (COG) of the shape is identified. An axes system with the COG as the original point, horizontal direction (from left to right) as X-axis and vertical direction (from bottom to top) as Y-axis is set up. Thus, the VO region is divided into four quadrants.

4.   The "end points" of the skeleton, i.e., the points that only have one 8-neighbor point, which is also part of the skeleton are detected (Figure 9c). The coordinates of these end points in the new axes system are obtained. Then, they are normalized by the maximum value of Euclidean distances of all the end points to COG. The purpose of the coordinate normalization step is to offset the effect of different body sizes.

5.   The mean x and y coordinates of the normalized end points in each quadrant are obtained and used as the features.

Note that, in the above algorithm, the end points of the skeleton may be from head, hands and feet. Also, they may be from joints, shoulders or even other non-body parts such as hat. The relations of these end points to the motion modeling will be discussed in the next sub-section.

Mapping from Low-Level Features to High-Level Semantics

After obtaining semantic features described previously from the extracted video objects, DBNs were used to model the temporal variation of the feature sets of each event.

A DBN for the sports video events unrolled in two time slices is shown in Figure 10. There are five hidden nodes representing the position of head, hands and feet. Each hidden node has four states representing their position relative to COG: upper-right (quadrant I), upper-left (quadrant II), lower-left (quadrant III) and lower-right (quadrant IV). Corresponding to the extracted features, there are four observation nodes representing the mean x and y coordinates in four quadrants. Thus, each observation node is a 2-D feature vector. As mentioned in the previous sub-section, the observed end points (observation nodes) do not necessarily correspond to the head, hands and feet (hidden nodes). But they can be considered to be excited indirectly by the motion of head, hands and feet. The dependency/independency of the variables are clearly shown in the DBN: in the five sports events we have, the chance that a head will appear in the lower part of the body is very rare. Thus, the head node only affect quadrants I and II. Similarly, the feet nodes only affect the III and IV quadrants. The hands, which are considered most flexible, affect the observation in all quadrants.

Experiments

We applied the DBN approach to model semantic events based on temporal variations of human behaviors within a video sequence. Kevin Murphy's Bayes Net Toolbox (BNT) (Murphy, 2001) was used for the DBN modeling.

In training stages, five different types of events were modeled separately by five DBNs. The observation features are modeled by Gaussian mixtures. The conditional probability distributions (CPDs) were learned from the data. After object extraction, video abstraction, and feature extraction, the probabilities are calculated for each DBN. The DBN with the maximum likelihood was considered as the correct event. We have 53

Figure 10: DBN for Human Body Motion in Five Sports Videos

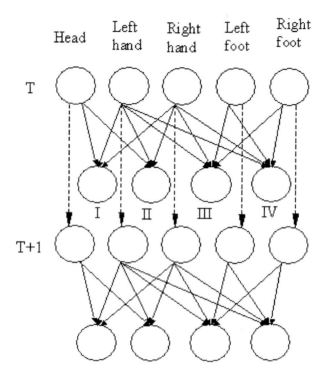

video clips for training/querying. The data set is randomly partitioned for training and querying for 25 times. Each time, two thirds of the sequences are used for training and the remaining one third are used for querying. Overall, an 88.2% average querying accuracy was obtained.

The other output of the system is the most probable explanation (MPE). In Figure 11, we show the MPE for a golf sequence. A "state vector," which indicates the spatial positions of the head, hands and feet in each frame, is obtained from MPE. 1, 2, 3 and 4 mean that the corresponding nodes are in quadrant I, II, III and IV, respectively. Although some error is involved (e.g., in the last frame, the right hand is calculated to be in quadrant IV with maximum probability, which is incorrect), we can see that a quite accurate explanation can be obtained.

DISCUSSION

In this chapter, we present a system for video analysis and interpretation based on objects. Based on extracted VOs, we modeled the system by DBNs, which can automatically generate descriptions for the video events. We showed that the object-based approach is effective for a complete characterization of video sequences, which includes both low-level signal features and high-level semantics about the contents.

Figure 11: Description of a Golf Video Event

Head 1	1	1	1	1	1	1
L. Hand 4	2	2	1	4	2	2
R. Hand 4	4	2	2	4	4	4
L. Foot 4	4	4	4	4	4	4
R. Foot 4	4	4	4	4	4	4

incorrect

There are some limitations in our scheme that open the doors for new exploration. First is that by considering only one video object, we discard the information contained in other video objects and the background, which may be very useful in the interpretation of video events. One possible solution is to use the object-based and frame-based approaches together to fully exploit the information contained in the video sequences. We have ongoing research that is trying to fuse both types of features together.

Another limitation is that the DBN structures in our work are domain-dependent, i.e., for different domains, different DBN structures need to be designed. Although this is good enough for some applications (e.g., modeling of the human behavior in constrained environments), the domain-dependence property of the proposed DBN modeling does limit the framework's extensibility. Theoretically, it is possible to learn the DBN structure directly from data. But, it is an extremely difficult problem and the result may not be satisfactory from the practitioner's point of view. The other possibility is to consider a more general structure of DBNs that will cover a bigger domain while keeping the computation tractable. The research on this issue is on the way.

The last limitation, as the readers may have noticed, is that the description generated by DBNs is very fine-grained. It works the best for simple video events. But for long video sequences involving various video events, this approach is unlikely to be satisfactory. For long video sequences, the most important semantic information is contained in the temporal structuring of the sub-events. This indicates that macro-grained modeling approaches, which allow the characterization of a temporal structure between video events, should be considered. Currently, we are exploring the appropriate models for long video sequences.

It is our belief that the preliminary work presented here will lead to satisfactory solutions for the "description generation" for MPEG-7 (see Figure 12), where multimedia indexing and retrieving are heavily depended on.

Figure 12: The Relationship Between the Presented System and MPEG-7

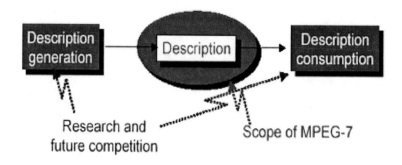

REFERENCES

Bilmes, J. (2000, July). Dynamic Bayesian multinets. *The 16th Conf. Uncertainty in Artificial Intelligence,* pp. 38-45, San Francisco, USA.

Boreczky, J. S. & Rowe, L. A. (1996). Comparison of video shot boundary detection techniques. *Proceedings of SPIE, 2670,* pp. 170-179.

Cowell, R. G., Dawid, A. P., Lauritzen, S. L., & Spiegelhalter, D. J. (1999). *Probabilistic Networks and Expert Systems.* Berlin-Heidelberg-New York: Springer-Verlag.

Ghahramani, Z. (1998). Learning dynamic Bayesian networks. *Adaptive Processing of Sequences and Data Structures,* pp. 168-197. Berlin-Heidelberg-New York: Springer-Verlag.

Haering, N., Qian, R. J., & x Sezan, R. J. (2000, September). A Semantic event-detection approach and its application to detecting hunts in wildlife Video. *IEEE Trans. Circuits and Systems for Video Technology, 10*(6), 857-867.

Kim, C. & Hwang, J.N. (2001, October). Object-based video abstraction using cluster analysis. *ICIP'2001,* vol. 2, pp. 7-10, Thessaloniki, Greece.

Kim, C. & Hwang, J.N. (2001, August). Video object extraction for object-oriented applications. *J. VLSI Signal Processing - Systems for Signal, Image, and Video Technology, 29*(1), 7-21. (moving background)

Kim, C. & Hwang, J.N. (2002, December). Object-based video abstraction for video surveillance systems. *IEEE Trans. Circuits and Systems for Video Technology, 12*(12), 1128-1138.

Kim, C. & Hwang, J.N. (2002, February). Fast and automatic video object segmentation and tracking for content-based applications. *IEEE Trans. Circuits and Systems for Video Technology, 12*(2), 122-129.

Mittal, A. & Cheong, L. F. (2001). Achieving semantic coupling in the domain of high-dimensional video indexing application. *Proceedings of SPIE, vol. 4305,* pp. 97-107.

Muller, S., Eickeler, S., & Rigoll, G. (2001). An integrated approach to shape and color-based image retrieval of rotated objects using hidden Markov models. *Int. J. of Pattern Recognition and Artificial Intelligence, 15*(1), 223-237.

Murphy, K. (2001). The Bayes net toolbox for matlab. *Computing Science and Statistics*, *33*.

Murphy, K. (2002). *Dynamic Bayesian networks: Representation, inference and learning*. Ph.D. dissertation, UC Berkeley.

Naphade, M. R. & Huang, T. S. (2001, March). A Probabilistic framework for semantic video indexing, filtering, and retrieval. *IEEE Trans. Multimedia*, *3*(1), 141-151.

Naphade, M. R., Kozintsev, I. V., & Huang, T. S. (2002, January). A factor graph framework for semantic video indexing. *IEEE Trans. Circuits and System and Video Technology*, *12*(1), 40-52.

Oliver, N.M., Rosario, B., & Pentland, A.P. (2000, August). A Bayesian computer vision system for modeling human interactions. *IEEE Trans. Pattern Analysis and Machine Intelligence*, *22*(8), 831-843.

Parker, J. R. (1997). *Algorithms for Image Processing and Computer Vision*. Wiley Computer Publishing.

Rabiner, L. (1989, February). A tutorial on hidden Markov models and selected applications in speech recognition. *Proceedings of the IEEE*, *77*(2), 257-286.

Rui, Y. & Huang, T. S. (1999). Image retrieval: Current techniques, promising, directions, and open issues. *J. Visual Communication and Image Representation*, 10, 39-62.

Starner, T. & Pentland, A. (1995). Visual recognition of American sign language using hidden Markov models. *Int. Work. Automatic Face and Gesture Recognition*, pp. 189-194. Zurich, Switzerland.

Taniquchi, Y., Akutsu, A., & Tonomura, Y. (1997). Panorama excerpts: Extracting and packing panoramas for video browsing. *Proceedings ACM Multimedia 97*, pp. 427-436. New York: ACM.

Tsutsumi, F. & Nakajima, C. (2001, October). Hybrid approach of video indexing and machine learning for rapid indexing and highly precise object recognition. *ICIP'2001*, vol. 2, Thessaloniki, Greece.

Vasconcelos, N. & Lippman, A. (2000, January). Statistical models of video structure for content analysis and characterization. *IEEE Trans. Image Processing*, *9*(1), 3-19

Zhong, D. & Chang, S. (1999, December). An integrated approach of content-based video object segmentation and retrieval. *IEEE Trans. Circuits and Systems for Video Technology*, *9*(8), 1259-1268.

Zweig, G. (1998). *Speech recognition by dynamic Bayesian networks*. Ph.D. dissertation, UC Berkeley.

SECTION V

MULTIMEDIA INDEXING TECHNIQUES

Chapter IX

Advances in Digital Home Photo Albums

Philippe Mulhem, IPAL-CNRS, Singapore

Joo Hwee Lim, Institute for Infocomm Research, Singapore

Wee Kheng Leow, National University of Singapore, Singapore

Mohan S. Kankanhalli, National University of Singapore, Singapore

ABSTRACT

In this chapter, we study the needs of digital home photo albums and the different components that are required to provide effective and efficient computer-based tools to match the users' expectations for such systems. We focus mainly on indexing and retrieval of photographic images using symbolic descriptions of image contents. We describe how symbolic labeling of image regions can be achieved, how the representation of image content is achieved using two different kinds of representations supporting different needs, and how the retrieval is performed on these image descriptions. Other features of digital home photo management are also described, and our proposal is evaluated on a genuine collection of 2,400 home photographs.

INTRODUCTION

The last few decades have witnessed a dizzying rate of technological innovation in the areas of computing and communication. While the effects of cheaper and faster computation power manifest explicitly in many places, slightly less obvious are the technological advances in sensor and signal processing technologies. Their impact is being increasingly felt in the form of digitization of all forms of communication and media. These advances have directly led to increased inexpensive communication bandwidth, which in turn has spurred the rapid acceleration of the Internet globally. In terms of consumer electronics devices, we are currently witnessing the mass-scale switchover to digital cameras from the traditional analog cameras. In fact, the year 2002 is considered to be a significant milestone since it is the first year when the sales of digital cameras has outstripped those of their analog predecessors.

The history of the invention of the camera is quite interesting. Joseph Nicéphore Niépce and Louis-Jacques Mandé Daguerre's invention of photography in 1825 was followed by the landmark contributions of George Eastman's dry photographic film with the associated camera in 1888 and Edwin Land's instant Polaroid photography in 1948. Essentially, the camera has democratized the preservation of images and, thus, it has had a tremendous impact on society. In the ancient times, only the kings and nobles could afford to engage artists to paint portraits, depict monuments and glorify conquests. With the invention of the camera, even ordinary people's lives started getting captured visually through this powerful medium. It basically eliminated the need of a skilled intermediary and simultaneously collapsed the time-period between the intent and production of a visual memory. Thus, the camera has been one of the first technological devices to be utilized on a large scale by people that demand neither the mastery of the technology nor the refinement of artistic skills. Hence, it rapidly became a mass-market consumer device. We are at an interesting technological cusp today. On one hand, the falling price of digital devices is rapidly pushing up the sales of digital cameras. On the other hand, increased global affluence coupled with the growing mobility of people is leading to an ever-greater use of the camera. Consequently, a huge amount of digital images is being generated everyday.

We are quite familiar with the traditional paradigm of handling photographs. Analog cameras are used with a film roll that can capture several photos, which are processed at one shot. The output of the rolls used for significant events such as birthdays, weddings, graduation ceremonies and travel are stored in a *home photo album*. This paradigm of capturing memories strongly resembles the book paradigm and quite easy to use for most people. Though it has some disadvantages in terms of limited use capabilities in terms of making copies or searching by only global album labels, it is a familiar and comfortable approach for most people.

Given that we are undergoing a paradigm shift in terms of camera technology, we can respond to this change in two ways. One way of responding to the challenge of managing large numbers of digital photographs is by faithfully mapping the analog photo album paradigm onto the digital arena, replicating both the look and functionality of the traditional approach. An alternative response would be to totally rethink and completely reengineer the way home users create, store, and manage *digital home photo albums*.

Thus, with more and more digital photos being accumulated, home users definitely need effective and efficient tools to organize and access their images. To address this genuine need, a three-year international collaborative project between CNRS, France, School of Computing; the National University of Singapore and Laboratories for Information Technology, Singapore was formed in 2000 to develop the next generation Digital Image/Video Album (DIVA) for home users. The goal of this chapter is to explain the work carried out in this DIVA international project. In particular, we will describe the needs of home users and possible solutions in the domain of management of digital images.

At the very outset, the DIVA project has adopted the second approach of having a fresh look at digital home photo albums in order to come up with an appropriate solution without being encumbered by habits and legacies of the past. Having settled on the approach, we came up with some fundamental assumptions related to digital home photo albums:

- A digital home photo album should not engender any *digital divide* between the ordinary home user and a technologically savvy home user. In particular, the digital home photo album should be intuitively easy to use for most users while offering the subtle flexibilities to the sophisticated user.

- Users take photographs (digital or otherwise) in order to *preserve* and *share* memories across space and time. Thus, sharing of home photos is at least as important as archiving the photographs.

- Given that sharing is important, users should be provided with extremely flexible means of *searching* and locating the appropriate photographs that are to be shared. This implies that the semantic content of the photographs needs to be represented along with the image.

- The user is likely to share his/her photographs with various people of different degrees of acquaintance and varying tastes. Hence, each presentation of shared photographs should be different — tailored to that particular individual or target group. Therefore, the ability to build *custom presentations* out of the same set of photographs is absolutely necessary.

- The digital home photo album of a user should adapt itself to the quirks and predilections of the user (instead of vice versa). For example, common content of the images such as the user's face, name and family members should be learned by the album over a period of time instead of being a memory-less stateless system. Thus, implicit and explicit *personalization* should be built into the system.

Given the above set of fundamental assumptions, we need to develop several technical pieces before we can solve the technological jigsaw puzzle. In particular, these technical considerations stemming from the fundamental assumptions need to be addressed:

1. Image capture and transfer: how should the image (and perhaps the camera parameters such as focal length, flash use, etc.) captured on the digital camera be transferred to the digital home photo album, which could reside on a computing device like a personal computer or possibly an embedded system consumer appliance like a portable image jukebox or perhaps be integrated with the camera itself.

2.   Image coding techniques: for efficient storage of the digital image.
3.   Image annotation: how to index the images with information related to the semantic content of the image. In other words, capturing the metadata about the digital photo.
4.   Representation of the metadata: which can facilitate flexible searching.
5.   Query languages: in order to pose the search constraints which enables efficient searching.
6.   User interfaces: which obliterates any digital divide by making the use very natural.
7.   Presentation tools: in order to customize the presentations for target audiences.
8.   Web interface: in order to use the worldwide web as a global channel for the sharing of images.
9.   Personalization: the system should have a means of personalizing explicitly the layout, the metadata and the sharing mechanisms. Moreover, it should strive for implicit personalization based on observed user behavior.

Thus, how to manage digital images is a challenging problem. We will now detail some of the efforts towards resolving a few of the above issues in the DIVA project. While we are taking an integrated approach of solving this problem in our project, our focus in this chapter is biased by the overall theme of this book, which basically deals with the content-related aspects. Hence, we will discuss in detail the content-based retrieval aspects while only briefly alluding to the other aspects.

USERS' NEEDS

Before going in detail into the existing work in content-based photographic images retrieval, we focus on the needs of users for the management of their home photographs. Even if the role of home photographs, i.e., a "bank of memory" (Chalfen, 1998), is somewhat clear, we had to get the users point of view about how home photograph management systems may help them.

The results presented here were obtained from a study carried out in 1999 on a panel of 37 persons. We intended to find out the current interest of users when organizing their images, and the consumer's expectations about the future of home photo management software.

Figure 1 shows how people currently retrieve and organize their photographs. In this figure, we present for each of the photographic points of view the relative ranked importance given by users. The points of view are: the *presentation* related to the colors/textures/shapes present in the images, the *content* related to the objects present in the images, their actions and their relations, the *context* related to the description of the date and the event at the origin of the photograph, and *connotation* related to the mood associated to the photograph. According to the Figure 1, we see that the *context* is the most important point of view to organize and retrieve images, and the *content* also plays a role in such photographs organization.

The second step is more related to the study of the potential uses expected by users for the future of home photograph systems. The question was for users to rank the expectations from first to fifth. The expectations proposed were: retrieval, organizing,

Figure 1: Existing Means to Organize Still Images

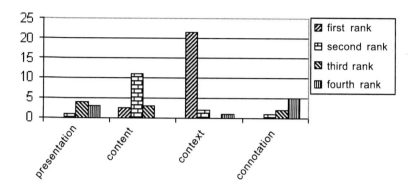

duplication of photographs, and gain of space in digital systems versus the paper. As we see in Figure 2, the users expectations are first related to retrieval and second to organization of photographs. These results are consistent with the findings of Rodden (1999). We conclude, then, that future home photo systems are expected to be able to handle queries and to help the user to organize her/his visual data. Organizing such visual data includes the creation of presentations like slide shows. FlipAlbum Suite (FlipAlbum, 2002) proposes to mimic the paper-based photo albums for presentation, whereas 3-D-Album (Photo Album Software, 2002) considers various 3-D styles for presenting photographs.

Because the retrieval and organization of the images are the most important aspects related to the management of home photographs, we consider in the next section the related works in the domain of still images indexing and retrieval before explaining our approaches based on symbolic descriptions of the image content (considered very important by users).

Figure 2: Expectations for Home Photo Management Systems

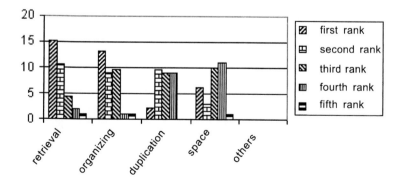

RELATED WORKS ON
CONTENT BASED IMAGE RETRIEVAL

Indexing and retrieval of images is a research field that has been studied for more than a decade. We describe the existing literature based on a simple classification that considers ascending approaches as descriptive approaches that go from the signal (i.e., signal-based), descending approaches more related to the conceptual representation (i.e., symbolic-based), and mixed approaches that use both symbolic and image processing techniques, and interpretation-based approaches.

At present, the overwhelming majority of existing approaches related to image retrieval are descriptive (Smeulder et al., 2000). For instance, consider QBIC (Faloustos et al., 1994; Holt & Weiss, 1997), VisualSeek (Smith et al., 1996a, 1996b), Virage (Gupta, 1995; Bach et al., 1996), and Netra (Ma et al., 1991). All of these approaches use color, texture and shape features to represent the content of images, but they never fill the gap between the description of objects and the actual symbols that correspond to the objects. Such approaches have the great advantage of avoiding promising impossible tasks: the user has to fill the gap between the interpretation and the description of the desired images when she/he asks a query. If the user does not perform this task properly then the results of such systems cannot be guaranteed. On the other hand, the significant advantages of such systems are, first, related to the fact that they can be applied on many kinds of photographs because they use only a little of priori features of image collections (except colors) and, second, that they are almost fully automatic.

Mixed approaches integrate human interaction and image processing techniques. For instance, the MiAlbum (Wenyin et al., 2000; Lu et al., 2000) uses relevance feedback sessions from users to "infer" the link between the features and keywords. MiAlbum counts on the number of relevance feedbacks (from a web site) to obtain accurate indexes. The Photobook (Minka & Picard, 1997) approach also uses interaction to propagate symbolic keywords along the image collections. For the still images, our approach is more related to the mixed approaches. We consider that face recognition belongs to this class, because the models of faces have to be learned by the system according to some input (face collection). Other works like Bradshaw (2000), Town and Sinclair (2000) or Luo and Etz (2002) are also based on more or less complex approaches to be able to apply symbolic labels to images or image regions.

Descending approaches consider only the interpretation of images. For instance, the EMIR2 model (Mechkour, 1995) used also in the FERMI-CG work (Ounis & Pasça, 1998) focuses on the representation of the interpretation of the image content in terms of objects and relations of objects using a knowledge representation formalism, the conceptual graphs (Sowa, 1984). The Symbolic Description of MPEG-7 (MPEG-7, 2001) also presents a modeling framework for objects and their inter-relations that can be applied on images. The advantage of such approaches is that they directly tackle the symbolic content of images, and are able to represent information that cannot, according to the state of the art in image analysis and computer vision, be extracted automatically. They also consider information that deals with purely symbolic characteristics (like generic/specific relationships between objects, or part-of relationships). It is well known, however, that such manual indexing data is not very consistent across human beings, and so great care has to be taken during such an indexing process. Another major drawback of such descending approaches is that the indexing of images is then a tedious process. However, speech analysis may ease the indexing drudgery and aid the retrieval process, like with Show&Tell (Srihari & Zhang, 2000), Shoebox (Mills et al., 2000) and SmartAlbum (Chen et al., 2002) systems. Sophisticated interaction techniques, like *drag-and-drop*, used in the PhotoFinder project (Schneiderman & Kang, 2000) or propagation techniques like in FotoFile (Kuchinski et al., 1999) can also help significantly. Other approaches intend to use image metadata coming for the camera itself, like (Gargi et al., 2002) using EXIF (EXIF 2.0, 1998) information stored with photographs taken by consumer digital cameras. In this case, the information extracted is numerical, and mixed approaches are devoted to detect and recognize faces. Considering one specific kind of meta-data, namely the date of creation of the photograph, the Calendar Browser (Graham et al., 2002) clusters images and generates a hierarchy to ease the navigation in the consumer image database.

From another perspective, efforts have also been made to develop ways for a consumer to easily browse through his collection of photographs. The PhotoFinder system (Kang & Schneiderman, 2000) presents a browser with a zooming function to provide continuity during the browsing. Fotofile (Kuchinski et al., 1999) proposes hyperbolic trees to rapidly access images.

In the context of home photographs, as we saw earlier in this chapter, the symbolic content of images is much more important than low-level features, that is why our work focuses on such symbolic representations of images. Because a home photo management system has to be easy to use by consumers, it has to be as automatic as possible. That is why we consider mixed approaches that try to extract the symbolic concepts from the image itself.

DIGITAL HOME PHOTO ALBUM INDEXING AND RETRIEVAL

We propose a new methodology to semantically index and retrieve photos. We advocate a learning-based approach that allows creation of semantically meaningful visual vocabularies (e.g., faces, crowd, buildings, sky, foliage, water, etc.) from examples. These semantic visual representations are further spatially aggregated and organized into conceptual graphs for describing the concepts and relations in the image contents. The home users can therefore query the system by visual example(s), by spatial arrangement of visual icons (i.e., a visual query language), and by concepts and relations in text, beyond the conventional indexing and retrieval based on low-level features such as colors, texture, and shapes.

Symbolic Labeling

As we explained earlier in this chapter, consumers think of images using symbols and not low-level features, even if this "high-level" representation is obviously related to the "low-level" pixels seen in the photographs. That is why a large amount of the work in the DIVA project has gone towards automatically associating symbolic descriptions to the photographs. We now explain the different steps that are involved in coming up with accurate descriptions of images. The two approaches used in the context of DIVA generate labels from the low-level image content through the use of probabilistic frameworks and by the learning of visual keywords.

Symbolic labeling can be framed as a problem of classifying an image region (or image patch, fixed-sized block) R to one of several semantic classes C_i, $i = 1, ..., M$. In practice, it is not possible to achieve perfect classification due to the presence of noise and ambiguity in the region features. A better approach is to represent the uncertainty of classification in the semantic labels and to defer the final decision to a latter stage at which the image structure can be taken into account using, for instance, the fuzzy conceptual graph matching method (Mulhem et al., 2001).

Let us denote by $Q_i(R)$ the confidence of classifying region R into semantic class C_i. Then, the symbolic labeling problem can be defined as follows:

Given a region R *and* M *semantic classes* C_i, i = 1, ..., M, *compute the confidence* $Q_i(R)$ *that* R *belongs to* C_i *for each* i.

A region R contains a set of features F_t of type $t = 1, ..., m$, each having a value v_t. Each feature F_t can contain more than one component, like color histograms, Gabor texture features, wavelet features, etc. The symbols F_t and v_t denote the *whole* feature and feature value instead of the individual component.

The standard method of computing $Q_i(R) = Q_i(v_1, ..., v_m)$ is the vector space approach: Regard each set of feature values as a vector $\mathbf{v} = [v_1, ..., v_m]^T$ in a linear vector space, and estimate Q_i using function approximation. It is well known that the various feature types are not independent of each other and the scales of the feature types are different. So, forming a linear vector space by assigning each feature type (or, more commonly, each feature component of each feature type) to an orthogonal dimension of the vector space is not expected to produce reliable results in general.

Instead, we adopt a probabilistic method of computing $Q_i(R)$ by estimating the conditional probability $P(C_i|v_t)$. The approach encompasses the following characteristics:

- It can make use of the dissimilarity measures that are appropriate for the various types of features (Leow & Li, 2001; Puzicha et al., 1999) instead of the Euclidean distance.
- It does not require the use of weights to combine the various feature types.
- It adopts a learning approach that can adapt incrementally to the inclusion of new training samples, feature types, and semantic classes.

The probabilistic labeling method consists of two stages: (1) semantic class learning and (2) region labeling.

Semantic Class Learning

The goal of the semantic class learning stage is to determine the conditional probabilities associated with each semantic class. This is accomplished by first partitioning the space of each feature type into discrete regions of approximately uniform probability density. An adaptive clustering algorithm is applied to cluster a set of training sample regions R_j, each assigned a pre-defined semantic class C_i, in the space of each feature type:

Adaptive Clustering
Repeat
> For each feature value v_t of each region,
>> Find the nearest cluster Ω_{tk} to v_t.
>> If no cluster is found or distance $d(\Omega_{tk}, v_t) \geq s$,
>>> create a new cluster with feature v_t;
>> Else, if $d(\Omega_{tk}, v_t) \leq r$,
>>> add feature value v_t to cluster Ω_{tk}.
>> For each cluster Ω_{ti},
>>> If cluster Ω_{ti} has at least Nm feature values,
>>>> update centroid of cluster Ω_{ti};
>>> Else, remove cluster Ω_{ti}.

The centroid of cluster Ω_{ti} is a generalized mean of the feature values in the cluster and the function $d(\Omega_{tk}, v_t)$ is a dissimilarity measure appropriate for the feature type t (Leow & Li, 2001; Puzicha et al., 1999). In the current implementation, the following feature types are used:

- *Adaptive color histograms:*

  An adaptive color histogram is obtained by performing adaptive clustering of the colors in an image (Leow & Li, 2001). Since different adaptive histograms can have different numbers of bins and different bin centroids, Euclidean distance and Euclidean mean cannot be applied on adaptive histograms. Instead, the weighted correlation dissimilarity measure (Leow & Li, 2001) is used to compute the dissimilarity between two adaptive histograms, which has been shown to give better performance than the Earth Mover's Distance (Leow & Li, 2001). For computing cluster centroids in region clustering, a special histogram merging operation is used, which has been shown to produce the correct mean of histograms (Leow, 2002).

- *MRSAR texture features:*

  The usual dissimilarity measure for MRSAR is the Mahalanobis distance and the Euclidean mean is used to compute cluster centroids.

- *Gabor texture features:*

  Weighted-mean-variance (WMV) as defined in (Ma & Manjunath, 1996) is a good dissimilarity measure for Gabor texture features. For computing the cluster centroids, Euclidean mean is used.

- *Edge histograms:*

  Normalized edge direction and magnitude histograms as defined for MPEG7 (MPEG-7, 2001) are extracted from the images. For these features, Euclidean distance and Euclidean mean are used for region clustering.

After the clustering has converged (or a fixed number of iterations has been performed), some training regions may remain unclustered. In this case, the cluster nearest to an unclustered training region can be expanded to include the region. This will result in clusters having different radii r_{tk}.

The clustering process produces a set of clusters Ω_{tk}, for each feature type t. After clustering, the conditional probability $P(C_i|\Omega_{tk})$ for semantic class C_i given cluster Ω_{tk} is estimated. Assuming that the distribution within each cluster is uniform, then $P(C_i|\Omega_{tk})$ can be estimated from the number of regions in the cluster:

$$P(C_i \mid \Omega_{tk}) = \frac{P(C_i, \Omega_{tk})}{P(\Omega_{tk})} = \frac{|C_i \cap \Omega_{tk}|}{|\Omega_{tk}|}$$

where $|\Omega_{tk}|$ denotes the number of regions in cluster Ω_{tk} and $|C_i \cap \Omega_{tk}|$ the number of regions in Ω_{tk} that belong to semantic class C_i.

To combine multiple feature types, we can determine the cluster combinations $\Psi(\tau, \kappa, n) = \{\Omega_{\tau(1),\kappa(1)}, ..., \Omega_{\tau(n),\kappa(n)}\}$, $\tau(i) \neq \tau(j)$ for $i \neq j$, that have high probabilities of associating to some semantic classes C_i:

$$P(C_i \mid \Psi(\tau, \kappa, n) = P(C_i \mid \Omega_{\tau(1),\kappa(1)}, ...\Omega_{\tau(n),\kappa(n)}))$$
$$= \frac{|C_i \cap \bigcap_l \Omega_{\tau(l),\kappa(l)}|}{|\bigcap_l \Omega_{\tau(l),\kappa(l)}|}.$$

The functions $\tau(l)$, $l = 1, ..., n$, denote a combination of feature types and $\kappa(l)$ a combination of cluster indices.

Region Labeling

After the learning stage, a region R can be labeled by determining the associated semantic classes. Given the region R, which contains a set of feature values v_t, the nearest clusters that contain the feature values v_t, for each feature type t, are determined. Next, the clusters found are matched with the stored cluster combinations, obtained during the learning stage, that are associated with some semantic classes. The confidence measure $Q_i(R)$ can now be computed from the conditional probabilities of the matching cluster combinations $\Psi(\tau, \kappa, n)$:

$$Q_i(R) = \max_{\tau, \kappa, n} P(C_i \mid \Psi(\tau, \kappa, n))$$

Note that $Q_i(R)$ as defined in the above equation is no longer a conditional probability:

- The C_i's in the equation may be conditioned on different sets of feature types.
- While $\sum_i P(C_i \mid \Psi(\tau, \kappa, n)) = 1$ for each cluster combination $\Psi(\tau, \kappa, n)$, the sum

$$\sum_i Q_i(R) \neq 1 \text{ in general.}$$

Nevertheless, $Q_i(R)$ is derived based on conditional probabilities and is, thus, a good measure of the confidence that region R belongs to class C_i.

Symbolic Indexing

Symbolic labeling is the first step to obtain symbolic descriptions of images. The next step is to represent the content of images in a powerful and efficient representation. This is achieved using two different *points of view* of images: the use of visual keywords that integrate the ambiguous interpretation of regions, and the use of extended conceptual graph formalism that is able to support the hierarchies of concepts and complex relationships.

Visual Keywords

The Visual Keyword approach (Lim, 2001) is a new attempt to achieve content-based image indexing and retrieval beyond the feature-based (e.g., Faloustos et al., 1994) and region-based (e.g., Smith et al., 1996a) approaches. Visual keywords are intuitive and flexible visual prototypes extracted or learned from a visual content domain with relevant semantics labels. An image is indexed as a spatial distribution of visual keywords whose certainty values are computed via multi-scale view-based detection.

The indexing process has four key components (square boxes) as shown in Figure 3. First, a visual vocabulary and thesaurus is constructed (keyword definition) from samples of a visual content domain. Then, an image to be indexed is compared against the visual vocabulary to detect visual keywords (keyword detection) automatically. Thirdly, the fuzzy detection results are registered as a *Fuzzy Object Map* (FOM) and further aggregated spatially (spatial summary) into a *Spatial Aggregation Map* (SAM). Last but not least, with the visual thesaurus, the SAM can be further abstracted (keyword abstraction) to a simpler representation, *Concept Aggregation Map* (CAM).

Visual keywords are visual prototypes specified or learned from domain-relevant regions of sample images. A set of labels $S^L_{VK} = \{C_i\}$ is assigned to these visual prototypes as a vocabulary. The labels C_i correspond to the semantic classes described later in this chapter. Figure 4 shows some examples of visual keywords used in our experiment.

Figure 3: Workflow of the Indexing Process Based on Visual Keywords

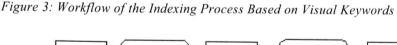
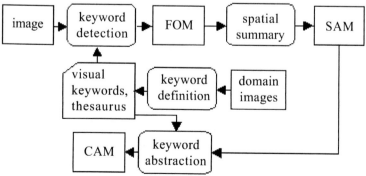

Figure 4: One Visual Keyword from Each Visual Class: Face, Crowd, Sky, Ground, Water, Foliage, Mountain/Rock and Building

An image to be indexed is scanned with square windows of different scales. Each scanned window is a visual token reduced to a feature vector similar to those of the visual keywords previously constructed. Figure 5 shows a schematic diagram of the architecture of image indexing (please refer to Lim, 2001 for details). The Fuzzy Object Map actually represents the probabilities of the different labels for the considered window.

Visual keywords can be regarded as coordinates that span a new pseudo-object feature space. The scale on each dimension is the probability of that visual keyword being detected at a specific spatial locality in the visual content (Figure 6).

Extended Conceptual Graphs

To handle the needs of consumers in the context of home photo retrieval, we also propose the use of the Conceptual Graph (CG) formalism (Sowa, 1984). A conceptual graph is a directed bipartite graph composed of two kids of nodes: concepts and relations. In the initial definition of (Sowa, 1984), a concept is itself composed by definition of a

Figure 5: Automatic Indexing with Fuzzy Recognition Values for Labeling

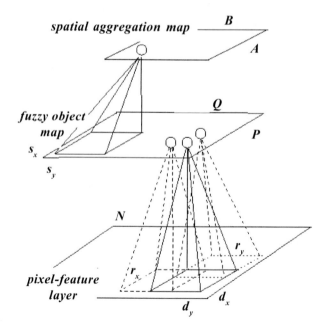

Figure 6: Transforming Feature Space into Visual Keyword Space for a Window of Coordinates (p, q)

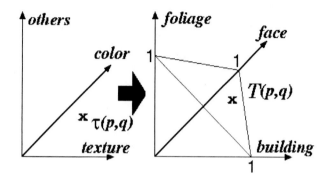

concept type and a referent. Concept types are organized in a hierarchy, representing for instance that the concept type Man is a specific of the concept type Human. In a concept, a referent can be generic, noted *, or individual, like *#john*. A generic referent only denotes any referent. The conformance relationship, namely Conf, exists between a concept type and individual referents that correspond to the concept type. For instance, Conf(Man, *#john*) may exists. Figure 7 presents the alphanumerical and graphical notations for a concept of type Man and of referent *#john*.

Relations are also organized in a lattice reflecting genericity/specificity (reflecting for instance the fact that the relation "*drink*" is a specific of "*ingesting*," but they do not contain any referent. We consider only binary relations in the following, even if the CG formalism allows n-ary relations. Figure 8 shows the alphanumerical and graphical notations for a relation *ingest*.

Figure 9 shows a graph representing "a man named John is walking on a road and is ingesting an apple" under it's alphabetical and graphical notations. To ease the explanation following, we call a triplet (concept, relation, concept) of a graph an *arch*. For instance, the graph of Figure 9 contains two arches.

Figure 7: Alphanumerical (Left) and Graphical (Right) Notations of a Concept

[Man: #john]   Man: #john

Figure 8: Alphanumerical (Left) and Graphical (Right) Notations of a Relation

(ingest)   ingest

Figure 9: Alphanumerical (Top) and Graphical (Bottom) Notations of a Graph

[Man: #john]->(walk)->[Road: *]
->(ingest)->[Apple: *]

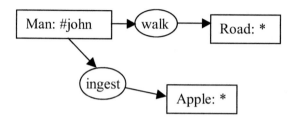

To be able to fit onto an image retrieval model, we use (as in standard text information retrieval systems in Salton & Buckley, 1988) weights that represent the importance of the objects in the graph description. In our case, a weight is assumed to be directly dependant on the relative surface of the objects in the images. Another important element, specific to the fact that the recognition process is not perfect, is to take into account the certainty of recognition in the concept representation.

This leads to the definition of an extension of the usual conceptual graphs, by taking into account the additional information related to conceptual graphs, namely the weights and certainty values. Figure 10 presents the alphanumerical and graphical description of a graph describing that a building *#b1*, having a weight of 0.4 and a certainty of recognition of 0.75, is at the left of a tree *#t1*, having a weight 0.2 and a certainty of recognition 0.9.

Having defined the conceptual graph formalism used to represent the content of images, we focus now on the model of images, i.e., the elements represented in this representation. The concepts types that are defined for the image model are composed of the objects that can occur in images, i.e., the set S^L_{VK}, organized in a hierarchy. Examples of concept types are "building," "foliage," etc. A concept type "Image" denotes one image and the concept type "Region" denotes a region in the image. Based on these concept types, the overall structure of the image model expresses the fact that an image is composed, with the relation "Comp," of regions uniquely identified by a referent, each

Figure 10: Alphanumeric (Top) and Graphical (Bottom) Extended Conceptual Graph

[Building: #b1 0.4 0.75]->(left_of)->[Tree: #t1 0.2 0.9]

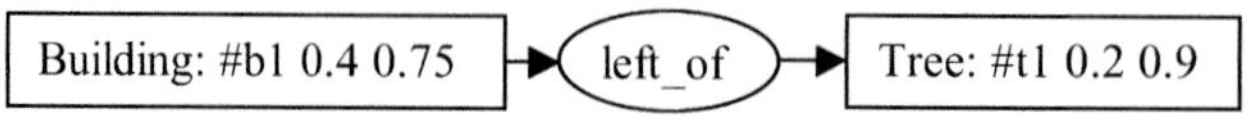

Building: #b1 0.4 0.75 → left_of → Tree: #t1 0.2 0.9

Figure 11: An Example of the Graph-Based Content Representation (Bottom) for One Image (Top)

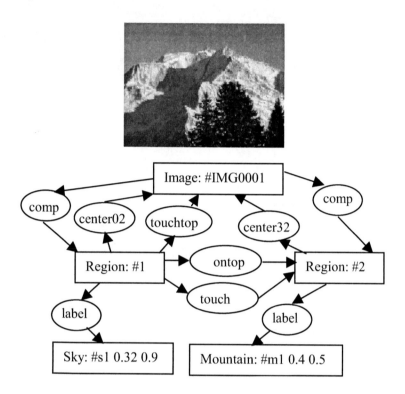

region being associated by a relation "Label" to an object type uniquely identified by a referent. The other relations between the concept Image of an image and its Regions describe the spatial position of center of gravity of the region (with the relations "center00", ..., "center44"), and if the regions touch the border of the photograph (touch_top, touch_bottom, touch_right, touch_left). Between region concepts, relations express if the region touches (relation "touch") and the relative position of regions ("left_of," "on_top," "under," "right_of"). Figure 11 presents on its top part a photograph and on its bottom part an excerpt of the extended graph that describes its content. In this figure, only the weights and certainty values of the object are presented.

That is such representation of the photograph contents that are used during the retrieval based on graphs.

Retrieval

The retrieval of images is based on the two representations presented before: the visual keywords and the extended conceptual graphs.

Visual Keywords

As SAM (or CAM) summarises the visual content of an image, similarity matching between two images can be computed as the weighted average of the similarities between the corresponding tessellated blocks of the images:

$$\lambda(x,y) = \frac{\sum_{(a,b)} \omega(a,b)\lambda(a,b)}{\sum_{(a,b)} \omega(a,b)}$$

and

$$\lambda(a,b) = 1 - \frac{1}{2}\left|SAM_x(a,b) - SAM_y(a,b)\right|$$

where $\omega(a,b)$ is the weight assigned to the block (a,b) in SAM and $\lambda(a,b)$ is computed using city block distance $|.|$ between two corresponding blocks (a,b) of the images. For the query processing of QBE in our experiment, we adopted the tessellation (and their relative weights $\omega(a,b)$) as depicted in Figure 12.

When multiple query examples (say q_1 to q_k) are selected for QBE, the RSV for an image d in the database is computed as $RSV(SAM_d, \{SAM_{qi}\}) = max_i(\lambda(d,q_i))$.

In summary, the VK approach provides a simple, compact, and efficient representation for multiple labeling of image elements. The simple and fast similarity matching process also takes care of absolute spatial relations as specified in the tessellation of SAM.

Extended Conceptual Graphs

The retrieval process using conceptual graphs is based on the fact that a query is also expressed under the form of a CG. Without going into details, a simple grammar composed of a list of objects names and relations is easily translated into a graph, for instance the string: "people left of foliage" is translated into the graph of Figure 13. In this figure, the concepts are all assumed to have a weight of one and a certainty of recognition of one.

The matching process is two fold:

- First, we select the images that answer the query. This selection is based on the projection operators on a conceptual graph (Sowa, 1984). The projection operator intends to determine if the query graph is a sub-graph of an image graph, taking into account the lattices of concept types and of relations. If we consider the query example of Figure 13, an image containing a photograph of John (a Man, and then

Figure 12: Tessellation and Weights for Similarity Matching in QBE

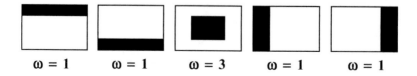

$\omega = 1$ $\omega = 1$ $\omega = 3$ $\omega = 1$ $\omega = 1$

Figure 13: A Query Graph Example

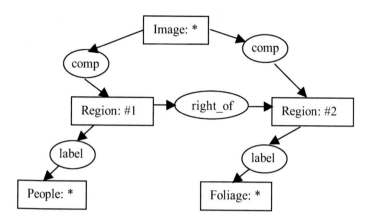

a people) at the right a pine tree (a specific of foliage) will be selected because the query graph is included, according to the concept type and relation hierarchies, in the image graph. Because a query graph may be projected into an image graph more than once, more than one projection may exist.

- Second, we compute the relevance status value (RSV) for one query graph g_q and one document graph g_d. This relevance value computation is related to the fact that ranking query answers is a must for any information retrieval system, thus, for image retrieval ones. This matching value is computed according to the weights of the matching arches a_q (a component of a graph of the form $[Type_{di}: referent_{di} \mid w_{di} \mid c_{di}] \rightarrow (Relation_{dj}) \rightarrow [Type_{dk}: referent_{dk} \mid w_{dk} \mid c_{dk}].$) and the weights of the matching concepts c_d of g_d. The relevance status value for one query graph g_q and one document graph g_d is defined as:

$$RSV(g_d, g_q) = \max_{p_q \in \pi_{g_q}(g_d)} \left(\sum_{c_d \text{ concept of } g_d} match_c(c_d, \pi\, c_d) \right.$$
$$\left. + \sum_{\substack{a_d \text{ arch of } g_d \text{ that} \\ \text{is corresponding to} \\ a_q \text{ of } p_q}} match_a(a_d, a_q) \right)$$

where $\pi_{g_q}(g_d)$ is the set of possible projections of the query graph into the image graph. The RSV formula may be compared to a dot product where the actual importance of arches and concepts of the image graph is one vector and the matching of the image parts and query parts forms another vector. The matching value $match_c$ between an image document concept $c_d [Type_{di}: referent_{di} \mid w_{di} \mid c_{di}]$ and a query concept $c_q [Type_{ql}: referent_{ql} \mid 1.0 \mid 1.0]$ takes into account the fact that the weight and the certainty of recognition play

Figure 14: The DIESKAU Interface

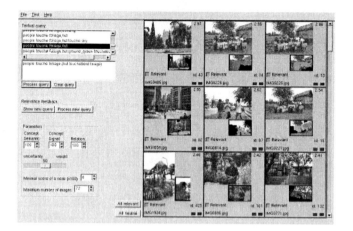

both a role during retrieval, and is computed as: $\sqrt[\tau]{w_{di}} \cdot {}^{1/}\sqrt[\tau]{c_{di}}$. The parameter τ is defined experimentally. The matching value of arches is based on the importance of the considered arch $[Type_{di}: referent_{di} \mid w_{di} \mid c_{di}] \rightarrow (Relation_{dj}) \rightarrow [Type_{dk}: referent_{dk} \mid w_{dk} \mid c_{dk}]$ of the document: $\min(\sqrt[\tau]{w_{di}} \cdot {}^{1/}\sqrt[\tau]{c_{di}}, \sqrt[\tau]{w_{dk}} \cdot {}^{1/}\sqrt[\tau]{c_{dk}})$; this value is inspired from a fuzzy logic interpretation of conjunction. We remind that these values are computed only when we know that the query graph has at least one projection into the image document graph, so we ensure the meaning of the computed values.

STILL PHOTOGRAPHS MANAGEMENT

As we emphasized previously, home photographs management systems are not only limited to the retrieval features. We present here two of the prototypes developed in the DIVA project: one, namely DIESKAU, concentrates more on indexing/retrieval using extended conceptual graphs, while the second, namely PhotoCorner, concentrates on retrieval, albums management and dynamic presentation tools.

The first one, DIESKAU (Digital Image rEtrieval System based on Knowledge representAtion and image featUres), allows precise descriptions of the targeted images using textual descriptions of images. The core of the system is based on an efficient implementation of the conceptual graphs formalism. Figure 14 presents a text query where a user looks for images containing people close to foliage and containing preferably a specific kind of building, namely a hut, touching one side of the photograph.

The results presented in the right-hand side of the figure shows the results obtained for this query. The lower left part of the interface allows the user to define the different uses of the parameters of the system during the retrieval process, namely putting more or less emphasize on the relations, concepts, certainty of recognition of importance. This interface allows, also, the use of query by example to retrieve images.

Figure 15: PhotoCorner Web-Based Interface

The DIESKAU interface is useful for very precise query expressions or fine-tuning of the retrieval process. However, consumers prefer more simple ways to retrieve images. That is why we describe a web-based online photo-sharing system (Figure 15), PhotoCorner, that allows home users to upload, manage, view, search, and share their photo albums anywhere from both web browsers as well as mobile wireless devices (e.g., PocketPC). The goal of such a system is the answer to the problem faced by home users that want to access their albums anytime, anywhere.

Images can be retrieved by several means, namely by text queries, by image examples and by sketching. Figure 15 presents on the right part a query based on sketching that expresses the fact that the user is looking for images containing people in the middle of the photograph, surrounded on the left and right-hand sides by foliage. The results are then presented in the center part of the figure. The right part of Figure 15 is dedicated to the different functions proposed by the system, like access to previously defined albums, access to friends' albums, and creation of albums.

The system also provides a user-friendly authoring tool for adventurous users to create their own slide show presentation styles for the photo albums, if they do not like the slide show templates provided. As the authoring tool is based on the open and declarative SMIL W3C standard (Synchronized Multimedia Integration Language, 2001), the users can enjoy a truly multimedia viewing experience of their memorable photos synchronized with background music, narrations, text captions, and transitions, over the web (desktop and TV) and on mobile devices. Figure 16 presents the authoring tool used to create such animated presentations. Going from top to bottom, the user decides the style she/he wants for the presentation, the "Slide Layout" part allows the user to define when to present the photographs and what information to display along the photographs themselves, the "Displaying of Photos" lists the photographs to be presented, as well as the transition effects that can be used between photographs. Figure 17 presents the first two images from the presentation generated in Figure 16.

Figure 16: PhotoCorner Authoring Tool

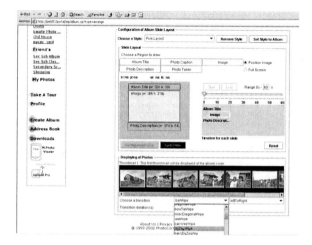

EXPERIMENTS

This section is dedicated to present evaluation results from the retrieval functionalities of the prototype.

Our experiments were conducted on a set of 2,400 real family photographs collected over a period of five years. Figure 18 displays typical photographs in this collection and Figure 19 shows some of the photographs with inferior quality (left to right): fading black and white, flashy, blur, noisy, dark, and over-exposed photographs. These inferior quality photographs could affect any automatic indexing system but they were kept in our test collection to reflect the complexity of original and realistic family photographs. The 2,400 photographs were indexed automatically as described in this chapter. The detection of faces in the photographs was further enhanced with specialized face detector (Rowley et al., 1998). The overall number of labels for VK and CG are 85 and 110, respectively. CG also uses 48 relations, and applies symmetry and transitivity among relations when needed.

Figure 17: Samples from Photographs Presentation

Figure 18: Typical Family Photographs Used in our Experiment

Figure 19: Some of the Inferior Quality Family Photographs

We defined 24 queries and their ground truths among the 2,400 photographs (Table 1): the queries cover a wide range of potential queries, like close-up portraits (queries Q1, Q5), relative locations of objects (queries Q10, Q12, etc.), absolute location of objects (queries Q2-4, Q24), and generic concepts ("large group of people," "indoor," "object," etc.). For each query listed in Table 1, we selected three relevant photographs as QBE input to the VK subsystem and constructed relevant textual query terms as QBS input to the CG subsystem. The query processing for QBE/VK, QBS/CG, and RSV integration are carried out according to the previous descriptions. We focus initially on the general results related to the experiment. Figure 20 presents the average recall/precision results (over the 24 queries) obtained for the VK and CG only and for the best combination of both. We first discuss the reason why the VK results are more precise than those of the CG.

The CG approach represents only the most probable label of an element recognized in a photograph. When the indexing is manually assisted we have very accurate descriptions. But here, the indexing is automatic and errors are inevitable, and this leads to the lack of precision of the CG approach in our results. On the contrary, the VK approach preserves the fuzziness of the labels during similarity matching and this helps to increase the quality of the results.

The combined result shows that our integrated approach attains an increase of precision (+8.1% compared to the VK approach), implying that the integrated approach outperforms each of the individual subsystems. We also notice that the improvement of the precision values at the 0.2 and 0.4 recall points is greater than 11%, which leads us to indicate that the combination seems to favor the increase of precision for low recall values. This is very important for a practical system to be used by home users. For the query Q11 for instance, "people between foliage," the average precision is 0.56 for the VK and 0.36 for the CG, but the combination provides an average precision of 0.62 (+10.7% over VK). This shows that, to a great extent, when the query is general, the query by example process is not appropriate and the use of a higher-level representation such as a CG that includes hierarchies of relevant concepts is useful even if the CG representation may not be perfect.

Table 1: The Queries Defined on the Family Photograph Collection

Q1: Close-up of people	Q13: People in front of building (or artifacts)
Q2: Small group of people at the center	Q14: People in front of mountain/rocks
Q3: Large group of people at the center	Q15: People between water
Q4: Any people at the center	Q16: People on one side of water
Q5: Close-up of people, indoor	Q17: Flowers in a garden
Q6: Small group of people, indoor	Q18: In a park or on a field
Q7: Large group of people, indoor	Q19: Close-up of building
Q8: Any people, indoor	Q20: Road/street scene in a city
Q9: Any people	Q21: Cityscape (view from far)
Q10: People near/besides foliage	Q22: Mountain (view from far)
Q11: People between foliage	Q23: At a (swimming) pool side
Q12: People near/besides building (or artifacts)	Q24: Object at the center, indoor

To be more precise about the results for low recall values, Table 2 presents the average precision values at 20, 30, 50, and 100 documents for the VK, CG and integrated approach. We chose these recall points from the fact that for image retrieval, the system is able to present 20 or 30 image thumbnails per page (or screen), and browsing a set of 50 or 100 images is not too painful for users (for instance, the well known Google web retrieval system (http://www.google.com) presents by default 20 query results for images and 10 query results for text).

If we analyse the results of Table 2 according to numbers of relevant documents, we notice that at 20 documents the recall value is increased by around 3%; so there is around 0.6 more document retrieved on 20 compared to the VK results. The same process applied to the 30, 50 and 100 document precision values gives that the combination finds around 1.5 more relevant documents in the first 30, 2.5 for the first 50 documents and 5.21 more relevant documents in the first 100. Both results shows that the combination of VK and CG approaches that consider different levels of representations provides better results that are worth the combined use of VK and CG approaches.

Figure 20: Recall vs. Precision

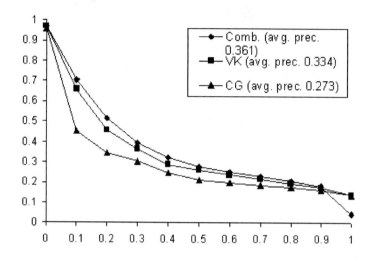

CONCLUSION

In this chapter, we have first analyzed the needs of digital home photo album users based on both the actual technological trends as well as by means of a user survey. This analysis brings out certain key points to be kept in mind for a designer of such digital albums:

- Need to build usable systems, especially given the enormous diversity of the users
- Need to share photos as well as store photos
- There will always be a plethora of data formats, capture and storage devices as well as communication channels
- Sharing can be on a global scale, yet should allow for crisp customization
- Albums must observe and learn (or be taught) quirks, preferences and nuances of its user

We have then described in detail about our efforts in the DIVA project to build innovative and functional tools that simplify the home users' effort in organizing, retrieving, viewing, and sharing their digital image albums. Since home photos are meant

Table 2: Precision at 20, 30, 50 and 100 Documents

	VK	CG	Comb.
Avg. prec. at 20 doc.	0.592	0.408	0.621
Avg. prec. at 30 doc.	0.517	0.363	0.569
Avg. prec. at 50 doc.	0.437	0.330	0.488
Avg prec. at 100 doc.	0.351	0.305	0.403

for sharing, we need to locate individual images from a collection that conveys a particular thought or mood or idea. In order to do this, adequate content description (metadata) needs to be captured and stored alongside the image. Hence, the ability to annotate photos based on their semantic content is a vital and challenging task. We have primarily emphasized our work on some novel content-based semantic indexing and retrieval techniques. The promising experimental results for these techniques have also been outlined. We subsequently presented our attempts on home photographs management via our DIESKAU and PhotoCorner systems, especially on the retrieval and authoring aspects.

Given that home photo collections already represent an enormous amount of our civilizations' heritage by capturing silhouettes of millions of peoples' daily lives — representing snapshots of celebrations as well as their relationships, building suitable digital albums is an extremely important technological endeavor which needs concentrated attention. We, therefore, believe that striving to achieve these eminently worthwhile goals will yield rich and satisfying research opportunities for technological innovations in the fields of image analysis and vision processing, efficient and effective data storage and retrieval, and human computer interaction among others. While work has already been started as in the case of the DIVA project and the works presented in the references section, a lot more remains to be done before our full set of objectives are met. Our long-term collective desire is to enrich the home users' visual experience in creating and enjoying their digital memories, thereby allowing users to fully participate in this age of visual literacy.

REFERENCES

Bach, J. R., Fuller, C., Gupta A., Hampapur A., Horowitz B., Humphrey, R., Jain R., & Fe Shu, C. (1996). The virage image search engine: An open framework for image management. *Proceedings SPIE Storage and Retrieval for Image and Video Databases, 2670,* (pp. 76-87).

Bradshaw, B. (2000). Semantic-based image retrieval: a probabilistic approach. *ACM Multimedia,* 167-176.

Chalfen, R. M. (1998). Family photograph appreciation: Dynamics of medium. *Interpretation and Memory, Communication and Cognition, 31*(2-3), 161-178.

Chen, J., Tan, T., & Mulhem, P. (2002). SmartAlbum – Toward unification of approaches for image retrieval. *International Conference on Pattern Recognition*, Québec (August, Vol. 3, pp. 983-986).

Faloutsos, C., Barber, R., Flickner, M., Hafner, J., Niblack, W., Petrovic, D., & Equitz, W. (1994). Efficient and effective querying by image content. *Journal of Intelligent Information Systems,* 3, 231-262.

FlipAlbum. (2002). http://www.flipalbum.com.

Gargi, U., Deng, Y., & Tretter, D. R. (2002). Managing and searching personal photo collections. *HP Laboratories Technical Report HPL-2002-67,* Palo Alto, USA.

Graham, A., Garcia-Molina H., Paepcke A., & Winograd, T. (2002). Time as essence for photo browsing through personal digital libraries. *International Workshop on Visual Interfaces for Digital Libraries*, Portland, USA.

Gupta, A. (1995). Visual information retrieval: A Virage perspective. *White paper, Virage Inc.*

Holt, B. & Weiss, K. (1997). The QBIC project in the department of art and art history at UC Davis. *The 60th ASIS Annual Meeting 1997, Digital Collections: Implications for users, Funders, Developers and Maintainers, 34*, (pp. 189-195).

Kang, H. & Schneiderman, B. (2000). Visualization methods for personal photo collections: Browsing and searching in the PhotoFinder. *ACM CIKM 2000*, (pp. 1539-1542). New York.

Kuchinski, A., Pering C., Creech, M. L., Freeze, D., Serra B., & Gwizdka, J. (1999). Fotofile: A consumer multimedia organization and retrieval system. *ACM CHI '99*, (pp. 496-503). Pittsburgh, PA.

Leow, W. K. (2002). The algebra and analysis of adaptive-binning color histograms. *Technical Report No. TRB8/02,* Dept. of Computer Science, School of Computing, National University of Singapore.

Leow, W. K. & Li R. (2001). Adaptive binning and dissimilarity measure for image retrieval and classification. In *Proceedings IEEE Conf. on Computer Vision and Pattern Recognition.*

Lim, J. H. (2001). Building visual vocabulary for image indexation and query formulation. *Pattern Analysis and Applications (Special Issue on Image Indexation), 4* (2/3), 125-139.

Lu, Y., Hu, C., Zhu, X., Zhang, H., & Yang, Q. (2000). A unified framework for semantics and feature based relevance feedback in image retrieval systems. *The 8th ACM Multimedia International Conference*, (November, pp. 31-37). Los Angeles, CA.

Luo, J. & Etz, S. (2002). A physics-motivated approach to detecting sky in photographs. *International Conference on Pattern Recognition,* (Canada, Vol. I, pp. 155-158).

Ma, W. Y. & Manjunath, B. S. (1996). Texture features and learning similarity. *Proceedings IEEE Conference on Computer Vision and Pattern Recognition,* (pp. 425-430).

Ma, W. Y. & Manjunath, B. S. (1997). NETRA: A toolbox for navigating large image databases. *IEEE International Conference on Image Processing (ICIP '97)*, (Vol. I, pp. 568-571).

Martinez, J. (ed.) (2001). MPEG-7 Committee. Overview of the MPEG-7 Standard (version 6.0), Report ISO/IEC JTC1/SC29/WG11 N4509.

Mechkour, M. (1995). An extended model for image representation and retrieval. *Proceedings of the International Conference on Database and Expert System Applications (DEXA '95)*, (UK, pp. 395-404).

Mills, T. J., Pye, D., Sinclair D., & Wood K. R. (2000). Shoebox: A digital photo management system. AT&T Technical Report 2000, 10.

Minka, T. P. & Picard, R. W. (1997). Interactive learning using a "society of models." *Special Issue of Pattern Recognition on Image Databases, 30*(4), 565-581.

Mulhem, P., Leow, W. K., & Lee Y. K. (2001). Fuzzy conceptual graph for matching images of natural scenes. *Proceedings of the International Joint Conf. on Artificial Intelligence,* (pp. 1397-1402).

Ounis, I. & Pasça, M. (1998). RELIEF: Combining expressiveness and rapidity into a single system. *ACM SIGIR* 1998, Melbourne, Australia, 266-274.

Photo Album Software. (2002). http://www.3d-album.com.

Puzicha, J., Buhmann, J. M., Rubner, Y., & Tomasi, C. (1999). Empirical evaluation of dissimilarity for color and texture. *International Conference on Computer Vision '99 (ICCV'99)*, (pp. 1165-1172). Kerkyra, Greece.

Rodden, K. (1999). How people organise their photographs? T*he BCS IRSG 21st Annual Colloquium on Information Retrieval Research (BCS Electronic Workshops in Computing)*. Glasgow, UK.

Rowley, H. A., Baluja S., & Kanade, T. (1998) Neural network-based face detection. *IEEE Trans. on PAMI*, 20(1), 23-38.

Salton, G. & Buckley, C. (1988). Term-weighting approaches in automatic text retrieval. *Information Processing and Management*, 24(5), 5513-523.

Schneiderman, B. & Kang, H. (2000, July). Direct annotation: A drag-and-drop strategy for labeling photos. *The International Conference on Information Visualisation (IV2000)*, (pp. 88-95). London.

Smith, J. R. & Chang, S. F. (1996a). VisualSeek: A Fully automated content-based image query system. T*he ACM Multimedia '96*, (pp. 426-237). Boston, MA, USA.

Smith, J. R. & Chang, S. F (1996b). Tools and techniques for color image retrieval. *IST & SPIE Proc. Storage and Retrieval for Image and Video Databases IV, 2670*, (pp. 87-98).

Sowa, J. F. (1984). *Conceptual Structures: Information Processing in Mind and Machines*. Reading, MA: Addison-Wesley.

Srihari, R. K. & Zhang, Z. (2000). Show&Tell: A semi-automated image annotation system. *IEEE Multimedia*, 7(3), 61-71.

Synchronized Multimedia Integration Language 2.0. (2001, August). W3C Recommendation, http://www.w3.org/TR/2001/REC-smil20-20010807.

Town, C. & Sinclair, D. (2000). Content-based image retrieval using semantic visual categories. *Technical report 2000.14, AT&T Laboratories*. Cambridge, UK.

Wenyin, L., Hu, C., & Zhang, H. (2000). iFind-a system for semantics and feature based image retrieval over Internet. *The 8th ACM Multimedia International Conference*, (November, pp. 477-478). Los Angeles, CA.

Chapter X

Algorithm for the Retrieval of Image with Emergence Index in Multimedia

Sagarmay Deb, University of Southern Queensland, Australia

Yanchun Zhang, Victoria University of Technology, Australia

ABSTRACT

We discuss here emergence phenomenon where we study the hidden meanings of an image. We present this concept in image database access and retrieval of images using this as an index for retrieval. This would give an entirely different search outcome than an ordinary search where emergence is not considered, as consideration of hidden meanings could change the index of a search. We talk about emergence, emergence index and accessing multimedia databases using emergence index to locate geographic areas in this paper along with the algorithm.

INTRODUCTION

Content-based image retrieval (CBIR) is a bottleneck of multimedia database access. Although plenty of research has been dedicated to this area during the last decade, it has yet to attain maturity. Original text-based approaches in image retrieval were time consuming and expensive as they involved manual processing of image data which could sometimes be very voluminous. Attempts have been made to combine text-based and content-based retrieval (Gudivada & Raghavan, 1995) and quite a few models like QBIC, Virage, Excalibur, Attrasoft, Pichunter, VisualSEEK, Chabot, and Photobook have been developed. Fully automated CBIR has been developed very recently using low-level features like color, texture, shape and spatial locations. A few models are now commercially available like QBIC, Virage, Excalibur, Attrasoft and others. Also, non-commercial models developed by universities and research institutions are available. But they do an approximate match between input and objects of image databases. Thorough image segmentation, which is vital to accurate retrieval, is not yet achieved.

CBIR has been defined in three levels. Level 1 talks about finding symmetry between input image and images of databases. To some extent, success has been achieved in this level. Level 2 is about finding semantic meanings out of the image like 'Find a double-decker bus in an image.' Only very limited success has been achieved in this field. One of the best known works in this field is of Forsyth and others (Forsyth et al., 1996) by successfully identifying the picture of a human being within an image and this technique has been applied to other objects. Level 3 is about finding inner meanings of an image like 'Find pain in an image.' This requires very sophisticated and complex logic and segmentation. Very little has been achieved so far in this level with state-of-the-art technology (Eakins & Graham, 1999).

Although quite a few commercial and non-commercial models are developed, none of them attempted to study the implicit meanings of the images. We achieve more accurate and different search outcomes when implicit meanings are also considered. For example, we can consider a square with one diagonal. This is the explicit meaning of the image. But when we consider implicit meanings, we end up getting two triangles in it. This is what we mean by emergence.

We will use content-based image retrieval where we would define our index, based on contents of the image, studying also the emergence phenomenon in the process for a more accurate search.

The chapter provides the definition and application of emergence index using pictures and the application of emergence index in image query processing. The section "Emergence Index" gives the definition and the section "Calculation of Emergence Index Using a Geographic Location" gives the calculation of emergence index and of establishing symmetry for a geographic location. "Algorithm for Accessing Databases with Emergence Index" presents the algorithm for accessing multimedia databases with emergence index. We make our conclusion at the end.

MAIN THRUST OF THE CHAPTER
Emergence Index

Features of an image, which are implicit or hidden, are emergent features if these can be made explicit.

Examples of Emergence

Shape emergence is associated with emergence of individual or multiple shapes. Figure 1 contains examples of shape emergence.

Figure 1: Two Emergent Shapes Derived from the Existing One [The first one is the existing shape whereas the other two are emergent shapes from the first (Gero, n.d.)].

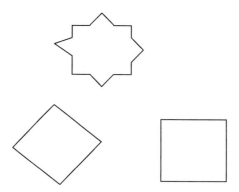

Definition of Emergence Index

Image retrieval where the hidden or emergent meanings of the images are studied and based on those hidden meanings as well as explicit meanings, where there is no hidden meaning at all, an index of search is defined to retrieve images is called emergence index.

Semantic Representation of Images

The symbolic representation of shapes could be defined using infinite maximal lines as:

$$I = \{N; constraints\} \tag{1}$$

where N is the number of infinite maximal lines, which effectively constitutes image I and constraints are limitations, which define behaviors or properties that come out from the infinite maximal lines (Gero, 1992).

Various Mathematical Tools that would be Used in the Definition of the Image

Geometric Property

There are four geometric properties involved in infinite maximal lines: (a) Two lines L_a and L_b are perpendicular, $L_a \perp L_b$. (b) Two lines L_a and L_b are parallel, $L_a // L_b$. (c) Two lines L_a and L_b are skewed, $L_a \times L_b$. (d) Two lines L_a and L_b are coincident, $L_a = L_b$.

Topological Property

Intersection and segment are two properties of a set of infinite maximal lines. If L_a and L_b are two infinite maximal lines then intersection I_{ab} would be denoted by (a) $L_a \times L_b => I_{ab}$, (b) $L_a \perp L_b => I_{ab}$ where => means 'implies.' The first case of the above is the skewness whereas the second case is perpendicularity of the geometric property.

The intersection cannot occur if $L_a // L_b$ or $L_a = L_b$. In other words, parallel behavior of two infinite maximal lines and also coincidence do not generate any intersection.

Properties of intersection (a) I_{ab} is the same as I_{ba}. (b) I_{ab} and I_{bc} are called a collinear intersection in L_b. (c) I_{abc} exists if L_a, L_b and L_c are concurrent.

The segment generated by two intersections is denoted by (I_{ab}, I_{bc}) and this segment lies obviously in infinite maximal line L_b.

There are three types of intersection groups: ordinary groups, adjacent groups and enclosed groups. These three groups indicate three kinds of topological structures, which define intersections and line segments in different ways. An ordinary group could be expressed by a pair of '(' and ')' parentheses. In this case, a line segment could be defined by two intersections. If L_a, L_b and L_c are three lines, then a segment of the line would be (I_{ab}, I_{cb}). The adjacent group is defined by a pair of angles '<' and '>' brackets. Here, only two adjacent intersections can represent a line segment of the order $<I_{ab}, I_{ac}>$. An enclosed group, defined by a pair of square '[' and ']' brackets represent a circuit of line segments. For a triangle it would be $[I_{ab}, I_{ac}, I_{bc}]$.

Dimensional Property

The length of the segment of two intersections is the dimensional property and is denoted by $d(I_{ab}, I_{bc})$ (Deb & Zhang, 2001a).

Calculation of Emergence Index Using a Geographic Location

In order to calculate the emergence index, we use the following equation.

$$EI = f(D,F,V,C,E) \tag{2}$$

where EI stands for emergence index, D for domain where the image belongs, F for features, V for variables which can define the features' constraints under which the features are defined, C for constraints and E for emergence characteristics of images.

We believe any image, static or in motion, could be expressed semantically in terms of the above-mentioned five parameters (Deb & Zhang, 2001).

Calculation of Feature

In this example of a map, we find a park, a lake, roads and residential areas, which cover the remaining part. This map is similar to any other map that could be drawn of part of a township. But, if we look carefully into the picture of the map, we see roads which surround the park and the lake, form the shape of a bowl. We take the shape of the bowl into a coordinate system to analyze it.

Let C_1, C_2, C_3, C_4 and C_5 be the coordinates defining basic vectors where C_1 corresponds to (x_1, y_1), C_2 corresponds (x_2, y_2) and so on.

It is clear C_1, C_2, C_3 and C_4 form a parallelogram. This parallelogram is obtained from the shape of the bowl by first destroying the original shape, then processing the unstructured shape giving rise to a new emergent shape of a parallelogram.

To represent the object of bowl, we use the following equation.

Figure 2: Geographic Location

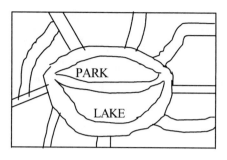

Figure 3: Coordinate System of Shape

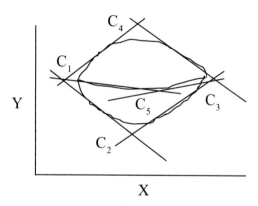

$$O_1 = f(w_1 F_1; w_2 F_2; w_3 F_3; \ldots; w_n F_n) \qquad (3)$$

where $w1$ is the weight of feature F_1, w_2 for F_2 and so on.

The bowl is composed of a lake, a park and surrounding streets. Since the lake is supposed to contain water, the color of the lake can be presumed to be blue and it occupies around 40% of the whole area of the bowl and the color of the water would be blue and is denoted by 2. We assume the park would occupy another 40% of the area and the color would be green which is denoted by 3. Let us assume streets occupy the remaining 20% of the bowl with the color black which is denoted by 5. Hence, if F1 is the standard color feature, then we calculate:

$$w_1 F_1 = (0.4 * 2, 0.4 * 3, 0.2 * 5)$$

Since O_1 would be composed of five coordinate points and if this object O_1 occupies 40% of total image, then the weight-feature factor would be:

$$w_2 F_2 = 0.4 * f((x_1, y_1), (x_2, y_2), \ldots \ldots (x_5, y_5))$$

where $(x_1, y_1), (x_2, y_2), \ldots \ldots (x_5, y_5)$ represents the shape of the object O_1.

Figure 4: Destruction of Original Image

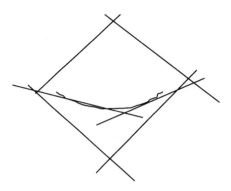

Figure 5: Emergent Shape

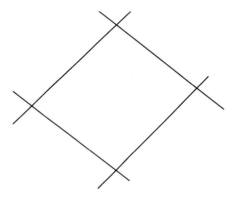

If the background is grass, which is green and occupies 50% of the image, and streets, which are black occupy the remaining 10%, then F_3, which represents background features, and w_3, which represents area covered, in a combined way would be:

$$w_3F_3 = (0.5 * 3, 0.1 * 5)$$

where 3 stands for green color and 5 for black.

If d_1, d_2, d_3, d_4, d_5 and d_6 are the distances between various coordinate points of the object O_1, then:

$$\text{Perimeter of } O_1 = \sum_{i=1}^{6} d_i$$

Since this covers the whole perimeter where there is no undefined or open part, the w_4 would be 1.0. Hence, weight-feature factor becomes in this case:

$$W_4F_4 = 1.0 * \sum_{i=1}^{6} d_i$$

Therefore, O_1 could be represented in this case as:

$$O_1 = f(w_1F_1; w_2F_2; w_3F_3; w_4F_4)$$
$$= ((0.4 * 2, 0.4 * 3, 0.2 * 5); (0.4* \; f((x_1,y_1), (x_2,y_2),......x_5,y_5))); (0.5 * 3, 0.1*5);$$
$$1.0 * \sum_{I=1} d_i).$$

Calculation of Domain
In the hierarchical domain structure since this is related to geographic location, images would lie in the directory containing geographic location.

Variables
In the example image, we have a lake, a park and streets that form a bowl O_1. We already defined the variables for this. They are $(x_1,y_1), (x_2,y_2), \ldots \ldots (x_5,y_5)$.

Constraints
According to our definition of symbolic representation of shape in Equation (1) in section Semantic Representation of Images:

$$I = \{N; constraints\}$$
$$For \; O_1, \; I = \{5; C_1, C_2, C_3, \ldots, C_5\}$$

Emergence
Although object O_1 is basically composed of a lake, a park and streets, it gives rise to the shape of a bowl as we pointed out earlier. This is the emergence output of the image. This is the example of an embedded shape emergence where emergence is a set of the whole image.

Calculation of Index of Input in the Form of a Bowl but Smaller in Size Compared to O_1 and Rotated
The input here comes in the form of a bowl with five intersections of straight lines that define the shape. The shape here is smaller than O_1 and is rotated. Let these intersections be $C_6, C_7, C_8, \ldots, C_{10}$. So the representation in this case is:

$$I = \{5; C_6, C_7, C_8, \ldots, C_{10}\}$$

Figure 6: Input in the Shape of a Bowl

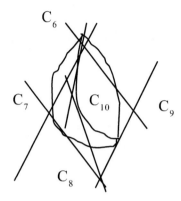

Establish Correspondence Between Input and O_1 of Section Calculation of Emergence Index Using a Geographic Location

Input $= \{5;[C_6,C_7,\ldots\ldots,C_{10}]\}$
$O_1 = \{5;[C_1,C_2,\ldots\ldots,C_5]\}$

Number of Intersections

The number of intersections in input is 5 and in O_1 it is also 5. Hence, they match.

Correspondence

Since the size of input is smaller than O_1, we cannot establish correspondence straightaway.

Let θ_1, θ_2, θ_3, $\ldots\theta_5$ be the angles at the points of intersection in O_1 and let θ_6, θ_7, $\theta_8,\ldots\theta_{10}$ be the angles at the points of intersection in input.

Now if
$$\theta_1 \Leftrightarrow \theta_6$$
$$\theta_2 \Leftrightarrow \theta_7$$
$$\theta_3 \Leftrightarrow \theta_8$$
$$\theta_4 \Leftrightarrow \theta_9$$
$$\theta_5 \Leftrightarrow \theta_{10}$$

then, correspondence between input and O_1 is established although input is smaller in size compared to O_1.

So, if the number of intersections are the same and angles at those intersections correspond to each other in input and O_1, then symmetry is established although input and O_1 are not of the same size.

Since the input is rotated from the vertical axis clockwise, we can obtain further symmetry in the following way.

Let $D_1, D_2, D_3, \ldots\ldots, D6$ be the infinite maximal lines defining the image and $\theta_1', \theta_2', \theta_3', \ldots\ldots, \theta_6'$ be the angles $D_1, D_2, D_3, \ldots\ldots, D_6$ made with the vertical axis, respectively.

Let $D_7, D_8, D9, ..., D_{12}$ be the infinite maximal lines defining the input and $\theta_7{}', \theta_8{}', \theta_9{}', ...,$ $\theta_{12}{}'$ be the angles $D_7, D_8, D_9, ..., D_{12}$ made with the vertical axis, respectively.

Now if
$$\theta_7{}' = \theta_1{}' + \theta$$
$$\theta_8{}' = \theta_2{}' + \theta$$
$$\theta_9{}' = \theta_3{}' + \theta$$
$$\theta_{10}{}' = \theta_4{}' + \theta$$
$$\theta_{11}{}' = \theta_5{}' + \theta$$
$$\theta_{12}{}' = \theta_6{}' + \theta$$

then, it is obvious that input makes a constant angle θ clockwise compared to the object of the image of the database for each and every infinite maximal line.

This establishes further symmetry although the image of the database is rotated by an angle θ.

When we want to locate a particular geographical area and we do not know where to look for it but if we know there are streets in the location that make a bowl, then we can quite easily find that location by having input as image of a bowl which can find the match with the emergent bowl of the map. This would be the advantage of applying this concept of emergence in image retrieval in practice.

Calculation and Establishing Symmetry Between Input and Images of Geographic Location after Emergence of a Different Shape

Calculation of Emergence Index of Emergent Shape

We have seen how emergence has given rise to the shape of a parallelogram from a bowl-shaped geographic region in section Calculation of Emergence Index using a Geographic Location. Now we go to calculate the emergence index of this parallelogram. This is the outcome of an illusory shape emergence where contours defining the shape are perceived though no contours are physically present.

In order to calculate the emergence index, we use the Equation (2) defined in section Calculation of Emergence Index using a Geographic Location here as well.

Calculation of Feature

Let C_1, C_2, C_3 and C_4 be the coordinates defining basic vectors where C_1 corresponds to (x_1, y_1), C_2 corresponds (x_2, y_2) and so on.

To represent the object of parallelogram, we use Equation (3) of Calculation of Emergence Index using a Geographic Location:

$$O_2 = f(w_1 F_1; w_2 F_2; w_3 F_3; .....; w_n F_n).$$

The parallelogram is composed of a lake, a park, surrounding streets and little bit of residential area. If the lake occupies around 35% of the whole area of the parallelogram and the color of water is blue then it is denoted by 2. We assume the park would occupy another 35% of the area and the color would be green which is denoted by 3. Let us assume streets occupy 20% of the bowl with black color which is denoted by 5. Also, if residential

Figure 7: Emergent Shape

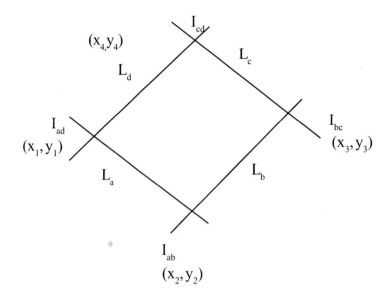

areas occupy the remaining 10% which is green then it would be denoted by 3. So, if F_1 is the standard color feature as we defined earlier then we calculate:

$$w_1 F_1 = (0.35 * 2, 0.45 * 3, 0.2 * 5)$$

Since O_2 would be composed of 4 coordinate points and if this object O_2 occupies 45% of the total image then the weight-feature factor would be:

$$w_2 F_2 = 0.45 * f((x_1, y_1), (x_2, y_2), \ldots \ldots (x_4, y_4))$$

where $(x_1, y_1), (x_2, y_2), \ldots \ldots (x_4, y_4)$ represent the shape of the object O_2.

If the background is grass, which is green and occupies 45% of the image, and streets, which are black occupy the remaining 10%, then F_3, which represent background features, and w_3, which represents area covered, in combined way would be:

$$w_3 F_3 = (0.45 * 3, 0.1 * 5)$$

where 3 stands for green color and 5 for black.

If d_1, d_2, d_3 and d_4 are the distances between various coordinate points of the object O_2, then:

$$\text{Perimeter of } O_2 = \sum_{i=1}^{4} d_i$$

Since this covers the whole perimeter where there is no undefined or open part, w_4 would be 1.0. Hence, weight-feature factor becomes in this case:

$$w_4F_4 = 1.0 * \sum_{i=1}^{4} d_i$$

Therefore, O_2 could be represented in this case as:

$$O_2 = f(w_1F_1; w_2F_2; w_3F_3; w_4F_4)$$
$$= ((0.35 * 2, 0.45 * 3, 0.2 * 5); (0.45 * f((x_1,y_1), (x_2,y_2), \ldots \ldots (x_4,y_4)));$$

$$(0.45 * 3, 0.1 * 5); 1.0 * \sum_{i=1}^{4} d_i$$

Calculation of Domain

In the hierarchical domain structure, since this is related to geographic location, images would lie in the directory containing geographic location.

Variables

For object O_2, the variables are obviously $(x_1,y_1),(x_2,y_2),\ldots,(x_4,y_4)$. The four sides are L_a, L_b, L_c and L_d.

Constraints

According to our definition of symbolic representation of shape in Equation (1) in section Semantic Representation of Images:

$$I = \{N; constraints\}$$

For O_2, the number of sides is 4 and the distances between (x_1,y_1), (x_2,y_2), (x_3,y_3), and (x_4,y_4) are the same. In other words:

$$d\{(x_1,y_1),(x_2,y_2)\} = d\{(x_2,y_2),(x_3,y_3)\} = d\{(x_3,y_3),(x_4,y_4)\} = d\{(x_4,y_4),(x_1,y_1)\}.$$
$$d(I_{ad},I_{ab}) = d(I_{ab},I_{bc}) = d(I_{bc},I_{cd}) = d(I_{cd},I_{ad}).$$

Then $L_a//L_c$, $L_b//L_d$ since opposite sides are parallel.

Since θ_1, θ_2, θ_3, θ_4 are the angles at the points of intersection in O_2 and it is a parallelogram, hence $\theta_1 = \theta_3$ and $\theta_2 = \theta_4$.

Emergence

The shape of the parallelogram out of a bowl is the outcome of illusory emergence as we mentioned earlier.

This completes the calculation of emergence index of Equation (2) in this case.

Calculation of Index of Input in the Form of a Parallelogram

If the input comes in the form of a parallelogram as shown in Figure 8, then we have the coordinates, which define the parallelogram as (x_{11},y_{11}), (x_{12},y_{12}), (x_{13},y_{13}) and (x_{14},x_{14}) representing C_{11}, C_{12}, C_{13} and C_{14}, respectively. The sides are L_e, L_f, L_g, L_h.

Also, the number of sides is 4 and the distances between (x_{11},y_{11}), (x_{12},y_{12}), (x_{13},y_{13}), and (x_{14},y_{14}) are same. In other words:

$$d\{(x_{11},y_{11}),(x_{12},y_{12})\}=d\{(x_{12},y_{12}),(x_{13},y_{13})\}=d\{(x_{13},y_{13}),(x_{14},y_{14})\}=d\{(x_{14},y_{14}),(x_{11},y_{11})\}.$$
$$d(I_{eh},I_{ef})=d(I_{ef},I_{fg})=d(I_{fg},I_{gh})=d(I_{gh},I_{eh}).$$

Then $L_e//L_g$, $L_f//L_h$ since opposite sides are parallel.

If θ_{11}, θ_{12}, θ_{13}, θ_{14} are the angles at the points of intersection and since it is a parallelogram, then $\theta_{11}=\theta_{13}$ and $\theta_{12}=\theta_{14}$.

Establish Correspondence Between the Input (Parallelogram) and Image

Ordinary Group Intersections in Each Image

Here we compare the representation of the input with O_2 in section Calculation of Emergence Index of Emergent Shape.

Input $= \{4;[I_{eh},I_{ef},I_{fg},I_{gh}]\}$
$O_2 = \{4;[I_{ad},I_{ab},I_{bc},I_{cd}]\}$

Figure 8: Input as a Parallelogram

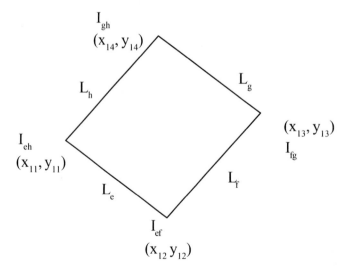

Number of Infinite Maximal Lines

We notice the number of infinite maximal lines in each case is 4.

Corresponding Equivalence

The corresponding equivalence of various segments is:

$$L_e \Leftrightarrow L_a \wedge L_f \Leftrightarrow L_b \wedge L_g \Leftrightarrow L_c \wedge L_h \Leftrightarrow L_d$$

Also, the corresponding equivalence of various intersections are:

$$I_{eh} \Leftrightarrow I_{ad} \wedge I_{ef} \Leftrightarrow L_{ab} \wedge I_{fg} \Leftrightarrow I_{bc} \wedge I_{gh} \Leftrightarrow I_{cd}$$

Number of Intersections

The number of intersections in each case is 4.

Geometric Constraints of Infinite Maximal Lines

Input has
$$I_{eh} \Leftrightarrow L_e \times L_h$$
$$I_{ef} \Leftrightarrow L_e \times L_f$$
$$I_{fg} \Leftrightarrow L_f \times L_g$$
$$I_{gh} \Leftrightarrow L_g \times L_h$$

O_2 has
$$I_{ad} \Leftrightarrow L_a \times L_d$$
$$I_{ab} \Leftrightarrow L_a \times L_b$$
$$I_{bc} \Leftrightarrow L_b \times L_c$$
$$I_{cd} \Leftrightarrow L_c \times L_d$$

Dimensional Constraints of Segments

Since the number of intersections in input and O_2 is same, we deduct

In input
$$L_e \times L_h \wedge L_e \times L_f \Leftrightarrow (I_{eh}, I_{ef})$$
$$L_e \times L_f \wedge L_f \times L_g \Leftrightarrow (I_{ef}, I_{fg})$$
$$L_f \times L_g \wedge L_g \times L_h \Leftrightarrow (I_{fg}, I_{gh})$$
$$L_g \times L_h \wedge L_e \times L_h \Leftrightarrow (I_{gh}, I_{eh})$$

So dimensional constraints in input are:
$$d(I_{eh}, I_{ef}), d(I_{ef}, I_{fg}), d(I_{fg}, I_{gh}), d(I_{gh}, I_{eh})$$

In O_2
$$L_a \times L_d \wedge L_a \times L_b \Leftrightarrow (I_{ad}, I_{ab})$$
$$L_a \times L_b \wedge L_b \times L_c \Leftrightarrow (I_{ab}, I_{bc})$$
$$L_b \times L_c \wedge L_c \times L_d \Leftrightarrow (I_{bc}, I_{cd})$$
$$L_c \times L_d \wedge L_a \times L_d \Leftrightarrow (I_{cd}, I_{ad})$$

So dimensional constraints in input are:
$$d(I_{ad}, I_{ab}), d(I_{ab}, I_{bc}), d(I_{bc}, I_{cd}), d(I_{cd}, I_{ad})$$

Corresponding Intersections

$$L_e \leftrightarrow L_a \wedge L_h \leftrightarrow L_d \wedge L_e \times L_h \wedge L_a \times L_d => I_{eh} \leftrightarrow I_{ad}$$
$$L_e \leftrightarrow L_a \wedge L_f \leftrightarrow L_b \wedge L_e \times L_f \wedge L_a \times L_b => I_{ef} \leftrightarrow I_{ab}$$
$$L_f \leftrightarrow L_b \wedge L_g \leftrightarrow L_c \wedge L_f \times L_g \wedge L_b \times L_c => I_{fg} \leftrightarrow I_{bc}$$
$$L_g \leftrightarrow L_c \wedge L_h \leftrightarrow L_d \wedge L_g \times L_h \wedge L_c \times L_d => I_{gh} \leftrightarrow I_{cd}$$

Corresponding Angles

If $\theta_1, \theta_2, \theta_3, \theta_4$ are the angles at the points of intersection of O_2 and $\theta_5, \theta_6, \theta_7, \theta_8$ are that of input and if $\theta_1 = \theta_5, \theta_2 = \theta_6, \theta_3 = \theta_7, \theta_4 = \theta_8$ then, corresponding angles are also the same.

Therefore, the input in the form of a parallelogram and image O_2 are symmetrical. Although the image O_2 is the emergence outcome of the bowl O_1, still this would be selected when the input is a parallelogram as a result of emergence.

Algorithm for Accessing Database with Emergence Index Plan

See the flow chart in Figure 9.

Algorithm for Retrieval without Emergence

If the image comes in the form of a map of section Calculation of Emergence Index using a Geographic Location and input as in section Calculation of index of input in the form of a bowl but smaller in size compared to O_1 and rotated, then we follow the next steps.

Input map of section Calculation of index of input in the form of a bowl but smaller in size compared to O_1 and rotated, input map of section Calculation of Emergence Index using a geographic location, image output selected images.

Step 1. Analysis of Input
Begin

Number of tangents = 6
Number of infinite maximal lines = 6 and they are $D_7, D_8, D_9, ..., D_{12}$.
Coordinate points are $C_6, C_7, C_8, C_9, C_{10}$.
Angles infinite maximal lines made with the next one are $\theta_6, \theta_7, \theta_8, ..., \theta_{10}$.
Angles infinite maximal lines made with the vertical axis are:
$\theta_7', \theta_8', \theta_9', \theta_{10}', \theta_{11}', \theta_{12}'$.
For color, weight-feature factor $w_1 F_1 = 1.0 * 0 = 0$ as for the whole input is color independent.
For shape, $w_2 F_2 = 0.3 * f((x_6, y_6), (x_7, y_7), ..., (x_{10}, y_{10}))$
if the bowl occupies 30% of the image.
For background, $w_3 F_3 = 0.7 * 0 = 0$ since background occupies 70% of the rest of the space and is color independent.
For distances between various coordinate points:

$$w_4 F_4 = 1.0 * \sum_{i=7}^{12} d_i$$

So feature $F = f(w_1F_1; w_2F_2; w_3F_3; w_4F_4)$

$$= (0; (0.3 * f((x_6, y_6), (x_7, y_7), \ldots, (x_{10}, y_{10}))); 0; 1.0 * \sum_{i=7}^{12} d_i).$$

Since this is an input image, there is no domain. Hence $D = 0$.
Variables are $V = (x_6, y_6), (x_7, y_7), \ldots, (x_{10}, y_{10})$.
Constraints are $C = \{5; (C_6, C_7, \ldots, C_{10})\}$.
As this is an input of a bowl, there is no emergence. Hence $E = 0$.
   So emergence index
   $EI = f(D, F, V, C, E)$

$$= \{0; (0; (0.3 * f((x_6, y_6), (x_7, y_7), \ldots, (x_{10}, y_{10}))); 0; 1.0 * \sum_{i=7}^{12} d_i);$$

$$(x_6, y_6), (x_7, y_7), \ldots, (x_{10}, y_{10}); (5; (C_6, C_7, \ldots, C_{10})); 0\}$$
End

Step 2. Analysis of Next Image
Begin
   Number of tangents = 6
   Number of infinite maximal lines = 6 and they are $D_1, D_2, D_3, \ldots, D_6$.
   Coordinate points are C_1, C_2, C_3, C_4, C_5.

Figure 9: Flow Chart

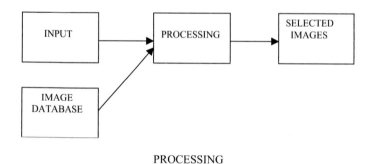

Angles infinite maximal lines made with the next one are θ_1, θ_2, θ_3,...., θ_5.

Angles infinite maximal lines made with the vertical axis are:

θ_1', θ_2', θ_3', θ_4', θ_5', θ_6'.

For color, weight-feature factor $w_1 F_1 = (0.4 * 2, 0.4 * 3, 0.2 * 5)$

For shape, $w_2 F_2 = 0.4 * f((x_1,y_1),(x_2,y_2),......,(x_5,y_5))$.

For background, $w_3 F_3 = (0.5 * 3, 0.1 * 5)$

For distances between various coordinate points:

$$w_4 F_4 = 1.0 * \sum_{i=1}^{6} d_i$$

So feature $F = f(w_1 F_1; w_2 F_2; w_3 F_3; w_4 F_4)$
$= ((0.4*2, 0.4*3, 0.2 * 5); (0.4 * f((x_1,y_1),(x_2,y_2),......,(x_5,y_5))); (0.5 *$

$3, 0.1*5); 1.0 * \sum_{I=1}^{6} d_i$

The domain path $D = D1/D2.2/D3.4/D4.7$ (directory containing geographic location)

Variables are $(x_1,y_1),(x_2,y_2),......,(x_5,y_5)$.

Constraints are $C = \{5; (C_1, C_2, ..., C_5)\}$.

Emergence E is the shape of a bowl
$= f((x_1,y_1),(x_2,y_2),......,(x_5,y_5))$.

Hence, emergence index

$EI = f(D,F,V,C,E)$
$= \{(D1/D2.2/D3.4/D4.7); ((0.4*2, 0.4*3, 0.2 * 5); (0.4* f((x_1,y_1),$

$(x_2,y_2),......,(x_5,y_5))); (0.5 * 3, 0.1*5); 1.0 * \sum_{I=1}^{6} d_i ; (x_1,y_1),(x_2,y_2),$

$......,(x_5,y_5); (5; (C_1,C_2, ...,C_5)); f((x_1,y_1),(x_2,y_2),......,(x_5,y_5))\}$.

End

Step 3. Find Correspondence

Begin

Compare the features F calculated for input and image, then

Color $w_1 F_1 (input) \neq w_1 F_1 (image)$.

Shape $w_2 F_2 (input) \neq w_2 F_2 (image)$

when we compare the percentage of the image occupied by the object, but

$N_{input} = N_{image}$ number of coordinates match, in each case being 5.

Background $w_3 F_3 (input) \neq w_3 F_3 (image)$.

Distances between various coordinate points $w_4 F_4 (input) = w_4 F_4 (image)$.

Although color, size and background of the input and image do not match, the other factors match.

Number of intersections in input and image is 5 and so they match.

If $\theta_1 \Leftrightarrow \theta_6$
$\quad \theta_2 \Leftrightarrow \theta_7$
$\quad \theta_3 \Leftrightarrow \theta_8$
$\quad \theta_4 \Leftrightarrow \theta_9$
$\quad \theta_5 \Leftrightarrow \theta_{10}$

then $Shape_{input} \Leftrightarrow Shape_{image}$ although input is smaller in size.

Since the number of intersections are the same and the angles correspond to each other, symmetry is established.

Also, $\theta_7' = \theta_1' + \theta$
$\quad \theta_8' = \theta_2' + \theta$
$\quad \theta_9' = \theta_3' + \theta$
$\quad \theta_{10}' = \theta_4' + \theta$
$\quad \theta_{11}' = \theta_5' + \theta$
$\quad \theta_{12}' = \theta_6' + \theta$

that proves input is rotated by a constant angle θ and further symmetry is established.
End

Step 4. Since they match, this image is selected and go to Step 2.

Algorithm for Retrieval with Emergence

If the image comes in the form of a map of section Calculation of emergence index using a geographic location and input as in section Calculation of index of input in the form of a parallelogram, then we follow the steps below.

Input map of section Calculation of index of input in the form of a parallelogram, input map of section Calculation of emergence index using a geographic location, image.

Output selected images.

Step 1. Analysis of Input
Begin
Number of infinite maximal lines = 4.
Coordinate points are $C_{11}, C_{12}, C_{13}, C_{14}$.
Four sides are L_e, L_f, L_g, L_h.
Four intersections are $I_{eh}, I_{ef}, I_{fg}, I_{gh}$.
Distances between four intersections are the same. In other words,
$\quad d(I_{eh}, I_{ef}) = d(I_{ef}, I_{fg}) = d(I_{fg}, I_{gh}) = d(I_{gh}, I_{eh})$.
For color, weight-feature factor $w1F1 = 1.0 * 0 = 0$ as for the whole input
is color independent.
For shape, $w_2F_2 = 0.45 * f((x_{11}, y_{11}), (x_{12}, y_{12}), \ldots\ldots, (x_{14}, y_{14}))$
if the bowl occupies 45% of the image.
For background, $w_3F_3 = 0.55 * 0 = 0$ since background occupies 55% of the
rest of the space and is color independent.
For distances between various coordinate points:

$$w_4F_4 = 1.0 * \sum_{i=5}^{8} d_i$$

So, feature $F = f(w_1F_1; w_2F2; w_3F_3; w_4F_4)$

$$= (0; (0.45 * f((x_{11},y_{11}),(x_{12},y_{12}),......,(x_{14},y_{14}))); 0; 1.0 * \sum_{i=5}^{8} d_i).$$

Since this is an input image, there is no domain. Hence $D = 0$.
Variables are $V = (x_{11},y_{11}),(x_{12},y_{12}),......,(x_{14},y_{14})$.
Constraints are $C = \{4; (C_{11}, C_{12}, ..., C_{14})\}$.
As this is an input of a parallelogram, there is no emergence. $E = 0$.
So emergence index
$\qquad EI = f(D,F,V,C,E)$

$$= \{0; (0; (0.45 * f((x_{11},y_{11}),(x_{12},y_{12}),......,(x_{14},y_{14}))); 0;$$

$$1.0 * \sum_{l=5}^{8} d_i);$$

$$(x_{11},y_{11}),(x_{12},y_{12}),......,(x_{14},y_{14}); (4; (C_{11},C_{12}, ...,C_{14})); 0\}$$

Step 2. Analysis of Image
Begin
Since the image is the same one we used in section Algorithm for Retrieval without Emergence, analysis of image remains same as in Step 2 of the section "Algorithm for Retrieval without Emergence."
End

Step 3. Find Correspondence
Begin
Compare the features F calculated for input and image, then
$\qquad$ Color $w_1F_1(\text{input}) \neq w_1F_1(\text{image})$.
$\qquad$ Shape $w_2F_2(\text{input}) \neq w_2F_2(\text{image})$
$\qquad\qquad$ when we compare the percentage of image occupied by
$\qquad\qquad$ the object, also
$\qquad\qquad$ $N_{\text{input}} \neq N_{\text{image}}$ number of coordinates does not match, in input it
$\qquad\qquad$ is 4 whereas in image, it is 5.
$\qquad$ Background $w_3F_3(\text{input}) \neq w_3F_3(\text{image})$.
$\qquad$ Distances between various coordinate points $w_4F_4(\text{input}) \neq w_4F_4(\text{image})$.
Hence the input and the image do not match.
End

Step 4. Since they do not match, this image is not selected and goes to Step 5.

Step 5. We study the emergence phenomenon in the image to see whether any symmetry could be established with the input parallelogram.

Begin

1. Original image – a bowl
2. To study the emergence, we have two options: hypothesis-driven search where an image is predefined and the particular unstructured image is searched to find a match of the predefined image and a data-driven search where a feature or a combination of features are passed through the unstructured image until some rule is satisfied to stop the process. We select a hypothesis-driven search because the image is predefined and the particular unstructured image is to be searched to find a match of the input image.
3. Destruction of original image

    a. Since we are considering the image of a map of section Calculation of emergence index using a geographic location, it has five coordinate points C_1, C_2, C_3, C_4, C_5. The image is represented by six infinite maximal lines which are $D_1, D_2, D_3, D_4, D_5, D_6$.

    b. We destroy the outer curve of the bowl and come up with Figure 4. It has still six infinite maximal lines and inside curves.

    c. This image now becomes an unstructured image.
4. Processing of unstructured image

    We further destroy the structure by removing inside curves and 2 infinite maximal lines D_5 and D_6.
5. New emergent image

    The image becomes an emergent shape with infinite maximal lines D_1, D_2, D_3 and D_4 in Figure 5.

    This has been shown in section Calculation of emergence index using a geographic location. We draw the analysis of an image from section Calculation of emergence index of emergent shape.

    Number of infinite maximal lines = 4.

    Coordinate points are C_1, C_2, C_3, C_4.

    Four sides are L_a, L_b, L_c, L_d.

    Four intersections are $I_{ad}, I_{ab}, I_{bc}, I_{cd}$.

    Distances between four intersections are the same. In other words,

    $d(I_{ad}, I_{ab}) = d(I_{ab}, I_{bc}) = d(I_{bc}, I_{cd}) = d(I_{cd}, I_{ad})$.

    For color, weight-feature factor is

    $w_1 F_1 = (0.35 * 2, 0.45 * 3, 0.2 * 5)$

    combination of blue, green and black.

    For shape, $w_2 F_2 = 0.45 * f((x_1, y_1), (x_2, y_2), \ldots, (x_4, y_4))$

    if the bowl occupies 45% of the image.

    For background, $w_3 F_3 = (0.45 * 3, 0.1 * 5)$

    combination of green and black.

    For distances between various coordinate points:

$$w_4 F_4 = 1.0 * \sum_{i=1}^{4} d_i$$

So feature $F = f(w_1F_1; w_2F_2; w_3F_3; w_4F_4)$
$= ((0.35 * 2, 0.45 * 3, 0.2 * 5); (0.45 * f((x_1,y_1), (x_2,y_2), \ldots\ldots (x_4,y_4)));$

$(0.45 * 3, 0.1 * 5);\ 1.0 * \sum_{i=1}^{4} d_i$

The domain path remains the same and is $D = D_1/D_{2.2}/D_{3.4}/D_{4.7}$.
Variables are $V = (x_1,y_1), (x_2,y_2), \ldots\ldots, (x_4,y_4)$.
Constraints are $C = \{4; (C_1, C_2, \ldots, C_4)\}$.
Emergent shape is that of a parallelogram.
So emergence index
$\quad EI = f(D, F, V, C, E)$
$= \{(D_1/D_{2.2}/D_{3.4}/D_{4.7});$
$\quad (0.35 * 2, 0.45 * 3, 0.2 * 5); (0.45 * f((x_1,y_1), (x_2,y_2), \ldots\ldots (x_4,y_4)));$

$\quad (0.45 * 3, 0.1 * 5); (1.0 * \sum_{i=1}^{4} d_i); (x_1,y_1), (x_2,y_2), \ldots\ldots, (x_4,y_4);$

$\quad (4; (C_1, C_2, \ldots, C_4)); f((x_1,y_1), (x_2,y_2), \ldots\ldots, (x_4,y_4))\}$
End

Step 6. Find Correspondence
Begin
Compare the features F calculated for input and emergent image, then
$\quad$ Color $w_1F_{1(input)} \neq w_1F_{1(image)}$.
$\quad$ Shape $w_2F_{2(input)} = w_2F_{2(image)}$
$\qquad$ when we compare the percentage of image occupied by
$\qquad$ the object, also
$\qquad N_{input} = N_{image}$ number of coordinates matches, in each case
$\quad$ being 4.
Background $w_3F_{3(input)} \neq w_3F_{3(image)}$.
Distances between various coordinate points $w_4F_{4(input)} = w_4F_{4(image)}$.
Although color and background of the input and image do not match, the other factors match.
$\quad$ Number of intersections in input and image is 4 and so they match.
$\quad$ Now we consider the following as shown in section to establish correspondence between the input (parallelogram) and image.

$\qquad$ Ordinary group intersections in each image
$\qquad$ Number of infinite maximal lines
$\qquad$ Corresponding equivalence
$\qquad$ Number of intersections
$\qquad$ Geometric constraints of infinite maximal lines
$\qquad$ Dimensional constraints of segments
$\qquad$ Corresponding intersections
$\qquad$ Corresponding angles

And we find the input and emergent shape match and they are both parallelograms. *End*

Step 7. Since they match, this image is selected and go to Step 2.

CONCLUSION

We have discussed accessing multimedia databases using emergence index to locate geographic location. We have shown how emergence can give rise to an altogether different meaning of a geographic area. This could help us explain and interpret geographic maps in a more accurate way.

Particularly if we know the pattern of road structures, like that of bowl as we have shown, then that map could be located by using that pattern as input. More research works need to be done to apply this concept in various practical problems. That way we should be able to find more meanings and hidden patterns of those images which not only would enable us to define them more accurately but also should establish more appropriate symmetry with other images when needed.

We have given an illustration in section Calculation of emergence index using a geographic location where input image finds symmetry with the example image of the multimedia database. Also we presented the algorithm for accessing multimedia databases. But, of course, there would be cases where input image would fail to find symmetry with images of the database. This would happen wherever the conditions set for symmetry, are not met. There would be some tolerance limit to accept symmetry. We would discuss this issue in our forthcoming paper.

Currently, we are working on the implementation of the theory we presented here.

REFERENCES

Deb, S. & Zhang, Y. (2001). Emergence index structure in image retrieval. *Tamkang Journal of Science and Engineering,* Tamkang University, Taipei, Taiwan, 4(1), 59-69.

Deb, S. & Zhang, Y. (2001a). Concepts of emergence index in image databases. *Distributed Multimedia Databases: Techniques and Applications,* 73-88.

Eakins, J.P. & Graham, M.E. (1999). Content-based image retrieval: A report to the JISC technology application program. Institute for Image Data Research, University of Northumbria at Newcastle, UK.

Forsyth, D.A., et al. (1996). Finding pictures of objects in large collection of images. In P.B. Heidon & B. Sandore (Eds.), *Digital Image Access and Retrieval: 1996 Clinic on Library Applications of Data Processing,* pp. 118-139. Graduate School of Library and Information Science, University of Illinois at Urbana-Champaign.

Gero, J.S. (1992). Shape emergence and symbolic reasoning using maximal lines. *Unpublished Notes,* Design Computing Unit, Department of Architectural and Design Science, University of Sydney, Australia.

Gero, J.S. (n.d.). *Visual Emergence in Design Collaboration.* Key Center of Design Computing, University of Sydney.

Gudivada, V.N. & Raghavan, V.V. (1995). *IEEE,* Content-Based Image Retrieval Systems.

SECTION VI

CONTENT-BASED AND SEMANTIC SEARCH AND RETRIEVAL METHODS

Chapter XI

An Efficient Content-Based Retrieval System for Large Image Database

Ching-Sheng Wang, Aletheia University, Taiwan

Timothy K. Shih, Tamkang University, Taiwan

ABSTRACT

Content-based image retrieval has become more desirable for developing large image databases. This chapter presents an efficient method of retrieving images from an image database. This system combines color, shape and spatial features to index and measure the similarity of images. Several color spaces that are widely used in computer graphics are discussed and compared for color clustering. In addition, this chapter proposes a new automatic indexing scheme of image databases according to our clustering method and color sensation, which could be used to retrieve images efficiently.

As a technical contribution, a Seed-Filling like algorithm that could extract the shape and spatial relationship feature of an image is proposed. Due to the difficulty of determining how far objects are separated, this system uses qualitative spatial relations to analyze object similarity. Also, the system is incorporated with a visual interface and a set of tools, which allows the users to express the query by specifying or sketching the images conveniently. The feedback learning mechanism enhances the precision of retrieval. The experience shows that the system is able to retrieve image information efficiently by the proposed approaches.

INTRODUCTION

Recent years have seen a rapid increase in the size of digital images collections. But, it is difficult for users to find and make use of the images well unless images are organized so as to allow efficient browsing, searching and retrieval. Most conventional image databases are text-annotated. As a result, image retrieval is based on keyword searching. Text-annotated images are simple and easy to manipulate. However, there are two major problems with this method. First, creating keywords for a large amount of images is time consuming. Moreover, the keywords are inherently subjective and not unique. With these disadvantages, automatic indexing and retrieval based on image content becomes more desirable for developing large volume image retrieval applications.

Content-Based Image Retrieval (CBIR) is an interesting but difficult research topic in information technology. It was proposed to overcome the difficulties faced by the manual annotation approach. Images could be indexed by their own visual content, such as color, shape, spatial relations, etc.; the main features for human beings as well as computers to recognize the image (shown in Figure 1).

Color feature is one of the most reliable visual features used in image retrieval. It is robust to background complication and is independent of image size and orientation. All color-based retrieval have two common issues: the selection of a proper color space and the proper color quantization scheme to reduce the color resolution in order to minimize the storage requirement and to increase the speed of color similarity measurement. But, there is no consistent agreement on the choice of a color space and quantization skill nowadays. Tominaga (1992) and Chang (1995) conducted color classification of natural color images at the C.I.E. L*a*b* color space. Wang and Yang (1997) reduced color resolution through hierarchical clustering, CNS (Color Name System) merging, and an equalization, quantization method according to the RGB and HVC color space. Wan and Kuo (1996) use a hierarchical color clustering method based on the pruned Oct-tree data structure with the RGB color space and calculate the average

Figure 1: Sketch of Visual Image Retrieval System

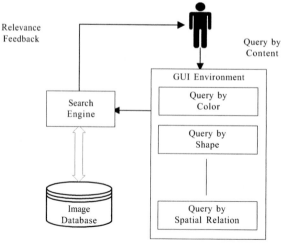

color with C.I.E. L*u*v* color space. In this chapter, we select the HIS color space to cluster color resolution according to human sensation.

The traditional way to represent a shape is through a set of features, extracted through image processing tools. An important criterion of shape feature representation is that shape features should be invariant to translation, rotation, and scaling, since human beings tend to ignore such variations for recognition and the retrieval purposes. Shape representation techniques are divided into two categories: boundary-based and region-based. Boundary based methods use only the contour or border of the object shape and completely ignore its interior. On the other hand, the region-based techniques take into account internal details (e.g., holes) besides the boundary details. The most successful representations for these two categories are Fourier Descriptor and Moment Invariant. The main idea of Fourier Descriptor is to use the Fourier transformed boundary as the shape feature (Pentlandn & Fu, 1977). The main idea of Moment Invariant is to use region-based moments, which are shape feature invariant to transformation. Motivated by the fact that most useful invariants were found by extensive experience and trial-and-error. Kapur et al. (1997) developed algorithms to systematically generate and search for a given geometry's invariant. Some recent work in shape representation included Chamfer matching (Borgefors, 1988; Barrow, 1977), Turning Function (Arkin, Chew, Huttenlocher, Kedem, & Mitchell, 1991) and Wavelet Descriptor (Chuang & Kuo, 1996). In this chapter, we proposed a series of methods to solve the image retrieval problems especially in shape representation and matching, such as defining the signature of the object, statistical recognition and species classification.

Spatial relations between entities (points, lines, regions and objects) often capture the most relevant and regular part of information in an image. Spatial relations between spatial entities can be classified according to their representation structure, into object-based structures and relation-based structures. Object-based structures treats spatial relations and visual information as one inseparable entity. Relation-based structures do not include visual information and preserve only a set of spatial relations, discarding all uninteresting relations. Regular grids, Quad-trees, R-Trees, R+-Trees and R*-Trees are widely used models in object-based representation (Nievergelt, Hinterberger, & Sevcik, 1984; Samet, 1984a, 1984b; Unnikrishnan, Shankar, & Venkatech, 1998; Samet, 1988). Relation-based representations require that pictorial objects in the image are represented by symbols (Tanimoto, 1976). The 2-D String, proposed by Chang and Liu (1984, 1987), is among the most popular representations based on symbolic projections. Many researchers propose temporal modeling of multimedia objects. The mechanism handles 1-D and 2-D objects, as well as 3-D objects, which treat a time line as the third axis based on the R-tree spatial data structure (Vazirgiannis, Theodoridis, & Timos Sellis, 1996). The discussion in (Wahl, Thomas et al., 1995) identified various temporal interaction forms and discussed their temporal dependencies. The work also integrated some interaction forms into a temporal model. The 2-D Projection Interval Relations (PIR) (Nabil, Anne, Ngu, & Shepherd, 1996) is based on both directional and topological temporal relations. Image retrieval algorithms were discussed based on PIR. The use of spatio-temporal relations serves as a reasonable semantic tool for the underlying representation of objects in many multimedia applications. In this chapter, we extend temporal interval relation by means of a complete analysis for spatial computation.

The index scheme in an image database is very important for improving retrieval performance. Index Structures ideally filter out all irrelevant images by checking image attributes with the user's query. They retain only relevant images without analyzing the entire database. Retrieval images are ranked in order of similarity to a query. The existing popular indexing techniques include k-d tree, priority k-d tree, quad-tree, K-D-B tree, h-B-tree, R-tree and its variants R+-tree and R*-tree (Guttman, 1984; Sellis, Roussopouls, & Faloutsos, 1987; Greene, 1989; Beckmann, Kriegel, Schneider, & Seeger, 1990; Rui, Chakrabarti, Mehrotra, Zhao, & Huang, 1997). In addition to the above approaches, clustering and Neural Nets, widely used in Pattern Recognition, are also promising indexing techniques (Duda & Hart, 1973; Zhang & Zhang, 1995). VisualSEEK developed a binary tree based indexing algorithm (Smith & Chang, 1996). Swain and Ballard (1991) used histogram intersection for color indexing. Pei and Shiue extracted the color contents of images and recorded the feature as an index in (Pei, Chang & Shiue, 1998). In Niu, Ozsu and Li (1997), Niu and Ozsu proposed an index scheme called 2-D-h trees for content-based retrieval of images. In our system, we propose a fast database indexing scheme based on our clustering method and MTM, which can effectively filter out the irrelevant images.

Several systems have been proposed in recent years in the research community of content-based information retrieval.

1. QBIC (Query By Image Content) by IBM
2. Virage by Virage, Inc.
3. Photobook by MIT Media Lab
4. VisualSEEk and WebSEEk by Columbia University
5. Picasso by the University of Florence, Italy
6. NeTra by the University of California, Alexandria Digital Library
7. RetrievalWare by Excalibur Technologies Corp.
8. IRIS by German Software Development Laboratory of IBM and the AI group of the University of Bremen
9. CORE by the University of Singapore

QBIC was the first commercial CBIR (Content Based Image Retrieval) system actually built (Flicker et al., 1995). Its system framework and techniques had great effects on later image retrieval systems. The QBIC system allows queries on a large image and video database, based on color, shape, texture, example images and sketches. The color features used in QBIC are the average (R,G,B), (Y,i,q), (L,a,b) and MTM (Mathematical Transform to Munsell) coordinates.

The Virage Search Engine supports querying of still images and video streams (Bach et al., 1996). Similar to QBIC, it supports visual queries based on color, composition (color layout), texture and structure (object boundary information). It also supports arbitrary combinations of the above four atomic queries. The user can adjust the weights associated with the atomic features according to their own purposes.

The Photobook system is a set of interactive tools for browsing and searching images (Pentland, Picard, & Sclaroff, 1996). The key idea behind this suite of tools is semantics preserving image compression, which reduces an image to a small set of perceptually significant coefficients. Photobook consists of three sub-books. There are the Appearance Photobook, Shape Photobook and Texture Photobook, which can extract the face, shape and texture, respectively. Users can query an image based on the corresponding features in each of the three sub-books, or on a combination of different mechanisms with a text-based description.

The VisualSEEK system (Smith et al., 1996), developed at the Columbia University Center for Telecommunication Research, supports retrieval of still images and video based on visual features and spatial layout. The visual features used in their systems are Color Set and Wavelet Transform based texture features. WebSEEk is a World Wide Web oriented text/image search engine. It supports queries based on both keywords and visual content.

The Picasso system, developed at the University of Florence, Italy, for still image retrieval (Del Bimbo, & Pala, 1997; Del Bimbo, Mugnaini, Pala, & Turco, 1998). Functions available are: query by global color similarity, color region similarity, color semantics (according to sensations induced in the observer), texture similarity and shape similarity. This system is particularly tailored to art image databases.

The Netra system, developed at University of California, Santa Barbara (Ma & Manjunath, 1997), is a Java-based system, designed to support retrieval from large image collections, according to color, shape and texture similarity. The main research feature of Netra is its Gabor filter based texture analysis.

Other systems (i.e., 7, 8 and 9 listed above) provide querying based on global color, color layout, shape, texture and semantic content (Alshuth, Termes, Klauck, Kreiss, & Roper, 1996; Wu, Narashihalu, Mehtre, Lam, & Gau, 1995). RetrievalWare emphasizes Neural Nets to retrieve images. It runs under many operating system platforms like: SG IRIX, IBM AIX, HO-UX, DEC OSF, SUNOS, SUN Solaris and MS Windows. IRIS provides querying by high-level concepts. Its application domains covered are technical drawing databases and shopping catalogues. CORE system provides the still image retrieval based on perceptual features.

Even though the above content-based image retrieval system provides many features for image querying, none of them combine global color, color region, color sensation, shape and qualitative spatial relation features to query the images. In this chapter, we discuss those features for extraction and measurement of the features of images. A total solution to the problem is then presented.

The rest of the chapter is organized as follows. A number of chosen color spaces including RGB, CMY, YUV, C.I.E. L*u*v* and HSI are discussed and compared in order to select the color space for color clustering. Then, the algorithms for extracting color, shape and spatial relation features are described. The similarity functions of image features are given and are followed by a discussion on the architecture and indexing scheme of image database. Next is a description of the procedure of image retrieval in our system. Finally, a short conclusion is given.

COLOR SPACE AND COLOR CLUSTERING

Selection of a proper color space and use of a proper color quantization scheme to reduce color resolution are common issues for all color-based retrieval methods (Wang, Yang, & Acharya, 1997; Swain & Ballard, 1991; Wan & Kuo, 1996). In this section, we describe the considerations for selecting color space and present our mechanism and procedure of color clustering and normalization of images, including the MTM transformer formulas obtained from the RGB to HSI color space.

Selection of the Color Space

A color space is a mathematical representation of a set of colors. Several color spaces exist for a variety of reasons. Some color spaces are widely used color spaces in computer graphics. All of the color space can be derived from the RGB information. There are several color spaces existing for a variety of reasons.

RGB Color Space

Red, green, and blue are three primary additive colors (individual components are added together to form a desired color) and are represented in three-dimensions. The RGB color space is the most prevalent choice for digital images because color-CRTs (computer display) use red, green, and blue phosphors to create the desired color. Also, it is easy for programmers to understand and program, since this color space has been widely used for a number of years. However, a major drawback of the RGB space is that it is senseless. It is difficult for the user to understand or get a sense of what color R = 100, G = 50, and B = 80 is and the difference between R = 100, G = 50, B = 50 and R = 100, G = 150, B = 150.

CMY Color Space

CMY color space is used for color printing. Cyan, magenta, and yellow are the complements of red, green and blue. They are called subtractive primaries because they are obtained by subtracting light from white. RGB to CMY can be obtained by a simple, but inaccurate transformation: C = 1-R, M = 1-G and Y = 1-B. Hence, CMY color space has the same drawback of RGB.

*C.I.E. L*u*v* Color Space*

Color is identified by two coordinates, x and y, in the C.I.E. L*u*v* Color Space. Lightness L* is based on perceptual measure of brightness and u* and v* are chromatic coordinates. Besides, color differences in an arbitrary direction are approximately equal in this color space. Thus, the Euclidean distance can determine the relative distance of two colors. But, its coordinate transformation to the RGB space is not linear.

YUV, YIQ and YCbCr Color Space

The YUV space is widely used in image compression and processing applications. Y represents the luminance of a color, while U and V represent the chromaticity of a color. The luminance (Y) component is separated from the chromatic components in this space. The YIQ color space is derived from the YUV color space. The I stands for In-phase and Q for Quadrature, which is the modulation method used to transmit the color information. YCbCr is a scale and offset version of the YUV color space. Those color spaces are difficult for users to deal with, because they do not directly refer to intuitive notions of hue, saturation and brightness.

HSI, HSV and HLS Color Space

The HSI color space was designed to be used more intuitive in manipulating color and to approximate the way humans perceive and interpret color. Three characteristics of color, hue, saturation and intensity, are defined so as to distinguish color components.

Figure 2: Procedure Diagram for Color Clustering and Normalization

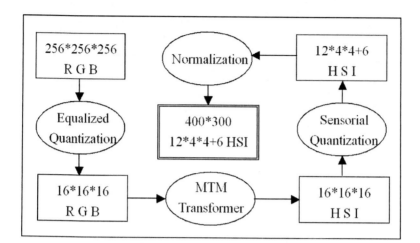

Hue describes the actual wavelength of a color by representing the color's name, for example, green, red or blue. Saturation is a measure of the purity of a color. For instance, the color red is a 100% saturated color, but pink is a low saturation color due to the amount of white in it. Intensity indicates the lightness of a color. It ranges from black to white. HLS (hue, lightness, and saturation) is similar to HSI; the term lightness is used rather than intensity. The different between HSI and HSV (hue, saturation, value) lies in the computation of the brightness component (I or V), which determines the distribution and dynamic range of both brightness (I or V) and saturation (S).

In our study, HSI is the color space employed because of its similarity and perceptibility features. Similarity means that two perceptually similar colors are in the same or neighboring quantized color bins, and that two non-similar colors are not in the same quantized color bin. Thus, the similarity between two colors can be determined based on the distance in the HIS color space. In addition, the HIS color space is defined based on human color perception. Users could choose the color they want easily by indicating the hue, saturation and intensity values independently. In addition, users can express queries based on values of hue, saturation and intensity in order to indicate the sensation of an image about warmth or coldness, gray or vividness and brightness or darkness.

Color Clustering

To achieve high storage and retrieval efficiency, the number of color bins used is normally much smaller than the real color space and total number of colors used to represent an image. Therefore, a number of colors have to be grouped into one bin. This is called color clustering. Ideally, colors clustered into the same bin should be more similar than colors of different bins.

The quantization scheme and the procedure for color clustering are shown in Figure 2. First, we equally quantize the RGB color space to change the number of color levels

Figure 3: The Clustering 12*4*4+6 HSI Color Pace

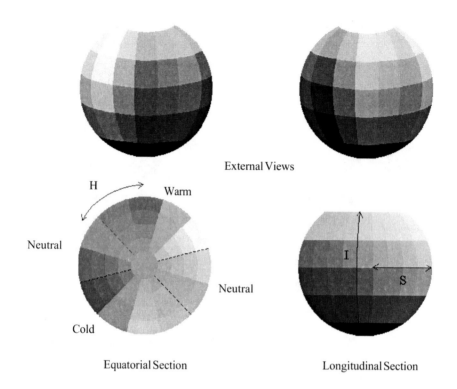

External Views

Equatorial Section

Longitudinal Section

from 256 to 16 levels in each axis. Second, we linearly convert the 16-level RGB color bins into HSI coordinates using the MTM transformer formulas:

$$H = \arctan 2(\sqrt{3}(G-B),(2R-G-B)),$$
$$S = 1 - \frac{\min(R,G,B)}{I},$$
$$I = \frac{(R+G+B)}{3}.$$

Also, we cluster the hue from 16 to 12 levels, since a hue is represented as circle and primary hues are located on the circle every 60 degrees (red, yellow, green, cyan, blue and magenta) in the HSI color space. In addition, because the human visual system is more sensitive to hues than to saturation or intensity, the H axis is quantized more finely than the S axis and the I axis. In our experiments, we quantized the HSI color space into 12 bins for hue, four bins for saturation, and four bins for intensity (shown in Figure 3). Besides, there are six degrees of intensity for gray color, which the saturation is smaller than 20% (we quantized the color into white or block bin if the intensity of this color is greater than top 10% or less than bottom 10%). Finally, we normalized the resolution of all the images to 400*300 pixels.

EXTRACTION OF FEATURES

In this section, we present our algorithms for extracting the features of an image. There are numerous standard image formats, including MP, GIF, JPEG, etc. Our feature extraction algorithm is based on the bitmap format, since its pixel stream can represent spatial information. For an image in another format, we convert it into the bitmap format only in the feature extraction phase. After feature extraction, the system saves its feature information and the image in the original format to the database. In brief, our system can process all kinds of image formats by converting them to the bitmap format in the feature extraction phase.

Color Feature Extraction

The extraction of color features includes two main procedures. First, the system reads the RGB value of pixels from the image file sequentially and then converts them to an HSI value by means of the MTM transformer. Second, the system constructs the color histogram of the image according to the number of pixels of each color within the image. Also, the system records the color sensation of the image, including warmth — coldness, gray — vividness and brightness — darkness, according to the average hue value, saturation value and intensity value of the image for filtering.

Shape Feature Extraction

There are three main steps of shape extraction: First, we extract the shapes of an image by the enhanced Seed Filling algorithm. Then, we normalize the shapes and convert them from region to contour by edge detection before the shape similarity measurement. In the first step, the system will record the color, location, height, width and area information of the objects for the similarity measurement and identify the color and spatial relations. The normalized contour that is generated by the second and the third steps is used in the measurement of shape similarity only.

Figure 4: Example of Processed Image (a) Original Image (b) Color Clustering Image (c) Shape Extraction Image (d) Refined Image

| (a) | (b) | (c) | (d) |

Shape Extraction

The procedure of the Seed Filling algorithm for extracting the region feature is described below:

Step 1: Quantization and Normalization the image

Step 2: Dividing the image. We divide an image into a number of boxes on the chessboard. The size of each box is 4*4 pixels and the representative color of a box is calculated by the average color of all pixels in the HSI color space.

Step 3: Filling the Seed. Starting from the upper-left corner, a box is chosen as a seed with the next box four units away both in the vertical and horizontal directions.

Step 4: Extract the objects. Starting from a seed box, the program looks at the left, right, up, and down directions. The program tries to combine as many boxes in a region as possible, if the color similarity between the seed box and the neighbor box is within a threshold.

The result of the front steps will contain many regions (see Figure 4c). Each region contains some boxes. We remove the scattered small regions, because in general it is useless to retrieve the image and will decrease the performance (see Figure 4d).

Edge Detection

Edge detection and edge tracing are very important tasks in the segmentation application of the image process system. There are two famous signal edge detectors: the Canny operator and the Shen-Castan (ISEF) method (Bach, 1986; Shen & Castan, 1992). The Canny algorithm convolves the image with the derivative of a Gaussian function and then performs non-maximum suppression and hysteresis threshold. The Shen-Castan algorithm convolves the image with the Infinite Symmetric Exponential Filter (ISEF), computes the binary Laplacian image, suppresses false zero crossings, performs adaptive gradient threshold, and also applies the hysteresis threshold. In our experience, the Canny's edge detector is the best that can be done under most certain specified circumstances. The non-maximum suppression is meant to ensure that the edge line is thinned and is only one pixel wide.

Shape Representation and Normalization

Technically, edge detection is the process of locating the edge pixels, and edge tracing is the process of following the edges, usually collecting the edge pixels into a list. This is done in a consistent direction, either clockwise or counterclockwise, around the objects. Chain coding (Freeman, 1974) is one of the methods of edge tracing. The result

Figure 5: Example Image and Result after Edge Detection Process

Figure 6: Turning Angle Representation of the Object

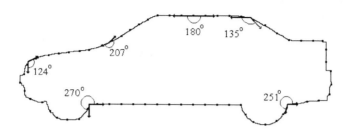

is a non-raster representation of the objects, which can be used to compute shape measurement or otherwise identify or classify the object. But, this method is influenced by the rotation and scale of the object.

In this chapter, we use the turning angle representation to describe the object. Shape representation is a set of turning angles $\theta=\{\theta(1), \theta(2), \theta(3), \ldots \theta(N)\}$ as shown in Figure 6. This method is invariant for translation and scale of the object. In addition, it is invariant for rotation after the normalization. The turning angle of the object can express the edge's subtle differences, including those in curvature and distance. Based on the turning angle variation, we classify feature tokens based on their curvature properties.

In our system, the edge is segmented into a fixed number of parts first. The turning points are selected from the edge by computing the local maximum curvature points in each segment. Therefore, the number of turning points in the image is fixed. This method is better than selecting the points just at the segment points that may lose the important turning angles.

Shape must be normalized before similarity measurement is performed. First, we normalize the length of the edge segments. Then, we find the centroid (center of mass) of the object. Consider the image shown in Figure 7. The vertical profile (orthogonal

Figure 7: Use of Orthogonal Projection to Find the Centroid of the Object

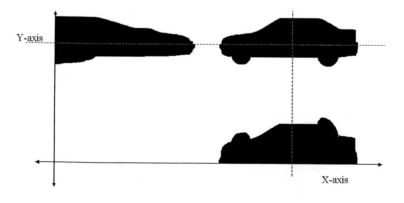

Figure 8: Starting Point of Turning Angle Representation

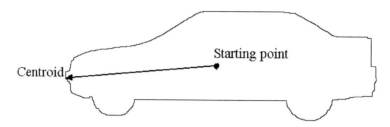

projection on the X-axis) appears below as a weight graph. We can easily compute the middle line of the mass. The horizontal profile (orthogonal projection on the Y-axis) appears on the left side of Figure 7. It is easy to find the centroid of the object.

After defining the centroid, the next step is to find the point of the boundary, which has the longest distance from the centroid to be the starting point of the turning angle representation (shown in Figure 8).

Spatial Relation Feature Extraction

After the shape is extracted, our system will analyze the spatial relation according to the 13 interval relations and five point-interval relations (as shown in Figure 9) of objects by projecting the shape from a 2-D space to two 1-D spaces. Our system will record the starting and ending points of the two objects in X and Y coordinates by splitting the shapes orthogonally to the coordinate axis (as shown in Figure 10), where As.x and Ae.x are the starting and ending points of the object A in X coordinate, As.y and Ae.y are the starting and ending points of the object A in Y coordinate. And, Bs.x, Be,x, Bs.y and Be,y are those of B. These points will be used to estimate the spatial relation of the two objects in X and Y coordinates based on the mechanism discussed in Shih, Timothy and Chang (1998).

Figure 9: The 13 Interval Relations and Five Point-Interval Relations

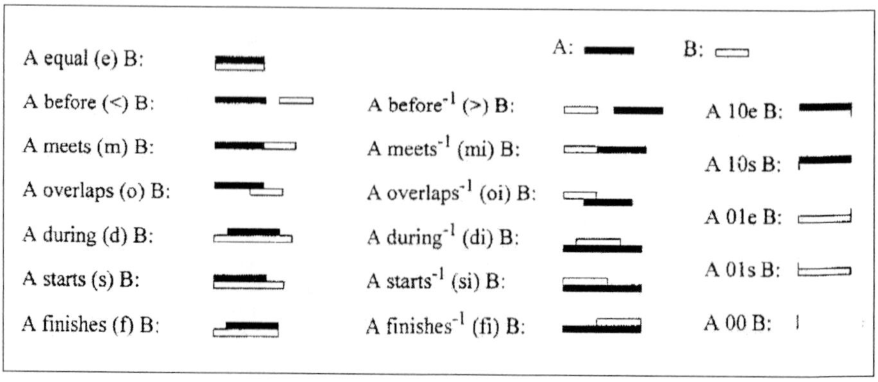

A equal (e) B:		A:	B:
A before (<) B:	A before^{-1} (>) B:	A 10e B:	
A meets (m) B:	A meets^{-1} (mi) B:	A 10s B:	
A overlaps (o) B:	A overlaps^{-1} (oi) B:	A 01e B:	
A during (d) B:	A during^{-1} (di) B:	A 01s B:	
A starts (s) B:	A starts^{-1} (si) B:	A 00 B:	
A finishes (f) B:	A finishes^{-1} (fi) B:		

Figure 10: The Orthogonal Projection of Shape in X and Y Coordinates

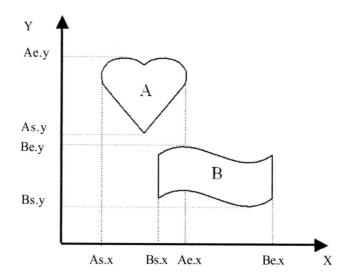

THE SIMILARITY MEASURE OF FEATURES

In our system, the similarity score of the images is integrated by three components: color similarity score named *CS*, shape similarity score named *SS* and spatial relation similarity score named *SRS*. Finally, the similarity score *S* is defined as following:

$$S = Wc * CS + Ws * SS + Wsr * SRS$$

Where *Wc*, *Ws* and *Wsr* are the weights of color, shape and spatial relation, which could be indicated by user or via training by our system.

The Similarity Measure of Color

We will present the similarity formula of two colors first. Then, we define the similarity of two images according to the similarity of their colors.

The Similarity of Two Colors

Let the hue, saturation and intensity value of color *C* are *H*, *S* and *I*. The similarity between two colors, *i* and *j*, is given by:

$$C(i, j) = W_h H(i, j) + S(i, j) + I(i, j)$$

where:

$$H(i,j) = \min\left(\left|H_i - H_j\right|, 12 - \left|H_i - H_j\right|\right)$$
$$S(i,j) = \left|S_i - S_j\right|$$
$$I(i,j) = \left|I_i - I_j\right|$$

And, we set $Wh = 2$. Because in our experience, the change of hue value affects the conceptual similarity is sensitive to the change of saturation and intensity value. Finally, the degree of similarity between two colors, i and j, is given by:

$$CS(i,j) = \begin{cases} 0 & \text{if } H(i,j) > H\max \\ 1 - \dfrac{C(i,j)}{C\max} & \text{otherwise} \end{cases}$$

where $Cmax = WhHmax + Smax + Imax$. In which, $Cmax$, $Hmax$, $Smax$ and $Imax$ are the maximum tolerant distance of the color, hue, saturation and intensity in the similar colors and $Hmax$ is two, because two colors are not perceived to be similar when the distance of their hue value exceeds 60 degrees (60/360=2/12) in the HIS color space. $Smax$ and $Imax$ are equal to $4-1 = 3$.

The Color Similarity of Two Images

The color similarity between two images shall be discussed in two fields: the difference of pixel numbers in the completely same color and the perceptual similar colors. In the first field, the similarity measure between query image Q and database image D for a color i can be determined as:

$$CSc(Q,D,i) = \min(Qi, Di)$$

And, the similarity measure between query image Q and database image D can be determined as the following formula for all colors:

$$CSc(Q,D) = \sum_{i=1}^{198} CSc(Q,D,i)/400*300$$

where 198 is the total number of colors in our clustering HIS color space ($12*4*4 + 6$ gray colors).

In the second field, the similarity measure between query image Q and database image D for a color i can be determined as:

$$CSp(Q,D,i) = Max\left(\min(Qi, Dj) \times CS(i,j)\right) \quad \forall j \in Cp$$

where Cp is the set of colors that are perceptually similar to color i. Then, the similarity formula between query image Q and database image D for all colors is:

$$CSp(Q,D) = \sum_{i \in C_D} CSp(Q,D,i)/Qi$$

Finally, we define the similarity formula of the images according to the color feature:

$$CS(Q,D) = Max(CSc(Q,D), CSp(Q,D))$$

The Similarity Measure of Shape

Given two shapes represented by their turning angle vectors $\theta 1$ and $\theta 2$, for the best match and partial similarity, we record the minimum distance between the two shapes by rotating one to match another. Then, the similarity distance between these two shapes is calculated:

$$SS_D (\theta 1, \theta 2) = \min(\sum_{i=1}^{N} |\theta 1(i) - \theta 2r(i)|),$$

where N is the fixed number of turning points in the image and $\theta 2r$'s are in the shape set of notation angle $\theta 2$. In this formula, if the segment is a straight line, we set the turning angle to 180 degrees for the segment.

Let the normalized similarity measurement degree be from 1(complete matching) to 0(most dissimilar matching). The measurement between the requested image and archive images will be:

$$SS(\theta 1, \theta 2) = 1 - \frac{SS_D(\theta 1, \theta 2)}{N * 360},$$

where $N * 360$ is the maximum distance measure of the requested image and archive images, the SS_D is the minimum distance measure of the requested image and archive images. If the archive images include the requested image, then SS_D is equal to 0, and SS is equal to 1. In addition, we set a threshold for disregarding dissimilar images. If SS_D is greater than the threshold, then it means that the requested image is dissimilar to the archive images. Then, we set the SS to 0.

The Similarity Measure of Spatial Relation

Before the similarity measure of spatial relation is obtained, we identify the object according to the weights of color, shape and the area of objects that are adjusted by the user. In this section, we will use the 2-D spatial relational representation proposed in Shih et al. (1998) to demonstrate the usefulness in the spatial domain. It is the simplest kind of spatial information of practical relevance. The 1-D spatial relation case can be handled by a simple modification of temporal interval relations.

Table 1: The Extended Point-Interval Relation Distance

EPIRD	<	>	D	di	o	oi	m	mi	s	si	f	fi	e	lo	lo	ol	ol	oo
<	0	8	4	4	2	6	1	7	3	5	5	3	4	6	2	2	6	4
>	8	0	4	4	6	2	7	1	5	3	3	5	4	2	6	6	2	4
D	4	4	0	4	2	2	3	3	1	3	1	3	2	4	4	2	2	4
Di	4	4	4	0	2	2	3	3	3	1	3	1	2	2	2	4	4	4
O	2	6	2	2	0	4	1	5	1	3	3	1	2	4	2	2	4	4
Oi	6	2	2	2	4	0	5	1	3	1	1	3	2	2	4	4	2	4
M	1	7	3	3	1	5	0	6	2	4	4	2	3	5	1	1	5	3
Mi	7	1	3	3	5	1	6	0	4	2	2	4	3	1	5	5	1	3
S	3	5	1	3	1	3	2	4	0	2	2	2	1	3	3	1	3	3
Si	5	3	3	1	3	1	4	2	2	0	2	2	1	1	3	3	3	3
F	5	3	1	3	3	1	4	2	2	2	0	2	1	3	3	3	1	3
Fi	3	5	3	1	1	3	2	4	2	2	2	0	1	3	1	3	3	3
E	4	4	2	2	2	2	3	3	1	1	1	1	0	2	2	2	2	2
Los	6	2	4	2	4	2	5	1	3	1	3	3	2	0	4	4	2	2
Loe	2	6	4	2	2	4	1	5	3	3	3	1	2	4	0	2	4	2
Ols	2	6	2	4	2	4	1	5	1	3	3	3	2	4	2	0	4	2
Ole	6	2	2	4	4	2	5	1	3	3	1	3	2	2	4	4	0	2
Oo	4	4	4	4	4	4	3	3	3	3	3	3	2	2	2	2	2	0

Let *EPIRD(r_i, r_j)* be an EPIRD index function that takes as input two relations, r_i, r_j ∈ *18REL*, and returns a similarity index from 0 to 8 as shown in Table 1. Note that, the lower the index, the closer the relation to the relations. Then, we have:

Assume that *A* and *B* are spatial relation strings of two object strings in different images and $SRS_x(A, B)$ and $SRS_j(A, B)$ are the similarity functions of *A* and *B* in the X and the Y coordinates. We define a normalized spatial relation similarity function of *A* and *B* as:

$$SRS(A, B) = (SRSx(A, B) + SRSy(A, B)) / 2$$

and

$$SRSx(A, B) = 1 - \frac{\sum_{i=1}^{min(m,n)-1} EPIRD(A(i)_x, B(i)_x) + 8 \times |m - n|}{8 \times (Max(m, n) - 1)}$$

$$SRSy(A, B) = 1 - \frac{\sum_{i=1}^{min(m,n)-1} EPIRD(A(i)_y, B(i)_y) + 8 \times |m - n|}{8 \times (Max(m, n) - 1)}$$

where $A(i)_x$, $A(i)_y$, $B(i)_x$ and $B(i)_y$ denotes the ith spatial relation of spatial relation string A and B in the X and the Y coordinates, m and n are of the number of spatial relations in spatial relation string A and B.

Qualitative representation of object positions has an advantage. It is difficult for a user to specify how far two objects are separated. But, using the before or the after relation, approximate reasoning can be used.

MANAGEMENT OF IMAGE DATABASE

In this chapter, we describe the architecture and index/filter mechanism of the image database. In our system, we propose a fast database indexing scheme according to our color clustering method. Based on this index scheme, filtering can eliminate the non-similar images effectively.

The Architecture of Database

The architecture of our image database is a tree (as shown in Figure 11). The image database has five layers according to our color clustering method. The first layer is the H (Hue), the second layer is S (Saturation), the third layer is I (Intensity), the fourth and fifth layers are corresponding color bins and disk storage image data. Based on this architecture, images can be stored and searched systemically.

In the case that we want to search the images, which have the same or similar hue only, we can top-down trace the database architecture from hue level to the subordinate saturation and intensity level and get the image information efficiently. If we want to search the image with the same hue and saturation and do not care about the intensity of the images, then we can get the images from the second level of the database. We can get the images that have the same/similar saturation or intensity based on our database architecture immediately, too.

In a word, our system can retrieve the image according to the color sensation of a query image including warm or cold indicated by hue, gray or vivid indicated by saturation and bright or dark indicated by intensity.

The Indexing Scheme

In the phase for creating and adding images to the database, the system analyzes and extracts the color, color sensation, shape and spatial relation features of the input image. According to the features, the indexing scheme assigns to the image with a unique image ID and saves its feature information and the original image to the proper address in the image database.

After quantization and normalization of the images, our system indexes the images according to their dominant colors. First, the system calculates the histogram and dominant colors of the image. The color histogram is an array that is computed by differentiating the colors within the image and counting the number of pixels of each color. From the color histogram, we can choose the dominant colors whose numbers of pixels exceed the threshold.

After getting the dominant colors, the system will save the unique image ID to each corresponding color bin. For example, if the unique ID of an image is 1, and the dominant

Figure 11: Structural Diagram of the Image Database

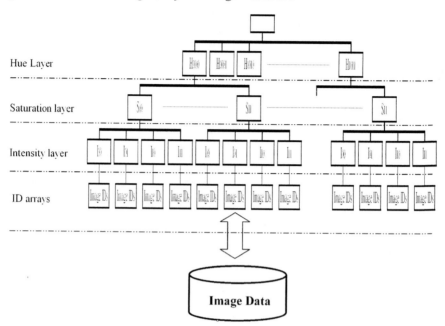

colors of this image are 37 (00100101), 38 (00100110), and 154(10011010). Then, the image ID will save to the ID arrays in the logical indexing addresses: 00100101, 00100110, and 10011010 (see Figure 12). According to this indexing scheme, the system could load the candidate images that have the same dominant colors and eliminate irrelevant images immediately before the more complex and expensive similarity measure.

The Filter Mechanism

For a small image database, sequentially searching the image during the retrieval process will be fast and provide acceptable response time. However, it is not feasible for large image databases. Therefore, we propose a filtering mechanism to eliminate irrelevant images before the more complex and expensive similarity measure.

First, our system will load the image ID arrays according to the dominant colors of the query image. Next, the system joins and ranks the image ID arrays according to their numbers of appearances. For example, if the dominant colors of an image are 37 (00100101), 38 (00100110), 39 (00100111), 152 (10011000) and 154 (10011010). Then, the image ID arrays of these color bins are 1,2,3; 1,2,8; 2,7,9; 2,3,7,9 and 1,2,9 (show in Figure 12). Furthermore, because image ID 2 appears five times, image ID 1 and 9 appear three times, image ID 3 and 7 appear twice and image ID 8 appears only once, the result of conjunction and ranking of these arrays is 2,1,9,3,7,8. After this step, the system can filter out irrelevant images effectively (ex: 4,5,6,10...).

Figure 12: Show a Filtering Example of a Query Image [the Dominant Colors of this Image are 37 (00100101), 38 (00100111), 152 (10011000) and 154 (10011010)]

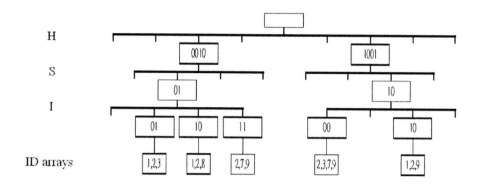

In addition to the filter mechanism described above, the system can filter the image based on human color sensation. According to chromatology, the hue value influences the sense of warmth or coldness, the saturation value influences the sense of gray or vividness, and the intensity value influences the sense of brightness or darkness. When a user indicates the color-sensation query by him/herself or analyzes the input image automatically by the system, the filter can load relevant image IDs from our special HSI indexing structure efficiently.

Figure 13: Overview of System Architecture

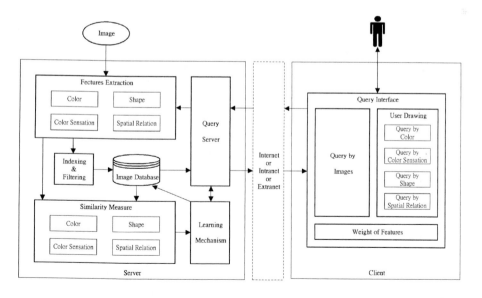

PROCEDURE OF IMAGE RETRIEVAL

In this section, we describe the query procedure of the system as shown in Figure 13. Our system includes two main sub-systems: the server sub-system and the client sub-system. The server sub-system handles the processes of feature extraction, database indexing/filtering, feature matching and system learning. The client sub-system handles the process of querying. In addition, we present here the implementation and query interface of our system.

The Procedure of Online Query

In the query phase, the user could retrieve the images by giving the sample images or sketching the image via our query interface that provides a lot of standard drawing tools. The following are the procedures of image query:

Step 1: User loads or sketches a query image, adjusts the weight of features and sends the query message.

Step 2: When query server receives the query message, it will pass the image and weight of features to the feature extraction mechanism and learning mechanism individually.

Step 3: After the extraction of features, the feature extraction mechanism will send the feature information of query image to the similarity measure mechanism and filtering mechanism.

Step 4: According to the feature information, filer mechanisms will get the feature record of relevant images from the image database for detail similarity measure.

Figure 14: Query by Sketched Image

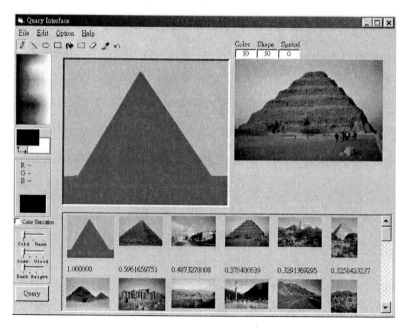

Figure 15: Query by Modified Image (Cut a Piece of Image)

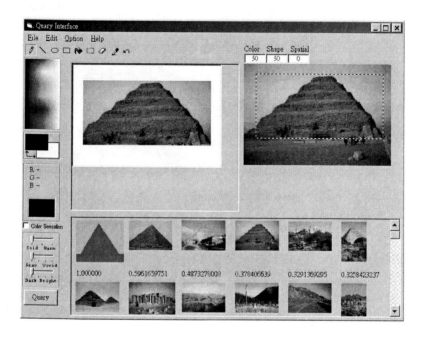

Figure 16: Query by Modified Image (Modify the Query Image)

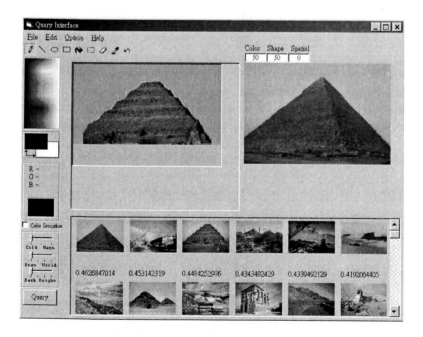

Figure 17: Query Example Based on Color

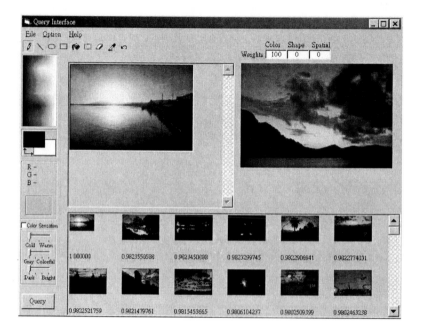

Step 5: Similarity measure mechanism will measure the similarity of features information between the query image and database images and return the results to the learning mechanism.

Step 6: Learning mechanism will rank the most similar database images to be the candidate images according to the similarity order that combines the weight and the similarity of features. Then, the learning mechanism will adjust the recommended weights of features according to the query image and candidate images. And, it will send the recommended weights to the query server and send the image IDs to the image database for returning the candidate images.

Step 7: Finally, query server will send the recommended weights and candidate images to the query interface at the client side.

Step 8: When the user receives the candidate images via query interface, he/her can pick the images that he/she wanted or choose some similar images for the next query.

In a new query with multiple images, the learning mechanism will rank the candidate images by the average of similarities between the candidate images and each of the query images. Then, the learning mechanism will adjust the recommended weights of features according to the query images and candidate images again. Repeating the above steps, the user will get the images he/she wanted easily.

Figure 18: Query Example Based on Shape

Figure 19: Query by Multiple Query Images

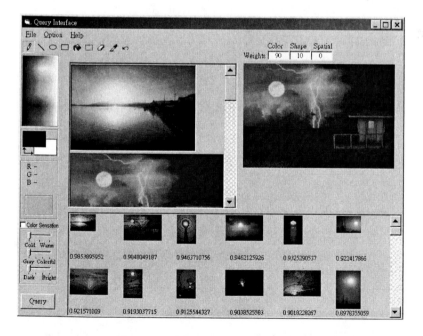

Figure 20: Query Example Based on Spatial Relations

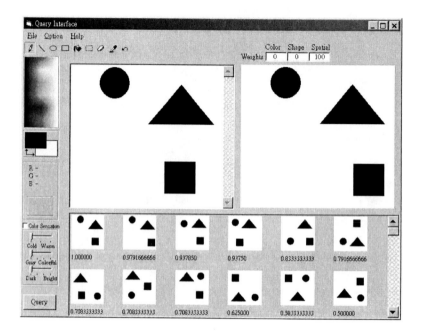

The Query Interface

We used Microsoft Visual Basic and C++ to develop our query interface and DLL (Dynamic Link Library). Our image database is developed by Microsoft SQL server, which connects the Visual Basic through the ODBC (Open Database Connectivity).

In the query interface (as shown in Figure 14), the user can use the drawing tools to sketch an image and adjust the weight of features. The user clicks on the query button after the query image is completed. Then, the query server returns the candidate images and similarity scores to the candidate area, which is at the bottom of the window. If the user wants to look at some image details, he/she can click on the candidate image and this image will be enlarged in the upper-right corner of the window. In addition to query by an example only, the user can use the drawing tools to modify the query image and process the query again (as showed in Figure 15 and Figure 16, the user cuts and pastes a piece of image and modifies the background for retrieval again).

Query Examples

Figure 17 and Figure 18 show two query examples based on the color and shape features, individually. The user loads an image sample file, puts it in the query area and sets the weight of color/shape feature to 100. The user clicks on the query button and the query server returns the candidate images and similarity scores to the candidate area.

If the user wants to search images dependent on the query results again, he/she can drag the candidate images from the candidate area to the query area. Click the query button again. Then, the query server returns the new candidate image and recommends weights of features based on the input query images (shown in Figure 19). This approach allows relevance feedback, which is based on the user's judgment to allow personal factors in image retrieval.

Figure 20 shows an example query based on the spatial relations. The user uses the drawing tools to sketch a circle, a triangle and a square, and adjusts the spatial relations among these three objects, including circle before the triangle, triangle during inverse the square in the X coordinate, square before the triangle, and triangle overlap the circle in the Y coordinate. After the user adjusts the weight of spatial features to 100 and clicks the query button, the query server will return the candidate images and similarity scores at the candidate area.

The example only shows the use of spatial relations in a content-based system. The qualitative approach has an advantage in terms of flexibility in dealing with uncertain information. That is, the user usually cannot be sure about the extract content of a picture. The qualitative approach is a method to represent such an uncertain query. That is the strength of our CBR system. Whether it is based on spatial relation, shapes identify matching, or color histogram similarity; our system considers various approaches and the integration of relevance feedback factors. The system provides a feasible solution toward CBR problems.

CONCLUSION

The main contributions of this chapter are the development of an intelligent content-based image retrieval system that includes the methodologies of feature extraction, the similarity measure functions of the features and the friendly visual query interface. This chapter proposes not only a color clustering method for speeding-up the similarity measurement, but also designs the image database indexing/filtering mechanism that could improve the efficiency of image retrieval according to the color sensation and chromatology. A revised Seed Filling algorithm for extracting the shape feature of an image and the turning angle representation to describe the object are proposed. According to the spatial information of the objects in the image, we use qualitative spatial relations to analyze object similarities due to the difficulty of determining how far objects are separated. For easy querying, a friendly visual interface with a number of drawing/ querying tools is provided. Besides, the feedback learning mechanism are integrated in this system. After training to adjust attribute weights, the system is able to retrieve information from the image database through the Internet with high results.

In our future research, we will incorporate other features like image texture or different color/shape representation methods into the system, and allow users to decide which features are suitable for his/her own application domain. We will extend the spatial relation of the objects to analyze the motion features for retrieving the video streams. In addition, we will improve the online retrieval performance through the Internet and enhance the personal feedback learning mechanism of the system for more efficient retrieval.

REFERENCES

Alshuth, P., Termes, C., Klauck, J., Kreiss, & Roper, M. (1996). IRIS image retrieval for images and video. *Proceeding of First Internal Workshop on Image Database and Multimedia Search*, Amsterdam (August, pp. 170-179).

Arkin, E. M., Chew, L., Huttenlocher, D., Kedem, K., & Mitchell, J. (1991). An efficiently computable metric for comparing polygonal shapes. *IEEE Trans. on Pattern Analysis and Machine Intelligent, 13*(March), 209-216.

Bach, J. R., Fuller, C., Gupta, A., Hampapur, A., Horowitz, B., Humphrey, R., & Jain, R. (1996). The Virage image search engine: An open framework for image management. *SPIE Storage and Retrieval for Still Image and Video Databases, 2760*, 76-87.

Barrow, H. G. (1977). Parametric correspondence and chamfer matching: Two new techniques for image matching. *Proceedings of the International Joint Conference on Artificial Intelligence*, (pp. 659-663).

Beckmann, N., Kriegel, H. P., Schneider, R., & Seeger, B. (1990). The R*- tree: An efficient and robust access method for points and rectangles. *Proceeding of ACM SIGMOD*, (pp. 322-331).

Bimbo, A.D. (1999). *Visual Information Retrieval*. San Francisco, CA: Academic Press.

Borgefors, G. (1988). Hierarchical chamfer matching: A parametric edge matching algorithm. *IEEE Trans. on Pattern Analysis and Machine Intelligent, 10*, (November, pp. 849-865).

Canny, J. (1986). A computational approach to edge detection. *IEEE Transactions on Pattern Analysis and Machine Intelligence, PAMI, 8*(6), 679-698.

Chang S. F. & Smith, J. R. (1995). Extracting multi-dimensional signal features for content-based visual query. *Proceeding of SPIE Symposium on Visual Communications and Signal Processing, 2501*(2), (May, pp. 995-1006).

Chang, S. K. & Liu, S. H. (1984). Picture indexing and abstraction techniques for pictorial databases. *IEEE Trans. on Pattern Analysis and Machine Intelligence, 6*(July), 475-484.

Chang, S. K., Shi, Q. Y., & Yan, C. W. (1987). Iconic indexing by 2-D strings. *IEEE Trans. on Pattern Analysis and Machine Intelligence, 9*(3), 413-427.

Chuang, G. C.-H. & Kuo, C.-C.J. (1996). Wavelet descriptor of planar curves: Theory and applications. *IEEE Trans. Image Proc., 5*(January), 56-70.

Del Bimbo, A. & Pala, P. (1997). Retrieval by elastic matching of user sketches. *IEEE Trans. on Pattern Analysis and Machine Intelligence, 19*(2), 121-132.

Del Bimbo, A., Mugnaini, M., Pala P., & Turco, F. (1998). Visual querying by colour perceptive regions. *Pattern Recognition, 31*(9), 1241-1253.

Duda, R. O. & Hart, P. E. (1973). *Pattern Classification and Scene Analysis*. John Wiley and Sons.

Flicker, M., Sawhney, H., Niblack, W., Ashley, J., Huang, Q., Dom, B., Gorkani, M., Hafner, J., Lee, D., Petkovic, D., Steele, D., & Yanker, P. (1995). Query by image and video content: The QBIC system. *IEEE Computer Magazine, 28*(9), 23-32.

Freeman, H. (1974). Computer processing of line drawing images. *Computer Survey, 6*, 57-97.

Greene, D. (1989). An implementation and performance analysis of spatial data access. *Proceedings of IEEE International Conference on Data Engineering*, 606-615.

Guttman, (1984). R-tree: a dynamic index structure for spatial searching. *Proceedings of the ACM SIGACT-SIGMOD Conf. Principles Database Systems*, (pp. 569-592).

Kapur, D., Lakshman, Y. N., & Saxena, T. (1995). Computing invariants using elimination methods. *Proceedings of the IEEE International Symposium on Computer Vision*, (pp. 97-102).

Ma, W. Y. & Manjunath, B. S. (1997). Netra: A toolbook for navigating large image databases. *ICIP '97*, Santa Barbara, CA, (October, pp. 568-571).

Nabil, M., Ngu, A H. H., & Shepherd, J. (1996). Picture similarity retrieval using 2D projection interval representation. *IEEE Transactions on Knowledge and Data Engineering, 8*(4), 533-539.

Nievergelt, J., Hinterberger, H., & Sevcik, C. (1984). The grid file: an adaptable, symmetric, multikey file structure. *ACM TODS, 9*(March), 38-71.

Niu, Y., Tamer Ozsu, M., & Li, X. (1997). 2D-h trees: An index scheme for content-base retrieval of image in multimedia systems. *IEEE International Conference on Intelligent Processing Systems*, (pp. 1710-1715).

Pei, S. & Shiue, H. (1998). Indexing and retrieval of color image database. *Conference on Computer Vision, Graphics and Image Processing*, Taipei, (pp. 196-199).

Pentland, A., Picard, R., & Sclaroff, S. (1996). Photobook: Content-based manipulation of image databases. *International Journal of Computer Vision. 18*(3), 233-254.

Person, E. & K. S. Fu (1977). Shape discrimination using Fourier descriptors. *IEEE Trans. Systems, Man and Cybernetics SMC, 7*(March 3, pp. 170-179).

Rui, Y., Chakrabarti, K., Mehrotra, S., Zhao, Y., & Huang, T. S. (1997). Dynamic clustering for optimal retrieval in high dimensional multimedia databases. *TR-MARS-10-97*.

Samet, H. (1984). A geographic information system using quadtrees. *Pattern Recognition, 6*, 674-656.

Samet, H. (1984). The quad-tree and related data structures. *ACM Computing Surveys, 16*(2), 187-259.

Samet, H. (1988). Hierarchical representations of collections of small rectangles. *ACM Computing Surveys, 20*(4), 271-309.

Sellis, T., Roussopouls, N., & Faloutsos, C. (1987). The R+ tree: A dynamic index for multi-dimensional objects. *In Proceedings of the 12th VLDB*, 507-518.

Shen, J. & Castan, S. (1992). An optimal linear operator for step edge detection. *Computer Vision, Graphics, and Image Processing: Graphical Model and Understanding, 54*(2), 112-133.

Shih, T. K. & Chang, A. Y. (1998). The algebra of spatio-temporal intervals. *12th International Conference on Information Networking*, Japan, (January 21-23, pp. 116-121).

Smith, J. R. & S. F. Chang (1996). VisualSEEK: A fully automated content-base image query system. *ACM International Conference Multimedia*, Boston, MA, (November, pp. 87-98).

Swain, M.J. & Ballard, H. (1991). Color index. *Internal Journal of Computer Vision, 7*(1), 11-32.

Tanimoto, S. L. (1976). An iconic/symbolic data structuring scheme. *Pattern recognition and artificial intelligence.* New York: Academic Press.

Tominaga, S. (1992, August). Color classification of natural color image. *COLOR research and application, 17*(4), 230-239.

Unnikrishnan, A., Shankar P., & Venkatech, Y. V. (1998). Threaded linear hierarchical quadtrees for computation of geometric properties of binary images. *IEEE Transactions on Software Engineering, 14*(5), 659-665.

Vazirgiannis, M., Theodoridis, Y., & Sellis, T. (1996). Spatio-temporal composition in multimedia applications. *International Workshop on Multimedia Software Development*, Berlin, Germany, (March 25-26, pp. 120-127).

Wahl, T. et al. (1995). TIEMPO: Temporal modeling and authoring of interactive multimedia. *International Conference on Multimedia Computing and Systems*, Washington DC, (May 15-18, pp. 274–277).

Wan, X. & Kuo, C.C.J. (1996). Color distribution analysis and quantization for image retrieval. *SPIE Storage And Retrieval for Image and Video Database IV*, (Vol. SPIE 2670, February, pp. 9-16).

Wang, J., Yang, W., & Acharya, R. (1997). Color clustering techniques for color-content-based image retrieval from image databases. *Proceedings of IEEE International Conference on Multimedia Computing and Systems*, (June 3-6, pp. 442-449).

Wu, J. K., Narashihalu, A, D., Mehtre, B.M., Lam, C. P., & Gau. Y. J. (1995). CORE: A content-based retrieval engine for multimedia information systems. *Multimedia Systems, 3*, 25-41.

Zhang, H. & Zhang, D. (1995). A scheme for visual feature based image indexing. *Proceedings of IS&T/SPIE Conf. on Storage and Retrieval for Image and Video Databases III*, (pp. 36-46).

Chapter XII

A Spatial Relationship Method Supports Image Indexing and Similarity Retrieval

Ying-Hong Wang, Tamkang University, Taiwan

ABSTRACT

The increasing availability of image and multimedia-oriented applications markedly impacts image/multimedia file and database systems. Image data are not well-defined keywords such as traditional text data used in searching and retrieving functions. Consequently, various indexing and retrieving methodologies must be defined based on the characteristics of image data. Spatial relationships represent an important feature of objects (called icons) in an image (or picture). Spatial representation by 2-D String and its variants, in a pictorial spatial database, has been attracting growing interest. However, most 2-D Strings represent spatial information by cutting the icons out of an image and associating them with many spatial operators. The similarity retrievals by 2-D Strings require massive geometric computation and focus only on those database images that have all the icons and spatial relationships of the query image. This study proposes a new spatial-relationship representation model called

"Two Dimension Begin-End boundary string" (2D BƐ-string). The 2D BƐ-string represents an icon by its MBR boundaries. By applying "dummy objects," the 2D BƐ-string can intuitively and naturally represent the pictorial spatial information without any spatial operator. A method of evaluating image similarities, based on the modified "Longest Common Subsequence" (LCS) algorithm, is presented. The proposed evaluation method can not only sift out those images of which all icons and their spatial relationships fully accord with query images, but for those images whose icons and/ or spatial relationships are similar to those of query images. Problems of uncertainty in the query targets and/or spatial relationships thus solved. The representation model and similarity evaluation also simplify the retrieval progress of linear transformations, including rotation and reflection, of images.

INTRODUCTION

The increasing availability of image and multimedia-oriented applications very significantly influences image/multimedia file and database systems. Image data are not well-defined keywords such as traditional text data used in searching and retrieving functions. Therefore, various indexing and retrieving methodologies have to be defined based on the characteristics of image data.

Abstracting the information in original images is very important in pictorial spatial application systems. These abstractions include how the image icons and their characteristics were recognized; how the symbolic image was encoded and constructed; how to index and retrieve these images; how to evaluate their similarity corresponding to a query image, and many others. All of these are very important issues in information and content-based retrieval.

Three basic types for image indexing and retrieval exist: (1) by features, for example, color, texture, or shape, of the icons in the images, as in the QBIC project (Huang & Jean, 1994), and the Virage search engine (Liang & Mou, 1996); (2) by size and location of the image icons, as in R-tree (Guttman, 1984), R*-tree (Beckmann, Kriegal, Schneider, & Seeger, 1990), Quadtree (Samet, 1989), and Mou's similarity method (Chien, 1998); (3) by relative position of the icons (called Spatial relationship), as in 2-D String (Chang, Shi, & Yan, 1987) and its variants (Chang, Jungert, & Li, 1988; Lee & Hsu, 1990; Lee, Yang, & Chen, 1992; Bach, et al., 1996; Liang & Mou, 1997; Hsu, Lee, & Lin, 1999; Sipser, 1997; Papadias & Theodoridis, 1995). Spatial relationships represent an important feature of objects (called icons) in an image (or picture).

The third type is most suited to those applications that are independent of the actual coordinates of icon objects, as in for example, 'find all images in which icon A is located on the left side and icon B on the right.' Spatial representation by 2-D String and its variants, in a pictorial spatial database, has attracted increasing attention. However, most of 2-D Strings represent the spatial information by cutting the icons out of an image, which are associated with many spatial operators. Their similarity retrievals require extensive geometric computation and focus only on those database images that include all of the icons and spatial relationships of the query image.

This investigation proposes a novel spatial knowledge representation model called, "Two Dimension Begin-End boundary string (2D BƐ-string)." The 2D BƐ-string need not cut any image's icons because it directly represents an icon by the boundaries of its MBR (Minimum Bounding Rectangle). By applying "**dummy** objects," the 2D Bε-string can intuitively and naturally represent the pictorial spatial information without any spatial operators. An algorithm is also introduced, which involves $O(n)$ space complexity in the best and worst case, to establish an image database using the proposed model.

A method of evaluating image similarities is also presented, according to the modified "Longest Common Subsequence" (LCS) algorithm (Cormen, Leiserson, & Rivest, 1990). The proposed evaluation method sifts out not only those images in which all of the icons and their spatial relationships fully accord with those of the query images, but also those images whose icons and/or spatial relationships are similar to those of the query image. Problems of uncertainty of the query targets and/or spatial relationships are thus solved. The modified LCS algorithm involves $O(mn)$ space and time complexity, where m and n are the numbers of icons in a query image and a database image, respectively. Retrieving the linear transformations of an image represented by a 2D Bε-string is simpler than other models of 2-D Strings. The transformations include 90, 180, 270 degrees clockwise rotations and reflections in the x- and y-axis.

The rest of this chapter is organized as follows. The chapter reviews the approaches of 2-D String and its variants and is followed with a section that proposes a new spatial knowledge representation model, called 2D Bε-string, and an algorithm to construct a symbolic picture using 2D Bε-string. Then, the chapter introduces a similarity retrieval algorithm, modified from LCS, and the corresponding similarity evaluation process. Next, the chapter presents a demonstration system, which is a visual retrieval system, implemented by 2D Bε-string and the modified LCS algorithm. The chapter finishes with concluding remarks and suggests directions for future work.

BACKGROUND

This section introduces relevant background theories and techniques.

Minimum Bounding Rectangle (MBR)

MBR is the most popular approximation to identify an object from images (Papadias & Theodoridis, 1995; Bowen & Um, 1999; Song, Whang, Lee, & Kim, 1999; Orlandic & Yu, 2000), and retains the most important characteristics of the object; position and extension. MBR is characterizes an object by minimum and maximum x and y coordinates (Zimbrao & De Souza, 1998). Figure 1 presents a coordinate system for a picture/image considered in this chapter. Symbols minX(A) and maxX(A) are minimum and maximum x coordinates of the MBR for an object, A. Symbols minY(A) and maxY(A) are minimum and maximum y coordinates of the MBR for an object, A.

Representation Models of 2-D String and its Variants

Chang, Shi and Yan (1987) proposed an approach, called '2-D String', to represent the spatial information of a picture or image. The 2-D String uses a symbolic projection of a picture on the x- and y-axes. They define two sets of symbols, V and A. Each symbol in V presents an icon object in an image. A is a set of spatial operators containing {'=', '<', ':'}. A 2-D String over V and A is defined by $(u, v) = (o_1 x_1 o_2 x_2 ... x_{n-1} o_n, o_{p(1)} y_1 o_{p(2)} y_2 ... y_{n-}$

Figure 1: MBR Presentation of an Object in a Picture/Image

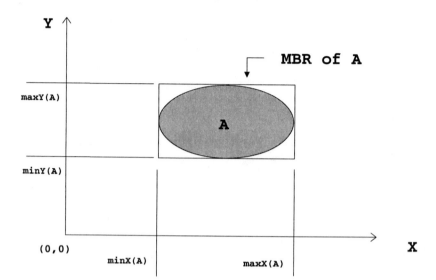

$_1 o_{p(n)}$), where $o_1 o_2 ... o_n$ is a 1-D string over V, $x_1 x_2 ... x_{n-1}$ and $y_1 y_2 ... y_{n-1}$ are 1-D strings over A; $o_{p(1)} o_{p(2)} ... o_{p(n)}$ is a permutation of $o_1 o_2 ... o_n$ on the y-axis. Therefore, n icon objects are in the picture/image and their spatial information is represented by operators, $x_1 x_2 ... x_{n-1}$ and $y_1 y_2 ... y_{n-1}$ on x-axis and y-axis, respectively. Figure 2 depicts an example of 2-D String.

The 2D G-string (Chang, Jungert, & Li, 1988), a variant of 2-D String, extends spatial relationships to two sets of spatial operators, R_1 and R_g, and cuts all the objects along their MBR boundaries. The set, R_1, defines local spatial relationships that are partially overlapping projections between two objects. The set, R_g, defines global spatial relationships, such that the projection of two objects are disjoining, adjoining or in the same position.

The 2D C-string (Lee & Hsu, 1990; Bach, et al., 1996), another variant of 2-D String, minimizes the number of cutting objects. The 2D C-string keeps the leading object uncut and addresses the problem of superfluous cutting objects generated by 2D G-string cutting progress. The worst case will involve $O(n^2)$ cutting objects.

Consequently, the 2D B-string (Lee, Yang, & Chen, 1992) does not use cutting, and instead, represents an object by two symbols. One of which indicates for the beginning boundary of that object; the other one represents the end. 2D B-string also reduces the spatial relationships to a single operator '=', such that two objects have the same boundary projection if '=' appears.

Similarity Retrieval and Evaluation

The basic similarity retrieval and evaluation approaches of 2-D String (Chang, Shi, & Yan, 1987), 2D G-string (Chang, Jungert, & Li, 1988), 2D C-string (Lee & Hsu, 1990) and 2D B-string (Lee, Yang, & Chen, 1992) are the same (Chan & Chang, n.d.). First, they

Figure 2: Example of 2D String Representation

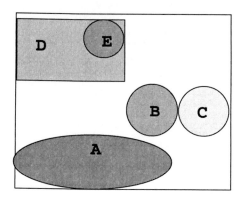

The 2D String is

(A=D:E<A=B<C, A<B=C<D:E)

always define three types of similarity, type-i (i = 0, 1, 2). Each is constrained according to some conditions. Type-1 is stricter than type-0; type-2 is stricter than type-1. Second, they compare all spatial relationship pairs between any two objects in the query image to pairs in an image in databases and build a type-i subgraph if the pair satisfies type-i constraints. Then, they find the **maximum complete subgraph** from each existing type-i graph. The number of objects in the maximum complete subgraph measures the similarity of the query image to images in databases.

The space and time complexity of examining all spatial relationship pairs is $O(n^2)$, where n is the number of objects in an image. Finding the maximum complete subgraph is an NP-complete problem (Kim & Um, 1999), and is a time consuming procedure is not suited to a large number of icon objects in an image.

SPATIAL REPRESENTATION MODEL USING 2D Bε-STRING

2D Bε-string Model

Several approaches have been proposed to represent an icon in an image. These include MBR (Minimum Bounding Rectangle) (Chang, Jungert, & Li, 1988; Lee & Hsu, 1990; Lee, Yang, & Chen, 1992; Bach, et al., 1996), MBE (Minimum Bounding Ellipse), MBC (Minimum Bounding Circle) (Chien, 1998), and others.

The approach presented here, 2D Bε-string, is based on MBR. Conceptually, it is similar to the 2D B-string approach. Both represent an object by its MBR boundaries and require nothing to be cut. However, 2D Bε-string states the spatial relationship between two boundary symbols in quite a different way. 2D B-string uses a **spatial operator** (=) to denote an **IDENTITY** between the projections of two boundaries. In 2D Bε-string, a

dummy object is used to describe the **DISTINCTION** between the projections of two boundaries.

The definition of 'Dummy Object' is as follows:

A 'Dummy Object' is an assumed virtual object; it is not a real object existing in an original image. It can be specified as any size of space and be memorized as symbol 'ε'.

2D Bε-string can be defined as:

$$(u, v) = (d_0 x_1 d_1 x_2 d_2 \ldots d_{n-1} x_n d_n, d_0 y_1 d_1 y_2 d_2 \ldots d_{n-1} y_n d_n)$$

where d_i is a dummy object ε, or a null string, $i = 0, 1, \ldots n$, and x_i and y_i are real icon objects which are either beginning or ending projected boundaries on the x- and y-axis, respectively, with $i = 1, 2, \ldots n$. d_i can be determined when the maximum size of an image, say X_{max} and Y_{max} along the x- and y-axes, respectively, is known. Set d_0 to ε if a space exists between the beginning boundary of the leftmost (bottommost) object and the left (bottom) edge of the image. Similarly, set d_n to ε if an interval exists between the ending boundary of the rightmost (topmost) object and the right (top) edge of the image. For the dummy objects, set d_i to ε if the boundary projections of x_i and x_{i+1} (y_i and y_{i+1}) differ from each other.

The 2D Bε-string in Figure 3, for example, is written as $(u, v) = (\varepsilon A_b \varepsilon B_b \varepsilon A_e C_b \varepsilon C_e \varepsilon B_e \varepsilon, \varepsilon B_b \varepsilon A_b \varepsilon B_e C_b \varepsilon C_e \varepsilon A_e \varepsilon)$. The dummy object, d_0, was set to ε because a space exists in front of the beginning boundary of object A on the x-axis. The dummy object d_6 was also set to ε because a space is in the behind object, B, on the x-axis. However, the dummy object, d_3, was set to null string, because the ending boundary of object A and the beginning boundary of object C are projected onto the same point on the x-axis. A similar case applies to the ending boundary of object B and the beginning boundary of object C on the y-axis.

Observably, 2D Bε-string has the following advantages:

First, the object location in the original image and the symbolic picture are mapped directly, as show in Table 1. No operator is required to represent the spatial relationship between objects. The approach is intuitive.

Figure 3: Image with Three Objects

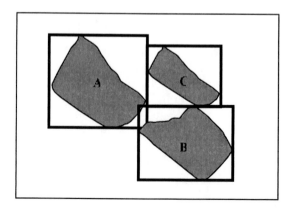

Table 1: Mapping of Spatial Relationships

	In symbolic picture	In original image
1	$\varepsilon A_b \varepsilon A_e \varepsilon C_b \varepsilon C_e \varepsilon$	(rectangles A and C, disjoint)
2	$\varepsilon A_b \varepsilon A_e C_b \varepsilon C_e \varepsilon$	(rectangles A and C)
3	$\varepsilon A_b \varepsilon C_b \varepsilon A_e \varepsilon C_e \varepsilon$	(rectangles A and C)
4	$\varepsilon A_b \varepsilon C_b \varepsilon C_e A_e \varepsilon$	(rectangles A and C)
5	$\varepsilon A_b \varepsilon C_b \varepsilon C_e \varepsilon A_e \varepsilon$	(rectangles A and C)
6	$\varepsilon A_b C_b \varepsilon A_e \varepsilon C_e \varepsilon$	(rectangles A and C)
7	$\varepsilon A_b C_b \varepsilon A_e C_e \varepsilon$	(rectangles A and C)
8	$\varepsilon A_b C_b \varepsilon C_e \varepsilon A_e \varepsilon$	(rectangles A and C)
9	$\varepsilon C_b \varepsilon A_b \varepsilon A_e \varepsilon C_e \varepsilon$	(rectangles A and C)
10	$\varepsilon C_b \varepsilon A_b \varepsilon A_e C_e \varepsilon$	(rectangles A and C)
11	$\varepsilon C_b \varepsilon A_b \varepsilon C_e \varepsilon A_e \varepsilon$	(rectangles A and C)
12	$\varepsilon C_b \varepsilon C_e A_b \varepsilon A_e \varepsilon$	(rectangles A and C)
13	$\varepsilon C_b \varepsilon C_e \varepsilon A_b \varepsilon A_e \varepsilon$	(rectangles A and C, disjoint)

Second, this approach of 2D Bε-string does not need to cut the objects from the image. It simplifies the construction of the image database. The space complexity for an image with n objects in the worst and best case is $O(n)$. In the worst case, all boundary projections are distinct and a space is left in the leftmost, bottommost, rightmost and topmost parts of an image ($4n+1$ symbols are required). In contrast, in the best case, all boundary projections are identical and exactly fit in an image (requiring $2n+1$ symbols only).

Third, the approach simplifies similarity retrieval because results of spatial reasoning need not be combined.

Table 2: Algorithm to Construct a Symbolic Picture

Convert-2D-Bε -String $(n, C, X_b, X_e, Y_b, Y_e, x_{max}, y_{max})$
1. // n ...number of objects in an image
2. // C ...object symbols in image, $C = \{c_1, c_2, ..., c_n\}$
3. // X_b ...begin boundaries on x-axis, $X_b = \{x_{b1}, x_{b2}, ..., x_{bn}\}$
4. // X_e ...end boundaries on x-axis, $X_e = \{x_{e1}, x_{e2}, ..., x_{en}\}$
5. // Y_b ...begin boundaries on y-axis, $Y_b = \{y_{b1}, y_{b2}, ..., y_{bn}\}$
6. // Y_e ...end boundaries on y-axis, $Y_e = \{y_{e1}, y_{e2}, ..., y_{en}\}$
7. // x_{max} ...maximum coordinate on x-axis
8. // y_{max} ...maximum coordinate on x-axis
9. // X_{be} ...2D Bε-string on x-axis, $X_{be} = \{v_0 x_1 v_1 x_2 v_2 ... v_{n-1} x_n v_n\}$, where $v_i =$ dummy object ε or null string; $i = 0, 1, ..., n$; $x_i = c_{bi}$ or c_{ei}, identifies the projection of beging boundary or end boundary of object c_i on x-axis, $i = 1, 2, ..., n$
10. // Y_{be} ...2D Bε-string on y-axis, $Y_{be} = \{v_0 y_1 v_1 y_2 v_2 ... v_{n-1} y_n v_n\}$, where $v_i =$ dummy object ε or null string; $i = 0, 1, ..., n$; $y_i = c_{bi}$ or c_{ei}, identifies the projection of beging boundary or end boundary of object c_i on y-axis, $i = 1, 2, ..., n$
11. // S...a sort based on x-axis, $S = \{s_i \mid s_i = x_{bi} c_i$ or $x_{ei} c_i, i = 1, 2, ..., 2n\}$
12. // T...a sort based on y-axis, $T = \{t_i \mid t_i = y_{bi} c_i$ or $y_{ei} c_i, i = 1, 2, ..., 2n\}$

Algorithm for Constructing a Symbolic Picture

By default, before converting an image to a symbolic picture represented by 2D Bε-string, all objects and their MBR coordinates must be abstracted from that image. Then, algorithm **Convert-2D-Bε-String**, shown in Table 2, is called to transform an original image into a symbolic picture. Lines one to 12 explain the meaning of the variables used in the input parameters and the conversion process. Lines 14 to 19 separately sort the input data by key coordinate and object identifiers, in ascending order on the x- and y-axes. Lines 21 to 32 construct the 2D Bε-string on the x-axis, and lines 34 to 45 construct the 2D Bε-string on the y-axis.

The time complexity of algorithm **Convert-2D-Bε-String** depends on the sorting algorithm in line 19. The time complexity of loops in lines 14 to 18, 24 to 30 and 37 to 43 is $O(n)$, and never exceeds that of the sorting algorithm. Ignoring the sorting algorithm, the space complexity of this algorithm is also $O(n)$.

Building an image database using 2D Bε-string, requires only algorithm **Convert-2D-Bε-String** to be called with the MBR coordinates and object identifiers of each image and the results of the 2D Bε-string to be saved in the database. Saving the 2D Bε-string with the MBR coordinates of objects in an image allows the location into which a new object is to be inserted and the MBR boundaries of that object to be easily found using the binary search method with MBR coordinates and the identifier of the new object as searching keys. This is because the 2D Bε-string uses an order datum to represent the relationship among the objects in an image. Whether a dummy object is to be inserted around this new object boundary is easy to determine. In contrast with insertion, dropping an object from an image, requires the dropping object to be searched sequen-

Table 2: Algorithm to Construct a Symbolic Picture (continued)

```
13.     // Combine MBR coordinate and object identifier as a key, sort the input data by
        ascending order
14.     for i = 1 to n
15.         sᵢ ← x_{bi}cᵢ
16.         s_{i+n} ← x_{ei}cᵢ
17.         tᵢ ← y_{bi}cᵢ
18.         t_{i+n} ← y_{ei}cᵢ
19.     Sorting S and T by ascending order
20          // Construct 2D Bε-string on x-axis
21          X_{be} ← "                        // Initilized by a null string
22          if x_b of s₁ ≠ 0 then              // Insert ε at the leftmost?
23              X_{be} ← ε
24          for i = 1 to 2n-1
25              if type of x in sᵢ is x_b then   // convert coordinate to
26                  X_{be} ← X_{be}c_{bi}        // boundary symbol
27              else                             // type of x in sᵢ is x_e
28                  X_{be} ← X_{be}c_{ei}
29              if x of sᵢ ≠ x of s_{i+1} then
30                  X_{be} ← X_{be}ε
31          if x_e of s_{2n} ≠ x_{max} then       // Insert ε at the rightmost?
32              X_{be} ← X_{be}ε
33          // Construct 2D Bε-string on y-axis
34          Y_{be} ← "
35          if y_b of t₁ ≠ 0 then              // Insert ε at the bottommost?
36              Y_{be} ← ε
37          for i = 1 to 2n-1
38              if type of y in tᵢ is y_b then   // convert coordinate to
39                  Y_{be} ← Y_{be}c_{bi}        // boundary symbol
40              else                             // type of y in tᵢ is y_e
41                  Y_{be} ← Y_{be}c_{ei}
42              if y of tᵢ ≠ y of t_{i+1} then
43                  Y_{be} ← Y_{be}ε
44          if y_e of t_{2n} ≠ y_{max} then       // Insert ε at the topmost?
45              Y_{be} ← Y_{be}ε
46      return X_{be}, Y_{be}
```

tially from the 2D Bε-string data. It is a direct deletion and the redundant dummy object, if found, to be deleted.

IMAGE SIMILARITY RETRIEVAL AND EVALUATION

Assessment of Similarity

The "Background" section discussed the symbolic image construction and the assessment of similarity, using 2D B-String. In order to decide which type, type-0, type-1 or type-2, of similarity it belongs to all spatial relationships for every pair of objects in a database image must be recorded to determine of which type is the similarity. However, this assessment does not address a situation in which only a few query objects are present in a database image. Moreover, the assessment of similarity as type-0, type-1 and type-2 is based on the maximum complete subgraph. Obtaining a maximum complete subgraph from C_2^m spatial relationships of m objects in a query image and C_2^n spatial relationships of n objects in the database image is rather time-consuming.

This chapter also uses the number of spatial relationships, formed by every pair of objects that simultaneously appear in the query image and the database image, as the assessment of similarity. However, the proposed method does not find a maximum complete subgraph but finds a longest common subsequence (LCS) (Cormen, Leiserson, & Rivest, 1990) of two 2D Bε-strings instead. After the LCS string is found, it is evaluated in relation to 2D Bε-strings of the query image and the database image.

The motivations for finding an LCS string in this work and finding a maximum complete subgraph in 2-D Strings from two images are different tunes rendered with equal skill. Both the LCS string and the subgraph are used to evaluate similarity. However, the time complexity of an LCS algorithm is $O(mn)$, where m and n are the number of objects in the query image and the database image, respectively. The complexity depends only on the length of 2D Bε-string in the query image and the database image. Not all the spatial relationships need be examined for every pair of objects because **"in the query image and the database image, all spatial relationships of every pair of objects in the LCS string are identical."** Therefore, similarity can be evaluated in a reasonable time.

Algorithms of Similarity Retrieval

This study presents an algorithm to find the longest common subsequence length of two 2D Bε-strings. Table 3 shows this algorithm, which is called, **2D-Bε-LCS-Length**. The algorithm is modified from the LCS algorithm in Cormen, Leiserson and Rivest (1990). Revising the original LCS algorithm depends on two considerations. First, LCS is prevented from picking dummy objects continuously, because a single dummy object sufficiently represents the relative spatial relationship between two boundary symbols. The *if*-statement in line 21 performs this evaluation. Second, the LCS paths-recording matrix in the original LCS algorithm is omitted by evaluating left and up paths first, as shown in lines 16 to 19, and then evaluating the left-up diagonal path, as shown lines 23 to 24. The LCS path can still be inferred from the matrix record of the LCS length.

Algorithm **2D-Bε-LCS-Length** uses two 2D Bε-strings, Q and D, as input parameters — one for the query image and the other one for the database image. The 2D Bε-string of a query image with m objects in, each dimension has $2m$ boundary symbols and up to $2m+1$ dummy objects. The maximum length of a 2D Bε-string in each dimension is $2m+(2m+1)$, that is, $4m+1$. The maximum length of 2D Bε-string of a database image with n objects is similarly derived as $4n+1$. The LCS length-inferring table W, requires $(1+(4m+1))(1+(4n+1))$ storage units; therefore, the space complexity is $O(mn)$.

Lines seven to eight and 10 to 11 of the algorithm in Table 2 show the initialization of the first row and first column in the LCS-length inferring table, W: each string symbol must be set once. These instructions are executed $4m+1$ and $4n+2$ times, respectively. The outer loop, in line 13, examines each row in W, $4m+1$ times. The inner loop, in lines 14 to 26, examines each cell of W, $(4m+1)*(4n+1)$ times. Thus, the time complexity is $O((4m+1)+(4n+2)+(4m+1)*(4n+1))$ the same as $O(mn)$.

Table 3: Algorithm to Determine LCS Length from Two Strings

2D-Bε-LCS-Length (Q, D)

1. $m \leftarrow length(Q)$
2. $n \leftarrow length(D)$
3. // Q is a 2D Bε-string of query image, $Q = \{q_i \mid q_i \in \{$dummy object ε or the boundary symbols of objects in query image$\}$, $i = 1, 2, ..., m\}$.
4. // D is a 2D Bε-string of database image, $D = \{d_j \mid d_j \in \{$dummy object ε or the boundary symbols of objects in query image$\}$, $j = 1, 2, ..., n\}$.
5. // LCS length is inferred in table W, $W = \{w_{i,j} \mid |w_{i,j}|$ is the LCS length of string $q_1, ..., q_i$ and $d_1, ..., d_j$. If the last symbol of LCS string is dummy object ε then $w_{i,j} < 0$ else $w_{i,j} \geq 0$, where $i = 0, 1, 2, ..., m, j = 0, 1, 2, ..., n\}$.
6. // Initialize the first column of inferring table W with zeros.
7. for $I \leftarrow 1$ to m do
8. $w_{i,0} \leftarrow 0$
9. // Initialize the first row of inferring table W with zeros.
10. for $j \leftarrow 0$ to n do
11. $w_{0,j} \leftarrow 0$
12. // From row 1 column 1, infer the value of each cell, row by row and column by column, until every cell has been evaluated.
13. for $i = 1$ to m do
14.   for $j = 1$ to n do
15. // Set current cell value to the value of the left or upper cell which has maximum absolute value.
16.   if $|w_{i-1,j}| \geq |w_{i,j-1}|$ then
17. $w_{i,j} \leftarrow w_{i-1,j}$
18.   else
19. $w_{i,j} \leftarrow w_{i,j-1}$
20. // Then check whether the value of q_i and d_j are equal and at least one of q_i and the last symbol on the LCS left-up diagonal path is not a dummy object.
21.   if $(q_i = d_j)$ and $((q_i \neq \varepsilon)$ or $(w_{i-1,j-1} \geq 0))$ then
22. // If all symbols are hold, then check whether to follow the left-up diagonal path.
23.   if $(|w_{i-1,j-1}| + 1) > |w_{i,j}|$ then
24. $w_{i,j} \leftarrow |w_{i-1,j-1}| + 1$
25.   if $q_i = \varepsilon$ then
26. $w_{i,j} \leftarrow -w_{i,j}$
27. return W

A recursive procedure is also specified for printing the longest common subsequence string of two 2D Bε-strings. Table 4 shows this algorithm. The initial invocation is **Print-2D-Bε-LCS** $(Q, W, length(Q), length(D))$. From the value of the last cell in the LCS-inferring table, W, this procedure decreases by i and/or j in the left and/or up direction in each recursive call, until either i or j reaches zero. Then, all symbols of the LCS string are printed out in the proper, forward order.

To find the longest common subsequence length of two 2D Bε-strings, the LCS string length of the current cell must be compared with that of the top one before the LCS string symbol is printed, according the revised procedure shown as Table 3. Therefore, the LCS path is determined from the up direction if the LCS string lengths are equal. The corresponding boundary symbol or dummy object is not a symbol of the LCS string. This symbol is thus ignored and is induced continuously along the up direction, as shown

Table 4: Algorithm to Print LCS String of Two 2D Bε-Strings

Print-2D-Bε-LCS (Q, W, i, j)
1.   // Q is a 2D Bε-string of query image, $Q = \{q_i \mid q_i \in \{$dummy object ε or the boundary symbols of objects in query image$\}$, $i = 1, 2, ..., m\}$.
2.   // W is the LCS-length inferring table of two 2D Bε-strings, and is induced by the algorithm in Table 3.
3.   if $i = 0$ or $j = 0$ then
4.   return
5.   if $|w_{i,j}| = |w_{i-1,j}|$ then
6.   Print-2D-Be-LCS($Q, W, i-1, j$)
7.   else if $|w_{i,j}| = |w_{i,j-1}|$ then
8.   Print-2D-Be-LCS($Q, W, i, j-1$)
9.   else
10.   Print-2D-Be-LCS($Q, W, i-1, j-1$)
11.   print q_i
12.   return

---

in lines five to six. However, if the lengths are unequal, the current cell's LCS string length must be compared with the left cell's length. If these lengths are the same, then the LCS is induced from the left direction. For the same reason as in the preceding case, if the corresponding boundary symbol or dummy object is not a symbol of the LCS string, this symbol is ignored and is induced continuously along the left direction, as shown in lines seven through eight. If the LCS is from neither the up nor the left direction, it must be induced from the left-up diagonal direction. The boundary symbol or dummy object associated with the current cell must be part of the LCS string. After recursively processing all the cells in the left/up direction, this symbol in the LCS string is printed out, as shown in lines nine to 11.

Lines six, eight and 10 are recursively called; each time, either i or j is reduced by one. This algorithm can print out all LCS string symbols after no more than $m+n$ recursions. The time complexity is $O(m+n)$.

Similarity Evaluation

After the LCS length and the LCS string are obtained from the query image and data images in each dimension of 2D Bε-string, how is similarity evaluated? Conceptually, the two images are more similar if the LCS string is longer. For example, the strings in one dimension of 2D Bε-string are:

Query image 1: $\varepsilon B_b \varepsilon C_b \varepsilon B_e \varepsilon A_b \varepsilon C_e \varepsilon A_e \varepsilon$,
Database image 1: $\varepsilon B_b \varepsilon B_e \varepsilon D_b \varepsilon A_b \varepsilon D_e \varepsilon A_e \varepsilon$,
LCS string 1: $\varepsilon B_b \varepsilon B_e \varepsilon A_b \varepsilon A_e \varepsilon$,
Database image 2: $\varepsilon B_b \varepsilon C_b \varepsilon B_e \varepsilon D_b \varepsilon A_b \varepsilon D_e \varepsilon C_e \varepsilon A_e \varepsilon$,
LCS string 2: $\varepsilon B_b \varepsilon C_b \varepsilon B_e \varepsilon A_b \varepsilon C_e \varepsilon A_e \varepsilon$.

The LCS strings 1 and 2 follow from query image 1 with database images 1 and 2, respectively, according to the LCS-length-inferring algorithm in Table 3 and the LCS path-discovering algorithm in Table 4. For a given query image string, database image

2 yields a better result than database image 1 because LCS string 2 is longer than LCS string 1. However, two database images with the same LCS string length may not have the same degree of similarity. For example:

Query image 2: $\varepsilon B_b \varepsilon C_b \varepsilon B_e A_b \varepsilon C_e \varepsilon A_e$,
Database image 3: $\varepsilon B_b \varepsilon B_e \varepsilon D_b \varepsilon A_b \varepsilon D_e \varepsilon A_e \varepsilon$,
LCS string 3: $\varepsilon B_b \varepsilon B_e A_b \varepsilon A_e$,
Database image 4: $\varepsilon B_b \varepsilon D_b \varepsilon B_e A_b \varepsilon D_e \varepsilon A_e \varepsilon$,
LCS string 4: $\varepsilon B_b \varepsilon B_e A_b \varepsilon A_e$,

The length of LCS strings 3 and 4 is the same, but database image 4 gives a better matching result than database image 3, because query image 2 requires object B and object A to be adjoined, that is, boundary symbols B_e and A_b must have the same projection. But in database image 3, object A is not adjoined to object B because spaces exist between boundary symbols B_e and A_b. The interval does not exist in database image 4. Accordingly, database image 4 has a better similarity than database image 3.

Following the above analysis, the similarity of preceding phenomena is assessed. The following notation is first defined over 2D Bε-string:

N: number of objects in a query image;
Q_x: string length along x-axis in a query image;
Q_y: string length along y-axis in a query image;
L_x: length of LCS string with dummy objects along x-axis;
L_y: length of LCS string with dummy objects along y-axis;
M_x: length of L_x string without dummy object;
M_y: length of L_y string without dummy object;
D_x: length of boundary symbols with spatial relationships in database image based on M_x;
D_y: length of boundary symbols with spatial relationships in database image based on M_y;
W_x: weight adjustment along x-axis, $0 \leq Wx \leq 1$;
W_y: weight adjustment along y-axis, $0 \leq Wy \leq 1$, and $Wx + Wy = 1$;
S_x: similarity along x-axis, $0 \leq Sx \leq 1$,

$$S_x = \begin{cases} 1-(Q_x + D_x - 2L_x)/(4N+1) & \text{if } M_x > 0, \\ 0 & \text{if } M_x = 0; \end{cases}$$

S_y: similarity along y-axis, $0 \leq Sy \leq 1$,

$$S_y = \begin{cases} 1-(Q_y + D_y - 2L_y)/(4N+1) & \text{if } M_y > 0, \\ 0 & \text{if } M_y = 0; \end{cases}$$

S: similarity of the query image to a database image,
$S = WxSx + WySy$, $0 \leq S \leq 1$.

The LCS string lengths L_x, L_y, M_x, and M_y can be obtained by the algorithm in Table 3 applied along the x and y axes. The values of M_x and M_y can be determined as the values L_x and L_y minus the number of dummy symbol, ε, in the LCS string, respectively. W_x and W_y stress the importance of similarity on the x-axis and y-axis, respectively.

As stated in the section, "2D Bε-String Model", an image with n objects has no more than $4n+1$ symbols on each dimension of its 2D Bε-string. $2n$ symbols are boundary symbols and the rest are $2n+1$ symbols; dummy objects are dispersed among the boundary symbols. Now each symbol is pictured as a bucket. Thus, an image with n objects has up to $4n+1$ buckets. If the symbol does not exist, then the associated bucket is considered empty. For example, query image 2 with three objects, A, B, and C, has at most $4*3+1=13$ symbols. The boundary string is $\varepsilon B_b \varepsilon C_b \varepsilon B_e A_b \varepsilon C_e \varepsilon A_e$. Bucket 7 (Figure 4) is empty due to the lack of a dummy object, ε, between B_e and A_b. The end of a boundary string also lacks a dummy object because the ending boundary of the object A is the same as the right-edge of the image; therefore, bucket 13 is empty. In another example, shown in database image 4, the boundary string $\varepsilon B_b \varepsilon D_b \varepsilon B_e A_b \varepsilon D_e \varepsilon A_e \varepsilon$ has an empty bucket 7 (Figure 4).

Comparing the query image (shown as Figure 4) with the database image (shown as Figure 5), buckets in the query image are categorized into four classes and the number of buckets in each class in Table 5 is summarized.

Class I: without a dummy object between two boundary symbols in both the query image and the database image: for example, bucket 7 is empty shown in Figure 4 and Figure 5.

Class II: without a dummy object between two boundary symbols in the query image, but with a dummy object of them in the database image: for example, the ending of boundary string, bucket 13, in the query image (Figure 4), but there is a dummy object in bucket 13 of the database image (Figure 5).

Class III: symbols in the query image but not in the database image; for example, the buckets 4, 5, 10 and 11 show on Figure 4 and Figure 5.

Class IV: symbols with same spatial relationships in both query image and database image; for example, the buckets 1, 2, 3, 6, 8, 9 and 12 present on Figure 4 and Figure 5.

Figure 4: Symbols in Buckets of Query Image 2

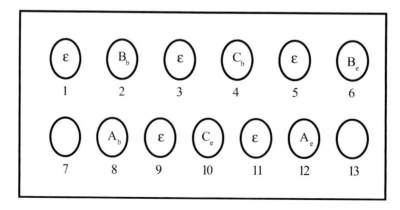

Figure 5: Symbols in Bucket of Database Image 4

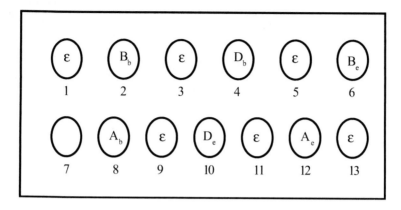

Classes I and IV together represent similar parts of a query image and a database image. The evaluated value of similarity can be also obtained from the complementary normalized portion of the total number of buckets in classes II and III. The total number of symbols in class I and IV along the x-axis and the y-axis are $(4n+1) - (Q_x - L_x + D_x - L_x)$ and $(4n+1) - (Q_y - L_y + D_y - L_y)$, respectively. The similarity on the x-axis (S_x) is $1 - (Q_x + D_x - 2L_x)/(4n+1)$ and that on the y-axis (S_y) is $1 - (Q_y + D_y - 2L_y)/(4n+1)$. Clearly, the similarity of the entire image is the sum of S_x and S_y with proper weights adjusting, that is, $S = W_x S_x + W_y S_y$.

Finally, an example is given to detailing the procedure of calculating the similarity. The query image in Figure 3 has three objects, so $N = 3$; the 2D Bε-string is represented as $(\varepsilon A_b \varepsilon B_b \varepsilon A_e C_b \varepsilon C_e B_e \varepsilon, \varepsilon B_b \varepsilon A_b \varepsilon B_e C_b \varepsilon C_e \varepsilon A_e \varepsilon)$ and the string lengths on the x-axis and the y-axis, (Q_x, Q_y), are $(12, 12)$, respectively.

The database image in Figure 6 has a 2D Bε-string $(\varepsilon E_b \varepsilon A_b \varepsilon_b \varepsilon A_e \varepsilon C_b \varepsilon F_b \varepsilon E_e \varepsilon C_e \varepsilon B_e \varepsilon F_e \varepsilon, \varepsilon E_b \varepsilon B_b \varepsilon E_e \varepsilon A_b \varepsilon B_e C_b \varepsilon F_b \varepsilon C_e \varepsilon A_e \varepsilon F_e \varepsilon)$. Table 6 and Table 7 show the LCS-length-inferring table on the x-axis and the y-axis of the query image and the database image with dummy objects, respectively. The symbols in column q_i and row d_j of Table 6 and Table 7 are the boundary string symbols along the associated axis, with dummy objects in the query

Table 5: Classify by Existence of Symbol in Buckets of a Query Image

Class	Symbol appears?	The symbol appeared in corresponding bucket in database image?	Number of buckets
I	No	No	?
II	No	Yes	$D_x - L_x$ in x-axis, $D_y - L_y$ in y-axis
III	Yes	No	$Q_x - L_x$ in x-axis, $Q_y - L_y$ in y-axis
IV	Yes	Yes	L_x in x-axis, L_y in y-axis

image and the database image, respectively. The LCS strings are $\varepsilon A_b \varepsilon B_b \varepsilon A_e C_b \varepsilon C_e \varepsilon B_e \varepsilon$ and $\varepsilon B_b \varepsilon A_b \varepsilon B_e C_b \varepsilon C_e \varepsilon A_e \varepsilon$; thus, the length pair (L_x, L_y) equals $(12, 12)$. The value of (M_x, M_y) can be determined by (L_x, L_y) minus the number of dummy objects in the LCS string of (L_x, L_y), respectively. The LCS strings of the query image and the database image without dummy objects are $A_b B_b A_e C_b C_e B_e$ and $B_b A_b B_e C_b C_e A_e$; thus, (M_x, M_y) equals $(6, 6)$. The boundary symbols with spatial relationships in the database image, based on strings of M_x and M_y, are $\varepsilon A_b \varepsilon B_b \varepsilon A_e \varepsilon C_b \varepsilon C_e \varepsilon B_e \varepsilon$ and $\varepsilon B_b \varepsilon A_b \varepsilon B_e C_b \varepsilon C_e \varepsilon A_e \varepsilon$; thus, (D_x, D_y) equals $(13, 12)$. Clearly, the similarity on the x-axis and the y-axis can be calculated as:

$$S_x = 1 - (Q_x + D_x - 2L_x)/(4N+1) \quad S_y = 1 - (Q_y + D_y - 2L_y)/(4N+1)$$
$$= 1 - (12 + 13 - 2*12)/(4*3+1) \qquad = 1 - (12 + 12 - 2*12)/(4*3+1)$$
$$= 1 - (25 - 24)/13 \qquad\qquad\qquad = 1 - (24 - 24)/13$$
$$= 1 - 0.0769 \qquad\qquad\qquad\qquad = 1 - 0.0$$
$$= 0.9231 \qquad\qquad\qquad\qquad\quad = 1.0$$

The weights adjustments along each axis (Wx, Wy) are given as $(0.5, 0.5)$. Then, for database image 5, the similarity $S = 0.5*0.9231 + 0.5*1.0 = 0.9616$.

Rotation and Reflection of an Image

The problems of rotating an image (90, 180, 270 degrees clockwise) or reflecting an image (in the x-axis or y-axis) are considered in 2-D String, 2D G-string, and 2D C-string. Similarity must be retrieved and evaluated eight times for an image. Thus, a proper transformation must be performed for a string in each dimension. Strings require a sophisticated formula to transform spatial operators, except when reversed (Li & Qu, 1998). Even though 2D B-string does not require cutting objects from an image, it still recalculates their ranks.

Figure 6: Database Image 5

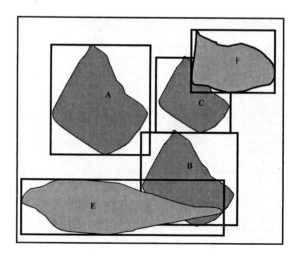

Table 6: LCS Length-Inferring Table with Dummy Objects on x-Axis

W_{ij}		0	1	2	3	4	5	6	7	8	9	10	11	12	13	14	15	16	17	18	19
		d_i	ε	E_h	ε	A_h	ε	B_h	ε	A_a	ε	C_h	ε	F_h	ε	E_e	ε	C_a	ε	B_a	ε
0	q_i	0	0	0	0	0	0	0	0	0	0	0	0	0	0	0	0	0	0	0	0
1	ε	0	-1	-1	-1	-1	-1	-1	-1	-1	-1	-1	-1	-1	-1	-1	-1	-1	-1	-1	-1
2	A_h	0	-1	-1	-1	2	2	2	2	2	2	2	2	2	2	2	2	2	2	2	2
3	ε	0	-1	-1	-1	2	-3	-3	-3	-3	-3	-3	-3	-3	-3	-3	-3	-3	-3	-3	-3
4	B_h	0	-1	-1	-1	2	-3	4	4	4	4	4	4	4	4	4	4	4	4	4	4
5	ε	0	-1	-1	-1	2	-3	4	-5	-5	-5	-5	-5	-5	-5	-5	-5	-5	-5	-5	-5
6	A_a	0	-1	-1	-1	2	-3	4	-5	6	6	6	6	6	6	6	6	6	6	6	6
7	C_h	0	-1	-1	-1	2	-3	4	-5	6	6	7	7	7	7	7	7	7	7	7	7
8	ε	0	-1	-1	-1	2	-3	4	-5	6	-7	-7	-8	-8	-8	-8	-8	-8	-8	-8	-8
9	C_a	0	-1	-1	-1	2	-3	4	-5	6	-7	-7	-8	-8	-8	-8	-8	9	9	9	9
10	ε	0	-1	-1	-1	2	-3	4	-5	6	-7	-7	-8	-8	-8	-8	-8	9	-10	-10	-10
11	B_a	0	-1	-1	-1	2	-3	4	-5	6	-7	-7	-8	-8	-8	-8	-8	9	-10	11	11
12	ε	0	-1	-1	-1	2	-3	4	-5	6	-7	-7	-8	-8	-8	-8	-8	9	-10	11	-12

If an image is represented in the 2D Bε-string, then the similarity retrieval of rotation and reflection of an image becomes very easy. Before evaluation, the string is only reversed, if necessary. The meaning, a dummy object between two adjoining boundary symbols, is not varied as the image is rotated or reflected because the dummy object is not a spatial operator.

Table 7: LCS Length-Inferring Table with Dummy Objects on y-Axis

W_{ij}		0	1	2	3	4	5	6	7	8	9	10	11	12	13	14	15	16	17	18	19	20
		d_i	ε	E_h	ε	B_h	ε	E_e	ε	A_h	ε	B_a	C_h	ε	F_h	ε	C_a	ε	A_a	ε	F_a	ε
0	q_i	0	0	0	0	0	0	0	0	0	0	0	0	0	0	0	0	0	0	0	0	0
1	ε	0	-1	-1	-1	-1	-1	-1	-1	-1	-1	-1	-1	-1	-1	-1	-1	-1	-1	-1	-1	-1
2	B_h	0	-1	-1	-1	2	2	2	2	2	2	2	2	2	2	2	2	2	2	2	2	2
3	ε	0	-1	-1	-1	2	-3	-3	-3	-3	-3	-3	-3	-3	-3	-3	-3	-3	-3	-3	-3	-3
4	A_h	0	-1	-1	-1	2	-3	-3	-3	4	4	4	4	4	4	4	4	4	4	4	4	4
5	ε	0	-1	-1	-1	2	-3	-3	-3	4	-5	-5	-5	-5	-5	-5	-5	-5	-5	-5	-5	-5
6	B_a	0	-1	-1	-1	2	-3	-3	-3	4	-5	6	6	6	6	6	6	6	6	6	6	6
7	C_h	0	-1	-1	-1	2	-3	-3	-3	4	-5	6	7	7	7	7	7	7	7	7	7	7
8	ε	0	-1	-1	-1	2	-3	-3	-3	4	-5	6	7	-8	-8	-8	-8	-8	-8	-8	-8	-8
9	C_a	0	-1	-1	-1	2	-3	-3	-3	4	-5	6	7	-8	-8	-8	9	9	9	9	9	9
10	ε	0	-1	-1	-1	2	-3	-3	-3	4	-5	6	7	-8	-8	-8	9	-10	-10	-10	-10	-10
11	A_a	0	-1	-1	-1	2	-3	-3	-3	4	-5	6	7	-8	-8	-8	9	-10	11	11	11	11
12	ε	0	-1	-1	-1	2	-3	-3	-3	4	-5	6	7	-8	-8	-8	9	-10	11	-12	-12	-12

The u and v are assumed to be the boundary strings of an image in the x-axis and the y-axis, respectively. They have m and n symbols, respectively; that is, $u = \{u_1u_2...u_{m-1}u_m\}$, $v = \{v_1v_2...v_{n-1}v_n\}$. The reversed string $u^{-1} = \{u_mu_{m-1}...u_2u_1\}$ is defined for u and $v^{-1} = \{v_nv_{n-1}...v_2v_1\}$ for v (shown as Table 7) summarizes the checklist of 2D Bε-strings between the original image and the image following rotation and/or reflection.

IMPLEMENTATION

A visualized image retrieval system is implemented using the proposed approaches of the 2D Bε-string spatial representation model and the modified LCS similarity evaluation algorithm. The system is divided into four parts. The first part converts MBR coordinate data of the original image into a symbolic picture represented in the 2D Bε-string. Part II randomly generates images, and calls part I to build a symbolic picture database. Each image includes an arbitrary number of objects. Each object is randomly assigned a set of MBR coordinate data. Part III performs similarity retrieval and evaluation. The final part handles the layout of the query image and the user interface interaction. Figure 7 shows the system's architecture.

After the retrieval system is begun (Figure 8), the user can load an image database from storage (Figure 9 and Figure 10), and browse them individually (Figure 11 and Figure 12). The user may place some available icons on the work area of the query image. He then drags them to an appropriate location and scales them appropriately (Figure 13). He hits the 'Search' button after he completes the layout of these icons in the query image. The system will transform the query image into a 2D Bε-string and compare it to the database images. The most similar image and its similarity information (Figure 14) are then displayed. Clicking on the '2D Bε-string' tab switches to the 2D Bε-string (Figure 15). The user may also browse less similar images (Figure 16).

Table 8: Checklist of 2D Bε-Strings after Rotation and Reflection

	Rotation/reflection	2D Bε-string
1	Original image	(u, v)
2	90 degree ckw	(v, u⁻¹)
3	180 degree ckw	(u⁻¹, v⁻¹)
4	270 degree ckw	(v⁻¹, u)
5	Reflect vs. x-axis	(u, v⁻¹)
6	Reflect vs. y-axis	(u⁻¹, v)
7	90 degree ckw and Reflect vs. x-axis	(v, u)
8	90 degree ckw and Reflect vs. y-axis	(v⁻¹, u⁻¹)

Figure 7: System Architecture

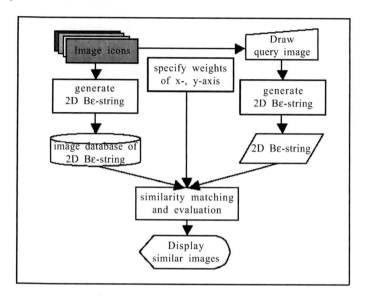

FUTURE TRENDS

The 2D Bε-string simplifies the representation of spatial relationships and improves the efficiency of similarity retrieval over those of other 2-D String methodologies. Even so, further research is required.

When an object area in an image differs greatly from its MBR area, the similarity is not obvious, whether 2D Bε-string or other 2-D Strings are used. Human vision is such that the size of an object is considered to be one factor that determines similarity.

Figure 8: After the Image Retrieval System has Loaded

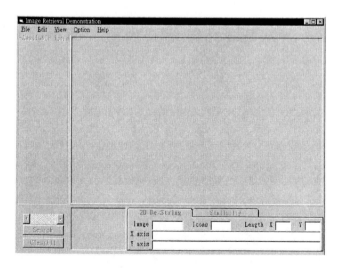

Figure 9: Loading an Image Database

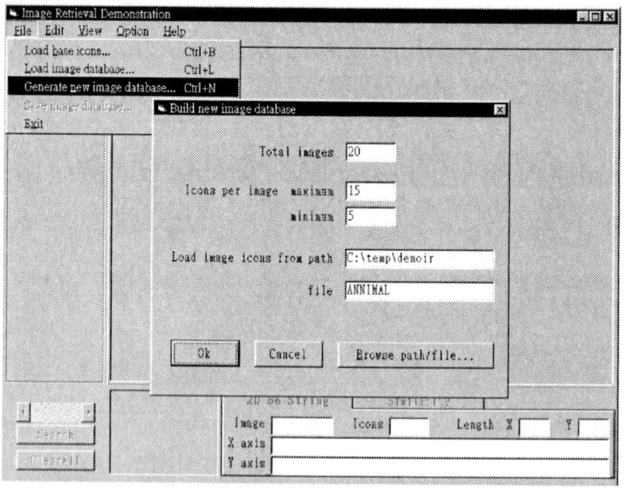

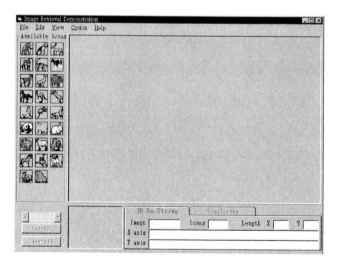

However, 2D Bε-string and other 2-D Strings lose this information while abstracting. The distance between objects is also lost. Consequently, size and distance information in the 2D Bε-string representation model is worthy of further study.

Similarity can be more accurately evaluated than as evaluated here. The original LCS algorithm does not calculate the number of LCS paths, nor does the algorithm presented here. For evaluating similarity of a query image from different images in the database, even for LCS strings with the same length and content, more LCS paths correspond to greater similarity. Thus, modifying the presented similarity retrieval and evaluation approaches to account for the number of LCS paths is an area of further study.

Figure 10: After a Database has Loaded

Figure 11: Select to View all Database Images

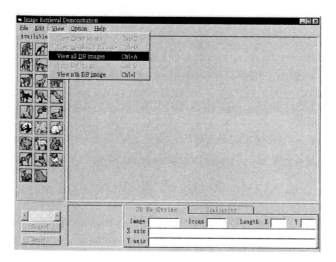

The 2D Bε-string representation model and similarity assessment can be easily expanded to retrieve objects in three-dimensions by directly adding the third dimension's string. For video data, adding extra temporal information as the third dimension allows a frame in a video to be indexed. The authors would also like to integrate the movement and velocity of objects in video images into the 2D Bε-string representation model in the near future.

Figure 12: View the First Database Image

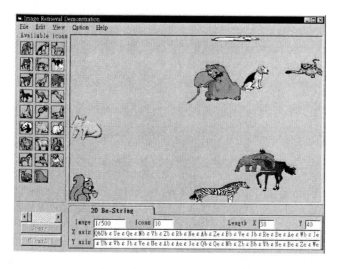

Figure 13: Arrange Icons in Query Image

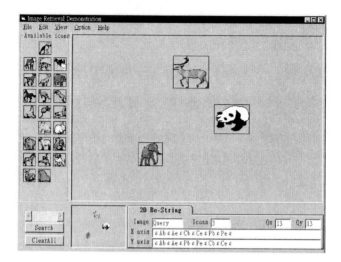

CONCLUSION

This investigation proposes a spatial representation model, called the "2D Bε-string spatial representation" model. The model does not require an icon object to be cut from an image; but it rather represents an object by its MBR boundaries. The model depicts the spatial relationship between two boundary symbols by applying a 'dummy object.' It can, thus, intuitively represent the spatial relationship in an image. Additionally, the 2D Bε-string is directly formed from the object boundaries; thus, an image with *n* objects

Figure 14: Most Similar Image and the Similarity

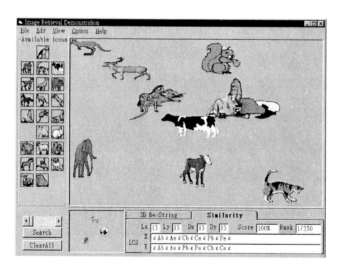

Figure 15: Most Similar Image and the 2D Bε-string

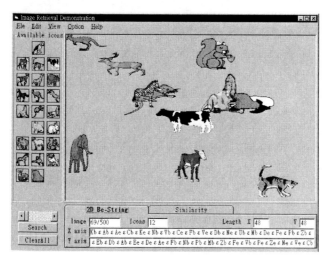

needs only between $2n$ and $4n+1$ storage units in each dimension. The space complexity of 2D Bε-string is $O(n)$.

An algorithm, **Convert-2D-Bε-String**, is introduced to convert an image with MBR coordinate data into a symbolic image, represented in the 2D Bε-string. The space and time complexity of this algorithm is $O(n)$ when it does not consider the sort requirement.

A similarity retrieval algorithm, **2D-Bε-LCS-Length**, is also presented. It is modified from the LCS algorithm for use in the 2D Bε-string representation model. All the space and time complexities of the proposed algorithm are $O(mn)$, where m is the number of icon objects in the query image and n is the number of object icons in the image database.

Figure 16: Next Similar Image and the Similarity

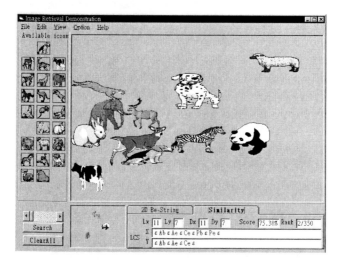

Moreover, an evaluation process is elucidated, which can evaluate all similarities, regardless of how the LCS string is matched, whether all objects of the query image appear in the database image or whether all of the spatial relationships appear between the pair of images. In retrieving similarities of rotation and reflection, the approach need only to reverse the string and then apply the method of similarity retrieval and evaluation, mentioned above. This process does not require any conversion of spatial operators. It is more efficient and much easier than the previous methodologies.

REFERENCES

Bach, J. R., Gupta, C. F. A., Hampapur, A., Horowitz, B., Humphrey, R., Jain, R., & Shu, C. (1996). The virage image search engine: An open framework for image management. *SPIE*, 2670.

Beckmann, N., Kriegel, H., Schneider, R., & Seeger, B. (1990). The R*-tree: An efficient and robust access method for points and rectangles. *Proceedings ACM SIGMOD International Conference On the Management of Data.*

Chan, Y. & Chang, C. (n.d.). Image retrieval based on tolerable difference of direction. *Proceedings of the 15th International Conference on Information Networking,* (January 31-February 2). Beppu, Japan.

Chang, S. K., Jungert, E., & Li, Y. (1988). Representation and retrieval of symbolic pictures using generalized 2D string. *Technical Report*, University of Pittsburgh, Pennsylvania, USA.

Chang, S. K., Shi, Q. Y., & Yan, C. W. (1987, May). Iconic indexing by 2-D strings. *IEEE Transactions on Pattern Analysis and Machine Intelligence,* 1(3), 413-428.

Chien, B. C. (1998). The Reasoning of Rotation and Reflection in Spatial Database. *Systems, Man, and Cybernetics*, IEEE International Conference, (Vol. 2, pp. 1582-1586).

Cormen, T. H., Leiserson, C. E., & Rivest, R.L. (1990). *Introduction to Algorithms.* MIT Press, 314-319.

Guttman, A. (1984). R-tree: A dynamic index structure for spatial searching. *Proceedings of the ACM SIGMOD International Conference on the Management of Data.*

Hsu, F.J., Lee, S. Y., & Lin, B. S. (1999, April). 2D C-tree spatial representation for iconic image. *Journal of Visual Languages & Computing,* 10(2), 147-164.

Huang, P. W. & Jean, Y. R. (1994). Using 2D C+-string as spatial knowledge representation for image database systems. *Pattern Recognition,* 27(9), 1249-1257.

Kim, B. & Um, K. (1999). 2D+ string: A spatial metadata to reason topological and directional relationships. *Proceedings Of 11th International Conference on Scientific and Statistical Database Management,* (pp. 112-121).

Lee, S. Y. & Hsu, F. J. (1990). 2D C-string: A new spatial knowledge representation for image database systems. *Pattern Recognition,* 23, 1077-1087.

Lee, S. Y., Yang, M. C., & Chen, J. W. (1992). 2D B-string: A spatial knowledge representation for image database systems. *Proceedings ICSC'92 Second International Computer Science Conference,* (pp. 609-615).

Li, X. & Qu, X. (1998). Matching spatial relations using DB-tree for image retrieval. *Pattern Recognition, Proceedings 14th International Conference,* (Vol. 2, pp. 1230-1234).

Liang, E. & Mou, D. (1997). *A Method of Computing Spatial Similarity Between Images.* Graduate Institute of Information Management, Tamkang University, Taiwan.

Liang, E. & Wu, S. (1996). *Similarity Retrieval of Image Database Based On Decomposed Objects.* Graduate Institute of Information Management, Tamkang University, Taiwan.

Liang, E. & You, G. (1999). *Similarity Retrieval Using String Matching in Image Database Systems.* Graduate Institute of Information Management, Tamkang University, Taiwan.

Nibalck, W., Barber, R., Wquitz, W., Flickner, M., Glasman, E., Yanker, D. P. P., Faloutsos, C., & Taubin, G. (1993). The QBIC Project: Querying images by content using color, texture and shape. *SPIE*, 1908.

Orlandic, R. & Yu, B. (2000). A study of MBR-based spatial access methods: How well they perform in high-dimensional spaces. *Proceedings Of International Database Engineering and Application Symposium,* (pp. 306-315).

Papadias, D. & Theodoridis, Y. (1995). Topological relations in the world of minimum bounding rectangles: A study with R-trees. *Proceedings of ACM SIGMOD Conference*, San Jose, CA, USA (pp. 71-79).

Samet, H. (1989). *Applications of Spatial Data Structures, Computer Graphics, Image Processing and GIS.* Addison-Wesley.

Sipser, M. (1997). *Introduction to the Theory of Computation.* PWS Publishing Company, 245-253.

Song, J.W., Whang, K., Lee, Y., & Kim, S.W. (1999). The clustering property of corner transformation for spatial database applications. *Proceedings of the 23rd Annual International Computer Software and Application Conference (COMPSAC '99)*, (pp. 28-35).

Zimbrao, G. & De Souza, J. M. (1998). A raster approximation for the processing of spatial joins. *Proceedings Of the 24th Annual International Conference on VLDB*, New York, USA (pp. 558-569).

Chapter XIII

A Stochastic Content-Based Image Retrieval Mechanism

Mei-Ling Shyu, University of Miami, USA

Shu-Ching Chen, Florida International University, USA

Chengcui Zhang, Florida International University, USA

ABSTRACT

Multimedia information, typically image information, is growing rapidly across the Internet and elsewhere. To keep pace with the increasing volumes of image information, new techniques need to be investigated to retrieve images intelligently and efficiently. Content-based image retrieval (CBIR) is always a challenging task. In this chapter, a stochastic mechanism, called Markov Model Mediator (MMM), is used to facilitate the searching and retrieval process for content-based image retrieval, which serves as the retrieval engine of the CBIR systems and uses stochastic-based similarity measures. Different from the common methods, our stochastic mechanism carries out the searching and similarity computing process dynamically, taking into consideration not only the image content features but also other characteristics of images such as their access frequencies and access patterns. Our experimental results demonstrate that the MMM mechanism together with the stochastic process can assist in retrieving more accurate results for user queries.

INTRODUCTION

The availability of today's digital devices and techniques offers people more opportunities than ever to create their own digital images. Moreover, the Internet has become the biggest platform to get, distribute and exchange digital image data. The rapid increase in the amount of image data and the inefficiency of traditional text-based image retrieval have created great demands for new approaches in image retrieval. As a consequence of such fast growth of digital image databases, the development of efficient search mechanisms has become more and more important. Content-Based Image Retrieval (CBIR) emerges and is dedicated to tackling such difficulties. CBIR is an active research area where the image retrieval queries are based on the content of multimedia data.

In contrast to the text-based approach, CBIR operates on a totally different principle, i.e., to retrieve the stored images from a collection of images by comparing the features that were automatically extracted from the images themselves. Content-based image retrieval involves a matching process between a query image and the images stored in the database. The first step of the process involves extracting a feature vector for the unique characteristics of each image. The features used for retrieval can be either primitive or semantic, but the extraction process must be automatic. A quantified similarity value between two images is obtained by comparing their feature vectors. The commonly used image features include color, shape and texture. Queries are issued through query by image example (QBE), which can either be provided or constructed by users, or randomly selected from the image database. A lot of research work has been done, which resulted in a number of systems and techniques, both in the academic and commercial domains. For example, IBM's QBIC system (Faloutsos, 1994; Flickner, 1995) and Virage's VIR engine (*http://www.virage.com*) are two of the most notable commercial image retrieval systems, while VisualSEEk (Smith, 1996) and PhotoBook (Pentland, 1994) are well-known academic image retrieval systems.

For large image collections, traditional retrieval methods such as sequential searching do not work well since it is time expensive and tends to ignore the relationships among all images by only considering the relationship between the query image and a single image in the database. Various kinds of data structures, approaches and techniques have been proposed to manage image databases and hasten the retrieval process.

The first aim of this chapter is to take an overview of the currently available content-based image retrieval (CBIR) systems. Then, with the focus on the searching process, we present a conceptually coherent framework that adopts a stochastic mechanism called Markov Model Mediator (MMM) for the content-based image retrieval problem. With an explicit model of image query patterns, given the target image, the proposed framework carries out the searching and similarity computing process dynamically by taking into consideration not only the image content features but also their access frequencies and access patterns.

We begin with the literature review as well as the motivations of the proposed mechanism. Then, the key components of the MMM mechanism and the stochastic process for information retrieval are introduced. After that, our experiments in applying the MMM mechanism to content-based image retrieval are presented and the experimental results are also provided. The future trends are discussed as well. Finally, a brief conclusion is given.

BACKGROUND

The objective of a CBIR system is to offer the user an efficient way in finding and retrieving those images that are qualified for the matching criteria of the users' queries from the database. Most of the existing CBIR systems retrieve images in the following manner. First, they build the indexes based on the low-level features such as color, texture and shape for the images in the database. The corresponding indexes of a query image are also generated at the time the query is issued. Second, they search through the whole database and measure the similarity of each image to the query image. Finally, the results are returned in a sorted order of the similarity matching level.

Lots of approaches for retrieving images on the basis of color similarity have been described in the literature, but most of them are actually variations of the same basic idea. The most commonly used matching technique is histogram intersection (Li, 2000). Variants of this technique are now used in a big proportion of the current CBIR systems. Methods of improving the original technique include the use of cumulative color histograms, combining histogram intersection with some element of spatial matching (Stricker, 1996) and the use of region-based color querying (Carson, 1997). As for texture similarity, the useful measures include the degree of *contrast, coarseness, directionality, regularity, periodicity, randomness*, etc. Alternative methods of texture analysis for retrieval include the use of Gabor filters (Ma, 1998) and fractals (Kaplan, 1998). Unlike texture, shape is a fairly well defined concept. Two main types of shape features are commonly used, namely (1) the *global* features such as aspect ratio, circularity and moment invariants and (2) the *local* features such as sets of consecutive boundary segments. Alternative methods proposed for shape matching include elastic deformation of templates (Zhong, 2000).

An impediment to research on CBIR is the lack of mapping between the high-level concepts and the low-level features. In order to overcome this problem and to better capture the subjectivity of human perception of the visual content, the concept of relevance feedback (RF) associated with CBIR was proposed in Rui (1997). Relevance feedback is an interactive process in which the user judges the quality of the retrieval results performed by the system by marking those images that the user perceives as truly relevant among the images retrieved by the system. This information is then used to refine the original query. However, even if the user provides a good initial query, it is still a problem of how to navigate through the image database.

No matter what information and what techniques are used for the construction of the image indexes, and no matter what similarity measurement strategies are employed, as far as the searching process is concerned, simple approaches such as sequential searching, are commonly put into operations to find the group of similar images for the queries. Such kinds of approaches may be adequate for small databases. However, as the scales and volumes of the databases increase considerably, they are deficient. Moreover, these approaches focus on only the relationship between the query image and the target image, neglecting the relationships among all the images within the database, which may result in inflexible and incomplete searching results.

There have been quite a few techniques being proposed and employed to alleviate the time consumption problem and to speed up the retrieval process, such as efficient indexing structures, compact representations, and pre-filtering techniques (Hafner, 1995). The QBIC system (Faloutsos, 1994; Flickner, 1995), for instance, uses the pre-filtering technique and the efficient indexing structure like R-trees to accelerate its searching performance. However, little has been done in considering the complicated relationships of the image objects to each other.

In this chapter, we present a content-based retrieval system that employs the Markov model mediator (MMM) mechanism to retrieve images, which functions as both the searching engine and image similarity arbitrator. In our previous studies, the MMM mechanism has been applied to multimedia database management (Shyu, 2000a, 2000c) and document management on the World Wide Web (WWW) (Shyu, 2000b, 2001a, 2001b). The MMM mechanism adopts the Markov model framework and the concept of the mediators. The Markov model is one of the most powerful tools available to scientists and engineers for analyzing complicated systems, whereas a mediator is defined as a program that collects and combines information from one or more sources, and finally yields the resulting information (Wiederhold, 1992). A Markov model consists of a number of states connected by transitions. The Markov property states that given the current state of the system, the future evolution is independent of its history. In other words, the states represent the alternatives of the stochastic process and the transitions contain probabilistic and other data used to determine which state should be selected next. All the transitions $S_i \rightarrow S_j$ such that $Pr(S_j \mid S_i) > 0$ are said to be allowed, the rest are prohibited. Markov models have been used in many applications. Some well-known examples are Markov Random Field Models in Frank (1986), and Hidden Markov Models (HMMs) (Rabiner, 1986). Some research works have been done to integrate the Markov model into the field of image retrieval. Lin et al. (Lin, 1997) used a Markov model to combine the spatial and color information. In their approach, each image in the database is represented by a pseudo two-dimensional hidden Markov model (HMM) in order to adequately capture both the spatial and chromatic information about that image. Wolf (1997) used the hidden Markov model (HMM) to parse video data. In Naphade (2001), the hidden Markov model was employed to model the time series of the feature vector for the cases of events and objects in their probabilistic framework for semantic level indexing and retrieval.

Our proposed CBIR system employs the MMM mechanism as well as the stochastic-based similarity measures for dynamic content-based image retrieval, which retrieves images with respect to the user queries. Our method also builds an index vector for each image within the database, but unlike the common methods mentioned above, our method considers not only the relationship between the query image and the target image, but also the relationships among all images in the database. A stochastic process that takes into account the image content features and other characteristics (such as the access frequencies and access patterns) of the images is proposed. Several experiments are conducted and the experimental results demonstrate that the MMM mechanism together with the stochastic process can assist in retrieving more accurate results for user queries.

THE STOCHASTIC MODEL
Markov Model Mediator (MMM) Mechanism

Markov model mediator (MMM) is a probabilistic-based mechanism that adopts the Markov model framework and the mediator concept (Shyu, 2000a, 2000b, 2000c, 2001a, 2001b). In our CBIR system, each image database is modeled by an MMM. The MMM mechanism is defined as follows.

Definition 1: An MMM is represented by a 5-tuple $\lambda = (S, F, A, B, \Pi)$, where S is a set of images called states; F is a set of distinct features of the images; A denotes the state transition probability distribution, where each entry (i, j) actually indicates the relationship between images i and j; B is the observation symbol probability distribution; and Π is the initial state probability distribution.

Each image database is modeled by an MMM, where S consists of all the images in the image database and F includes all the distinct features for the images in S. The elements in S and F determine the dimensions of A and B. If there are totally n images in S, and the number of distinct features in F is m, then the dimensions of A is $n \times n$, while B has the size of $n \times m$. The relationships of the images are modeled by the sequences of the MMM states connected by transitions. A training data set consisting of the access patterns and access frequencies of the queries issued to the database is used to train the model parameters for an MMM.

Formulation of the Model Parameters

Each MMM has three probability distribution matrixes: A, B, and Π. These matrixes are critical for the stochastic process and can be obtained from the training data set.

Matrix B: The Observation Symbol Probability Distribution

The observation symbol probability B denotes the probability of observing an output symbol from a state. Here, the observed output symbols represent the distinct features of the images and the states represent the images in the database. Since an image has one or more features and one feature can appear in multiple images, the observation symbol probabilities show the probabilities that a feature is observed from a set of images.

In this study, we consider the following features: color information and object location information for the images in the image database. Since the color feature is closely associated with image scenes and it is more robust to changes due to scaling, orientation, perspective and occlusion of images, it is the most widely used visual feature in image retrieval (Ma, 1999). Humans perceive a color as a combination of three stimuli, R (red), G (Green), and B (Blue), which form a color space. Separating chromatic information and luminance information can generate more color spaces such as RGB, YIQ,

YUV, CIE LAB, CIE LUV, and HSV. None of them can be used for all applications (Androutsos, 1999; Aslandogan, 1999; Cheng, 2001, 2000; Ma, 1999; Rui, 1999). RGB is the most commonly used color space primarily because color image acquisition and recording hardware are designed for this space. However, the problem of this space is the close correlation among the three components, which means that all three components will change as the intensity changes. This is not good for color analysis. YIQ and YUV are used to represent the color information in TV signals in color television broadcasting. CIE LAB and CIE LUV are often used in measuring the distance between two colors because of their perceptual uniformity. However, its transformation from the RGB space is computationally intensive and dependent on a reference white.

In our CBIR system, color information is obtained for each image from its HSV color space. The whole color space is divided into 12 sub-spaces according to the combinations of different ranges of hue (H), saturation (S), and intensity values (V). The HSV color space is chosen for two reasons. First, it is perceptual, which makes HSV a proven color space particularly amenable to color image analysis (Androutsos, 1999; Cheng, 2001, 2000). Secondly, the benchmark results in Ma (1999) shows that the color histogram in the HSV color space performs the best. For information of object locations, the SPCPE algorithm proposed in Sista (1999) and Chen (2000) is used. The minimal bounding rectangle (MBR) concept in R-tree (Guttman, 1984) is adopted so that each object is covered by a rectangle. The centroid point of each object is used for space reasoning so that any object is mapped to a point object. When these features are integrated into the queries, the semantic level meaning in the users' queries can be captured.

In our experiments, each image has a feature vector of 21 elements. Within the 21 features, 12 are for color descriptions and nine are for location descriptions. The color features considered are 'black,' 'white' (w), 'red,' 'red-yellow' (ry), 'yellow' (y), 'yellow-green' (yg), 'green,' 'green-blue' (gb), 'blue' (b), 'blue-purple' (bp), 'purple' (p), and 'purple-red' (pr). Colors with a number of pixels less than 5% of the total number of pixels are regarded as non-important and the corresponding positions in the feature vector have a value of 0. Otherwise, we put the corresponding percentage of that color component to that position. As for the location descriptions, each image is divided into 3×3 equal-sized regions. The image can be divided into a coarser or finer set of regions if necessary. As shown in Figure 1, the nine regions are ordered from left to right and top to bottom: L1, L2, L3, L4, L5, L6, L7, L8, and L9. When there is an object in the image whose centroid falls into one of the nine regions, the value 1 is assigned to that region. Objects with their

Figure 1: Object Locations and their Corresponding Regions

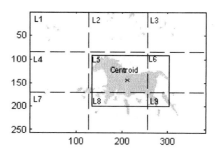

Figure 2: Three Sample Images (Img1 – Img3)

areas less than 8% of the total area are ignored.

In order to capture the appearance of a feature in an image, we define a temporary matrix ($\mathcal{BB}$) whose rows are all the distinct images and columns are all the distinct features, where the value in the $(p, q)^{th}$ entry is greater than zero if feature q appears in image p, and 0 otherwise. Then, the observation symbol probability distribution $\mathcal{B}$ can be obtained via normalizing $\mathcal{BB}$ per row. In other words, the sum of the probabilities that the features are observed from a given image should be 1.

Matrix $\mathcal{BB}$ consists of image feature vectors for all images. Figure 2 gives three example images and Table 1 illustrates their associated feature vectors. The observation symbol probability distribution $\mathcal{B}$ can be obtained via normalizing $\mathcal{BB}$ per row as shown in Table 2. In other words, the sum of the probabilities that the features are observed from a given image should be 1. We consider that the color and location information are of equal importance, such that the sum of observed probability of color features should be equal to that of location features (0.5 each).

Training Data Set

A set of training data is used to generate the training traces that are the central part of the stochastic process. Definition 2 gives the information that is available in the training data set. Based on the information in the training data set, we calculate the

Table 1: $\mathcal{BB}$ Matrix — Image Feature Vectors of Sample Images

	black	w	red	ry	y	yg	green	gb	b	bp	p	pr	L1	L2	L3	L4	L5	L6	L7	L8	L9
img1	0.11	0	0.83	0.06	0	0	0	0	0	0	0	0	0	0	0	0	1	0	0	1	0
img2	0	0	0	0	0	0	0	0	1	0	0	0	0	0	0	0	1	0	0	0	0
img3	0.53	0	0	0.30	0	0	0.17	0	0	0	0	0	0	0	0	0	1	0	0	0	0

Table 2: $\mathcal{B}$ Matrix — Normalized Image Feature Vectors of Sample Images

	black	w	red	ry	y	yg	green	gb	b	bp	p	pr	L1	L2	L3	L4	L5	L6	L7	L8	L9
img1	0.06	0	0.41	0.03	0	0	0	0	0	0	0	0	0	0	0	0	0.25	0	0	0.25	0
img2	0	0	0	0	0	0	0	0.5	0	0	0	0	0	0	0	0	0.5	0	0	0	0
img3	0.26	0	0	0.15	0	0	0.09	0	0	0	0	0	0	0	0	0	0.5	0	0	0	0

relative affinity measurements of the images in the image database (as shown in Definition 3).

Definition 2: The training data set consists of the following information:
* *The value N that indicates the number of images in the image database d.*
* *A set of queries $Q = \{q_1, q_2, ..., q_q\}$ that are issued to the database in a period of time. Each query shows the access patterns and access frequencies of the images. Let $use_{m,k}$ denote the usage pattern of image m with respect to query q_k per time period, where the value of $use_{m,k}$ is 1 when m is accessed by q_k, and 0 otherwise. The value of $access_k$ denotes the access frequency of query q_k per time period.*

Definition 3: The relative affinity measurements indicate how frequently two images are accessed together. The relative affinity relationship between two images m and n is defined as follows:

$$aff_{m,n} = \sum_{k=1}^{q} use_{m,k} \times use_{n,k} \times access_k \qquad (1)$$

Table 3 gives eight example queries issued to the image database with their corresponding access frequencies. The access patterns of the three sample images in the database versus the eight example queries are shown in Table 4. In this table, the entry $(i, j) = 1$ indicates that the ith image is accessed by the jth query (i.e., q_j).

Matrix A: The State Transition Probability Distribution

The state transition probability distribution (matrix A) is constructed by having $a_{m,n}$ be the element in the $(m, n)^{th}$ entry in A, where:

$$a_{m,n} = \frac{f_{m,n}}{f_m} \qquad (2)$$

Table 3: Eight Example Queries and their Frequencies (access$_k$)

Query Type	Feature Required	Frequency
q1	black / L1	1200
q2	blue	1500
q3	white / red / L5	2500
q4	yellow / L5	1750
q5	green / gb	1250
q6	purple / L9	2220
q7	ry / L5	1870
q8	bp	1345

Table 4: The Access Patterns of the Sample Images

	q1	q2	q3	q4	q5	q6	q7	q8
img1	1	0	1	1	0	0	1	0
img2	0	1	1	1	0	0	1	0
img3	1	0	1	1	1	0	1	0
... ...	... ...	... ...	... ...	... ...	... ...	... ...	... ...	... ...

$$f_{m,n} = \frac{aff_{m,n}}{\sum_{m \in d} \sum_{n \in d} aff_{m,n}} \tag{3}$$

$$f_m = \sum_n f_{m,n} \tag{4}$$

In this formulation, $f_{m,n}$ is the joint probability that refers to the fraction of the relative affinity of images m and n in the database d with respect to the total relative affinity for all the images in d, f_m is the marginal probability, and $a_{m,n}$ is the conditional probability that refers to the state transition probability for an MMM.

Matrix Π: The Initial State Probability Distribution

The preference of the initial states for queries can be obtained from the training traces. For any image $m \in d$ the initial state probability is defined as the fraction of the number of occurrences of image m with respect to the total number of occurrences for all the images in d from the training traces.

$$\Pi = \{\pi_m\} = \frac{\sum_{k=1}^{q} use_{m,k}}{\sum_{l=1}^{N} \sum_{k=1}^{q} use_{l,k}} \tag{5}$$

Stochastic Process for Information Retrieval

The need for efficient information retrieval from databases is strong. Usually the cost for query processing is expensive and time-consuming. Meanwhile, the results may not be very satisfactory. Probabilistic models offer a way to perform the searching process more efficiently and accurately. We capture the most matched images through a dynamic programming algorithm that conducts a stochastic process in calculating the current edge weights and the cumulative edge weights.

Assume N is the total number of images in the databases and each query is denoted as $query = \{o_1, o_2, ..., o_T\}$, where T is the total number of features requested in the query. We define the edge weights and the cumulative edge weights as follows.

Definition 4: $W_t(i, j)$ is defined as the edge weight of the edge $S_i \to S_j$ at the evaluation of the tth feature (o_t) in the query, where $1 \leq i, j \leq N$ and $1 \leq t \leq T$.

Definition 5: $D_t(i, j)$ is defined as the cumulative edge weight of the edge $S_i \to S_j$ at the evaluation of the tth feature (o_t) in the query, where $1 \leq i, j \leq N$ and $1 \leq t \leq T$.

Based on Definitions 4 and 5, the *dynamic programming algorithm* is given as follows:

At $t = 1$, we define

$$W_1(i, j) = \begin{cases} \pi_{S_i} b_{S_i}(o_1) & i = j \\ 0 & otherwise \end{cases} \tag{6}$$

$$D_1(i, j) = W_1(i, j) \tag{7}$$

The values of $W_{t+1}(i,j)$ and $D_{t+1}(i,j)$, where $1 \leq t \leq T-1$, are calculated using the values of $W_t(i,j)$ and $D_t(i,j)$ as follows:

$$W_{t+1}(i, j) = \max_k (D_t(k,i) a_{S_i,S_j}) b_{S_j}(o_{t+1}) \tag{8}$$

$$D_{t+1}(i, j) = (\max_k D_t(k,i)) + W_{t+1}(i, j) \tag{9}$$

As we mentioned before, $\mathcal{A} = \{a_{S_i, S_j}\}$ denotes the states transition probability distribution, $\mathcal{B} = \{b_{S_j}(o_k)\}$ is the observation symbol probability distribution, and $\Pi = \{\pi_{S_j}\}$ is the initial state probability distribution.

The image retrieval steps using the dynamic programming algorithm in the stochastic process are shown in Table 5. As can be seen from the result, our method can give a good ordering using this stochastic process.

In Step 3, since we already obtained matrices $W_1(i,j)$ and $D_1(i,j)$ from Step 2, and the second feature o_2 is known, the content of $W_2(i,j)$ and $D_2(i,j)$ can be determined. The value of $D_t(i, j)$ (obtained in Step 4) represents the cumulative edge weight for the joint event that $\{o_1, o_2, ..., o_T\}$ is observed. In the filtering step (Step 6), $D_T(q, j)$ together with $sumD_t(j)$ (where $1 \leq t \leq T$) are used as the filter to retrieve the candidate images with respect to query image q. In this step, when there are images with identical $D_T(q, j)$ values, we go to the matrix $sumD_T(j)$ to find different values to order them. If we fail to order them by the values in $sumD_T(j)$, we have to trace down to the next matrix $sumD_{T-1}(j)$ and continue the process until we reach the first matrix $sumD_1(j)$. We also take into consideration the characteristics of $sumW_t(j)$. From our observations, if the jth image does not have the tth feature in the query, the value of $sumW_t(j)$ would be zero. Taking advantage of this characteristic, we can exclude some of the images that do not have any feature desired in the query from the final result. Therefore, in Step 7, we use $W_T(q, j) + W_T(j, q)$ to reflect the possibility that the jth image matches the issued query. In other words, it indicates the matching percentage of the jth image in the image database to the query image q with respect to the features $\{o_1, o_2, ..., o_T\}$.

Table 5: Image Retrieval Steps Using the Stochastic Model

---

1. Given the query image q, obtain its feature vector $query = \{o_1, o_2, ..., o_T\}$, where T is the total number of non-zero features of the query image q.

2. Upon the first feature o_1, calculate $W_1(i, j)$ and $D_1(i, j)$ according to Equations (6) and (7).

3. Move on to calculate $W_2(i, j)$ and $D_2(i, j)$ according to Equations (8) and (9).

4. Continue to calculate the next values for the W and D matrices until all the features in the query have been taken care of.

5. Upon each feature in query, we can obtain a pair of matrices: $W_t(i, j)$ and $D_t(i, j)$. We then sum up each column in matrices $W_t(i, j)$ and $D_t(i, j)$. Namely, we calculate $sumW_t(j) = \sum_i W_t(i, j)$ and $sumD_t(j) = \sum_i D_t(i, j)$.

6. Find the candidate images by sorting their corresponding values in $D_t(q, j)$, $sumD_T(j)$, $sumD_{T-1}(j)$, ..., or $sumD_1(j)$. First, an image is ranked according to its value in $D_T(q, j)$. If there exist several images that have the same value, then $sumD_T(j)$ values are used for ranking. If several images have the same $sumD_T(j)$ value, then $sumD_{T-1}(j)$ values are used and the process continues until $sumD_1(j)$.

7. Select the top ranked images from the output of Step 6, and rank them to the user based on their values in $W_T(q, j) + W_T(j, q)$.

EXPERIMENTS

Experimental Image Database System

In our image database, there are 1,500 color images of various dimensions that are used to carry out the experiments. With the purpose of supporting semantic level meaning in the users' queries, both the color information and object location information are considered in our experiments. In addition, the query-by-example strategy is used for query issuing in our experiments. Based on the training data set of this image database, first we need to construct the model parameters for the MMM mechanism for the database.

Constructions of the Model Parameters

Each MMM has three probability distributions ($\mathcal{A}$, $\mathcal{B}$, and Π). The state transition probability distribution $\mathcal{A}$ can be obtained according to Equations (1) to (4). In order to calculate $\mathcal{B}$, first we need to construct $\mathcal{BB}$ based on the images and their features in the experimental database. Based on $\mathcal{BB}$, $\mathcal{B}$ can be obtained using the procedure aforementioned. The initial state probability distribution for experimental database can be determined by using Equation (5). The constructions of these model parameters can be performed off-line.

Once the model parameters of the MMM for the image database is constructed, the stochastic process shown in Table 5 is used for image retrieval.

Stochastic Process for Example Queries

For a given query image issued by a user, the stochastic process with the proposed dynamic programming algorithm will be carried on to dynamically find the matched images for the user's query. A series of W_t and D_t matrices are generated according to Equations (6) to (9). The qualifying degrees of the images with respect to the certain query image are estimated by the values in the resulting W_t and D_t matrices according to rules described in Table 5.

In this section, we use a set of example queries to demonstrate the effectiveness of our stochastic model. For each set of query results, the qualifying possibilities of the images are in the descending order from the *top left* to the *bottom right*. The searching results are listed and analyzed as well. As can be seen from the experimental results, our method effectively extracts the images that contain the features specified in the query image and ranks them appropriately.

Query I

Query Image ID: #2265

In this query example, the query image #2265 has one color feature and one location feature which are 'blue' (b) and 'L5.' Below gives the corresponding $\mathcal{B}$ matrix entry for it:

	black	w	red	ry	y	yg	green	gb	b	bp	p	pr	L1	L2	L3	L4	L5	L6	L7	L8	L9
img2265	0	0	0	0	0	0	0	0	0.5	0	0	0	0	0	0	0	0.5	0	0	0	0

Figure 3: Snapshot of Query I

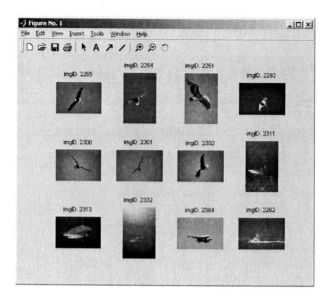

Since there are two features in the query image, two W matrices and two D matrices will be generated. The system is supposed to return those images that have the desired features in the ordering of similarity. The snapshot of the retrieval result screen containing the top 12 images is shown in Figure 3. As can be seen from this figure, the 'blue' color is the dominating color in all the retrieved images. Moreover, they all have an object located at 'L5' (the centre location). It should also be noted that some images are excluded from the query results because their values in $sumW_T(j)$ are zeros, which means they do not have the corresponding features ('blue' or 'L5').

Query II

Query Image ID: #2001

In this query, the major features of this query image include four components: 'blue' (b), 'white' (w), 'yellow-green' (yg), and 'L5' (the centre location) with the $\mathcal{B}$ matrix at the top of the following page:

black	w	red	ry	y	yg	green	gb	b	bp	p	pr	L1	L2	L3	L4	L5	L6	L7	L8	L9
0	0.17	0	0	0	0.17	0	0	0.16	0	0	0	0	0	0	0	0.5	0	0	0	0

The most qualified images to this query are those that have all of the above three-color features and an object at the L5 location (i.e., the centre location). Images that have only one of the desired features are less satisfactory. The snapshot of this example query is given in Figure 4. All the retrieved top 12 images have the above mentioned color features and have the object(s) at location 'L5.'

Query III

Query Image ID: #2197

Similar to the previous query example, there are four features, which are 'red,' 'purple-red,' 'L1,' and 'L5.' Two of them are the color features and the other two are the object location descriptions. Figure 5 exhibits the top 24 images retrieved from the image database. The final query results are good and the ranking is reasonable.

Figure 4: Snapshot of Query II

Figure 5: Snapshot of Query III

FUTURE TRENDS

The current CBIR systems are promising and reflect the increasing interest in the field of content-based image retrieval. However, there are still a number of open research issues to be addressed. For example, it is critical to develop the suitable evaluation criteria and benchmarks for CBIR systems. Some future trends include:

- *Automatic or semi-automatic methods of object extraction for image retrieval:* It has been recognized that the searching for images in large databases can be greatly facilitated by the use of semantic information such as object location and type. However, using the current technique of computer vision cannot extract the object information easily. For example, even though the unsupervised image segmentation is applied in our framework to obtain the object information, we still have to find a trade-off between the accuracy and performance. Considering that users may upload their own query image (which is not in the database) during the content-based retrieval, the real-time feature extraction could be a big issue to affect the users' will to use the system. There is an increasing need to derive more efficient yet good enough methods of segmenting images to distinguish objects of interest from their background. The main goal is to bridge the semantic gap, bringing some measure of automation to the processes of indexing and retrieving images by the type of object or scene depicted.

- *Indexing standard and query language support for image databases:* Currently, there are neither the standards in indexing the features and the subject taxonomies for image databases, nor the standard for hierarchical representation of an image when taking into consideration the objects inside the image. These standards are essential in expressing complex semantics and supporting the manipulation of content-based queries on image objects. Once the feature representations of image objects follow the same standards, it becomes possible to develop a suitable query language exclusively designed for image databases.

- *Support for automatic video indexing and retrieval:* Recently, lots of research work has been done on automatic video segmentation. After video is segmented into smaller units such as shots or scenes, each unit is represented by its key frames. Then, the complex spatial-temporal semantics can be obtained by parsing the content of these key frames, which forms the basis for supporting advanced video retrieval techniques such as query-by-motion facilities. MPEG-7 (Moving Picture Experts Group) standard (*http://media.wiley.com/product_data/excerpt/ 87/04714867/0471486787.pdf*) is the first to take into consideration the issue of multimedia content representation. This standard will define a standard for describing every aspect of the content of a multimedia object, including the specifications of a video's image features. MPEG-7 will definitely have an impact on CBIR and will probably guide the development of future CBIR systems.

- *Better user interaction, especially the improved techniques for collecting users' feedback:* User's relevance feedback has been adopted in most recent efforts towards the research of CBIR. In order to get better results, the user may be asked to browse a bunch of images through iterations and to provide the detailed ranking for similarity for the images. The fact is that a heavy and unnecessary burden of responsibility is brought to the user. In addition, it is highly probable that this burden will have a negative effect on a user's perception of the effectiveness and efficiency of the system.

CONCLUSION

Currently, Content-Based Image Retrieval (CBIR) technology is still immature but with great potential. In this chapter, a review of the recent efforts and techniques in CBIR is given, followed by the discussion of the current problems in the CBIR systems from the efficiency concern of the searching process. In response to this issue, in this chapter, the Markov model mediator (MMM) mechanism is applied to the image databases for content-based image retrieval. A stochastic process based on the MMM mechanism is proposed to traverse the database and find the similar images with respect to the query image. This approach performs similarity comparison based on not only the relationship between the query image and the target image, but also the relationships among all the images within the database, such as their access patterns and access frequencies. Joint color/layout similarity measurement is supported in this system to offer more complete distinction descriptions of the images and better retrieval effectiveness. Several experiments were conducted and the experimental query-by-example image query results to the proposed retrieval system were reported. The fact that the proposed stochastic content-based CBIR system utilizes the MMM mechanism and supports both spatial and color information offers more flexible and accurate results for user queries. The experimental results exemplify this point and the overall retrieval performance of the presented system is promising. Besides modelling the relationship of image objects within a single database, the MMM mechanism also has the capability (although not shown in this chapter) to model the relationships among distributed image databases so as to guide the efficient search across the distributed image databases.

ACKNOWLEDGMENT

For Shu-Ching Chen, this research was supported in part by NSF EIA-0220562 and NSF CDA-9711582.

REFERENCES

Androutsos, D. (1999). *Efficient indexing and retrieval of color image data using a vector-based approach.* Ph.D. Dissertation. Department of Electrical and Computer Engineering, University of Toronto.

Aslandogan, Y. A., & Yu, C. T. (1999). Techniques and systems for image and video retrieval. *IEEE Trans. On Knowledge and Data Engineering, 11*(1), 56-63.

Carson, C. S., Belongie, S., Greenspan, H., & Malik, J. (1997). Region-based image querying. In *Proceedings of IEEE Workshop on Content-Based Access of Image and Video Libraries*, San Juan, Puerto Rico, (pp. 42-49).

Chen, S.-C., Sista, S., Shyu, M.-L., & Kashyap, R.L. (2000). An indexing and searching structure for multimedia database systems. *IS&T/SPIE Conference on Storage and Retrieval for Media Databases 2000*, (pp. 262-270).

Cheng, H.D. & Sun, Y. (2000). A hierarchical approach to color image segmentation using homogeneity. *IEEE Transactions on Image Processing, 9*(12), 2071-2082.

Cheng, H.D., Jiang, X.H., Sun, Y., & Wang, J.L. (2001). Color image segmentation: Advances and prospects. *Pattern Recognition, 34*, 2259-2281.

Faloutsos, C., Barber, R., Flickner, M., Hafner, J., Niblack, W., Petkovic D., & Equitz, W. (1994). Efficient and effective querying by image content. *Journal of Intelligent Information Systems, 3*(3/4), 231-262.

Flickner, M., Sawhney, H., Niblack, W., Ashley, J., Huang, Q., Dom, B., Gorkani, M., Hafner, J., Lee, D., Petkovic, D., Steele, D., & Yanker, P. (1995). Query by image and video content: The QBIC system. *IEEE Computer, 28*(9), 23-31.

Frank, O. & Strauss, D. (1986). Markov graphs. *Journal of the American Statistical Association, 81*, 832-842.

Guttman, A. (1984). R-tree: A dynamic index structure for spatial search. *Proc. ACM SIGMOD*, (pp. 47-57).

Hafner, J., Sawhney, H. S., Equitz, W., Flickner, M., & Niblack, W. (1995). Efficient color histogram indexing for quadratic form distance functions. *IEEE Transactions on Pattern Analysis and Machine Intelligence, 17*(7), 729-736.

Kaplan, L. M., Murenzi, R., & Namuduri, K. R. (1998). Fast texture database retrieval using extended fractal features. In *Storage and Retrieval for Image and Video Databases VI, Proc. SPIE, 3312*, (pp. 162-173).

Li, Z.-N., Tauber, Z., & Drew, M. S. (2000). Locale-based object search under illumination change using chromaticity voting and elastic correlation. In *Proc. IEEE International Conference on Multimedia and Expo (II) 2000*, (pp. 661-664).

Lin, H. C., Wang L. L., & Yang, S. N. (1997). Color image retrieval based on hidden Markov models. *IEEE Transactions on Image Processing, 6*(2), 332-339.

Ma, W.-Y. & Manjunath, B. S. (1998). A texture thesaurus for browsing large aerial photographs. *Journal of the American Society for Information Science, 49*(7), 633-648.

Ma, W.-Y. & Zhang, H.J. (1999). Content-based image indexing and retrieval. *Handbook of Multimedia Computing*, CRC Press.

Naphade, M. R. & Huang, T. S. (2001). A probabilistic framework for semantic indexing and retrieval in video. *IEEE Transactions on Multimedia, 3*(1), 141-151.

Pentland, A., Picard, R.W., & Sclaroff, S. (1994). Photobook: Tools for content-based manipulation of image databases. In *Proc. Storage and Retrieval for Image and Video Databases II, 2185*, (pp. 34-47), SPIE.

Rabiner, L. R. & Huang, B. H. (1986). An introduction to hidden Markov models. *IEEE ASSP Magazine, 3*(1), 4-16.

Rui, Y. & Huang, T. S. (1999). Image retrieval: Current techniques, promising directions and open issues. *Journal of Visual Communication and Image Representation, 10*(4), 39-62.

Rui, Y., Huang, T. S., & Mehrotra, S. (1997). Content-based image retrieval with relevance feedback in MARS. In *Proceedings of the 1997 International Conference on Image Processing (ICIP'97)*, (pp. 815-818).

Shyu, M.-L., Chen, S.-C., & Haruechaiyasak, C. (2001a). Mining user access behavior on the www. *IEEE International Conference on Systems, Man, and Cybernetics*, (pp. 1717-1722).

Shyu, M.-L., Chen, S.-C., & Kashyap, R. L. (2000a). A probabilistic-based mechanism for video database management systems. *IEEE International Conference on Multimedia and Expo (ICME2000)*, (pp. 467-470).

Shyu, M.-L., Chen, S.-C., & Kashyap, R. L. (2000c). Organizing a network of databases using probabilistic reasoning. *IEEE International Conference on Systems, Man, and Cybernetics*, 1990-1995.

Shyu, M.-L., Chen, S.-C., & Shu, C.-M. (2000b). Affinity-based probabilistic reasoning and document clustering on the www. *The 24th IEEE Computer Society International Computer Software and Applications Conference (COMPSAC)*, (pp. 149-154).

Shyu, M.-L., Chen, S.-C., Haruechaiyasak, C., Shu, C.-M., & Li, S.-T. (2001b). Disjoint web document clustering and management in electronic commerce. *The Seventh International Conference on Distributed Multimedia Systems (DMS'2001)*, (pp. 494-497).

Sista, S. & Kashyap, R. L. (1999). Unsupervised video segmentation and object tracking. *IEEE International Conference on Image Processing*.

Smith, J. R. & Chang, S. F. (1996). VisualSEEK: A fully automated content-based image query system. In *Proceedings ACM International Conf. Multimedia*, (pp. 87-98).

Stricker, M. & Dimai, A. (1996). Color indexing with weak spatial constraints. In *Storage and Retrieval for Image and Video Databases IV, Proc SPIE 2670*, (pp. 29-40).

Wiederhold, G. (1992). Mediators in the architecture of future information systems. *IEEE Computers, 25*(3), 38-49.

Wolf, W. (1997). Hidden Markov model parsing of video programs. Presented at the *International Conference of Acoustics, Speech and Signal Processing*.

Zhong, Y., Jain, A.K., & Dubuisson-Jolly, M.-P. (2000). Object tracking using deformable templates. *IEEE Trans. on Pattern Analysis and Machine Intelligence, 22*(5), 544-549.

SECTION VII

DYNAMIC
USER INTERFACE

Chapter XIV

Mind the Gap: Content-Based Image Retrieval and the User Interface

Colin C. Venters, University of Manchester, UK

Richard J. Hartley, Manchester Metropolitan University, UK

William T. Hewitt, University of Manchester, UK

ABSTRACT

The user interface is the principal component responsible for facilitating human-computer interaction in an information retrieval system and provides the medium between the end user and the system. Query formulation is a core activity in the process of information retrieval and a number of query paradigms have been proposed for specifying a query Q_n in an image database I. Despite being identified as one of the major research areas, few studies have investigated the user interface for specifying visual queries and the area remains an open research issue. This chapter presents an overview of user interface research activity and related areas in the field of content-based image retrieval.

INTRODUCTION

The success and value of any information resource can be maximized by ensuring that its content is effectively exploited and is effortlessly accessible by those users whose information needs it is intended to satisfy. Millions of digital images[1] are now generated on a daily basis and the number continues to grow with advances in technology. For example, a Landsat V satellite broadcasts $85x10^6$ bits of data every second and a typical image from a single scene consists of $6100x6100$ pixels in seven spectral bands, e.g., 250MB of image data (Sonka, Hlavac, & Boyle, 1998). The Landsat satellite program has been in operation for 30 years and provides continuous coverage on a 16-day, 233-orbit cycle. Similarly, based on preliminary calculations, van Beard (1991) estimated that a single 14"x17" radiograph could be digitised at 2000^2, 12-bit pixels (6MB). This combined with other factors, such as an examination requiring several radiographs and the number of examinations per year, suggested that an image database for a typical 500-bed hospital would require approximately 15 terabytes of storage per year. Comparison with a previous investigation suggested that 4000^2, 12-bit pixels (24MB) was a more realistic estimation (Pizer & van Beard, 1989).

The increase in volume of digital image data has exacerbated the general image retrieval problem, posing new challenges for the medium's overall information management and its utility as an information resource. The creation of image repositories is of no value unless there are efficient and effective methods for the retrieval of the image data. Research has investigated only a small number of the problems inherent in the development of visual information management systems. A considerable amount of research activity has been directed at the development and advancement of retrieval algorithms for content-based image retrieval (CBIR) and arguably this effort has only delivered limited success (Venters & Cooper, 2000). However, many research topics in this field, which are considered fundamental to the advancement of CBIR as a viable retrieval tool, have been largely ignored. As Jain (1993) stated, "in failing to address any of these areas, one may either address only theoretical issues or may work in a microcosm that will, at best, be extremely narrow in its utility and extensibility." Only when there is a seamless integration of multiple research activities can the goal of effective CBIR be achieved (Rui, Huang, & Chang, 1999).

Information retrieval (IR) systems present special difficulties for end users who are trying to discover something they do not know while interacting with what may be an

Figure 1: Landsat TM Image

Figure 2: MRI Scan

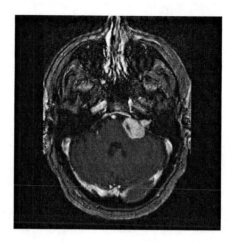

unfamiliar computer-based system (Shaw, 1991). The user interface provides the medium between the end-user and the system and is crucial to effective human-computer interaction. Several commentators have highlighted the need to design and develop new user interface metaphors and paradigms for specifying visual queries (Chang & Hsu, 1992; Gudivada & Raghavan, 1995; Aigrain, Zhang, & Petkovic, 1996; Besser, 1996; Jain, 1996; Gupta & Jain, 1997; Rui, Huang, & Chang, 1999; Del Bimbo, 1999; Eakins, 2001). However, despite being identified as one of the major research areas of the field, few studies have investigated the user interface. The requirement for end users to communicate their information needs accurately and effectively is crucial in any information retrieval system. How this may be achieved in practice with content-based image retrieval systems is not readily apparent (Eakins & Graham, 1999). Clearly, there is a growing need to ignite interest in user interface research within the CBIR community.

   This chapter seeks to provide a review of user interface research activity in the field of content-based image retrieval in order to provide a platform for future research. Following the introduction there are brief reviews of approaches to CBIR and a prototype CBIR system is outlined. Image query paradigms are summarised and this is followed by an explanation of various approaches to image query by example. We then examine approaches to query specification that attempt to go beyond the query by a visual example paradigm. In the following section research into image information seeking behaviour is examined and, finally, there is a consideration of the evaluation of the user interface. The chapter concludes by identifying future research directions.

CONTENT-BASED IMAGE RETRIEVAL

   While there have been significant technological advances with image data capture and storage, developments in effective image retrieval have not kept pace with image production (Chang & Hsu, 1992; Mostafa & Dillon, 1996). Several novel approaches to the problem of retrieving digital image data have been devised which focus on the

Figure 3: Simplified Model of a Content-Based Image Search

automatic extraction, indexing, and retrieval of images by their visual attributes and characteristics; content-based image retrieval (CBIR) is the general term used to describe the overall approach. Its origins lie in the subject areas of artificial intelligence, computer vision, image processing, pattern recognition, and signal processing. Advancement of the approach has been attributed to the early experiments conducted by Kato et al. (1991) into the automatic retrieval of images by colour and shape feature (Eakins & Graham, 1999). At its simplest level, it involves a direct matching operation between a query image and a database of stored images (Figure 3).

At a more detailed level, the process involves computing a feature vector or global signature for the unique visual properties of an image. Similarity is calculated by comparing the feature vector of the query image against the feature vectors of images stored in a database. The visual distance D between images can be measured by a function such as Euclidean distance where d is a distance function and s_1 and s_2 are generic stimuli (Figure 4).

Other distance functions include the L_1 and L_2 distances, weighted Euclidean distance, city-block distance, and Minkowsky distance. The result of this process is a quantified similarity score that measures the visual distance between the two images, represented by the feature vectors, in a 2-D feature space (Figure 5) (Del Bimbo, 1999).

The most common image matching feature characteristics are colour, shape, and texture. Colour retrieval techniques allow images to be retrieved on the basis of their global or local distribution of colour. Global colour features analyse the overall distribution of colour within the entire image for both the dominant colour and the variation of colour throughout the image independent of its location. Examples of this approach include colour histogram intersection (Swain & Ballard, 1991), colour moments (Stricker & Orengo, 1995), and colour sets (Smith & Chang, 1995). The positions of the colour values are not significant and as a result this feature retrieves a high proportion of false positives. To improve retrieval, local colour techniques divide an image into n sub-

Figure 4: Euclidean Distance

$$d(s_1, s_2) = \sqrt{(x_2 - x_1)^2 + (y_2 - y_1)^2}$$

blocks and then extract the colour values from each block. Image similarity is based on the position of the colour values. Examples of this approach include quadtree-based colour layout (Lu, Ooi, & Tan, 1994), colour tuple histogram (Rickman & Stonham, 1996), and colour correlogram (Huang, Kumar, Mitra, Zhu, & Zabih, 1997). Chromatic-based retrieval is effective in retrieving images containing identical and similar regions or distributions of colour within an image.

Shape retrieval techniques can be differentiated by the techniques they employ: feature-based representations or shape transformation. Feature-based representations allow images to be retrieved on the basis of either their boundary (parametric external) or regions (parametric internal). Parametric external methods can describe both the external and internal boundary of an object. Parametric internal methods use simple geometric attributes of the shape, digital moments, or the first coefficients of transform such as 2D Fourier (Del Bimbo, 1999). Rui et al. (1999) suggest that the most successful parametric internal methods are Fourier descriptor (Zahn & Roskies, 1972) and moment invariant (Hu, 1962). With this approach, shapes are represented as feature vectors and similarity is measured as a distance in a multi-dimensional feature space. Colour, position and absolute orientation of the lines have no value. According to the shape transformation model, a shape is considered as a template that is deformed in order to improve its match with the target image (Del Bimbo, 1999). Examples of this approach were proposed by Sclaroff and Pentland (1993) and Del Bimbo and Pala (1997).

Texture features analyse areas for periodicity, randomness, and roughness of fine-grained textures in images. Colour, position and absolute orientation of the features have no value. Examples of this approach include co-occurrence matrix (Haralick, Shanmugam, & Dinstein, 1973), texture representations (Tamura, Mori, & Yamawaki, 1978), and wavelets (Chang & Kuo, 1993.). A number of recent publications have surveyed the feature matching techniques utilized in the process of content-based image retrieval and readers are directed to those publications for detailed descriptions of the techniques and approaches used (Idris & Panchanathan, 1997; Del Bimbo, 1999; Lew, 2001).

Figure 5: Euclidean Distance in a 2-D Metric Space

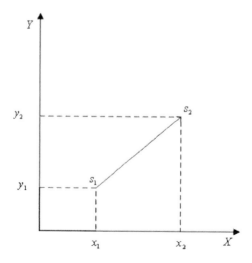

The holy grail of content-based image retrieval is to search a database in order to retrieve all images that are similar, perceptually and semantically, to the image query (Eakins, Huang, Panchanathan, & Marchand-Maillet, 2002). The paradigm potentially provides a non-semantic method for the retrieval of digital images and has reached a relative stage of maturity with existing techniques (Eakins, 2002). Commentators have proposed a broad and diverse range of promising application areas in which to apply the technology including art gallery and museum management, architectural and engineering design, fabric and fashion design, medical and scientific database management, remote sensing and earth resource management, and trademark and copyright database management (Jain, 1993; Gudivada & Raghaven, 1995; Del Bimbo, 1999; Eakins & Graham, 1999).

Despite these predictions there is insufficient evidence to support such claims and it is currently unclear whether any of the proposed fields are viable application areas for the technology. For example, Venters and Cooper (2001a) investigated the feasibility of applying content-based image retrieval technology to the field of radiology. The purpose of their study was to determine to what extent content-based image retrieval would be considered 'useful' in the field of radiology. The results of this study suggested that the technology is 'unlikely' to be useful in this particular field. Participants were generally positive about the concept of the technology but were extremely sceptical about its application in the field of radiology given its apparent fuzzy matching features and the difficulty of formulating a visual query accurately, quickly, and succinctly.

Wong (1998) highlighted other challenges of applying CBIR technology to the field of medical science. Supporters of the technology have promoted this approach as a powerful information retrieval tool, which can complement the traditional information retrieval paradigm or be utilised as a novel query mechanism for the retrieval of images from large repositories of digital image data (Eakins & Graham, 1999). Nevertheless, the difficulties involved in developing effective and efficient content-based image retrieval systems are problematic (Rosenfeld, 1984; Eakins, 1992). Little independent empirical evidence exists to verify the effectiveness of this approach and there are still a significant number of open research issues to be addressed if this technique is to bear fruit (Rui, Huang, & Chang, 1999).

CONTENT-BASED
IMAGE RETRIEVAL SYSTEMS

A plethora of content-based image retrieval systems and their user interfaces have been reported (Kato, Kurita, & Shimogaki, 1991; Bach, Fuller, Gutpa, Hampapur, Horowitz, Humphrey, Jain, & Shu, 1996; Huang, Mehrotra, & Ramchandran, 1996; Pentland, Picard, & Sclaroff, 1996; Smith, & Chang, 1997; Del Bimbo, Mugnani, & Turco, 1998; Laaksonen, Koskela, Laakso, & Oja, 2000; Wang, 2000; Ciocca, Gagliardi, & Schettini, 2001). The increasing number of systems is a reflection of the growing research activity and current interest in the field of image retrieval. The majority of these image retrieval 'systems' are research prototypes designed to test and demonstrate the performance of a retrieval algorithm. They support a range of retrieval features, functionality, and performance that have been summarised in recent reviews, and can be differentiated according to whether they deal with 2-D static, 2-D dynamic or 3-D image data (Venters & Cooper, 2000; Venters & Cooper, 2001b; Veltkamp & Tanase, 2002).

One of the earliest reported image retrieval systems was ImageQuery developed at the University of California at Berkeley during the late 1980s (Besser, 1990). While not a content-based image retrieval system in the strictest sense, the system combined traditional text retrieval with a visual browsing feature to query the database and provided additional image processing tools to analyse or alter an image. The system was originally designed to explore user interface issues in a first-generation image database but subsequently became the focus of a development project to provide a uniform and common user interface to three distributed image collections held at Berkley (Lynch, 1991; Besser, 1996).

Arguably the best-known content-based image retrieval system is QBIC (Query by Image Content) developed by IBM at the Almaden Research Centre (Niblack, Barber, Equitz, Flickner, Glasman, Petkovic, Yanker, Faloutsos, & Taubin, 1993). QBIC was designed as an open framework that could be utilised for both 2-D static and dynamic image retrieval. Several user interfaces have been designed for the system since it was first reported in the early 1990s. The first public release had two main user interfaces - one for controlling the database population process and the other for interrogating the database. The query interface allowed users to specify colour, texture, and shape properties of an image query. Each matching feature had an associated picker. For example, the colour picker consisted of a set of standard RGB (Red, Green, Blue) sliders and a colour patch displaying the selected colour. The system also supported additional colour wheels and HIS (Hue, Intensity, Saturation) colour pickers. All the features could be used individually or in combination. The system displayed the retrieval results in rank order and employed relevance feedback to allow iterative query refinement. Other utility functions included features to display image similarity scores or view the full-scale image.

Lee et al. (1994) reported an alternative design of the QBIC user interface separated into two main windows: the query specification window and the query results window. The query specification window formed a hierarchy of three levels: the query window, the feature window, the editors and the sample window. The query window allowed the user to specify singular or multiple queries in the form of icons. Queries were restricted to objects or scenes; an icon with a rectangle represented a scene and one without a rectangle represented an object. Creating multiple icons in the query window formed multiple queries. The feature window allowed the user to control the weighting of the feature values used during runtime. Each available feature had an enable button, a feature type field, editor or sampler radio buttons, a value picker, and a weight slider. Features were enabled or disabled by selecting a radio button and features were weighted by adjusting the slider. The editors and sample window allowed feature values to be set or selected. The query results window was divided into two areas, the results area and the holding area. The retrieval results were displayed in the results area in rank order and employed relevance feedback to allow iterative query refinement. Images of interest could be moved to the holding area for use as queries at a later stage.

Bird et al. (1996) describe the design of a prototype user interface for use within the textile industry using QBIC as the underlying retrieval engine. The purpose of the interface was to enrich the early stages of the design process by enabling designers to explore new ideas for textile patterns. It was divided into three sections from left to right: search parameters, results, and a theme board. The interface was modelled on the process of you input, we output, you play. The theme board was the central feature of the interface and was based on the designers current working practice, allowing them to compare and explore combinations of textile patterns from the retrieved results. The design of the user interface was based on several considerations. For example, the language used in the interface should be intuitive to the designer; the word Finish was used in favour of the ubiquitous Quit. Bird et al. provide one of the more detailed descriptions of the design of a content-based image retrieval system user interface and the underlying principles behind that design. However, it is not clear whether their user interface was subject to usability testing.

Flickner et al. (1997) reflected that one of the key challenges that remains in making the technology pervasive and useful is the design of the user interface. They suggested that the user interface must be designed to let users easily select content-based properties, allow these properties to be combined with each other and with text or parametric data, let users reformulate queries, and navigate the database. It is impossible to assess the usability of the user interfaces developed for QBIC based purely on their descriptions in the literature. Bird et al. (1999) stated that the user interface was too complex for general users of QBIC. Similarly, the user interface described by Lee et al. (1994) appears to be designed from a systems perspective, and from its description appears overly complicated and difficult to use. No empirical or informal evaluations of those QBIC user interfaces described have ever been publicly reported and it is generally unclear why the interfaces were designed in the manner they were. This situation is generally symptomatic for all reported content-based image retrieval system user interfaces.

IMAGE QUERY PARADIGMS

Query[2] formulation is a core activity in the process of information retrieval (Catarci, Costabile, Levialdi, & Batin, 1997). A number of query paradigms have been proposed for specifying a query Q_n in an image database I. Several database query languages[3] have been proposed to support image query expression in both first- and second-generation image retrieval systems and are based on either the relational or tabular data models. The most widespread languages are extensions of the Structured Query Language (SQL) proposed by Codd (1970). With this approach the user formulates the query in the form of a query statement. Examples include ISQL (Assmann, Venema, & Hohne, 1986), PROBE (Orenstein & Manola, 1988) and Spatial SQL (Egenhofer, 1991). A major criticism levelled at these languages is the potential complexity of the query statement required to express a simple query (Catarci, Costabile, Levialdi, & Batin, 1997). An example of a PSQL style query is shown in Figure 6. The query selects all cities in the area (4±4,11±9) having a population ≥ 450,000.

Chang and Jungert (2001) proposed to simplify the expression of SQL queries with ΣQL. The language is based upon a single operator, σ, that acts on the extended multimedia static structure (MSS) proposed by Chang et al. (1995) and is suitable for audio, image, text, and video or multimedia databases. An example of a ΣQL query is shown in Figure 7.

Figure 6: PSQL Query (Roussopoulos, Faloutsos, & Sellis, 1988)

SELECT city, state, population, location
FROM cities
ON us-map
WHERE location within window (4±4,11±9)
AND population ≥ 450,000

The introduction of the new keyword 'CLUSTER' allows the parameters of the σ operator to be grouped as t_1, t_2, t_3; the keyword indicates that objects belonging to the same class must share some common value or characteristic. In the above example, the subscript t_n indicates three predetermined values. To extract these values from the source I, the ΣQL query can be expressed as $\sigma(t_1, t_2, t_3)I$, and can be translated into the equivalent SQL syntax shown in Figure 8. The query language differs significantly from previously proposed query languages in its use of a single operator that can be mapped into an SQL-like query language to reduce the complexity of the SELECT statement.

As an alternative to the relational-based query language approach, Zloof (1977) proposed Query by Example (QBE). This is based on a tabular data model and employs a tabular query structure to express queries. The user specifies an example output of the query by directly constructing entries into relational skeletons instead of writing lengthy queries, and the system identifies the goal by generalizing an example. QBE is a revision of Codd's relational calculus language SQL. Several examples have been based on this approach including Aggregate by Example (Klug, 1981), Time by Example (Tansel, Arkun, & Ozsoyoglu, 1989), Generalised Query by Example (Jacobs & Walczak, 1983), Office by Example (Whang, Ammann, Bolmarcich, Hanrahan, Hochgesang, Huang, Khorasani, Krishnamurthy, Sockut, Sweeney, Waddle, & Zloof, 1987), and Natural Forms Query Language (NFQL) (Embley, 1989). The languages share a commonality in the method of query expression, and differ only in their expansion or revision of the QBE paradigm to serve different application areas.

Two languages specifically developed for image databases were Query by Pictorial Example (QPE) and PICQUERY. QPE, proposed by Chang and Fu (1980), was implemented as part of the REDI (RElational Database system for Images) database that comprised

Figure 7: Query (Chang & Jungert, 2001)

SELECT t
CLUSTER t_1, t_2, t_3
FROM I

Figure 8: Query by Pictorial Example Relations (Chang & Fu, 1980)

```
ROADS(FRAME, ROID, X1, Y1, X2, Y2)
RONAME(FRAME, ROID, NAME)
POS(FRAME, XSIZE, YSIZE, XCEN, YCEN, LOC)
CITIES(FRAME, CIID, X1, Y1, X2, Y2)
CINAME(FRAME, CIID, NAME)
```

LANDSAT images and digitised maps. Descriptions of linear features were represented internally by their x and y coordinates and stored in a relational database with additional data. Queries could be specified from the relations outlined in Figure 8.

The user formulates the query by entering an example of a possible answer in the appropriate cell as an alphanumeric string. Example elements that were underlined are those that must be resolved when the system processes the query. An example of a QPE query for area similarity is shown in Table 1, Table 2, and Table 3.

The query is to retrieve one image frame whose road network pattern is most similar to the query example. The ROADS processing set is applied to the image with location*, which is the image currently being displayed on the screen (Table 1). The results of the ROADS processing set is inserted as the pictorial relation TEMP with default domains X1, Y1, X2, Y2 (Table 2). The spatial operator SIM-LL measures the similarity of the relative positions, rather than the co-ordinates of the line segments specified in the two given relations (Table 3). A criticism levelled at this approach was that when a user formulates the query, the internal structure and operations of the database were visible (Del Bimbo, 1999). Similarly, if several tables are to be completed the responsibility is placed on the user to establish the connections between columns of different tables in order to execute the query.

Joseph and Cardenas (1988) proposed a similar approach with PICQUERY. The language was designed as a non-procedural, conversational language for non-programmers, which operated either directly on images, or image elements that had been

Table 1: QPE Query for Area Similarity (Step 1)

POS	FRAME	XSIZE	YSIZE	XCEN	YCEN	LOC
						*

Table 2: QPE Query for Area Similarity (Step 2)

TEMP	X1	Y1	X2	Y2
I(ROADS)				

Table 3: QPE Query for Area Similarity (Step 3)

ROADS	FRAME	ROID	X1	Y1	X2	Y2
	P.X		SIM-LL.(TEMP)			

previously extracted and labelled with a name. Queries could involve different types of operations on the image data including point set, metric, image manipulation, pattern recognition or user defined functions. Queries are constructed by completing the fields of tabular forms with the appropriate information. The tabular forms had a predefined layout according to the operations used in the query. An example of a query to identify region similarity is shown in Table 4.

Here, the operation is to find a portion of a given region object that is similar to another region object. The portion in Region $Name_2$ with similar temperatures to portions in Region $Name_1$ is to be identified and named FRAPT if the operation is successful. In contrast to QPE, they attempted to simplify the language by restricting a query to a singular table to reduce the complexity of the operation.

The range and variety of query languages proposed over the years illustrate the diversity of data sources and operations that can be carried out on the data. Many of the query languages are based upon extensions of SQL. These query languages have constructs to allow the end users to formulate their information needs or queries through alphanumeric strings and Boolean combinations in order to interrogate the database.

To use a command language users are required to learn the primitives and the syntax of the query language. Such languages are usually efficient but difficult to learn as interaction is based on recall as opposed to recognition. Ozoyoglu and Wang (1993) suggested that ease of learning was one of the major features of all example-based languages. The system can be used with limited prior knowledge and requires learning only a small number of concepts. Languages based on the tabular data model reduce the cognitive load on the user as interaction is based on recognition. However, Yen and Scamell's (1993) comparison experiment of SQL and QBE suggested that query language type leads to a difference in user performance and satisfaction only at a theoretical level. At a practical level, the results suggested that query language type had no affect on user performance. The results also suggested that under certain conditions query complexity had a significant effect on user performance and the order of exposure to different query languages could lead to differences.

Eakins and Graham (1999) comment that text-based queries hardly seem an obvious choice for formulating visual queries. However, the way in which a query is expressed

Table 4: PICQUERY (Joseph & Cardenas, 1988)

Picture₁	Region Name₁	Picture₂	Region Name₂	Basis	Name for Similar Portion
PIC_1	EGYPT	PIC_2	FRANCE	Temperature	FRAPT

ultimately depends on the nature and complexity of the query itself. In context, text-based queries may be an entirely appropriate and valid method for specifying a query.

QUERY BY VISUAL EXAMPLE

Content-based image retrieval requires the user to provide or create a visual example or representation of their query image Q_n as the basis of the search from the image archive I. Query by Visual Example (QVE) is the general term used to describe this approach. Several examples of this approach to query specification have been reported in the literature. Del Bimbo (1999) and Lew and Huang (2001) distinguish between different methods of QVE: query by browsing, query by icon, query by image, query by painting, and query by sketch. Each of these will be considered briefly.

Query by Browsing

Query by browsing permits users to browse the database by three methods: unstructured, semi-structured, and structured browsing. The simplest method of query by browsing is unstructured browsing where the user is presented with a complete view of all the images contained in the database. Generally, the images are presented as thumbnails, ordered by filename, that the user can scroll through. Semi-structured browsing allows the user to search through the image collection by choosing example images. The system computes a similarity ranking on image features and disregards the least similar images after each iteration until the user is satisfied with the set of images left in the retrieval loop. Examples of this approach were proposed by Laaksonen et al. (2000) and Vendrig et al. (2001). With structured browsing, images are clustered into predefined, hierarchal classes based on a visual property such as colour. The images are presented as thumbnails and the user can move through the hierarchy until satisfied. Examples of this approach were proposed by Lai et al. (1999) and Brodley et al. (1999).

The concept of browsing has been recognised in the field of information retrieval as a fundamental part of human information seeking behaviour (Wilson, 1981; Ellis, 1989). Marchionini (1995) states that browsing is an approach to information seeking that is both informal and opportunistic. Nevertheless, the viability of browsing as an access strategy is heavily dependent on the size of the image collection and the effectiveness of any classification by which a physical order is imposed (Enser, 1995). No empirical studies have measured the ceiling or threshold of the maximum number of images a user is willing to search through in order to find a suitable image.

Query by Icon

Query by icon allows the user to select an icon that represents a high-level concept of a category or idea. Icons are commonly found in graphical user interfaces (GUI) and are a graphic representation of an entity, metaphor or an artefact. Similar to iconic-based visual query languages, the user physically places object icon(s) on a query canvas to specify relative locations, orientations, and sizes of objects within the desired image (Gupta & Jain, 1997). Several examples of this approach have been proposed over the years by Angelaccio et al. (1990); Del Bimbo et al. (1993); Papantonakis and King (1995); Aslandogan, Thier, and Yu (1996); Chvada and Wood (1997); Lee and Whang (2001). Lew and Huang (2001) suggest that the iconic query paradigm is the most intuitive query method, but that it is restricted to a vocabulary of visual concepts that can be reliably understood by the VIR system.

Query by Image

Query by image allows the user to provide an example image as a representation of their query. The example can be either an image selected externally or internally from the system. Di Lecce and Guerriero (1999) characterize this as query by external pictorial example and query by internal pictorial example. Query by external pictorial example permits the user to submit their own image to the system and is generally perceived as the simplest approach to query formulation. However, it is based on the assumption that the user has a suitable representative image to use as the basis of their query. Query by internal pictorial example is query by browsing where the user selects an image from the system's database. All the images contained in the database are presented or a selection is generated randomly in a n-dimensional matrix. Similar to the problems associated with query by browsing, the main disadvantages of this method are providing suitable access mechanisms to retrieve the internal example and the size of the image collection the user is willing to search through in order to find a suitable image.

Query by Painting

Query by painting allows the user to manually specify the percentage or the distribution of colour values. For example, the user is able to specify the percentages of colour within a composition, such as 50% green, 25% yellow, and 25% red (Figure 9). Similarly, the user is able to specify the x, y positions of the of colour values on the query canvas (Figure 10). Examples of this approach were proposed by Flickner et al. (1995) and Del Bimbo et al. (1998).

Query by Sketch

Query by sketch allows the user to draw a sketch of the desired image by combining several features commonly found in computer graphic applications. The sketch represents a template of either a completed object or scene. Kato et al. (1992) were the first to provide a query by sketch but other examples of this approach have since been proposed by Chuah, Roth, and Kerpedjiev (1997); Del Bimbo (1997); Muller, Eickeler, and Rigoll (1998); Di Sciascio and Mongiello (1999). As Korfhage (1997) indicates, queries formulated by this method are simplistic, relatively crude sketches of the desired query image and that the tool has a limited functionality for expressing more complex image queries. Eakins (1992) stressed that drawing a shape query is inherently time consuming and requires a certain modicum of artistic ability. Similarly, the effectiveness of shape matching features are highly sensitive to noise and pixel arrangement in the query image. Bird et al. (1999) demonstrated that the user blamed their own artistic drawing ability when query results where unsuccessful.

Query by image, painting and sketch are the most widespread interaction methods of query formulation found in content-based image retrieval systems. As Zachary and Iyengar (1999) suggest, a good query method will be natural to use as well as capturing enough information from the user to extract meaningful results. However, supporting the

Figure 9: Colour Percentages (QBIC)

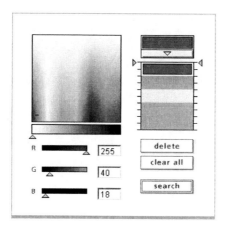

expression of image queries by these modes of interaction is a non-trivial problem. Eakins (1992) stresses, the more complex the query in terms of shape and structure, the more difficult it will be for the user to express and produce a meaningful visual example. Similarly, Chang and Jungert (2001) state that most visual query systems (VQSs) restrict human-computer interaction to only one kind of interaction paradigm. They suggest that the presence of several paradigms, each one with its different characteristics and advantages, will help both naïve and experienced users in interacting with the system.

BEYOND QUERY BY VISUAL EXAMPLE

Alternative methods have been proposed to extend the QVE paradigm. Gupta and Jain (1997) note that while most systems are limited in the query types they can handle, i.e., colour, shape, and texture, they suggest that image query specification should not

Figure 10: Colour Distribution (QBIC)

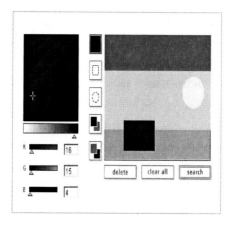

be performed exclusively within the query by visual example paradigm but extended through a range of different tools that serve as a visual information retrieval query language. They proposed a nine-component query language framework that included: image processing, feature-space manipulation, object specification, measurement specification, classification, spatial arrangement, temporal arrangement, annotation, and data definition. For example, the spatial arrangement tool would allow the user to specify location sensitive queries and move query objects denoted by the object specification tool to reposition them in the place of interest. Similarly, the feature-space manipulation tool would allow the user to explore the feature space and to specify nearest neighbour queries where each image is viewed as a point in a n-dimensional feature vector space, i.e., find the nearest x images within distance d of the query image Q_n.

They argue that while most systems support this type of query, it is executed blindly and does not allow the user to interactively navigate in the feature space or modify query conditions based on this interaction. While there may be merit in their suggestions, what they propose is not strictly a query language but a set of image processing or image manipulation tools that could assist the user in modifying an existing image.

Several visualization tools for image browsing have been proposed based on Gupta and Jain's (1997) feature-space manipulation tool. Cinque et al. (1998) developed a new version of VIBE[4] (Visualization Browsing Environment) known as ImageVIBE. Queries are initially expressed in the form of keywords or a sketch. Images retrieved from the database can be based on both textual and geometrical attributes and are displayed in a user defined 2-D multi-dimensional information space. The image space is displayed as a 2-D feature space with a number of user-defined points or regions of interest that correspond to meaningful colour or shape attributes. The position of the attributes in the display is dependent on their similarity according to the points of interest. For example, an object returned by a query may be presented in an information space defined by keywords, together with geometrical attributes.

Santini and Jain (1997) extended this to a non-immersive 3-D environment where images were clustered in the user defined 3-D feature space by feature similarity. See also (Gupta, Santini, & Jain, 1997). Del Bimbo (1999) suggests that the use of such visualization tools and techniques could specifically improve the effectiveness of the query by browsing paradigm. However, they still do not overcome the primary challenge of providing an effective method for specifying an initial query.

Assfalg et al. (2000) argue that virtual reality (VR) provides a realistic reproduction of a user's natural environment, particularly where images represent real-world scenes. They propose that the use of a non-immersive 3-D environment is a natural and effective interface to perform query by content. Their approach permits the user to navigate and edit the virtual space and to take photographs. This interaction provides the basis upon which to query the image database. They propose an extension of the query by browsing and query by image paradigms based on a new interaction metaphor: query by photograph. This enables the user to take snapshots of their current view and to use the resultant image to query the database. They argue that the photographer metaphor does not constrain the user to a predefined set of images. Nevertheless, it does constrain them to a pre-defined VR world, and it is difficult to assess how these environments could support the diversity and range of image data. The application of a non-immersive 3-D environment in information retrieval is not new (Hyldegaard, 1997). VR potentially represents the next generation of user interfaces for information retrieval. How they can be effectively applied in an operational setting is unclear and introduces a new avenue for further research.

Buford et al. (2002) take an unconventional approach to user interface design. They conducted an investigation into the human perception of images in order to produce a specification of desirable interface elements to develop a generic visual query interface for image databases based on the relation to particular types of image query. They postulated that the traditional user-centred design was inappropriate as the interface was not intended to be limited to a particular user group and the fundamentals issues of how queries may be expressed have not been addressed. Based on their theoretical work on the process of visual cognition, basic sensory input through to complex cognitive associations, they derived a taxonomy of nine types of image content: perceptual primitives, geometric primitives, visual extensions, semantic units, contextual abstraction, cultural abstraction, technical abstraction, emotional abstraction and metadata. One of the main difficulties of developing an effective retrieval mechanism arises from the subjectivity of human visual perception (Eysenck & Keane, 2000).

Research on the human perception of images has demonstrated the diversity of human perception and the complexity of extrapolating the findings into a coherent and generalisable theory for information retrieval (Panofsky, 1968; Shatford Layne, 1994; Svenonius, 1994; Burke, 1997; Hidderley & Rafferty, 1997). In contrast to their approach, Besser (1995) suggests that it will be collections of segmented studies that will provide a rich and detailed understanding of specific aspects of the field of visual information retrieval (VIR), which will contribute towards future developments of general VIR models and frameworks. If we accept the basic premise of HCI then — the user interface must match the tasks, activities and goals of the end user population for whom it is being developed (Preece, 1994) — the user interface is likely to be of limited use. The litmus test of the user interface would have been in its evaluation but the final results of the research are still keenly awaited.

USER INTERACTION

Retrieval is commonly obtained through an interactive session (Del Bimbo, 1999). To initiate a CBIR search, the user provides or creates the visual representation of their information need and then selects the features, range of model parameters, and similarity measure that are important. Smeulders et al. (2000) defined an abstract query space to represent user interaction in a content-based image retrieval system (Figure 11).

Figure 11: Abstract Query Space (Smeulders, Worring, Santini, Gupta, & Jain, 2000)

$$Q = \{I_Q, F_Q, S_Q, Z_Q\}$$

Figure 12: Image Object Model (Rui & Huang, 2001)

$$O = O(D, F, R)$$

To start a query session, an instantiation of $Q = \{I_Q, F_Q, S_Q, Z_Q\}$ is created. Where I_Q is the selection of images from the image archive I, F_Q is the selection of features derived from the images in I_Q, S_Q is the similarity function, and Z_Q is the goal dependent semantics. The query space forms the basis of user interaction in a content-based image retrieval system, specifying queries and displaying results. Rui and Huang (2001) highlight the flaw in this approach. They state that an image object O can be modelled as a function of the image data D, features F, and representations R (Figure 12).

Where D is the raw image data, $F = \{f_i\}$, $i = 1, ..., I$ is a set of visual features associated with the image object, such as colour, texture or shape, and $R_i = \{r_{ij}\}$, $j = 1, ..., J_i$ is a set of representations for a given feature such as colour histogram or colour moments. Each representation of r_{ij} is a vector consisting of multiple components where K_{ij} is the length of the vector r_{ij}, i.e., $r_{ij} = \lfloor r_{ij_1}, ..., r_{ij_k}, ..., r_{ij}k_{ij} \rfloor$. The proposed image model has three levels of information abstraction — objects O, features F, and representations R — which increase the granularity of information, and different weights exist to reflect a particular entity's importance to its upper level U at the object level, at the feature level, and at the representation level. They suggest that specifying object O, feature F and R representation level weights imposes a dual burden on the user of the retrieval system and its developers. For example, specifying the object level weights U imposes a burden on the user as it requires them to have comprehensive knowledge of the visual features used in the retrieval system and how they relate to their information need. Similarly, specifying feature and representation level weights V_i and W_{ij} imposes a burden on system developers who do not know which r_{ij} and r_{ijk} match users perception of the image content.

In general, the majority of content-based image retrieval systems exemplify these interaction models although research activity has only explored specific elements. The models emphasise that user interaction is a complex interplay between the user and the system, suggesting that only highly skilled and specialised users would be able to utilise the system effectively to obtain relevant retrieval results.

IMAGE INFORMATION SEEKING BEHAVIOUR

Seeking information is a fundamental human function, vital to survival (Large, Tedd, & Hartley, 1999). In the context of textual information, research into information seeking behaviour has a history going back nearly 40 years. Much of it has been reviewed in the pages of the Annual Review of Information Science and Technology and significant attempts have been made to draw this research into a unified theory of information behaviour. Within this theory, Wilson (2000) differentiates between information behaviour, information seeking behaviour, information searching behaviour, and information use behaviour. In the context of this section we adopt Wilson's definition of information seeking behaviour: the purposive activity of seeking for information as a consequence of a need to satisfy some goal, as opposed to information searching behaviour that is concerned with the micro-level of behaviour employed by the searcher in interacting with information systems. Wilson (1981, 2000) proposed a general model of information behaviour — the totality of human behaviour in relation to sources and channels of information, including both active and passive information seeking and information use (Figure 13).

Figure 13: Model of Information Behaviour (Wilson, 2000)

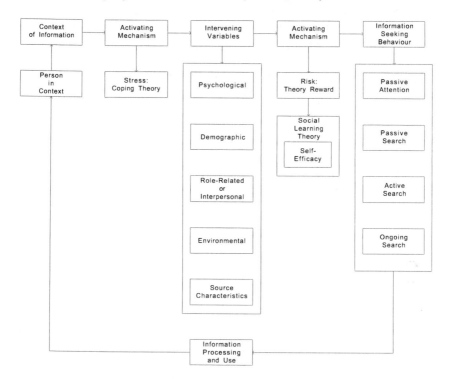

Wilson (2000) states that the study of information behaviour in the field of information science is a well-defined area of research and the benefits of this accumulated knowledge are beginning to show. This observation only strictly applies to the area of text retrieval; research into visual information seeking behaviour has a much shorter history. Nevertheless, there has been considerable activity in recent years.

In an early investigation, Batley (1988) investigated the image information seeking behaviour of users of a database containing 950 images in order to identify the visual information search strategies employed. An experimental retrieval environment was developed that allowed for three search types: keyword, specific browsing, and seren-dipitous browsing. The study included forty one participants drawn from four distinct user groups: school children aged between 12 and 17 years, undergraduate librarianship students, postgraduate Master of Education students, and librarians. From this small study, she concluded that the major influences on image information seeking behaviour were the information need and the individual user's characteristics. In addition, she identified five factors that influenced visual information search strategies: the nature of the information itself, the database structure, the task or information need, the user, and the interface.

The results of the study suggested that information need and individual user characteristics would largely determine visual information search strategies adopted by the end user. For example, where a query was clearly defined, end users would generally employ a keyword-based search as opposed to browsing. Browsing strategies were more likely to be adopted where the query or information need was less clearly defined.

Sustained effort to develop an understanding of visual information seeking behaviour has been undertaken by two groups in the United Kingdom. Over a period of time and with various colleagues, Enser, at the University of Brighton, has undertaken a series of studies of information seeking behaviour. In a major piece of research based upon the Hulton Deutsch picture collection, 2,722 requests were analysed (Enser & McGregor, 1992). From this examination they deduced that queries could be allocated to one or other of four categories on two dimensions. These were referred to as unique and non-unique and refined or non-refined. An example of unique would be 'The Parthenon' and an example of non-unique would be 'goats.' Therefore, an example of a unique refined query might be 'Margaret Thatcher giving a press conference' whilst an example of non-unique refined would be 'nurses looking exhausted.'

When compared with the field of text retrieval, his observation concluded that users of visual information do not behave in the same way as users of text retrieval systems, who generally express their queries at a higher level of abstraction than is necessary (Cousins, Enser, & Hartley, 1989). However, he recognised there was a process of pre-meditation.

The study was subsequently extended to investigate a further 1,749 queries derived from seven image collections, of which five were archives of still images and two were archives of moving images (Armitage & Enser, 1997). This research led to an extended method of analysis that was based upon Panofsky's (1969) framework of image analysis.

Conniss et al. (Conniss, Ashford, & Graham, 2000) conducted an investigation into the visual information seeking behaviour of a small number of users from ten wide ranging organisations which included three picture libraries, a museum, an architectural company, a broadcasting organisation, a police force, a newspaper, an art history department, and a radiology department. In contrast to Enser's work, they used a qualitative approach and studied the information seeking behaviour of 45 individuals selected using purposive sampling and whose information seeking habits were recorded through a mixture of questionnaires, informal observation, in-depth interviews, and documentation. They concluded that images could be categorised as: specific, where only one image will satisfy the request (e.g., a specific painting or X-ray); semi-specific, where only one of a subset is acceptable (e.g., specific conditions or criteria are attached, such as Impressionist paintings, conceptual, or abstract) and where images have some semantic notion, or context, or abstract element; or vague, where the searcher is unsure exactly what is required or has only 'fuzzy criteria.'

Clearly, there is some similarity between this categorisation and the initial categorisation devised by Enser and McGregor (1992). That very different approaches to studying user queries have produced results which are at least broadly similar should perhaps offer some confidence in their results. The overall results of the study suggested that the image seeking process is influenced by the complex interaction between contextual factors that contribute significantly to the way in which a user searches and ultimately selects and uses images. They suggest that these factors are critical in bringing about a specific information need, in influencing the source(s) of information chosen, which search strategies are adopted, and when the search is terminated.

Keister (1994) described a review of user query data that was used to aid the development of an automated picture retrieval system for the Prints and Photographs Collection at the National Library of Medicine (NLM). The results of the study suggested that requests could be grouped into two categories: visual (concerned with the content depicted in the image) and topical (concerned with the theme). The investigation also highlighted a dichotomy in the way in which different patron groups expressed their information need. For example, picture professionals used art and graphics jargon; health professionals used specific terms that matched the subject matter of the National Library of Medicine's collection; museum and academic clients generally had precise references to the images they required. She implies that this behaviour can be attributed in some way to a generic cognitive information processing model shared by each specific group. Unfortunately, the size of the study was not reported and nor was the study based on accurate recordings of the queries as presented by the users. Nevertheless, the report suggests that many if not all the requests could be categorised using the analytical framework developed by Enser and colleagues.

Hastings (1995) studied the image seeking behaviour of art historians in their use of the collection of West Indian paintings at the University of Central Florida. Her investigation resulted in the categorisation of queries into four levels of complexity ranging from those she determined to be simple queries (Level 1) to complex queries (Level 4). The examples she provides of each type of query suggest considerable agreement with the Armitage and Enser (1997) analysis, although a complete mapping between the approaches has not been undertaken. Ornager (1997) studied the information seeking behaviour of 30 journalists and 33 archivists using 17 newspaper photographic archives. Using a combination of quantitative and qualitative questions administered through structured interviews, she concluded that queries could be categorised as:

- Named person (who).
- Named phenomena (what).
- Geographical information (where).
- Time information (when).
- Specific events (what).
- Moods and emotions (shown or expressed).
- Associative meanings (what).
- Size of photo.

Again, there is some similarity between this analysis and that of Armitage and Enser. Arguably, that there is not the same complexity of query type as indicated in their facet analysis is explained by the fact that Ornager has studied only newspaper archives, whereas, the Armitage and Enser analysis is based upon a greater variety of image archives. Similarly, Markkula and Sormunen (1998) conducted an investigation into the information seeking behaviour of journalists in order to ascertain the requirements for a digital newspaper photo archive. The results suggested that specific information needs dominate the use of the archives, and highlighted that journalist requests fell into four categories: concrete objects, themes or abstractions, background information, and specific images.

In 1993, Enser (1993) remarked that the literature of image database and retrieval applications offered no systematic study of user demand for visual information sources. However, since that time there has been considerable effort to understand the needs of those seeking images in a variety of contexts, not the least of which was the substantial studies undertaken by Enser himself. The crucial point which emerges from these studies is that users seek images which demonstrate semantic similarity to their information needs and that these needs appear to be categorisable into a limited number of groups. Given that CBIR systems retrieve material by primitive features, there remains a considerable semantic gap between user requirements and CBIR system capabilities. The only proviso that might be added to this is that our understanding of user image information seeking behaviour has largely been developed in situations where the users have not been exposed to CBIR systems and where their information seeking behaviour has doubtless been conditioned by the available systems.

USER INTERFACE EVALUATION

Evaluation in the field of content-based image retrieval has focused primarily on measuring retrieval performance. Information retrieval systems have traditionally been evaluated by two measures — precision and recall — which have their origins in the Cranfield retrieval tests in the 1960s (Figure 14). Precision is a measure of the proportion of the returned items that are relevant to the query and recall is a measure of the proportion of relevant items in the database that are returned by the query.

Several alternative measures have been proposed for assessing retrieval performance in image databases (Mehtre, Kankanhalli, & Lee, 1997; Narasimhalu, Kankanhalli, & Wu, 1997; Del Bimbo & Pala, 1997; Eakins, Graham, & Boardman, 1997). Despite criticism surrounding the reliability and validity of the measures in assessing retrieval effectiveness, both from the fields of text and image retrieval, effectiveness measures have been widely adopted in evaluation experiments in the field of content-based image retrieval. As van Rijsbergen (1979) states, effectiveness is purely a measure of the ability of the system to satisfy the user in terms of the relevance of documents retrieved, and information retrieval systems can be evaluated from several different perspectives. Lancaster and Warner (1993) report that studies have consistently demonstrated that accessibility and ease of use are the principal factors affecting the selection of an information source.

Emerging attempts have shifted their focus away from effectiveness measures to consider user satisfaction and to seek to understand its importance (Dunlop, 2000; Johnson, Griffiths, & Hartley, 2001). From an HCI perspective, evaluation is concerned

Figure 14: Precision and Recall Measures

$$precision = \frac{A(q) \cap R(q)}{A(q)} \qquad recall = \frac{A(q) \cap R(q)}{R(q)}$$

with gathering data about the usability of a design or product by a specified group of users, for a particular activity, within a specified environment or work context (Preece, Rogers, Sharp, Benyon, Holland, & Carey, 1994). Usability is defined as a measure of the ease with which a system can be learned or used, its safety, effectiveness and efficiency, and the attitude of its users towards it (Nielsen, 1993). In contrast with evaluation experiments of retrieval effectiveness, experimentation focusing specifically on human-computer interaction in image databases is strictly limited.

McLean et al. (1995) reported one of the earliest known usability studies of the Promenade image retrieval system, which was designed to operate over the Internet using Mosaic as the client interface. The interface provided a range of functionality to the user: to develop queries, display thumbnail sketches of retrieval output, and download full sized images for processing. The overall aim of the experiment was to determine the usability of the Promenade system by casual users, particularly in terms of its learnability, and it was also designed to assess whether there was a correlation between user experiences with other applications and use of the Promenade systems, e.g., X-Windows, Unix, Mosaic and the Internet in general.

The participants were composed of 19 undergraduate computer science students, 10 male and nine female, with subject knowledge in the field of human-computer interaction, who had diverse backgrounds and varying degrees of experience with other systems. None of the participants had any prior experience of the Promenade system or the National Agriculture Library services, or any subject expertise in the field of Botany, particularly of plant nomenclature or classification systems.

The results suggested that previous experience with UNIX and the Internet resulted in improved performance when using the system. However, the participant with no experience demonstrated the best overall experience with the system. This raises serious concerns and casts doubt over the reliability and validity of the experiment and its findings.

Mostafa and Dillon (1996) conducted an experiment into the usability of a user interface that supported multiple image query models. They postulated that for effective access to images the design of the database interface must be based on principles that match the actual querying needs of the end users. The ViewFinder interface was designed as a client to a database server to support visual and textual querying by end users. A second interface was designed for comparative purposes and supported text-based keyword queries. The evaluation involved 18 library and information science graduate students, seven male and 11 female, who had no experience of either user interface. The results of the experiment demonstrated that both user interfaces were easy to use with an average of 80% search success rates achieved, 83% and 84% respectively. Users generally preferred keyword queries as opposed to visual queries for known item queries, while visual queries were more frequently used for topical searches. The results support the findings of Batley (1988); there is a direct relationship between the user, their information need, and their visual information seeking behaviour. However, they concede that the tasks were not sufficiently taxing to induce any variance in retrieval performance.

Bird et al. (1999) report the results of a usability study using the QBIC image engine. Their objective was to assess usability by examining user response to three specific areas: reaction to the interface, interaction specifically with the query options, and expectations when formulating their queries. Twenty-five participants from a variety of backgrounds and with a range of experience took part in the evaluation including curators, graphic designers, photographers, librarians, and IT specialists. Query formulation was restricted to query by image and query by sketch, and the matching feature was limited to colour layout. The results highlighted a number of specific usability issues with the user interface and suggested a number of guidelines for the development of future user interfaces. For example, the drawing canvas area was square, whereas the images used in the experiment were either portrait or landscape. They concluded that user expectations were dependent on previous experience and that any user interface needs to provide the flexibility to accommodate this range of experience.

Lai et al. (2000) reported the results of the user-centred evaluation of the CHROMA image retrieval system. The overall aim of the study was to test the hypothesis that structured browsing would facilitate effective image retrieval where the user had only a vague concept of their information need. The experiment was designed to compare the system's two search facilities: the navigation tool and the sketch tool. The navigation tool provides access to a hierarchical set of 10 dominant colour groupings. The user navigates this space by selecting the dominant image colour and then by selecting minor colours within that group. The sketch tool provides a standard drawing facility for users to construct an outline of the approximate contents of their query in terms of predominate colours and the spatial location of objects.

Twenty-four first year undergraduates, 12 male and 12 female, aged 22 to 31, participated in the study. The subjects had no prior experience of image retrieval systems, but all had experience of using text-based retrieval systems. The result of the experiment suggested that the navigational tool was an effective image retrieval tool in supporting their original hypothesis.

The results reaffirmed the relationship between browsing and non-specific queries; however, the sample population is too small to have statistical significance. This is by no means a new finding and Lai et al. acknowledge that Batley (1988) had concluded that browsing was an essential information seeking strategy in an earlier experiment. In light of what information is available about the image information seeking behaviour of end users, the results suggest that high-level concepts can be matched to low-level features where colour is a primary factor. Despite their claim that the results obtained are sufficiently clear-cut and warrant no further experiments, it does present an interesting avenue for further exploration in testing the boundaries of their findings.

Rose et al. (2000) reported a comparative evaluation of the ANVIL system user interface. The system was designed for the retrieval of images annotated with short captions, and used NLP (Natural Language Processing) techniques to extract dependency structures from these captions and then apply a matching algorithm to recursively explore and compare them. ANVIL was designed to operate as a W3 image retrieval server accessible through a W3 client interface.

Two user interfaces were developed for the system: 1-D and 2-D. In both the 1-D and 2-D interfaces, queries were entered into a text box as an alphanumeric string with the retrieval results being displayed either as a ranked list or in a 2-D feature space. In the 2-D interface, the query results utilised a 2-D spatial layout that clustered the output based on distance from each other. The query image was positioned at the centre of the display with other matching images in proximity to the distance proportional to their similarity to the original query. The aim of their evaluation was to test the hypothesis that the 2-D interface enhanced user interaction for abstract tasks more successfully than the 1-D user interface.

Sixteen individuals participated in an experiment. The results of the evaluation suggested that both interfaces had an overall positive usability score. The 2-D client interface scored marginally higher in the tests but did not yield statistically significant results to support their hypothesis and the null hypothesis could not be rejected. They suggested that the results should be treated as exploratory rather than conclusive and concluded that whatever type of approach is used for query formulation and display of results, an equilibrium needs to be struck to cater to the needs of different types of users.

Venters et al. (2001c) reported the preliminary results of an inquiry into the usability of a visual query interface. The purpose of the evaluation was to assess the usability of the interface and to determine whether the proposed user interface features improved the human-computer interaction. For comparison purposes two user interfaces were used in the experiment: single feature and multi-feature. The single-feature interface allows the user to browse through categories of visual surrogates and select an image(s) on the basis of its visual properties. The multi-feature interface reflected the proposed features identified during the user analysis stage and included shape-building, browsing, sketching, and scanning tools.

The experiment was segmented by image type, user group, and use function. The image type consisted of a set of device marks supplied by the UK Trademark Registry. The participants in the study were purposefully selected to produce a group who shared similar task orientation, motivation, systems expertise, and domain knowledge. The use function was restricted to the retrieval of images by shape similarity. The ARTISAN (Eakins, Shields, & Boardman, 1996) shape retrieval system was used as the underlying retrieval engine. Twenty-eight information professionals from the UK Patent Information Network participated in the experiment.

The results of the evaluation suggested that both interfaces had an overall positive usability score. However, the single feature interface was the preferred user interface of choice by the majority of participants. Similarly, the browsing feature in the multi-feature interface was also the preferred feature. The results of the study, in part, reflect the nature of the majority of their queries — ambiguous, vague and imprecise — and reveal an intuitive display of current information seeking behaviour. This supports evidence from previous studies that browsing is a core strategy of information seeking behaviour. This is not a new finding but suggests that even when presented with a set of alternative, user-defined query tools to aid expression of non-specific queries, a complete paradigm shift in user perception may be required if content-based image retrieval is to be adopted as a viable retrieval tool.

A limited number of studies have focused on user interfaces for visual query formulation and modest attempts have been made to measure their usability. The studies emphasise that attention to usability issues during the system life cycle can result in an overall positive interaction score and lead to improvements for the interface under examination. In general, the participants involved in the experiments are drawn from a homogenous population and have no direct relationship to the tasks, activities, and goals of the end-user population. While this may be considered a limiting factor in extrapolating the findings to a sound, general theory there is sufficient evidence to suggest that there is a direct relationship between the user, their information need, and their visual information seeking behaviour that impacts on which query tools are utilised to express that need.

The results of the studies suggest that the user interface should offer the user different interaction mechanisms for expressing a query, depending on both the experience of the user and the type of query. However, the tasks may not be adequately broad in their scope to induce any significant variance in the results obtained. What is not clear is the usability of different methods of QVE in supporting the range of users and their information needs. Given the small number of studies, there is little empirical evidence to support the use of any interface metaphor or paradigm and there is insufficient evidence to suggest that the presence of several paradigms will help both naïve and experienced users in interacting with the system. The validity of the query by visual example paradigm and its effectiveness in supporting image query expression remains an open and valid research issue that now requires critical attention. The problem of what type of user interface is required to support human-computer interaction in a content-based image retrieval environment remains unsolved.

CONCLUSION

This chapter presented an overview of user interface research activity and related areas in the field of content-based image retrieval. There have been considerable developments in the field, some of which have been reported in this chapter. However, as we have demonstrated, there are two huge gaps which must be bridged before CBIR can move from being an interesting laboratory-based curiosity to being a tool of practical value for image retrieval. One of those gaps is the development of viable means of presenting user queries to CBIR systems. Effective retrieval algorithms are of little use if there is no means by which the typical end-user can present queries to that algorithm. Research on user interface design for image retrieval systems is embryonic and more research into improved methods of query formulation and refinement is required. Particular problems include how to specify an initial query to the system and how best to refine parameters if system output fails to meet user requirements. The other is the closing of the semantic gap: the chasm which exists between the ability of systems to deal with the primitives of colour, shape and texture and the real needs of users, which were considered in the section of this chapter devoted to image seeking behaviour. Attempts are underway to address this specific challenge (Grosky, 2002).

Del Bimbo (1999) argues that QVE is a paradigm particularly suited to express the perceptual aspects of low to intermediate features of visual content. It is clear that users and potential users of image retrieval systems seek information using queries which are at a higher semantic level than colour, shape and texture. In the short term, there are two probable approaches: first to identify any highly specialist areas where queries can be expressed as primitive features and second, as stressed by Enser (2000), to attempt the combination of CBIR with concept-based approaches to image retrieval such as those proposed by Brodley et al. (1999), Lew (2000), and Zhou and Huang (2002). Finally it can be argued that there is also the need to develop robust approaches to the evaluation of CBIR systems, which consider both the effectiveness of the system and its usability for the intended audience. Effectiveness without usability and usability without effectiveness are equally redundant. While it can be argued that much has been achieved within the field of CBIR, it is very clear that very much more remains to be done.

REFERENCES

Aigrain, P., Zhang, H., & Petkovic, D. (1996). Content-based image retrieval of visual media: A state of the art review. *Multimedia Tools and Applications, 3*, 179-202.

Angelaccio, M., Catarci, T., & Santucci, G. (1990). QBD*: A graphical query language with recursion. *IEEE Transactions on Software Engineering, 16*, 1150-1163.

Armitage, L. H. & Enser, P. G. B. (1997). Analysis of user need in image archives. *Journal of Information Science, 23* (4), 287-299.

Aslandogan, Y. A., Thier, C., & Yu, C. (1996). A system for effective content based image retrieval. *Multimedia '96: Proceedings of the Fourth ACM International Conference on Multimedia*, (pp. 429-430).

Assfalg, J., Del Bimbo, A., & Pala, P. (2000). Virtual reality for image retrieval. *Journal of Visual Languages and Computing, 11*, 105-124.

Assmann, K., Venema, R., & Hohne, K. H. (1986). The ISQL language: A software tool for the development of pictorial information systems in medicine. In S-K. Chang, T. Ichikawa, & P. Ligomenides (Eds.), *Visual Languages* (pp. 261-283).

Bach, J. R., Fuller, C., Gutpa, A., Hampapur, A., Horowitz, B., Humphrey, R., Jain, R., & Shu, C.-F. (1996). The virage image search engine: An open framework for image management. *Storage and Retrieval for Still Image and Video Databases IV, Proceedings of SPIE, 2670*, (pp. 76-87).

Batley, S. (1988). Visual information retrieval: Browsing strategies in pictorial databases. *Online Information '88: Proceedings of the 12th International Online Information Meeting*, London (December 6-8, pp. 373-381).

Besser, H. (1990). Visual access to visual images: The UC Berkley image database project. *Library Trends, 38*, 787-798.

Besser, H. (1995). Getting the picture on image databases: The basics. *Database*, (April/May), 12-19.

Besser, H. (1996). Image databases: The first decade, the present, and the future. *Digital Image Access and Retrieval: 1996 Clinic on Library Applications of Data Processing*, Graduate School of Library and Information Science, University of Illinois at Urbana-Champaign 1996, 17.

Bird, C., Elliott, P. J., & Griffiths, E. (1996). User interfaces for content-based image retrieval. *IEE Colloquium on Intelligent Image Databases*, London, 1-4.

Bird, C., Elloitt, P. J., & Hayward, P. M. (1999). Content-based retrieval for European image libraries. *The Challenge of Image Retrieval: CIR99, The 2nd UK Conference on Image Retrieval, Forte Posthouse Hotel*, Newcastle upon Tyne, United Kingdom, (February 25-26)..

Brodley, C. E., Kak, A. C., Shyu, C., Dy, J., Broderick, L. S., & Aisen, A. M. (1999). Content-based retrieval from medical image databases: A synergy of human interaction, machine learning and computer vision. *AAAI/IAAI '99: The Proceedings of the Sixteenth National Conference on Artificial Intelligence and Eleventh Conference on Innovative Applications of Artificial Intelligence*, Orlando, FL, USA, (July 18-22, pp. 760-767). MIT Press.

Burford, B., Briggs, P., & Eakins, J. P. (2002). *A Taxonomy of the Image: On the Classification of Content for Image Retrieval.* Institute for Image Data Research, University of Northumbria. Unpublished.

Burke, M. (1997). Meaning, multimedia and the Internet: Subject retrieval challenges and solutions. *Library and Information Studies: Research and Professional Practice: Proceedings of the 2nd British-Nordic Conference on Library and Information Studies,* Queen Margaret College, Edinburgh, Scotland, (pp. 61-78).

Catarci, T., Costabile, M. F., Levialdi, S., & Batini, C. (1997). Visual query systems for databases: A survey. *Journal of Visual Languages and Computing, 8*(2), 215-260.

Chang, H., Hou, T., Hsu, A., & Chang, S-K. (1995). The management and applications of tele-action objects. *ACM Journal of Multimedia Systems, 3*(5-6), 204-216.

Chang, N.-S. & Fu, K-S. (1980, November). Query by pictorial example. *IEEE Transactions on Software Engineering, 6*(6), 519-524.

Chang, S.-K. & Hsu, A. (1992). Image information systems: Where do we go from here? *IEEE Transactions on Knowledge and Data Engineering, 4*(5), 431-442.

Chang, S.-K & Jungert, E. (2001). Query languages for multimedia search. M.S. Lew (Ed.), *Principles of Visual Information Retrieval.* Springer-Verlag, Advances in Pattern Recognition, 199-217.

Chang, T. & Kuo, C.-C. J. (1993). Texture analysis and classification with tree-structured wavelet transform. *IEEE Transactions on Image Processing, 2*(4), 429-441.

Chavda, M. & Wood, P. (1997). Towards an ODMG-compliant visual object query language. *VLDB '97: Proceedings of 23rd International Conference on Very Large Data Bases,* Athens, Greece, (August 26-29, pp. 456-465).

Chen, H-L. (2001). An analysis of image retrieval tasks in the filed of art history. *Information Processing & Management,* 37, 701-720.

Chuah, M. C., Roth, S. F., & Kerpedjiev, S. (1997). Sketching, searching, and custom visualizations: A content-based approach to design retrieval. M.T. Maybury (Ed.), *Intelligent Multimedia Information Retrieval,* (pp. 83-111). AAAI Press.

Cinque, L., Levialdi, S., Malizia, A., & Olsen, K. A. (1998). A multidimensional image browser. *Journal of Visual Languages and Computing, 9*(1), 103-117.

Ciocca, G., Gagliardi, I., & Schettini, R. (2001). Quicklook2: An integrated multimedia system. *Journal of Visual Languages and Computing, 12,* 81-103.

Codd, E. F. (1970). A relational model of data for large shared data banks. *Communications of the ACM, 13*(6), 377-387.

Conniss, L. R., Ashford, A. J., & Graham, M. E. (2001). Information seeking behaviour in image retrieval: VISOR I. *Institute for Image Data Research,* 1-147, (Library and Information Commission Research Report 95).

Cousins, S., Enser, P. G. B., & Hartley, R.J. (1989). Enhancing the subject search performance of online public access catalogues: Experiments with query representation. *Prospects for Intelligent Retrieval: Informatics,* (10), 107-118.

Del Bimbo, A. (1999). *Visual Information Retrieval.* Morgan Kaufmann.

Del Bimbo, A. & Pala, P. (1997). Visual image retrieval by elastic matching of user sketches. *IEEE Transactions on Pattern Analysis and Machine Intelligence, 19*(2), 121-132.

Del Bimbo, A., Campanai, M., & Nesi, P. (1993). A three-dimensional iconic environment for image database querying. *IEEE Transaction on Software Engineering, 19*(10), 997-1011.

Del Bimbo, A., Mugnani, P. P., & Turco, F. (1998). Visual querying by colour perceptive regions. *Pattern Recognition, 31*(9), 1241-1253

Di Lecce, V. & Guerriero, A. (1999). An evaluation of the effectiveness of image features for image retrieval. *Journal of Visual Communication and Image Representation, 10*, 353.

Di Sciascio, E. & Mongiello, M. (1999). Query by sketch and relevance feedback for content-based image retrieval over the web. *Journal of Visual Languages and Computing, 10*, 565-584.

Djeraba, C., Bouet, M. & Briand, H. (1998). Concept-based query in visual information systems. *Proceedings of IEEE Advances in Digital Libraries Conference*, Santa Barbara, CA, USA, (April 22-24, pp. 299-308).

Dunlop, M. D. (2000). Reflections on Mira: Interactive evaluation in information retrieval. *Journal of American Society for Information Science, 51*(14), 1269-1274.

Eakins, J. P. (1992). Pictorial information systems: Prospects & problems. *Proceedings of the 14th British Computing Society Information Retrieval Specialist Group Research Colloquium.* Lancaster, UK, (pp. 102-123).

Eakins, J. P. (2001). Trademark image retrieval. M. S. Lew (Ed.), *Principles of Visual Information Retrieval* (p. 345). Springer-Verlag, Advances in Pattern Recognition.

Eakins, J. P. (2002). Towards intelligent image retrieval. *Pattern Recognition, 35*, 3-14.

Eakins, J. P. & Graham, M. E. (1999). *Content-Based Image Retrieval.* JISC, 27.

Eakins, J. P., Graham, M. E., & Boardman, J. M. (1997). Evaluation of a trademark image retrieval system. *Proceedings of the 19th Annual BCS-IRSG Colloquium on IR Research*, Robert Gordon University, Aberdeen, Scotland, (April 8-9, pp. 178-187).

Eakins, J. P., Huang, T. S., Panchanathan, & Marchand-Maillet, S. (2002). Bridging the semantic gap. *CIVR2002: Challenge for Image & Video Retrieval. Proceedings of the International Conference on Image and Video Retrieval*, The Brunei Gallery, SOAS, London, UK, (July 18-19).

Eakins, J. P., Shields, K., & Boardman, K. J. M. (1996). ARTISAN: A shape retrieval system based on boundary family indexing. *Storage and Retrieval for Image and Video Databases IV, Proceedings of the Society of the Photo-Optical Instrumentation Engineers, 2670*, San Jose, CA, USA, (pp. 17-28). SPIE-The International Society for Optical Engineering.

Egenhofer, M. (1991). Spatial SQL: A query and presentation language. *IEEE Transaction on Knowledge Data Engineering, 5*(2), 161-174.

Ellis, D. (1989). A behavioural approach to information retrieval systems design. *Journal of Documentation, 45*(3), 171-212.

Embley, D. W. (1989). NFQL: The natural forms query language. *ACM Transactions on Database Systems, 14*(2), 168-211.

Enser, P. G. B. (1993). Query analysis in a visual information retrieval context. *Journal of Document & Text Management, 1*(1), 25-52.

Enser, P. G. B. (1995). Progress in documentation pictorial information retrieval. *Journal of Documentation, 51*(2).

Enser, P. G. B. (2000). Visual image retrieval: Seeking the alliance of concept-based and content-based paradigms. *Journal of Information Science, 26*(4), 199-210.

Enser, P. G. B. & McGregor, C. G. (1992). *Analysis of Visual Information Retrieval Queries*. London: British Library, (British Library Research & Development Report, no. 6104).

Enser, P. G. B. & Sandom, C. J. (2002). Retrieval of archival moving imagery – CBIR outside the frame? *CIVR: Challenge for Image & Video Retrieval. International; Conference on Image and Video Retrieval*, London, UK, (July 18-19, pp. 206-214).

Eysenck, M. W. & Keane, M. T. (2000). *Cognitive Psychology*. (4th ed.). Psychology Press.

Flickner, M., Sawhney, H., Niblack, W., Ashley, J., Huang, Q., Dom, B., Gorkani, M., Hafner, J., Lee, D., Petkovic, D., Steele, D., & Yanker, P. (1997). Query by image and video content: The QBIC system. *IEEE Computer, 28*, 23-32.

Gonzalez, R. C. & Woods, R. E. (1993). *Digital Image Processing*. Prentice Hall.

Grosky, W. (2002). *Workshop on Multimedia Semantics: 29th Annual Conference on Current Trends in Theory and Practice of Informatics*, Devet skal Hotel, Milovy, Czech Republic, (November 28-29).

Gudivada, V. N. & Raghaven, V. V. (1995). Content-based image retrieval systems. *IEEE Computer*, (September), 18-22.

Gupta, A. & Jain, R. (1997). Visual information retrieval. *Communications of the ACM, 40*(5), 71-79.

Gupta, A., Santini, S., & Jain, R. (1997). In search of information in visual media. *Communications of the ACM, 40*(12), 35-42.

Haralick, R. M., Shanmugam, K., & Dinstein, I. (1973). Texture features for image classification. *IEEE Transactions on Systems, Man. and Cybernetics*, SMC-3(6).

Hastings, S. (1995). Query categories in a study of intellectual access to digitized art images. *ASIS'95: Proceedings of the 58th ASIS Annual Meeting, ASIS*, (pp. 3-8).

Hidderley, R. & Rafferty, P. (1997). Democratic indexing: An approach to the retrieval of film. *Library and Information Studies: Research and Professional Practice: Proceedings of the 2nd British-Nordic Conference on Library and Information Studies*, Queen Margaret College, Edinburgh, Scotland, (pp. 90-102).

Hu, M. K. (1962). Visual pattern recognition by moment invariants, computer methods in image analysis. *IRE Transactions on Information Theory*, 8.

Huang, J., Kumar, S., Mitra, M., Zhu, W.-J., & Zabih, R. (1997). Image indexing using color correlogram. *CVPR '97: Proceedings of the IEEE Conference on Computer Vision and Pattern Recognition*, Puerto Rico, (June 17-19, pp. 762-768).

Huang, T., Mehrotra, S. & Ramchandran, K. (1996). Multimedia analysis and retrieval system (MARS) project. *Digital Image Access and Retrieval: 1996 Clinic on Library Applications of Data Processing, Graduate School of Library and Information Science*, University of Illinois at Urbana-Champaign 101-117.

Hyldegaard, J. (1997). Visual information seeking: Browsing and navigating through a desktop VR user interface. *Library and Information Studies: Research and Professional Practice: Proceedings of the 2nd British-Nordic Conference on Library and Information Studies*, Queen Margaret College, Edinburgh, Scotland, (pp. 79-89).

Idris, F. & Panchanathan, S. (1997). Review of image and video indexing techniques. *Journal of Visual Communication and Image Representation, 8*(2), 146-166.

Jacobs, B. E. & Walczak, C. A. (1983). A generalized query-by-example data manipulation language based on database logic. *IEEE Transactions on Software Engineering, SE-9*(1), 40-56.

Jain, R. (1993). NSF workshop on visual information retrieval management systems. *Storage and Retrieval for Image and Video Databases: Proceedings of the International Society for Optical Engineering*, San Jose, CA, USA, (February 2-3, pp. 198-218).

Jain, R. (1996). Visual information retrieval in digital libraries. *Digital Image Access and Retrieval: 1996 Clinic on Library Applications of Data Processing, Graduate School of Library and Information Science*, University of Illinois at Urbana-Champaign 1996, 67-85.

Johnson, F. C., Griffiths, J. R., & Hartley, R. J. (2001). *DEVISE: A Framework for the Evaluation of Internet Search Engines Resource*. The Council for Museums, Archives and Libraries (Library and Information Commission Report 100).

Jorgensen, C. (1996). Indexing images: Testing an image description template. In *ASIS'96: Proceedings of the 59th Annual Conference of the American Society for Information Science*, Renaissance Harborplace, Baltimore, MD, USA, (October 19-24, pp. 209-213).

Joseph, T. & Cardenas, A. F. (1988). PICQUERY: A high level query language for pictorial database management. *IEEE Transactions on Software Engineering 14*(5), 630-638.

Kato, T., Kurita, T., & Shimogaki, H. (1991). Intelligent visual interaction with image database systems: Towards the multimedia personal interface. *Journal of Information Processing, 14*(2), 134-143.

Kato, T., Kurita, T., Otsu, N., & Hirata, K. (1992). A sketch retrieval method for full colour image database: Query by visual example. *Computer Vision and Applications: Proceedings of ICPR*, 530-533.

Keister, L. H. (1994). User types and queries: Impact on image access systems. In R. Fidel, T. Bellardo Hahn, M. Rasmussen, & P.J. Smith (Eds.), *Challenges in Indexing Electronic Text and Images*, (pp. 7-22). ASIS.

Klug, A. C. (1981). ABE: A query language for constructing aggregates-by-example. *SSDBM: Proceedings of the First LBL Workshop on Statistical Database Management*, Lawrence Berkeley Laboratory, Melno Park, CA, USA, (December 2-4, pp. 190-205).

Korfhage, R. R. (1997). *Information Storage and Retrieval*. John Wiley & Sons.

Laaksonen, J., Koskela, M., Laakso, S., & Oja, E. (2000). PicSOM: Content-based image retrieval with self-organising maps. *Patter Recognition Letters, 21*, 1199-1207.

Lai, T.-S., Tait, J., & McDonald, S. (2000). A user-centred evaluation of visual search methods for CBIR. *The Challenge for Image Retrieval: CIR2000, Third UK Conference on Image Retrieval*, Old Ship Hotel, Brighton, UK, (May 4-5).

Lancaster, F. W. & Warner, A. J. (1993). *Information Retrieval Today*. Information Resources.

Large, A., Tedd, L. A., & Hartley, R. J. (1999). *Information Seeking in the Online Age: Principles and Practice*. Bowker Saur.

Lee, D., Barber, R., Niblack, W., Flickner, M., Hafner, J., & Petkovic, D. (1994). Query by image content using multiple objects and multiple features: User Interface issues.

ICIP '94: Proceedings of the International Conference on Image Processing, Austin, Texas, USA, (November 13-16, pp. 76-80). IEEE Computer Society.

Lee, S. K. & Whang, K-Y. (2001). VOQL. *Journal of Visual Languages and Computing, 12,* 413-433.

Lew, M. S. (2000). Next-generation web searches for visual content. *IEEE Computer,* 46-53.

Lew, M. S. & Huang, T. S. (2001). Visual information retrieval: Paradigms, applications, and research issues. In M.S. Lew (Ed.), *Principles of Visual Information Retrieval,* (p. 3). Springer-Verlag, Advances in Pattern Recognition.

Lu, H., Ooi, B., & Tan, K. (1994). Efficient image retrieval by colour content. *ADB '94: Proceedings of the First International Conference on Applications of Databases,* Vadstena, Sweden, (June 21-23 pp. 95-108). Lecture Notes in Computer Science 819, Springer.

Lynch, C. A. (1991). The technologies of electronic imaging. *Journal of the American Society for Information Science, 42*(8), 583.

Marchionini, G. (1995). *Information Seeking in Electronic Environments.* University of Cambridge Press.

Markkula, M. & Sormunen, E. (1998). Searching for photos: Journalists' practices in pictorial IR. *The Challenge of Image Retrieval Workshop, University of Northumbria at Newcastle,* Newcastle upon Tyne, UK, (February 5).

McLean, S., Spring, M. B., Rasmusses, E., & Williams, J. G. (1995). Online image databases: Usability and performance. *The Electronic Library, 13*(1), 27-41.

Mehtre, B. M., Kankanhalli, M. S., & Lee, W. F. (1997). Shape measures for content based image retrieval: A comparison. *Information Processing & Management, 33*(3), 319-337.

Mostafa, J. & Dillion, A. (1996). Design and evaluation of a user interface supporting multiple image query models. *ASIS '96: Proceedings of the 59th Annual Conference of the American Society for Information Science,* Baltimore, MD, USA, (October 21-26).

Muller, S., Eickeler, S., & Rigoll, G. (1998). Image database retrieval of rotated objects by user sketch. *CBAIVL: Proceedings of the IEEE Workshop on Content-Based Access of Image and Video Libraries,* Santa Barbara, CA, USA, (June 21, pp. 40-44).

Narasimhalu, A. D., Kankanhalli, M. S., & Wu, J. (1997). Benchmarking multimedia databases. *Multimedia Tools and Applications,* 4, 333-356.

Niblack, W., Barber, R., Equitz, W., Flickner, M., Glasman, E., Petkovic, D., Yanker, P., Faloutsos, C., & Taubin, G. (1993). The QBIC project: Querying images by content using colour, texture and shape. *Storage and Retrieval for Image and Video Databases I: Proceedings of the Society of the Photo-Optical Instrumentation Engineers,* 1908, San Jose, California, USA, (pp. 173-187).

Nielsen, J, (1993). *Usability Engineering.* AP Professional, 26.

Olsen, K. A., Korfhage, R. R., Sochats, K. M., Spring, M. B., & Williams, J. G. (1993). Visualization of a document collection: The VIBE system. *Information & Processing Management, 29*(1), 69-82.

Orenstein, J. A. & Manola, F. A. (1988). PROBE spatial data modeling and query processing in an image database application. *IEEE Transactions on Software Engineering, 14*(5), 611-628.

Ornager, S. (1997). Image retrieval: Theoretical analysis and empirical user studies on accessing information in images. *ASIS '97: Proceedings of the 60th ASIS Annual Meeting*, (pp. 202-211).

Ozoyoglu, G. & Wang, H. (1993). Example-based graphical database query languages. *IEEE Computer*, 25-38.

Panofsky, E. (1955). *Studies in Iconology: Humanistic Themes in the Art of the Renaissance*. Harper Row.

Papantonakis, A. & King, P. J. H. (1995). Syntax and semantics of Gql, a graphical query language. *Journal of Visual Languages and Computing, 6*, 3-25.

Pentland, A., Picard, R., & Sclaroff, S. (1996). Photobook: Tools for content-based manipulation of image databases. *International Journal of Computer Vision, 18*, 233-254.

Pizer, S. M., & van Beard, D. (1989). Medical image workstation: State of science & technology. *The Journal of Digital Imaging, 2,* 185-193.

Preece, J., Rogers, Y., Sharp, H., Benyon, D., Holland, S., & Carey, T. (1994). *Human-Computer Interaction*. Addison-Wesley.

Rickman, R. M. & Stonham, T. J. (1996). Content-based image retrieval using color tuple histograms. *Storage and Retrieval for Still Image and Video Databases IV: Proceeding of the International Society for Optical Engineering,* San Jose, CA, USA, (Vol. 2670, pp. 2-7).

Rose, T., Elworthy, D., Kotcheff, A., & Clare, A. (2000). ANVIL: A system for the retrieval of captioned images using nlp techniques. *The Challenge for Image Retrieval: CIR2000, Third UK Conference on Image Retrieval*, Old Ship Hotel, Brighton, UK, (May 4-5).

Rosenfeld, A. (1984). *Multi-Resolution Image Processing and Analysis*. Springer.

Roth, I. (1986). An introduction to object perception. In I. Roth & J.P. Frisby (Eds.), *Perception and Representation: A Cognitive Approach*. Open University Press.

Rui, Y. & Huang, T. S. (2001). Relevance feedback techniques. In M.S. Lew (Ed.), *Principles of Visual Information Retrieval* (p. 219). Springer-Verlag, Advances in Pattern Recognition.

Rui, Y., Huang, T. S., & Chang, S-F. (1999). Image retrieval: Current techniques, promising directions, and open issues. *Journal of Visual Communication and Image Representation, 10*(1), 39-62.

Salton, G. & McGill, M. J. (1983). *Introduction to Modern Information Retrieval*. McGraw-Hill.

Santini, S. & Jain, R. (1997). Visual navigation in perceptual databases. *Visual '97: Proceedings of the 2nd International Conference on Visual Information Systems*, Sea Lodge Hotel, San Diego, CA, USA, (December 15-17).

Sclaroff, S. & Pentland, A. (1993). A modal framework for correspondence and recognition. *ICCV '93: Proceedings of the 4th IEEE International Conference on Computer Vision,* Berlin, Germany, (May).

Shatford Layne, S. (1994). Some issues in the indexing of images. *Journal of the American Society for Information Science, 45*(8), 583-588.

Shaw, D. (1991). The human-computer interface for information retrieval. *Annual Review of Information Science and Technology, 26*, ASIS.

Smeulders, A. W. M., Worring, M., Santini, S., Gupta, A., & Jain, R. (2000). Content-based image retrieval at the end of the early years. *IEEE Transaction on Pattern Analysis and Machine Intelligence, 22*(12).

Smith, J. R. & Chang, S.-F. (1995). Single color extraction and image query. *ICIP '95: Proceedings of the IEEE International Conference on Image Processing, 3* Washington D.C., (October 23-26, pp. 528-531).

Smith, J. R. & Chang, S-F. (1997). Querying by color regions using the visualseek content-based visual query system. In M.T. Maybury (Ed.), *Intelligent Multimedia Information Retrieval,* AAAI Press.

Sonka, M., Hlavac, V., & Boyle, R. (1999). *Image Processing, Analysis, and Machine Vision.* 2nd edition. PWS Publishing.

Stricker, M. A. & Orengo, M. (1995). Similarity of color images. *Storage and Retrieval for Image and Video Databases III: Proceeding of the International Society for Optical Engineering,* San Jose, CA, USA, (Vol. 2420, pp. 381-392).

Svenonius, E. (1994). Access to non-book materials: The limits of subject indexing for visual and aural languages. *Journal of the American Society for Information Science, 45*(8), 600-606.

Swain, M. & Ballard, D. (1991). Color indexing. *International Journal of Computer Vision, 7*(1), 11-32.

Tamura, H., Mori, S., & Yamawaki, T. (1978). Texture features corresponding to visual perception. *IEEE Transactions on Systems, Man. and Cybernetics,* SMC-8 (6).

Tansel, A. U., Arkun, M. E., & Ozsoyoglu, G. (1989). Time-by-example query language for historical databases. *IEEE Transactions on Software Engineering, 15*(4), 464-478.

van Beard, D. (1991). Computer human interaction for image information systems. *Journal of the American Society for Information Science, 42*(8), 600-608.

van Rijsbergen, K. (1979). *Information Retrieval.* Butterworths.

Veltkamp, R. C. & Tanase, M. (2002). A survey of content-based image retrieval systems. In O. Marques & B. Furht (Eds.), *Content-Based Image and Video Retrieval,* (pp. 47-101). Kluwer.

Vendrig, J., Worring, M., & Smeulders, A. W. M. (2001). Filter image browsing: Interactive image retrieval by using database overviews. *Multimedia Tools and Applications, 15*(1), 83-103.

Venters, C. C. & Cooper, M. D. (2000). *A Review of Content-Based Image Retrieval Systems.* JISC.

Venters, C. C. & Cooper, M. D. (2001a). *Content-Based Image Retrieval: An Evaluation of the Technology in the Field of Radiology and Magnetic Resonance Imaging.* Manchester Visualization Centre, University of Manchester.

Venters, C. C. & Cooper, M. D. (2001b). *Content-Based Image Retrieval Systems: A Preliminary Investigation into Systems Performance.* Manchester Visualization Centre, University of Manchester.

Venters, C. C., Hartley, R. J., Cooper, M. D., & Hewitt, W. T. (2001c). Query by visual example: Assessing the usability of content-based image retrieval system user interface. *PCM2001: Advances in Multimedia Processing: Proceedings of the Second IEEE Pacific-Rim Conference on Multimedia 2001:* Beijing, Republic of China, (October 24-26, pp. 514-521).

Wang, J. Z. (2000). SIMPLIcity: A region-based image retrieval system for picture libraries and biomedical image databases. *Proceedings of the 8 ACM International Conference on Multimedia*, Marina del Rey, CA, USA, (October, pp. 483-484). ACM Press.

Whang, K-Y., Ammann, A., Bolmarcich, A., Hanrahan, M., Hochgesang, G., Huang, K-T., Khorasani, A., Krishnamurthy, R., Sockut, G. H., Sweeney, P., Waddle, V. E., & Wilson, T. (1981). On user studies and information needs. *Journal of Documentation, 37*, 3-15.

Wilson, T. (2000). Human information behaviour. *Informing Science, 3*(2), 49-55.

Wong, S. T. C. (1998). CBIR in medicine: Still a long way to go. *CBAIVL: Proceedings of the IEEE Workshop on Content-Based Access of Image and Video Libraries*, Santa Barbara, CA, USA, (June 21, p. 114).

Yen, M. Y-M. & Scamell, R. W. (1993). A human factors experimental comparison of SQL and QBE. *IEEE Transactions on Software Engineering, 19*(4), 390-409.

Zachary, J. & Iyengar, S. (1999). Content-based image retrieval systems. *ASSET '99; IEEE Symposium on Application-Specific Systems and Software Engineering & Technology*, Richardson, TX, USA, (March 24-27).

Zahn, C. T. & Roskies, R. Z. (1972). Fourier descriptors for plane closed curves. *IEEE Transactions on Computers*.

Zhou, X. S. & Huang, T. S. (2002). Unifying keywords and visual contents in image retrieval. *IEEE MultiMedia, 9*(2), 23-33.

Zloof, M. M. (1977). Query-by-example: A data base language. *IBM Systems Journal, 16*(4), 324-343.

Zloof, M. M. (1987). Office-by-example: An integrated office system and database manager. *ACM Transactions on Office Information Systems, 5*(4), 393-427.

ENDNOTES

[1] A digital image is an image $f(x, y)$ that has been discretized both in spatial co-ordinates and brightness and consists of a set of elements, defined on an n-dimensional regular grid that has the potential for display. It can be considered a matrix whose row and column indices identify a point in the image and the corresponding matrix element values identifies the grey level at that point. The elements of such a digital array are called image elements, picture elements, pixels, or pels (Gonzalez & Woods, 1993).

[2] A query is a formal expression of an information need (Korfhage, 1997).

[3] A query language is a set of formally defined operators that allow queries to be expressed to a database. The execution of the query produces a set of results that are extracted from the data.

[4] VIBE was developed by Olsen et al. (1993).

[5] Perception is the process by which sensory stimulation is organised into usable experiences of objects, events, sounds and tastes (Roth, 1986).

Chapter XV

Face Animation: A Case Study for Multimedia Modeling and Specification Languages

Ali Arya, University of British Columbia, Canada

Babak Hamidzadeh, University of British Columbia, Canada

ABSTRACT

This chapter will discuss the multimedia modeling and specification methods, especially in the context of face animation. Personalized Face Animation is and/or can be a major user interface component in modern multimedia systems. After reviewing the related works in this area, we present the ShowFace streaming structure. This structure is based on most widely accepted industry standards in multimedia presentations like MPEG-4 and SMIL and extends them by providing a higher level Face Modeling Language (FML) for modeling and control purposes and by defining image transformations required for certain facial movements. ShowFace establishes a comprehensive framework for face animation consisting of components for parsing the input script, generating and splitting the audio and video "behaviors," creating the required images and sounds, and eventually displaying or writing the data to files. This component-based design and scripted behavior make the framework suitable for many purposes including web-based applications.

INTRODUCTION

Specifying the components of a multimedia presentation and their spatial/temporal relations are among basic tasks in multimedia systems. They are necessary when a client asks for a certain presentation to be designed, when a media player receives input to play, and even when a search is done to retrieve an existing multimedia file. In all these cases, the description of the contents can include raw multimedia data (video, audio, etc.) and textual commands and information. Such a description works as a Generalized Encoding, since it represents the multimedia content in a form not necessarily the same as the playback format, and is usually more efficient and compact. For instance a textual description of a scene can be a very effective "encoded" version of a multimedia presentation that will be "decoded" by the media player when it recreates the scene.

Face Animation, as a special type of multimedia presentation, has been a challenging subject for many researchers. Advances in computer hardware and software, and also new web-based applications, have helped intensify these research activities, recently. Video conferencing and online services provided by human characters are good examples of the applications using face animation. Personalized Face Animation includes all the information and activities required to create a multimedia presentation resembling a specific person. The input to such a system can be a combination of audio/visual data and textual commands and descriptions. A successful face animation system needs to have efficient yet powerful solutions for providing and displaying the content, i.e., a content description format, decoding algorithms, and finally an architecture to put different components together in a flexible way.

Although new streaming technologies allow real-time download/playback of audio/video data, bandwidth limitation and it's efficient usage still are, and probably will be, major issues. This makes a textual description of multimedia presentation (e.g., facial actions) a very effective coding/compression mechanism, provided the visual effects of these actions can be recreated with a minimum acceptable quality. Based on this idea, in face animation, some researches have been done to translate certain facial actions into a predefined set of "codes." Facial Action Coding System (Ekman & Friesen, 1978) is probably the first successful attempt in this regard. More recently, MPEG-4 standard (Battista, et al., 1999) has defined Face Animation Parameters to encode low-level facial actions like jaw-down, and higher level, more complicated ones like smile.

Efficient use of bandwidth is not the only advantage of multimedia content specifications like facial action coding. In many cases, the "real" multimedia data does not exist at all and has to be created based on a description of desired actions. This leads to the whole new idea of representing the spatial and temporal relation of the facial actions. In a generalized view, such a description of facial presentation should provide a hierarchical structure with elements ranging from low-level "images," to simple "moves," to more complicated "actions," to complete "stories." We call this a Structured Content Description, which also requires means of defining capabilities, behavioural templates, dynamic contents, and event/user interaction. Needless to say, compatibility with existing multimedia and web technologies is another fundamental requirement, in this regard.

Having a powerful description and specification mechanism, also is obviously powerful in search applications that currently suffer when looking for multimedia content. MPEG-7 standard (Nack & Lindsay, 1999) is the newest arrival in the group of research projects aiming at a better multimedia retrieval mechanism.

Considering three major issues of Content Delivery, Content Creation, and Content Description, the following features can be assumed as important requirements in a multimedia presentation systems (Arya & Hamidzadeh, 2002):

1. Streaming, i.e., continuously receiving/displaying data
2. Structured Content Description, i.e., a hierarchical way to provide information about the required content from high-level scene description to low-level moves, images, and sounds
3. Content Creation (Generalized Decoding), i.e., creating the displayable content based on the input. This can be decoding a compressed image or making new content based on the provided textual description.
4. Component-based Architecture, i.e., the flexibility to rearrange the system components, and use new ones as long as a certain interface is supported.
5. Compatibility, i.e., the ability to use and work with widely accepted industry standards in multimedia systems.
6. Minimized Database of audio/visual footage.

The technological advances in multimedia systems, speech/image processing, and computer graphics, and also new applications especially in computer-based games, telecommunication, and online services, have resulted in a rapidly growing number of publications regarding these issues. These research achievements, although very successful in their objectives, mostly address a limited subset of the above requirements. A comprehensive framework for face animation is still in conceptual stages.

The *ShowFace* system, discussed later, is a step toward such a framework. It is based on a modular structure that allows multimedia streaming using existing technologies and standards like MPEG-4, Windows Media and DirectX/DirectShow (http://www.microsoft.com/windows/directx), and XML (http://www.w3.org/XML). The components independently read and parse a textual input, create audio and video data, and mix them together. Each component can be replaced and upgraded as long as it conforms to the ShowFace Application Programming Interface (SF-API). SF-API also allows other programs like web browsers to connect to ShowFace components directly or through a wrapper object called *ShowFacePlayer*. The system uses a language specifically designed for face animation applications. Face Modeling Language (FML) is an XML-based structured content description language that describes a face animation in a hierarchical way (from high-level stories to low-level moves), giving maximum flexibility to the content designers. Receiving FML scripts as input, *ShowFace* generates the required frames based on a limited number of images and a set of pre-learned transformations. This minimizes the image database and computational complexity, which are issues in existing approaches, as reviewed later.

In Section 2, some of the related works will be briefly reviewed. This includes different approaches to multimedia modeling and specification (content description in general), multimedia systems architectures to support those specification mechanisms, and eventually, content creation methods used in related multimedia systems. The basic concepts and structure of the *ShowFace* system will be discussed in Section 3 to 5. This includes the proposed Face Modeling Language (FML) and the system structure and components for parsing the input and creating the animation. Some experimental results and conclusions will be the topics of Sections 6 and 7, respectively.

RELATED WORK
Multimedia Content Description

The diverse set of works in multimedia content description involves methods for describing the components of a multimedia presentation and their spatial and temporal relations. Historically, one of the first technical achievements in this regard was related to video editing where temporal positioning of video elements is necessary. The SMPTE (Society of Motion Picture and Television Engineers) time coding (Ankeney, 1995; Little, 1994) that precisely specifies the location of audio/video events down to the frame level is base for EDL (Edit Decision List) (Ankeney, 1995; Little, 1994) that relates pieces of recorded audio/video for editing. Electronic Program Guides (EPGs) are another example of content description for movies in the form of textual information added to the multimedia stream.

More recent efforts by SMPTE are focused on Metadata Dictionary, which targets the definition of the metadata description of the content (see http://www.smpte-ra.org/mdd). These metadata can include items from title to subject and components. The concept of metadata description is a base for other similar researches like Dublin Core (http://dublincore.org), EBU P/Meta (http://www.ebu.ch/pmc_meta.html), and TV Anytime (http://www.tv-anytime.org). Motion Picture Expert Group is also another major player in standards for multimedia content description and delivery. MPEG-4 standard, which comes after MPEG-1 and MPEG-2, is one of the first comprehensive attempts to define the multimedia stream in terms of its forming components (objects like audio, foreground figure, and background image). Users of MPEG-4 systems can use Object Content Information (OCI) to send textual information about these objects.

A more promising approach in content description is MPEG-7 standard. MPEG-7 is mainly motivated by the need for a better more powerful search mechanism for multimedia content over the Internet but can be used in a variety of other applications including multimedia authoring. The standard extends OCI and consists of a set of descriptors for multimedia features (similar to metadata in other works), schemes that show the structure of the descriptors, and an XML-based description/schema definition language.

Most of these methods are not aimed at and customized for a certain type of multimedia stream or object. This may result in a wider range of applications but limits the capabilities for some frequently used subjects like human faces. To address this issue MPEG-4 includes Face Definition Parameters (FDPs) and Face Animation Parameters (FAPs). FDPs define a face by giving measures for its major parts, as shown in Figure 1. FAPs on the other hand, encode the movements of these facial features. Together they allow a receiver system to create a face (using any graphic method) and animate based on low-level commands in FAPs. The concept of FAP can be considered a practical extension of Facial Action Coding System (FACS) used earlier to code different movements of facial features for certain expressions and actions.

After a series of efforts to model temporal events in multimedia streams (Hirzalla et al., 1995), an important progress in multimedia content description is Synchronized Multimedia Integration Language (SMIL) (Bulterman, 2001), an XML-based language

designed to specify the temporal relation of the components of a multimedia presentation, especially in web applications. SMIL can be used quite suitably with MPEG-4
object-based streams.

There have also been different languages in the fields of virtual reality and computer
graphics for modeling computer-generated scenes. Examples are Virtual Reality Modeling Language (VRML, http://www.vrml.org) and programming libraries like OpenGL
(http://www.opengl.org).

Another important group of related works are behavioural modeling languages and
tools for virtual agents. BEAT (Cassell et al., 2001) is an XML-based system, specifically
designed for human animation purposes. It is a toolkit for automatically suggesting
expressions and gestures, based on a given text to be spoken. BEAT uses a knowledge
base and rule set and provides synchronization data for facial activities, all in XML
format. This enables the system to use standard XML parsing and scripting capabilities.
Although BEAT is not a general content description tool, it demonstrates some of the
advantages of XML-based approaches. Other scripting and behavioural modeling
languages for virtual humans are considered by other researchers as well (Funge et al.,
1999; Kallmann & Thalmann, 1999; Lee et al., 1999). These languages are usually simple
macros for simplifying the animation, or new languages, which are not using existing
multimedia technologies. Most of the time they are not specifically designed for face
animation.

Multimedia Content Creation

In addition to traditional recording, mixing, and editing techniques in the film
industry, computer graphics research has been long involved in multimedia, especially
in image/video creation. Two main categories can be seen in these works: 3-D geometrical
models (Blanz & Vetter, 1999; Lee et al., 1999; Pighin et al., 1998) and 2-D image-based
methods (Arya & Hamidzadeh, 2002; Bregler et al., 1997; Ezzat & Poggio, 1998; Graf et
al., 2000).

The former group involves describing the scene using 3-D data (as in VRML and
OpenGL) and then rendering the scene (or sequence of frames) from any point of view.
These techniques need usually complicated 3-D models, data and computation, but are
very powerful in creating any view provided the model/data is inclusive enough. Due to
the way images are generated and their inability to include all the details, most of these
methods do not have a very realistic output. In the case of face animation, 3-D techniques
are used by many researchers (Blanz & Vetter, 1999; Lee et al., 1999; Pighin et al., 1998).
To reduce the size of required data for model generation, some approaches are proposed
to create 3-D models based on a few (two orthogonal) 2-D pictures (Lee et al., 1999).

It is shown that any view of a 3-D scene can be generated from a combination of a
set of 2-D views of that scene or by applying some transformations on them (Arya &
Hamidzadeh, 2002; Ezzat & Poggio, 1998). This fact is base for the latter group of
techniques, i.e., 2-D image-based. In a talking head application, Ezzat et al. (Ezzat &
Poggio, 1998) use view morphing between pre-recorded visemes (facial views when
pronouncing different phonemes) to create a video corresponding to any speech. Optical
flow computation is used to find corresponding points in two images, solving the
correspondence problem for morphing. Bregler et al. (1997) combine a new image with
parts of existing footage (mouth and jaw) to create new talking views. Both these

approaches are limited to a certain view where the recordings have been made. No transformation is proposed to make a talking view after some new movements of the head. In a more recent work based on MikeTalk, (Graf et al., 2000) recording of all visemes in a range of possible views is proposed, so after detecting the view (pose) proper visemes will be used. This way talking heads in different views can be animated but the method requires a considerably large database.

Defining general image transformations for each facial action and using facial feature points to control the mapping seem to be helpful in image-based techniques. TalkingFace (Arya & Hamidzadeh, 2002) combines optical flow and facial feature detection to overcome these issues. It can learn certain image transformations needed for talking (and potentially expressions and head movements) and apply them to any given image. Tiddeman et al. (2001) show how such image transformations can be extended to include even facial texture.

Multimedia Systems Architectures

Different architectures are proposed for multimedia systems. They try to address different aspects of multimedia, mostly streaming and playback. The main streaming systems, aimed at web-based transmission and playback, are Microsoft Windows Media, Apple QuickTime, and Real Networks RealVideo (Lawton, 2000).

Different architectures are also proposed to perform facial animation, especially as an MPEG-4 decoder/player (Pandzic, 2001). Although they try to use platform-independent and/or standard technologies (e.g., Java and VRML), they are usually limited to certain face models and lack a component-based and extensible structure and do not propose any content description mechanism more than standard MPEG-4 parameters.

STRUCTURED CONTENT DESCRIPTION IN *SHOWFACE*

Design Ideas

Describing the contents of a multimedia presentation is a basic task in multimedia systems. It is necessary when a client asks for a certain presentation to be designed, when a media player receives input to play, and even when a search is done to retrieve an existing multimedia file. In all these cases, the description can include raw multimedia data (video, audio, etc.) and textual commands and information. Such a description works as a Generalized Encoding, since it represents the multimedia content in a form not necessarily the same as the playback format and is usually more efficient and compact. For instance a textual description of a scene can be a very effective "encoded" version of a multimedia presentation that will be "decoded" by the media player when it recreates the scene.

Although new streaming technologies allow real-time download/playback of audio/video data, bandwidth limitation and it's efficient usage still are, and probably will be, major issues. This makes a textual description of multimedia presentations (in our case facial actions) a very effective coding/compression mechanism, provided the visual effects can be recreated with minimum acceptable quality.

Efficient use of bandwidth is not the only advantage of facial action coding. In many cases, the "real" multimedia data does not exist at all and has to be created based on a description of desired actions. This leads to the whole new idea of representing the spatial and temporal relation of the facial actions. In a generalized view, such a description of facial presentation should provide a hierarchical structure with elements ranging from low-level "images," to simple "moves," to more complicated "actions," to complete "stories." We call this a Structured Content Description, which also requires means of defining capabilities, behavioural templates, dynamic contents, and event/user interaction. Needless to say, compatibility with existing multimedia and web technologies is another fundamental requirement, in this regard.

Face Modeling Language (FML) is a Structured Content Description mechanism based on eXtensible Markup Language. The main ideas behind FML are:

- Hierarchical representation of face animation
- Timeline definition of the relation between facial actions and external events
- Defining capabilities and behaviour templates
- Compatibility with MPEG-4 FAPs
- Compatibility with XML and related web technologies

FACS and MPEG-4 FAPs provide the means of describing low-level face actions but they do not cover temporal relations and higher-level structures. Languages like SMIL do this in a general purpose form for any multimedia presentation and are not customized for specific applications like face animation. A language bringing the best of these two together, customized for face animation, seems to be an important requirement. FML is designed to do so.

Fundamental to FML is the idea of Structured Content Description. It means a hierarchical view of face animation capable of representing simple individually-meaningless moves to complicated high-level stories. This hierarchy can be thought of as consisting of the following levels (bottom-up):

- Frame, a single image showing a snapshot of the face (Naturally, may not be accompanied by speech)
- Move, a set of frames representing a linear transition between two frames (e.g., making a smile)
- Action, a "meaningful" combination of moves
- Story, a stand-alone piece of face animation

The boundaries between these levels are not rigid and well defined. Due to the complicated and highly expressive nature of facial activities, a single move can make a simple yet meaningful story (e.g., an expression). The levels are basically required by the content designer in order to:

- Organize the content
- Define temporal relation between activities
- Develop behavioural templates, based on his/her presentation purposes and structure.

Figure 1: FML Timeline and Temporal Relation of Face Activities

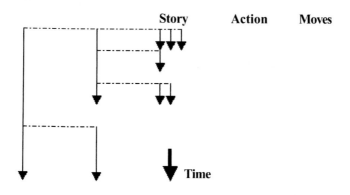

FML defines a timeline of events (Figure 1) including head movements, speech, and facial expressions, and their combinations. Since a face animation might be used in an interactive environment, such a timeline may be altered/determined by a user. So another functionality of FML is to allow *user interaction* and in general *event handling* (Notice that user input can be considered a special case of *external event*). This event handling may be in the form of:

- Decision Making; choosing to go through one of possible paths in the story
- Dynamic Generation; creating a new set of actions to follow

A major concern in designing FML is compatibility with existing standards and languages. Growing acceptance of MPEG-4 standard makes it necessary to design FML in a way it can be translated to/from a set of FAPs. Also, due to the similarity of concepts, it is desirable to use SMIL syntax and constructs, as much as possible.

Primary Language Constructs

FML is an XML-based language. The choice of XML as the base for FML is based on its capabilities as a markup language, growing acceptance, and available system support in different platforms. Figure 2 shows the typical structure of an FML.

An FML document consists, at higher level, of two types of elements: **model** and **story**. A **model** element is used for defining face capabilities, parameters, and initial configuration. A **story** element, on the other hand, describes the timeline of events in face animation. It is possible to have more than one of each element but due to possible sequential execution of animation in streaming applications, a **model** element affects only those parts of a document coming after it.

A face animation timeline consists of facial activities and their temporal relations. These activities are themselves sets of simple moves. The timeline is primarily created using two time container elements, **seq** and **par** representing sequential and parallel move-sets. A **story** itself is a special case of sequential time container. The begin times

Figure 2: FML Document Map — Time-Container and Move-Set will be Replaced by FML Time Container Elements and Sets of Possible Activities, Respectively

```
<fml>
    <model>           <!-- Model Info -->
        <model-info />
    </model>
    <story>           <!-- Story Timeline -->
        <action>
            <time-container>
                <move-set>
                    < . . . >
                <move-set>
                    < . . . >
            </time-container>
            < . . . >
        </action>
        < . . . >
    </story>
</fml>
```

of activities inside a **seq** and **par** are relative to previous activity and container begin time, respectively.

FML supports three basic face activities: talking, expressions, and 3-D head movements. They can be a simple move (like an expression) or more complicated (like a piece of speech). Combined in time containers, they create FML Actions. This combination can be done using nested containers, as shown in Figure 4.

FML also provides the means for creating a behavioral model for the face animation. At this time, it is limited to initialization data such as a range of possible movements and image/sound databases, and simple behavioral templates (subroutines). But, it can be extended to include behavioral rules and knowledge bases, especially for interactive applications. A typical **model** element is illustrated in Figure 5, defining a behavioral template used later in **story**.

Event Handling and Decision Making

Dynamic interactive applications require the FML document to be able to make decisions, i.e., to follow different paths based on certain events. To accomplish this **excl** time container and **event** element are added. An event represents any external data, e.g., the value of a user selection. The new time container associates with an event and allows waiting until the event has one of the given values, then it continues with action corresponding to that value.

Figure 3: FML Primary Time Container

```
<seq begin="0">
    <talk begin="0">Hello World</talk>
    <hdmv begin="0" end="5" type="0" val="30" />
</seq>
<par begin="0">
    <talk begin="1">Hello World</talk>
    <exp begin="0" end="3" type="3" val="50" />
</par>
```

Compatibility

The XML-based nature of this language allows the FML documents to be embedded in web pages. Normal XML parsers can extract data and use them as input to an FML-enabled player, through simple scripting. Such a script can also use XML Document Object Model (DOM) to modify the FML document, e.g., adding certain activities based on user input. This compatibility with web browsing environments, gives another level of interactivity and dynamic operation to the FML-based system, as illustrated later in this chapter.

Another aspect of FML is its compatibility with MPEG-4 face definition/animation parameters. This has been achieved by:

- Translation of FML documents to MPEG-4 codes by the media player.
- Embedded MPEG-4 elements (**fap** element is considered to allow direct embedding of FAPs in FML document).

Case Studies

Static Document

The first case is a simple FML document without any need for user interaction. There is one unique path the animation follows. The interesting point in this basic example is the use of loop structures, using **repeat** attributes included in any activity.

Figure 4: Nested Time Container

```
<action>
<par begin="0">
<seq begin="0">
        <talk begin="0">Hello World</talk>
    <hdmv begin="0" end="5" type="0" val="30" />
</seq>
    <exp begin="0" end="3" type="3" val="50" />
</par>
</action>
```

Figure 5: FML Model and Templates

```
<model>
    <img src="me.jpg" />
    <range dir="0" val="60" />
    <template name="hello" >
<seq begin="0">
    <talk begin="0">Hello</talk>
        <hdmv begin="0" end="5" dir="0" val="30" />
</seq>
    </template>
</model>
<story>
    <behavior template="hello" />
</story>
```

The **event** element specifies any external entity whose value can change. The default value for **repeat** is 1. If there is a numerical value, it will be used. Otherwise, it must be an **event** id, in which case the value of that **event** at the time of execution of related activity will be used. An FML-compatible player should provide means of setting external events values. *ShowFacePlayer* has a method called *SetFaceEvent,* which can be called by the owner of a player object to simulate external events.

Event Handling

The second example shows how to define an external event, wait for a change in its value, and perform certain activities based on the value. An external event corresponding to an interactive user selection is defined first. It is initialized to –1 that specifies an invalid value. Then, an **excl** time container, including required activities for possible user selections, is associated with the event. The **excl** element will wait for a valid value of the event. This is equivalent to a pause in face animation until a user selection is done.

It should be noted that an FML-based system usually consists of three parts:

- FML Document
- FML-compatible Player
- Owner Application

Figure 6: FML Decision Making and Event Handling

```
<event id="user" val="-1" />
<excl ev_id="user">
    <talk ev_val="0">Hello</talk>
    <talk ev_val="1">Bye</talk>
</excl>
```

Figure 7: Repeated Activity — Using Event is not Necessary

```
<event id="select" val="2" />
< . . . >
<seq repeat="select">
    <talk begin="0">Hello World</talk>
<exp begin="0" end="3" type="3" val="50" />
</seq>
```

In a simple example like this, it could be easier to simply implement the "story" in the owner application and send simpler commands to a player just to create the specified content (e.g., face saying Hello). But in more complicated cases, the owner application may be unaware of desired stories or unable to implement them. In those cases, e.g., interactive environments, the owner only simulates the external parameters.

Dynamic Content Generation

The last FML example to be presented illustrates the use of XML Document Object Model (DOM) to dynamically modify the FML document and generate new animation activities.

The simplified and partial JavaScript code for the web page shown in Figure 8 looks like this:

```
function onRight()
{
   var fml = fmldoc.documentElement;
   var new = fmldoc.createElement("hdmv");
   new.setAttribute("dir","0");
   new.setAttribute("val","30");
   fml.appendChild(new);
}
```

Figure 8: Dynamic FML Generation

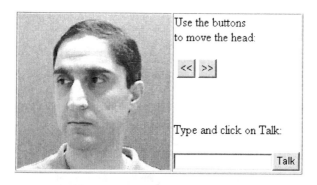

Figure 9: JavaScript Code for FML Event shown in Figure 6

```
function onLoad()
{
    facePlayer.ReadFML("test.fml");
    facePlayer.Run();
}

function onHelloButton()
{
    facePlayer.SetFaceEvent(
        "user", 0);
}

function onByeButton()
{
    facePlayer.SetFaceEvent(
        "user", 1);
}
```

More complicated scenarios can be considered, using this dynamic FML generation, for instance, having a form-based web page and asking for user input on a desired
behavior and using templates in **model** section of FML.

CONTENT CREATION IN *SHOWFACE*
Feature-Based Image Transformation (FIX)

The FML parser component of *ShowFace* system determines the visual activities
required in the face. These activities are transitions between certain face *states* like a
viseme or expression. In a training phase, a set of image-based transformations is learned
by the system, which can map between these face states. Transformations are found by
tracking facial features when the model is performing the related transitions, and then
applied to a given image, as illustrated in Figure 10. A library of transformations is created
based on the following facial states:

* Visemes in full-view
* Facial expressions in full-view
* Head movements

For group 1 and 2, mappings for all the transitions between a non-talking neutral
face and any group member are stored. In group 3 this is done for transitions between
any two neighbouring states (Figure 11).

Each transformation is defined in the form of $T = (F, M)$ where T is the transformation,
F is the feature set in the source image, and M is the mapping value for features. Source
image information is saved to enable scaling and calibration, which is explained later. The

Figure 10: Facial Features and Image Transformations — (a) Model State 1, (b) Model State 2, (c) Target Character in State 1, (d) Target Character in State 2

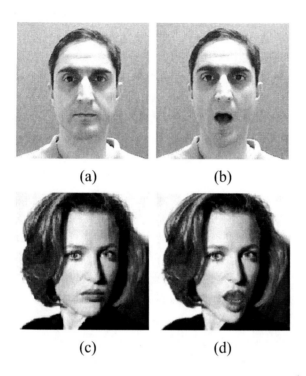

(a)   (b)

(c)   (d)

feature set for each image includes face boundary, eyes and eyebrows, nose, ears, and lips. These feature lines and the facial regions created by them are shown in Figure 12.

The solid lines are feature lines surrounding feature regions, while dashed lines define face patches. The patches are defined in order to allow different areas of the face to be treated differently. Covisibility is the main concern when defining these face patches. Points in each patch will be mapped to points in the corresponding patch of the target image, if visible.

The transformations are done by first applying the mapping vectors for the feature points. This is shown in Figure 13. Simple transformations are those which have already

Figure 11: Moving Head States — The Same Three States Exist for Rotating to the Left, in Addition to a Full-View Image at the Center

Figure 12: Facial Regions are Defined as Areas Surrounded by Two Facial Feature Lines, e.g., Inside Eyes or Between Lower Lip and Jaw (Some face patches are removed (b) for simplicity.)

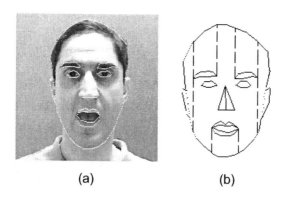

(a)   (b)

been learned, e.g., T_{12} and T_{13} (assuming we only have *Image-1*). Combined transformations are necessary in cases when the target image is required to have the effect of two facial state transitions at the same time, e.g., T_{14}.

Due to the non-orthographic nature of some head movements, combined transformations involving 3-D head rotation cannot be considered a linear combination of some known transformations. Feature mapping vectors for talking and expressions (which are learned from frontal view images) need to be modified when applied to "moved" heads.

$$T_{14} = a\,T_{12} + b\,T'_{13}$$
$$T'_{13} = f_p(T_{12},\, ,T_{13}) = T_{24}$$

where f_p is Perspective Calibration Function and a and b are coefficients between 0 and 1 to control transition progress. T_{13} will also be scaled based on face dimensions in source/target images.

When the *Image-2* is given, i.e., the new image does not have the same orientation as the one used in learning, the required transformation is *T24, which* still needs scaling/perspective calibration based on T_{13} and T_{12}.

Facial Region Transformation

The stored transformations only show the mapping vectors for feature lines. Non-feature points are mapped by interpolating the mapping values for the feature lines surrounding their regions. This is done based on the face region to which a point belongs.

Face regions are grouped into two different categories:

- Feature islands, surrounded by one or two "inner" feature lines
- Face patches, covering the rest of the face as shown in Figure 4-b.

The mapping vector for each point inside a group-1 region is found using the following formula:

Figure 13: Feature Transformation — T_{ij} is the Transformation Between Image-i and Image-j

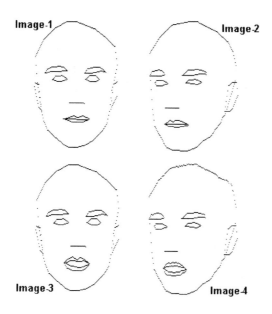

$$\mathbf{d}_{r,c} = w(\mathbf{d}_{u,c}, \mathbf{d}_{l,c})$$

where the function *w* is a weighted average with distance as the weights, *r* and *c* are row and column in the image for the given point, *u* and *l* are the row number for top and bottom feature points, and *d* is the mapping vector.

Face patches are defined based on covisibility, i.e., their points are most likely to be seen together. Defining the patches is necessary in order to preserve the geometric validity of the transformation. The mapping vector of each point in a patch is the weighted average of mapping of all the patch corners. Extra checking is performed to make sure a point inside a patch will be mapped to another point in a corresponding patch of the target image.

Sample Images

Figure 14 shows some sample outputs of the image transformations.

Speech Synthesis

To achieve the best quality with minimum database requirements, *ShowFace* uses a concatenative approach to speech synthesis. Diphones (the transitions between the steady-state of a phoneme to the steady-state of another) are used as the basis of this approach. An off-line diphone-extraction tool is designed to create a database of diphones from existing audio footage. This database is normalized for power and pitch to provide a smooth initial set. The diphones are then dynamically connected based on the phoneme list of a given text to be spoken.

Figure 14: Transformed Faces — Mapped from 7-a: (a) Frown, (b) Smile, (c and d) Visemes for Sounds "oo" and "a" in "root" and "talk", (e) Rotate to Right, and (f) Non-Frontal Talking

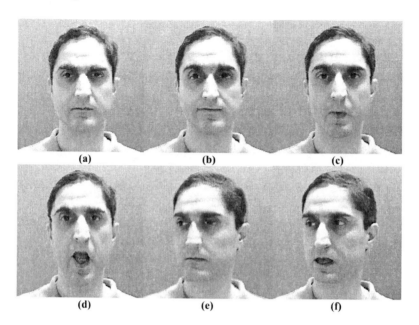

An FFT-based comparison of diphones finds the best connection point for two diphones at run time. This results in a dynamic time length calculation for diphones and words, which will then be used to find the necessary duration of the corresponding visual transitions and the number of frames to be generated, in order to achieve a lip-synchronized audio-visual stream.

SHOWFACE FRAMEWORK
System Architecture

The basic structure of the *ShowFace* system is illustrated in Figure 15. Five major parts of this system are:

- Script Reader, to receive an FML script from a disk file, an Internet address, or any text stream provider
- Script Parser, to interpret the FML script and create separate intermediate audio and video descriptions (e.g., words and viseme identifiers)
- Video Kernel, to generate the required image frames
- Audio Kernel, to generate the required speech
- Multimedia Mixer, to synchronize audio and video streams

ShowFace relies on the underlying multimedia technology for audio and video display. The system components interact with each other using the ShowFace Applica-

Figure 15: Component-Based ShowFace *System Structure*

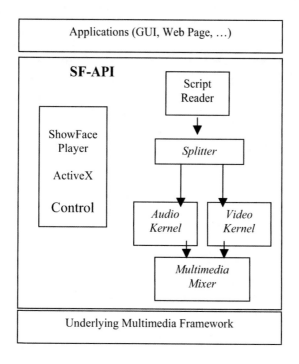

tion Programming Interface, SF-API, a set of interfaces exposed by the components and utility functions provided by the *ShowFace* run-time environment. User applications can access system components through SF-API, or use a wrapper object called *ShowFacePlayer*, which exposes the main functionality of the system, and hides programming details.

ShowFace system is designed and implemented with the concept of openness in mind. By that we mean the ability to use and connect to existing standard components and the independent upgrade of the system modules. To make most use of existing technologies, *ShowFace* components are implemented as Microsoft DirectShow filters.

DirectShow is a multimedia streaming framework, which allows different media processing to be done by independent objects called *filters*, which can be connected using standard Component Object Model (COM) interfaces. DirectShow will be installed as part of many application programs like browsers and games and comes with a set of filters like audio and video decoders and renderers. This allows *ShowFace* objects to access these filters easily and rely on multimedia streaming services provided by DirectShow, e.g., receiving data from a URL reader or MPEG-4 decoder and sending data to a video player or file writer.

The *ShowFacePlayer* wrapper object is implemented as an ActiveX control, which can be easily used in web pages and other client applications. An off-line tool, *ShowFace*

Studio, is also developed to assist in detecting the features, creating the maps and recording the FML scripts. Some samples of transformed faces are shown in Figure 4.

CONCLUDING REMARKS

Reviewing the most important works in the area of multimedia specification and presentation, it's been shown that a comprehensive framework for face animation is a requirement, which has not been met. Such a framework needs to provide:

- a structured content description mechanism,
- an open modular architecture covering aspects from getting input in standard forms to generating audio/video data on demand,
- efficient algorithms for generating multimedia with minimum use of existing footage and computational complexity.

An approach to such a framework, ShowFace System, is proposed. Unlike most of the existing systems, ShowFace is not limited to an off-line application or a media player object, but provides a complete and flexible architecture. The component-based architecture uses standard interfaces to interact internally and also with other objects provided by an underlying platform, making maximum use of existing technologies like MPEG-4, XML, and DirectX. These components can be used separately or in a combination controlled by the animation application.

An XML-based Face Modeling Language (FML) is designed to describe the desired sequence of actions in form of a scenario. FML allows event handling and a sequential or simultaneous combination of supported face states and will be parsed to a set of MPEG-4 compatible face actions. The Main contributions of FML are its hierarchical structure, flexibility for static and dynamic scenarios, and dedication to face animation. Compatibility with MPEG-4 and the use of XML as a base are also among the important features in the language. Future extensions to FML can include more complicated behaviour modeling and better coupling with MPEG-4 streams.

The image-based transformations used in the video kernel are shown to be successful in creating a variety of facial states based on a minimum input of images. Unlike 3-D approaches, these transformations do not need complicated modeling and computations. On the other hand, compared to usual 2-D approaches, they do not use a huge database of images. They can be extended to include facial textures for better results and the system allows even a complete change of image generation methods (e.g., using a 3-D model), as long as the interfaces are supported.

Better feature detection is a main objective of our future work, since any error in detecting a feature point can directly result in a wrong transformation vector. This effect can be seen in cases like eyebrows where detecting the exact corresponding points between a pair of learning images is not easy. As a result, the learned transformation may include additive random errors, which cause non-smooth eyebrow lines in transformed feature sets and images.

A combination of pre-learned transformations is used to create more complicated facial states. As discussed, due to the perspective nature of head movements, this may not be a linear combination. Methods for shrinking/stretching the mapping vectors as a function of 3-D head rotation are being studied and tested. Another approach can be defining the mapping vectors in terms of relative position to other points rather than numeric values. These relational descriptions may be invariant with respect to rotations.

REFERENCES

Ankeney, J. (1995). Non-linear editing comes of age. *TV Technology*, (May).

Arya, A. & Hamidzadeh, B. (2002). ShowFace MPEG-4 compatible face animation framework. *Int. Conf. Computer Graphics and Image Processing (CGIP)* Hawaii.

Battista, S., et al. (1999). MPEG-4: A multimedia standard for the third millennium. *IEEE Multimedia*, (October).

Blanz, V. & Vetter, T. (1999). A morphable model for the synthesis of 3D faces. *ACM SIGGRAPH*.

Bregler, C., et al. (1997). Video rewrite: Driving visual speech with audio. *ACM Computer Graphics*.

Bulterman, D. (2001). SMIL-2. *IEEE Multimedia*, (October).

Cassell, J. et al. (2001). BEAT: The behavior expression animation toolkit. *ACM SIGGRAPH*.

Ekman, P. & Friesen, W.V. (1978). *Facial Action Coding System*. Consulting Psychologists Press Inc.

Ezzat, T. & Poggio, T. (1998). MikeTalk: A talking facial display based on morphing visemes. *IEEE Conference on Computer Animation*.

Funge, J., et al. (1999). Cognitive modeling: Knowledge, reasoning, and planning for intelligent characters. *ACM SIGGRAPH*.

Graf, H.P., et al. (2000). Face analysis for the synthesis of photo-realistic talking heads. *IEEE Conference on Automatic Face and Gesture Recognition*.

Hirzalla, N., et al. (1995). A temporal model for interactive multimedia scenarios. *IEEE Multimedia*, (Fall).

Kallmann, M. & Thalmann, D. (1999). A behavioral interface to simulate agent-object interactions in real time. *IEEE Conference on Computer Animation*.

Lawton, G. (2000). Video streaming. *IEEE Computer*, (July).

Lee, W. S., et al. (1999). MPEG-4 compatible faces from orthogonal photos. *IEEE Conference on Computer Animation*.

Little, T.D.C. (1994). Time-based media representation and delivery. In J.F. Koegel Buford (Ed.), *Multimedia Systems*. ACM Press.

Nack, F. & Lindsay, A.T. (1999). Everything you wanted to know about MPEG-7. *IEEE Multimedia*, (July).

Pandzic, I.S. (2001). A web-based MPEG-4 facial animation system. *International Conference Augmented Virtual Reality & 3D Imaging*.

Pighin, F., et al. (1998). Synthesizing realistic facial expressions from photographs. *ACM SIGGRAPH*.

Tiddeman, B., et al. (2001). Prototyping and transforming facial textures for perception research. *IEEE CG&A,* (September).

About the Authors

Sagarmay Deb is an international consultant and researcher in Information Technology. He has been to many places of the world for consulting and research. He did his postgraduate studies in the USA. His research interests are multimedia databases, content-based image retrieval, various indexing techniques and electronic commerce. He contributes to books on multimedia databases. He attends international conferences and also writes research papers for international journals. Deb is also a reviewer of contributions to international conferences and journals. Currently, he is with the University of Southern Queensland, Australia, and is involved in the research works. Marquis Who's Who, a well-known publisher of biographies of people of notable achievements, has selected his biography for publication.

* * * * * *

Hussein Abdel-Wahab received a PhD in 1976 and an MS in 1973 both from the University of Waterloo in computer communications and a BS in electrical engineering from Cairo University in 1969. Currently, he is a full professor of computer science at Old Dominion University, USA. In addition, he is an adjunct professor of computer science at the University of North Carolina at Chapel Hill and a faculty member at the Information Technology Lab of the National Institute of Standards and Technology. Prior to that he held faculty positions at North Carolina State University, the University of Maryland and Rochester Institute of Technology. He served as a consultant to many organizations including IBM, MCNC and MITRE Corp. He is the principle investigator in designing and implementation of XTV, a pioneer X-window-based Teleconferencing system. His main research interests are collaborative desktop multimedia conferencing systems and real-time distributed information sharing. His research has been supported by NSF, ONR, IBM, MCNC, MITRE, ARPA among others. He is a senior member of IEEE Computer Society and a member of the Association for Computing Machinery.

Ali Arya received a BS degree in electrical engineering from Tehran Polytechnic, Iran, in 1990, and currently is a PhD candidate at the Department of Electrical and Computer Engineering, University of British Columbia, Canada. He has worked as a research engineer, system analyst, and project manager in different research centers and industry-related companies, including Tehran Cybernetic Arm Project, Iran, and Honeywell-Measurex, Canada. His research interests include multimedia, computer graphics, real-time systems, and web-based applications. He is also an instructor for "Systems Software Engineering" and "Software Project Management" in UBC.

Lokesh R. Boregowda obtained his BE degree in electronics from M.S. Ramaiah Institute of Technology, Bangalore, India (1991); ME degree in electronics from the University Visveswaraya College of Engineering, Bangalore, India (1994-1995); and a PhD from the Indian Institute of Science, Bangalore, India (2002). He has worked as a faculty member in electronics and communication engineering for a period of five years. He also worked as research consultant for a project on face detection and recognition at I.I.Sc., in collaboration with Samsung (SDS, Korea). His interests are computer vision, image understanding, face recognition technology and human interaction systems. He is currently working as a principal software engineer (R &D — Algorithms) at Honeywell India Software Operations Pvt. Ltd., Bangalore.

Yung-Kuan Chan received his MS degree in computer science in 1991 from New Mexico Institute of Mining and Technology, USA. He received his PhD in computer science and information engineering in 2000 from National Chung Cheng University, Chiayi, Taiwan. From 2001-2002, he worked as an assistant professor at the Department of Information Management, Chaoyang University of Technology. Since August 2002, he has worked as an assistant professor at the Department of Computer Science and Information Engineering, National Huwei Institute of Technology. His research interests include image retrieval, image compression, and image hiding.

Shu-Ching Chen received his PhD from the School of Electrical and Computer Engineering at Purdue University, West Lafayette, Indiana, USA, in December 1998. He also received master's degrees in computer science, electrical engineering, and civil engineering from Purdue University. He has been an assistant professor in the School of Computer Science (SCS), Florida International University (FIU), USA, since August 1999. He is currently the director of the Distributed Multimedia Information System Laboratory and the associate director of the Center for Advanced Distributed System Engineering (CADSE). Dr. Chen's research interests include distributed multimedia database systems and information systems, data mining, databases, and multimedia communications and networking.

Tung-Shou Chen was born in Taichung, Taiwan, Republic of China, on October 14, 1964. He received BS and PhD degrees from National Chiao Tung University in 1986 and 1992, respectively, both in computer science and information engineering. He served at the Computer Center, Chinese Army Infantry School, Taiwan, from 1992-1994. During the academic years 1994-1997, he was on the faculty of the Department of Information Management at National Chin-Yi Institute of Technology, Taichung, Taiwan. From

August 1998 to July 2000, he was the dean of student affairs and a professor of the Department of Computer Science and Information Management at Providence University. Since August 2000, he has been a professor of the Department of Information Management at National Taichung Institute of Technology, Taichung, Taiwan. His current research interests include data structures, image cryptosystems, and image compression.

Waleed E. Farag received his BS in electronics and communications engineering from Zagazig University (Egypt) in 1993 with distinct honor. He then obtained his master's degree in computer engineering from the same university in 1997. In 1998, he joined the PhD program at the Department of Computer Science, Old Dominion University (USA) where he got his PhD in 2002. Dr. Farag joined the Department of Computer Science at Indiana University of Pennsylvania (USA) as a faculty member in Fall 2002. His research interest includes information hiding and network security, video and image indexing and retrieval techniques, distance learning applications, artificial neural networks, optimization techniques, multimedia applications, wireless and mobile computing, and parallel computer architecture. He is a reviewer for a number of IEEE conferences and is an IEEE member.

Y. Y. Gao received BE and ME degrees from Tsinghua University, China, in 1998 and 2000, respectively. She worked in Lucent Technologies Optical Networking (China) Co., Ltd. from 2000-2001. She is now pursuing her PhD degree at Michigan State University, USA. Her current research interests include image processing, computer vision and video compression. She has publications in the field of image segmentation and content-based image retrieval. She is an associate member of IEEE.

Babak Hamidzadeh received MS and PhD degrees in computer science and engineering from the University of Minnesota in Minneapolis, in 1989 and 1993, respectively. In that period, he also worked as a research associate at The Systems and Research Center of Honeywell Inc., and as a research scientist at The Research and Technology Center of Alliant Techsystems Inc. for more than three years. From 1993-1996, he was an assistant professor of Computer Science and Computer Engineering at The Hong Kong University of Science and Technology. Currently, he is an associate professor of Electrical and Computer Engineering at The University of British Columbia, Canada. He is also a member of the IEEE Computer Society, a fellow of the BC Advanced Systems Institute and the holder of a Canada Research Chair in Information Technology. His areas of research include resource management and scheduling, real-time computing, parallel and distributed processing, database systems, multimedia, and communication networks.

Richard J. Hartley is the head of the Department of Information and Communications, Manchester Metropolitan University, UK. He graduated in chemistry at UMIST and has a master's in the design and evaluation of information systems from the University of Wales. He was a lecturer in the Department of Information and Library Studies at the University of Wales Aberystwyth, and reader in the Department of Information and Library Management at the University of Northumbria. He is a fellow of the Chartered Institute of Library and Information Professionals and has written extensively on various areas of information seeking behavior and information retrieval.

William T. Hewitt is the head of Supercomputing, Visualization and E-Science (SVE), and director of the International AVS Centre at Manchester Computing, University of Manchester, UK. He graduated with a first class honors degree in applied mathematics from University College of North Wales. His research interests are systems and software tools for HPCN, distributed computing, applications of high speed networks, Grid, high-performance 3D interactive visualization, parallel algorithms for rendering, radiosity and free-form curves and surfaces, particularly NURBs. He is an honorary lecturer in the Department of Computer Science, University of Manchester, and a visiting lecturer at University College of North Wales.

Yu-an Ho received BS degrees in 2002 from the Department of Information Management at the National Taichung Institute Technology, Taichung, Taiwan. His interests include image retrieval and image hiding.

Jenq-Neng Hwang received BS and MS degrees, both in electrical engineering from the National Taiwan University, Taipei, Taiwan, in 1981 and 1983, respectively. After two years of obligatory military service, he enrolled as a research assistant in 1985 at the Signal and Image Processing Institute, Dept. of Electrical Engineering, University of Southern California, where he received his PhD in December 1988. He was also a visiting student at Princeton University, New Jersey (1987-1989). In the summer of 1989, Dr. Hwang joined the Department of Electrical Engineering of the University of Washington in Seattle (USA), where he is currently a professor. He has published more than 180 journal, conference papers and book chapters in the areas of image/video signal processing, computational neural networks, multimedia system integration and networking. Dr. Hwang is the co-author of an edited book *Handbook of Neural Networks for Signal Processing* (CRC Press, July 2001). He received the 1995 IEEE Signal Processing Society's Annual Best Paper Award (with Shyh-Rong Lay and Alan Lippman) in the area of neural networks for signal processing. Dr. Hwang is a fellow of IEEE. Dr. Hwang served as the secretary of the Neural Systems and Applications Committee of the IEEE Circuits and Systems Society (1989-1991), and was a member of the Design and Implementation of Signal Processing Systems Technical Committee in IEEE Signal Processing Society. He is also a founding member of the Multimedia Signal Processing Technical Committee of the IEEE Signal Processing Society. He served as the Chairman of the Neural Networks Signal Processing Technical Committee in the IEEE Signal Processing Society from 1996-1998, and the Society's representative to the IEEE Neural Network Council from 1997 to 2000. He served as associate editor for the *IEEE Transactions on Signal Processing* and the *IEEE Transactions on Neural Networks*, and is currently an associate editor for *IEEE Transactions on Circuits and Systems for Video Technology*. He is also on the editorial board of the *Journal of VLSI Signal Processing Systems for Signal, Image, and Video Technology*. He is a guest editor for *IEEE Trans. on Multimedia*, special issue on Multimedia over IP in March/June 2001. Dr. Hwang was the conference program chair of the 1994 IEEE Workshop on Neural Networks for Signal Processing held in Ermioni, Greece, September 1994. He was the general co-chair of the International Symposium on Artificial Neural Networks held in Hsinchu, Taiwan, R.O.C., December 1995. He also chaired the tutorial committee for the IEEE International Conference on Neural Networks (ICNN'96) held in Washington, DC (June 1996). He was the program co-chair of the

International Conference on Acoustics, Speech, and Signal Processing (ICASSP), Seattle (1998).

Mohan S. Kankanhalli obtained his B-Tech (electrical engineering) from the Indian Institute of Technology, Kharagpur, in 1986 and his MS and PhD in computer and systems engineering from the Rensselaer Polytechnic Institute in 1998 and 1990, respectively. He then joined the Institute of Systems Science (ISS — now Institute for Infocomm Research) in October 1990. He mainly worked on content-based multimedia information retrieval in multimedia groups. He left ISS in June 1997 and spent the 1997-1998 academic year at the Department of Electrical Engineering of the Indian Institute of Science, Bangalore. He has been with the Department of Computer Science of the School of Computing at the National University of Singapore since May 1998. His current research interests are in multimedia information systems (image/audio/video content processing, multimedia retrieval) and information security (multimedia watermarking, image/video authentication). He is leading the Digital Image and Video Albums collaborative research project at the School of Computing.

Wee Kheng Leow graduated from the National University of Singapore in 1985 and 1988 with BS and MS degrees, and obtained his PhD from The University of Texas at Austin in 1994. He is now an associate professor at the Department of Computer Science, School of Computing, National University of Singapore. He is also the associate director of the Centre for Information Mining and Extraction (CHIME) at the School of Computing, National University of Singapore. His research interests include computer vision, medical image analysis, multimedia matching and retrieval, and robotics planning and control.

Joo Hwee Lim received his BS (Hons I) and MS (by research) degrees in computer science from the National University of Singapore in 1989 and 1991, respectively. He joined the Institute for Infocomm Research, Singapore, in October 1990. He has conducted research in connectionist expert systems, neural-fuzzy systems, handwriting recognition, multi-agent systems, and content-based retrieval. He was the head of the Information-Base Functions KRDL Lab under the Real World Computing Partnership funded by METI, Japan and currently a key member of the Digital Image and Video Album project under the CNRS-NUS-I2R international research collaboration. He has published more than 30 referenced international journals and conference papers in his research areas including content-based processing, pattern recognition, and neural networks.

Y. Luo received an MS degree in electrical engineering from the University of Michigan, USA (2002) and a BS in electronics engineering from Tsinghua University, Beijing, China (2000). He is currently a research scientist at the Vision Group at the Advanced Research and Development Department, TRW Automotive, Michigan, USA. His research interests are in image processing, pattern recognition, machine vision and learning, including stereo vision, image classification, object detection and tracking, neural networks, image understanding, content-based image and video retrieval, etc.

Ying Luo received a BS degree from Xidian University (China) in 1994 and an MS degree from the University of Washington (2001). He is currently a PhD candidate at the information processing Lab (IPL), Department of Electrical Engineering, University of Washington. His research interests include video analysis, modeling and multimedia database.

M. Monsignori is a research contractor at the University of Florence, Department of Systems and Informatics and is with EXITECH (Italy). His research interests include industrial automation, object-oriented technology, distributed systems, and watermarking music sheets. Monsignori received his degree in engineering in informatics from the University of Florence, and worked on VISICON, OPTAMS and WEDELMUSIC projects of the European Commission.

Philippe Mulhem is currently the director of the Image Processing and Applications Laboratory (IPAL) located in Singapore. It is a joint laboratory between the French Centre National de la Recherche Scientifique, the National University of Singapore and the Institute for Infocomm Research of Singapore. He is also a member of CLIPS-IMAG laboratory of Grenoble. His works focus on formalization and experimentation of image, video and multimedia documents indexing and retrieval. He obtained his PhD from the Joseph Fourier University, Grenoble, France (1993).

P. Nesi is a full professor at the University of Florence, Department of Systems and Informatics, Italy. His research interests include object-oriented technology, real-time systems, quality, system assessment, testing, formal languages, physical models, computer music, and parallel architectures. He has spent a period of his life at the IBM Almaden Research Center, USA. Nesi received a PhD in electronic and informatics engineering from the University of Padoa. He has been the general chair of the WEDELMUSIC conference, IEEE Press, and of several other international conferences: IEEE ICSM, OQ, CSMR. He is the coordinator of the following research and development multipartner projects: MOODS (Music Object Oriented Distributed System, http://www.dsi.unifi.it/~moods/), WEDELMUSIC (WEB Delivering of Music Score, www.wedelmusic.org), and MUSICNETWORK (The Interactive Music Network, www.interactivemusicnetwork.org). Contact Dr. Nesi at *nesi@dsi.unifi.it* or at *nesi@ingfi1.ing.unifi.it*.

Timothy K. Shih is a professor and the chairman of Department of Computer Science and Information Engineering at Tamkang University, Taiwan, R.O.C. He is a senior member of IEEE and a member of ACM. His research interests include multimedia computing and networking, distance learning, e-commerce, and content-based multimedia information retrieval. Dr. Shih received his PhD in computer engineering from Santa Clara University in 1993. He has edited many books and published more than 260 papers and book chapters, as well as participated in many international academic activities, including the organization of many international conferences and special issues of international journals.

K. K. Shukla is presently on the faculty of the Department of Computer Engineering, Institute of Technology, Banaras Hindu University, India. He is a senior member of the IEEE and Computer Society of India, a life member Indian Society for Technical Education and a member of the Institute of Engineers (India). Dr. Shukla has to his credit 75 international and national publications in the area of AI and neural network applications. He has contributed a chapter in the Academic Press, USA book: *Softcomputing & Intelligent Systems*. He has also authored a book, *Neurocomputers* published by Narosa. His name appears in the Marquis's Who's Who world directory. His current areas of interest are neural network applications, evolutionary computation and image processing.

Mei-Ling Shyu has been an assistant professor at the Department of Electrical and Computer Engineering, University of Miami (USA), since January 2000. She received her PhD from the School of Electrical and Computer Engineering, Purdue University, West Lafayette, Indiana, USA, in 1999. She also received her MS in computer science, MS in electrical engineering and MS in restaurant, hotel, institutional, and tourism management from Purdue University in 1992, 1995, and 1997, respectively. Her research interests include multimedia networking, wireless communications and networking, data mining, multimedia database systems, multimedia information systems, and database systems.

Richa Singh was born in 1980. She obtained BTech in 2002. She is presently working at the Indian Institute of Technology, Kanpur, India. She has worked on various face detection and recognition projects. Her current areas of interest are pattern recognition, image and video processing, biometric authentication techniques and neural network.

Sanjay K. Singh obtained a BE, MTech and PhD in computer engineering. He is a certified Novell engineer and certified Novell administrator. He is currently a faculty member in IET Jaunpur (India). He has worked in the industry for more than two years on projects such as face detection and recognition. His areas of interest are image processing, face recognition technology, man-machine interaction systems and data acquisition systems.

M. Spinu is a contract professor at the University of Florence, Department of Systems and Informatics, Italy. His research interests include object-oriented technology, distributed systems, watermarking, web services, security, and transaction models. Spinu received a PhD in informatics and telecommunication engineering from the University of Florence, and has worked on MOODS, WEDELMUSIC, and MUSICNETWORK projects of the European Commission.

Shamik Sural completed his PhD in 2000. He is currently an assistant professor in the School of IT at the Indian Institute of Technology, Kharagpur, India. Dr. Sural has worked for more than 10 years in IT consulting projects in both India and the USA. During this period, he managed and executed large application software projects involving n-tier client server architecture, rational unified process and SEI CMM Level 5 certified software quality management techniques. His research interests are in the areas of image processing, pattern recognition and multimedia databases. He is a member of the IEEE.

Mayank Vatsa was born in 1980. He obtained BTech in 2002. He is presently working at the Indian Institute of Technology, Kanpur, India. He has worked on various face detection and recognition projects. His current areas of interest are pattern recognition, image and video processing, biometric authentication techniques and artificial intelligence.

Colin C. Venters is a research associate at Manchester Visualization Centre (MVC), University of Manchester, UK. He graduated with an upper second-class degree in information science from the University of Northumbria. In 1996, he was awarded a three-year British Academy Information Science Scholarship for his post-graduate research. His scientific interests lie in the fields of computer vision, signal and image processing, image databases, pattern recognition, multimedia information retrieval, and human-computer interaction. He is a member of the Association for Computing Machinery (ACM), the British Computing Society (BCS), and the Institute of Electrical & Electronic Engineers (IEEE).

Ching-Sheng Wang is an assistant professor at the Department of Computer and Information Science of Aletheia University, Taipei, Taiwan. He received a BS in computer science and information engineering from Tamkang University in 1994, and MS and PhD degrees in information engineering from the Tamkang University, in 1997 and 2001, respectively. His research interests include content-based information retrieval, VRML 3D object retrieval, multimedia presentation and multimedia database systems.

Ying-Hong Wang received a BS degree in information engineering from Chung-Yuan University, Taiwan, in 1986 and MS and PhD degrees in information engineering from the TamKang University, Taiwan, in 1992 and 1996, respectively. From 1988-1990, he worked in the Product Development Division of the Institute of Information Industry (III). From 1992-1996, he was a lecturer in the department of information engineering of TamKang University. Since the fall 1996, he has been an associate professor in the Department of Information Engineering of TamKang University. He has nearly 80 technological papers published in international journals and international conference proceedings and has also joined many international activities and served on program committees as workshop chair, session chair and so on. He had been invited as visiting researcher at the University of Aizu, Japan, from January to March 2002. His current research interests are software engineering, multimedia database systems, wireless multimedia, and mobile agents.

Tzong-Der Wu received his PhD in electrical engineering from the University of Washington, Seattle (USA), in 1999. Dr. Wu is the project manager of the Multimedia Technologies Laboratory, Institute for Information Industry, Taiwan. He is also an adjunct professor at the National Taiwan University of Science and Technology and National Taipei University of Technology. His research interests include video coding, indexing and networking. Dr. Wu has been awarded one patent and has published about 30 technical papers including two book chapters in the area of video technology.

Chengcui Zhang is a research assistant at the school of Computer Science at Florida International University (USA), pursuing a PhD in computer science. Her research interests are in multimedia data mining, video segmentation and indexing, and image retrieval. She received her BS and MS in Computer Science from Zhejiang University in China.

Y. J. Zhang received a PhD in applied science from the State University of Liège, Liège, Belgium (1989). From 1989 to 1993, he was with the Delft University of Technology, Delft, The Netherlands, as a post-doc fellow and research scientist. In 1993, he joined Tsinghua

University, Beijing, China, where he is a professor of image engineering since 1997. He is on sabbatical leave as a visiting professor at National Technological University, Singapore, in 2003. His research interests are mainly in the area of image engineering, that includes image processing, image analysis and image understanding, as well as their applications. He has authored more than 200 research papers and book chapters, and he is the author of eight technical books including two monographs: *Image Segmentation* and *Content-based Visual Information Retrieval* (Science Press). He is the vice president of the China Society of Image and Graphics, the deputy editor-in-chief of the *Journal of Image and Graphics*, and on the editorial board of several international and national journals. He has served as the program co-chairs of The First and Second International Conferences on Image and Graphics (ICIG'2000, ICIG'2002). He is a senior member of IEEE.

Yanchun Zhang is currently an associate professor in the Department of Mathematics and Computing at the University of Southern Queensland. He got his PhD in computer science from the University of Queensland (1991). His research areas cover database and information systems, object-oriented and multimedia database systems, distributed and multi-database systems, database support for cooperative work, electronic commerce, Internet/web information systems, web data management and visual database processing. He is a regular contributor to international journals and conferences. He is an editor-in-chief of *World Wide Web* (*WWW Journal*) and *Internet and Web Information Systems* (*IWIS Journal*) from Kluwer Academic Publishers. He is a chairman of International Web Information Systems Engineering Society (WISE Society).

Index

L

M

N

O

P

Q

R

NEW from Idea Group Publishing